LONG ROAD TO
LIQUOR
CITY

ONI PRESS

AN ONI PRESS PUBLICATION

LONG ROAD TO LIQUOR CITY

Written by
MACON BLAIR

Illustrated, Colored
& Lettered by
JOE FLOOD

Designed by Kate Z. Stone
Edited by Charlie Chu
with Desiree Wilson

PUBLISHED BY ONI PRESS, INC.

Joe Nozemack Founder & Chief Financial Officer
James Lucas Jones Publisher
Charlie Chu V.P. of Creative & Business Development
Brad Rooks Director of Operations
Melissa Meszaros Director of Publicity
Margot Wood Director of Sales
Sandy Tanaka Marketing Design Manager
Amber O'Neill Special Projects Manager
Troy Look Director of Design & Production
Kate Z. Stone Senior Graphic Designer
Sonja Synak Graphic Designer
Angie Knowles Digital Prepress Lead
Ari Yarwood Executive Editor
Sarah Gaydos Editorial Director of Licensed Publishing
Robin Herrera Senior Editor
Desiree Wilson Associate Editor
Michelle Nguyen Executive Assistant
Jung Lee Logistics Coordinator
Scott Sharkey Warehouse Assistant

onipress.com
facebook.com/onipress
twitter.com/onipress
onipress.tumblr.com
instagram.com/onipress

@maconblair
@joefloodcomics

First edition: February 2019

ISBN 978-1-62010-461-3
eISBN 978-1-62010-462-0

PRINTED IN CHINA.

Library of Congress Control Number: 2018950258

1 3 5 7 9 10 8 6 4 2

Macon and Joe would like to offer hundred-proof gratitude
to Charlie Chu and Desiree Wilson and everyone at Oni Press
for seeing it through, to Rick Spears for hooking it up,
and to Dollar Bill Lacey for giving it a name.

And to Liz, Phoebe, Lee, Buck, and Sonny, for all the rest.
—mb & jf

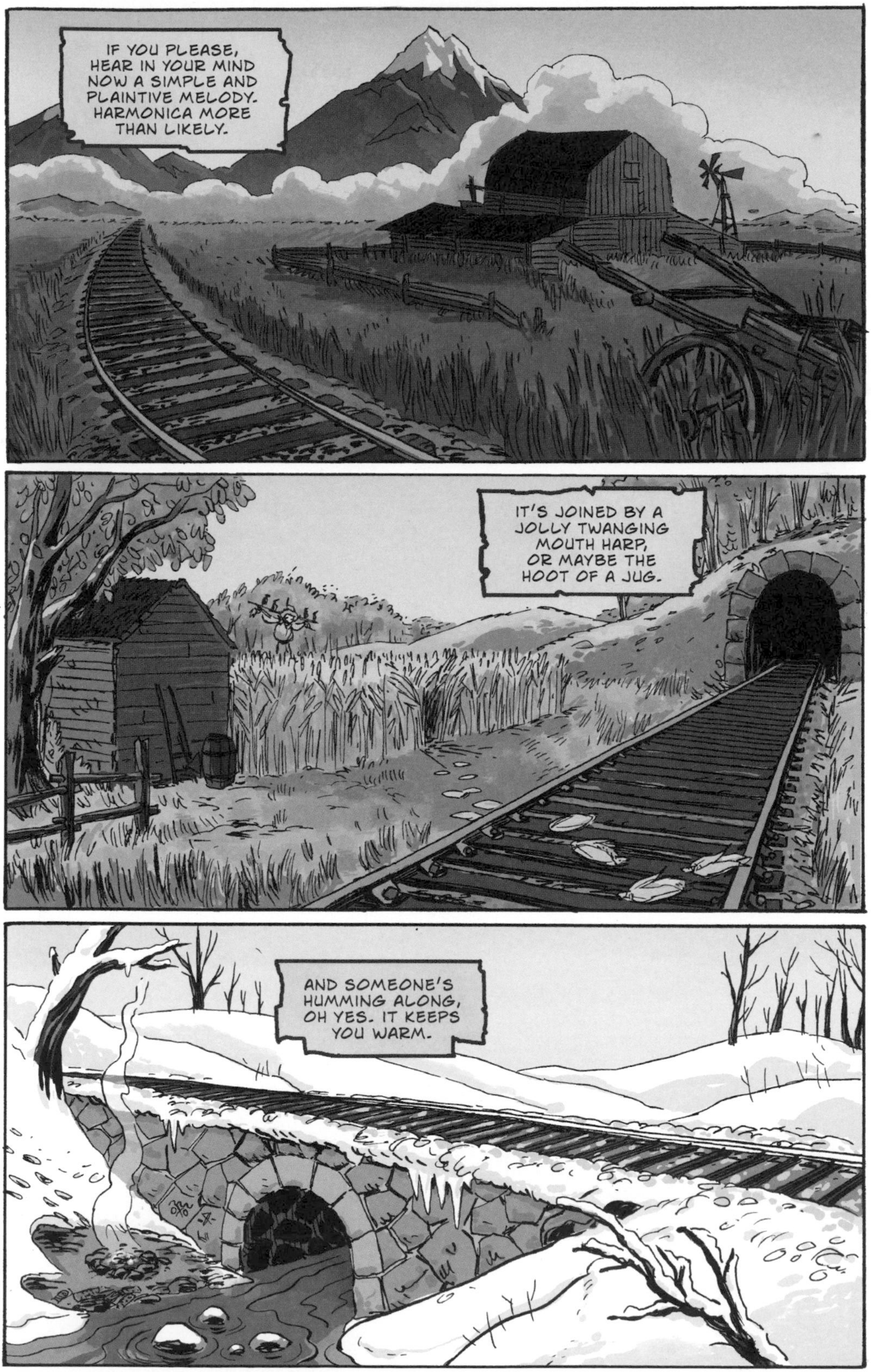
IF YOU PLEASE, HEAR IN YOUR MIND NOW A SIMPLE AND PLAINTIVE MELODY. HARMONICA MORE THAN LIKELY.
IT'S JOINED BY A JOLLY TWANGING MOUTH HARP, OR MAYBE THE HOOT OF A JUG.
AND SOMEONE'S HUMMING ALONG, OH YES. IT KEEPS YOU WARM.

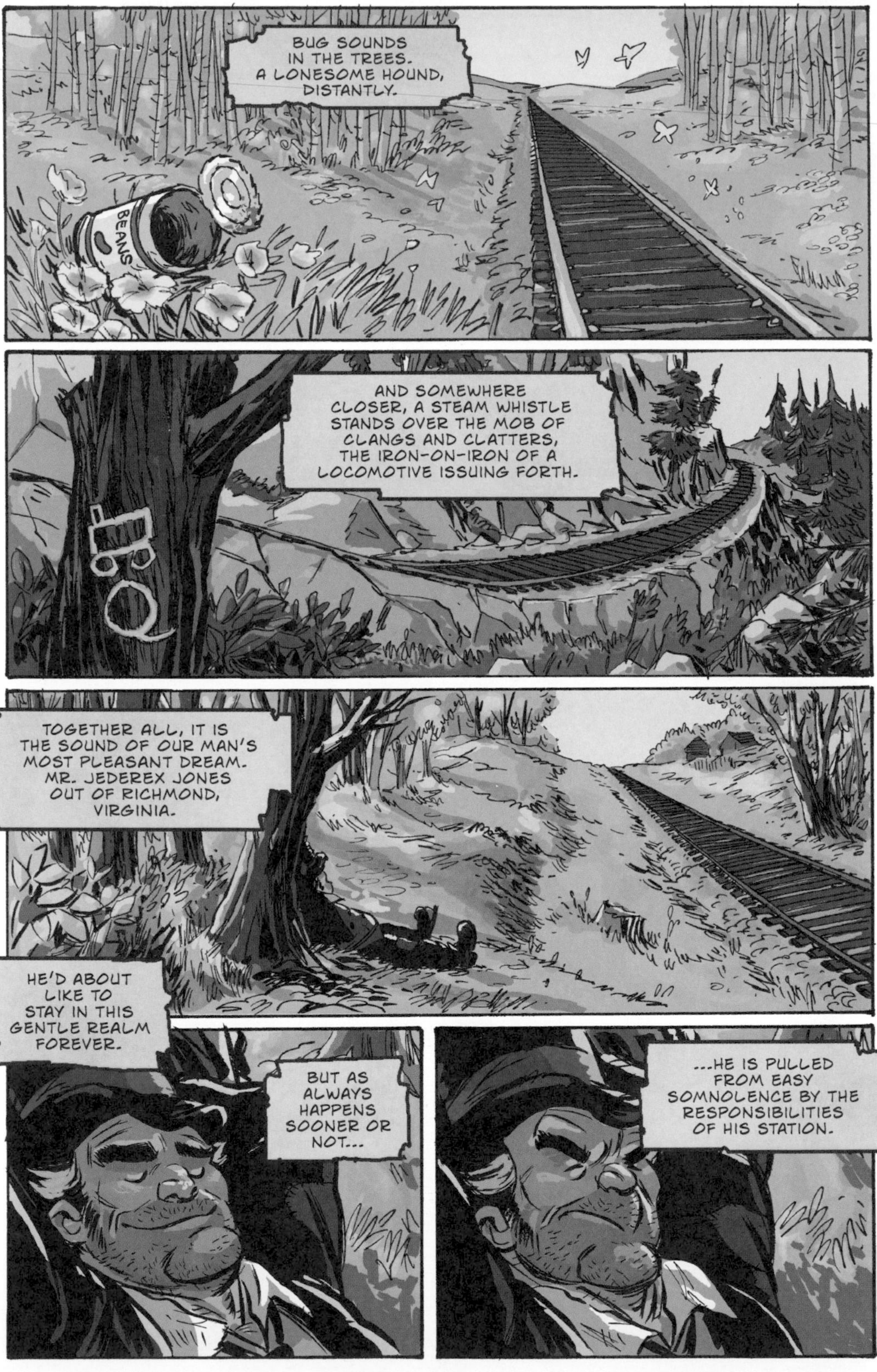
BUG SOUNDS IN THE TREES. A LONESOME HOUND, DISTANTLY.
BEANS
AND SOMEWHERE CLOSER, A STEAM WHISTLE STANDS OVER THE MOB OF CLANGS AND CLATTERS, THE IRON-ON-IRON OF A LOCOMOTIVE ISSUING FORTH.
TOGETHER ALL, IT IS THE SOUND OF OUR MAN'S MOST PLEASANT DREAM. MR. JEDEREX JONES OUT OF RICHMOND, VIRGINIA.
HE'D ABOUT LIKE TO STAY IN THIS GENTLE REALM FOREVER.
BUT AS ALWAYS HAPPENS SOONER OR NOT...
...HE IS PULLED FROM EASY SOMNOLENCE BY THE RESPONSIBILITIES OF HIS STATION.

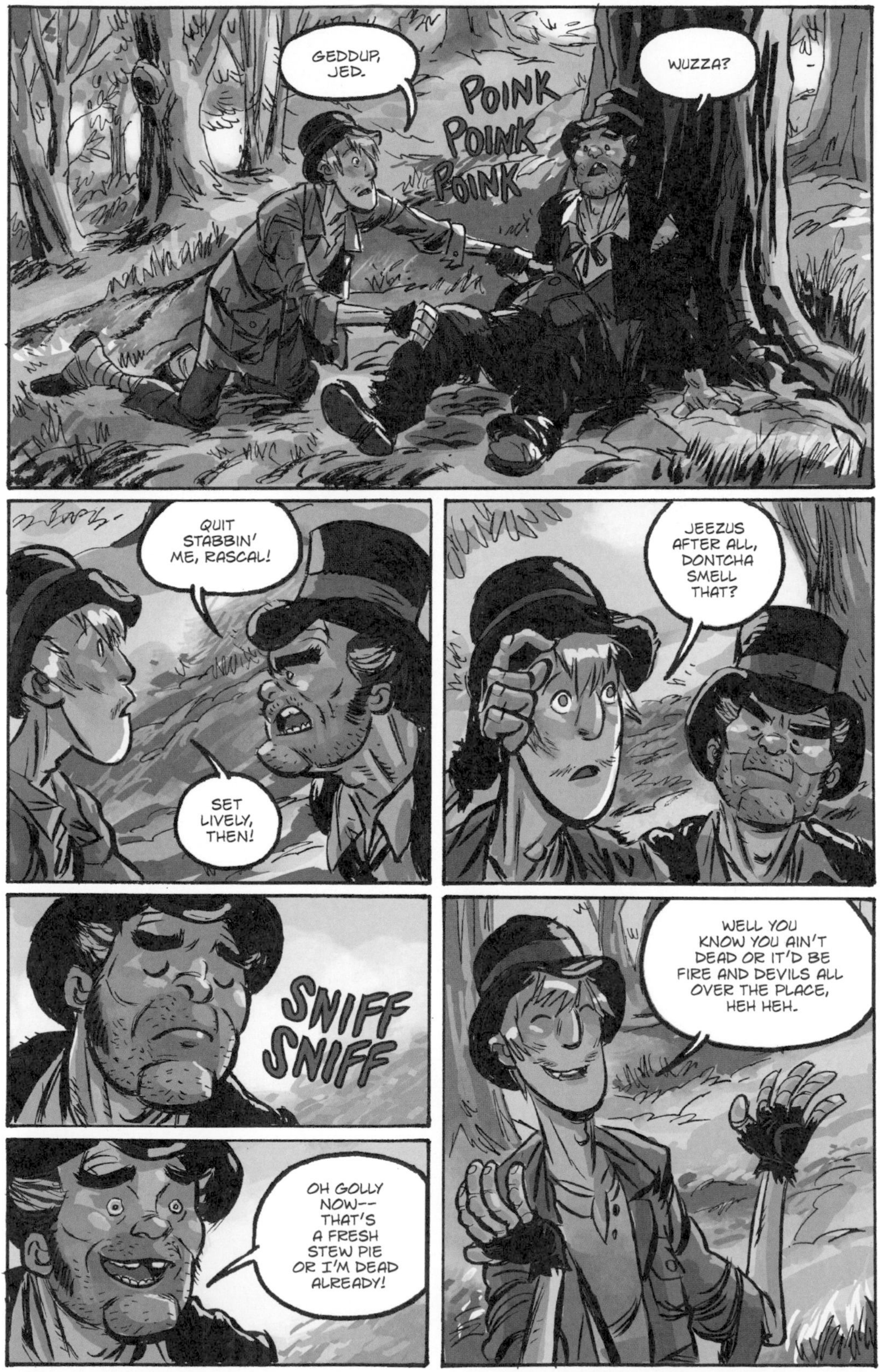
GEDDUP, JED.
POINK POINK POINK
WUZZA?
QUIT STABBIN' ME, RASCAL!
SET LIVELY, THEN!
JEEZUS AFTER ALL, DONTCHA SMELL THAT?
SNIFF SNIFF
OH GOLLY NOW-- THAT'S A FRESH STEW PIE OR I'M DEAD ALREADY!
WELL YOU KNOW YOU AIN'T DEAD OR IT'D BE FIRE AND DEVILS ALL OVER THE PLACE, HEH HEH.

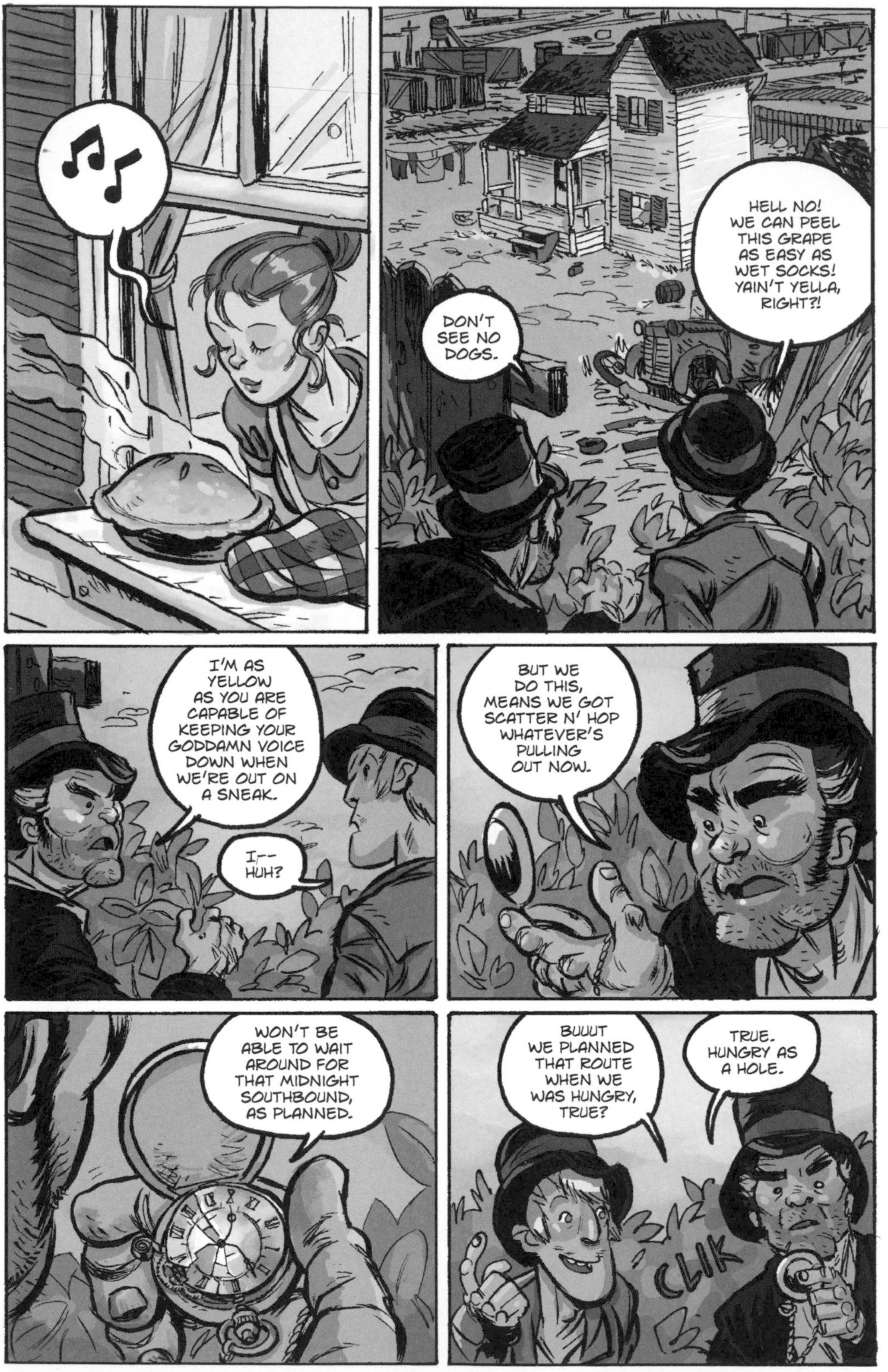
DON'T SEE NO DOGS.
HELL NO! WE CAN PEEL THIS GRAPE AS EASY AS WET SOCKS! YAIN'T YELLA, RIGHT?!
I'M AS YELLOW AS YOU ARE CAPABLE OF KEEPING YOUR GODDAMN VOICE DOWN WHEN WE'RE OUT ON A SNEAK.
I-- HUH?
BUT WE DO THIS, MEANS WE GOT SCATTER N' HOP WHATEVER'S PULLING OUT NOW.
WON'T BE ABLE TO WAIT AROUND FOR THAT MIDNIGHT SOUTHBOUND, AS PLANNED.
BUUUT WE PLANNED THAT ROUTE WHEN WE WAS HUNGRY, TRUE?
TRUE. HUNGRY AS A HOLE.
CLIK

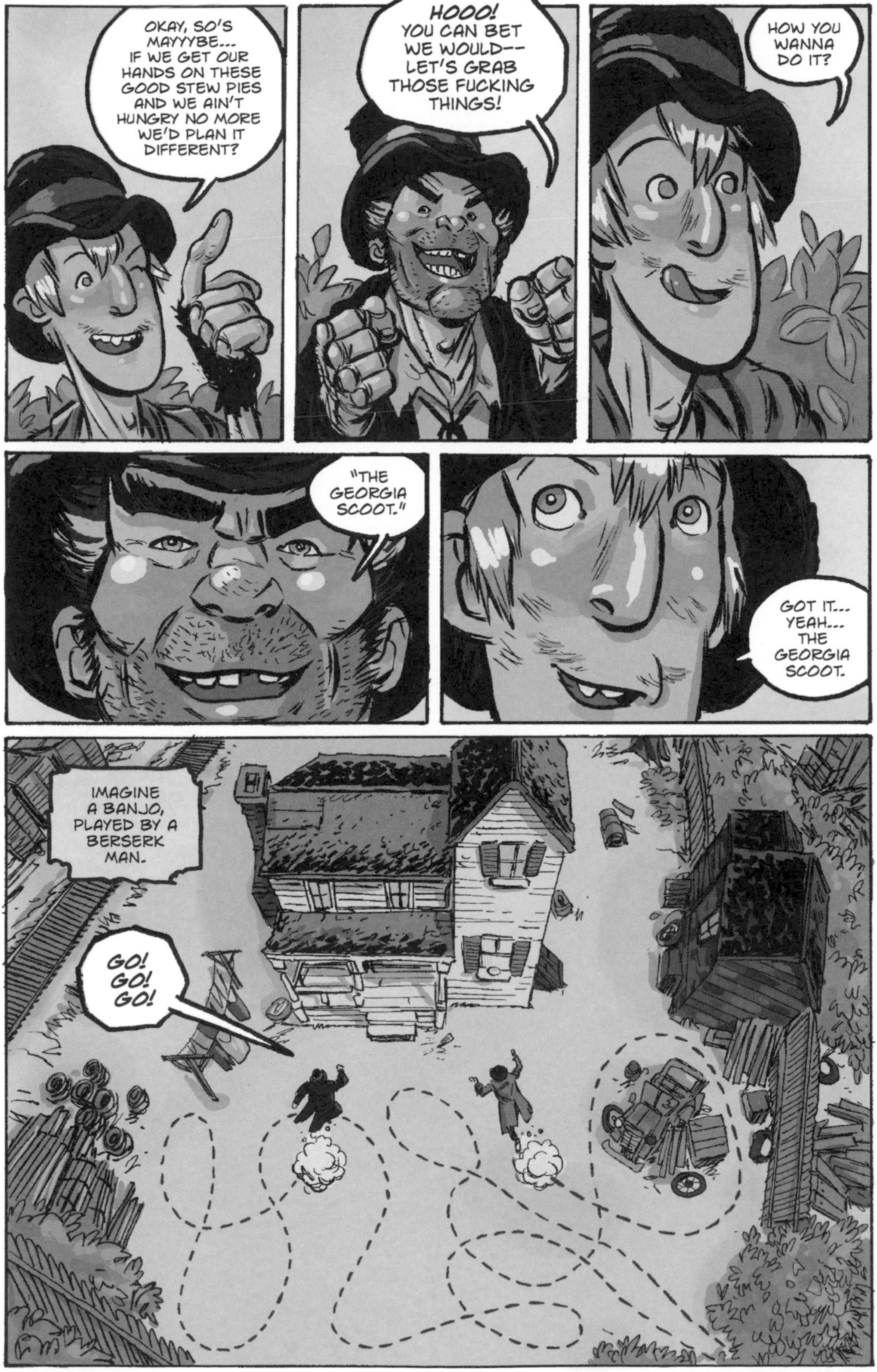
OKAY, SO'S MAYYYBE... IF WE GET OUR HANDS ON THESE GOOD STEW PIES AND WE AIN'T HUNGRY NO MORE WE'D PLAN IT DIFFERENT?
HOOO! YOU CAN BET WE WOULD-- LET'S GRAB THOSE FUCKING THINGS!
HOW YOU WANNA DO IT?
"THE GEORGIA SCOOT."
GOT IT... YEAH... THE GEORGIA SCOOT.
IMAGINE A BANJO, PLAYED BY A BERSERK MAN.
GO! GO! GO!

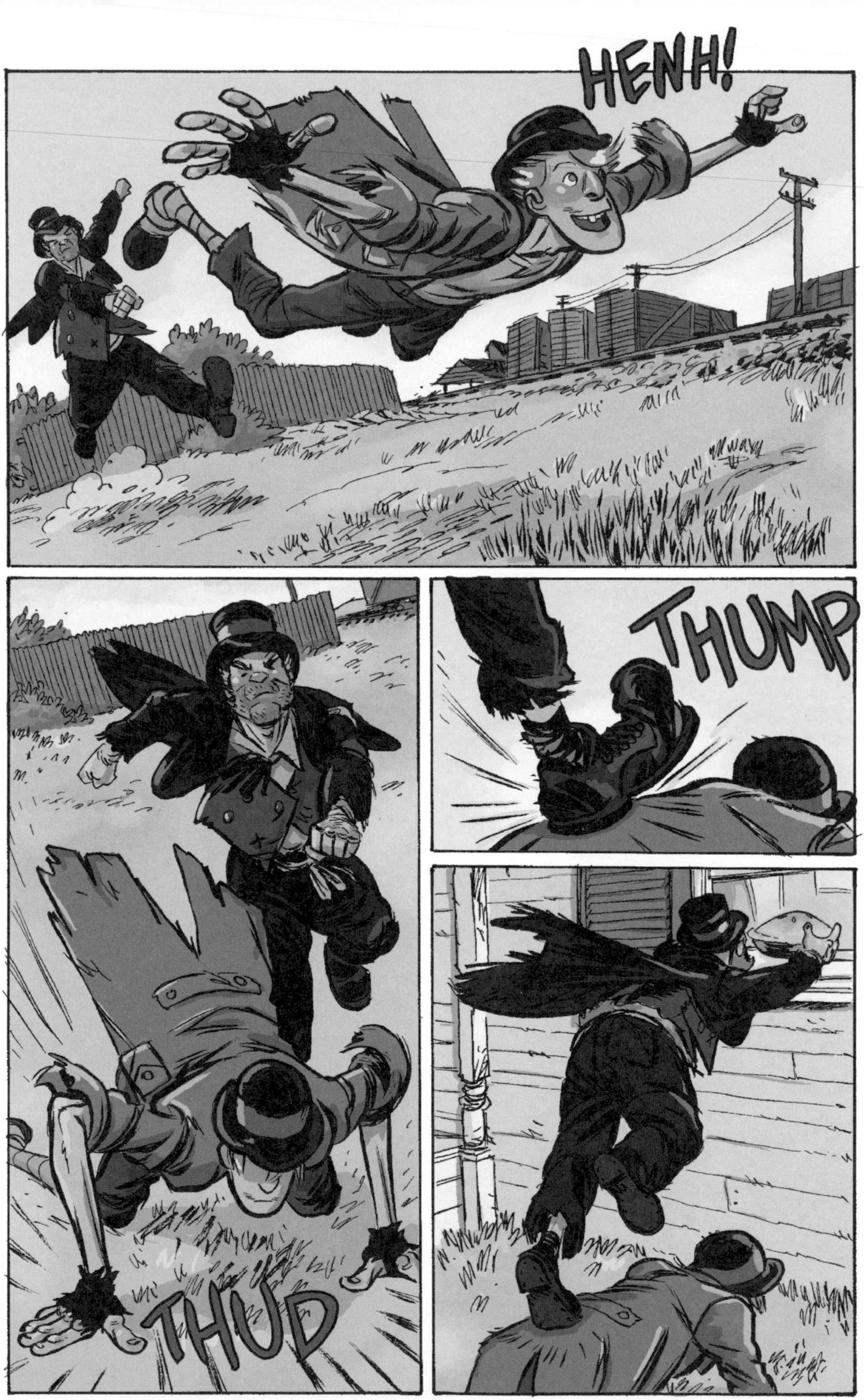
HENH!
THUMP
THUD

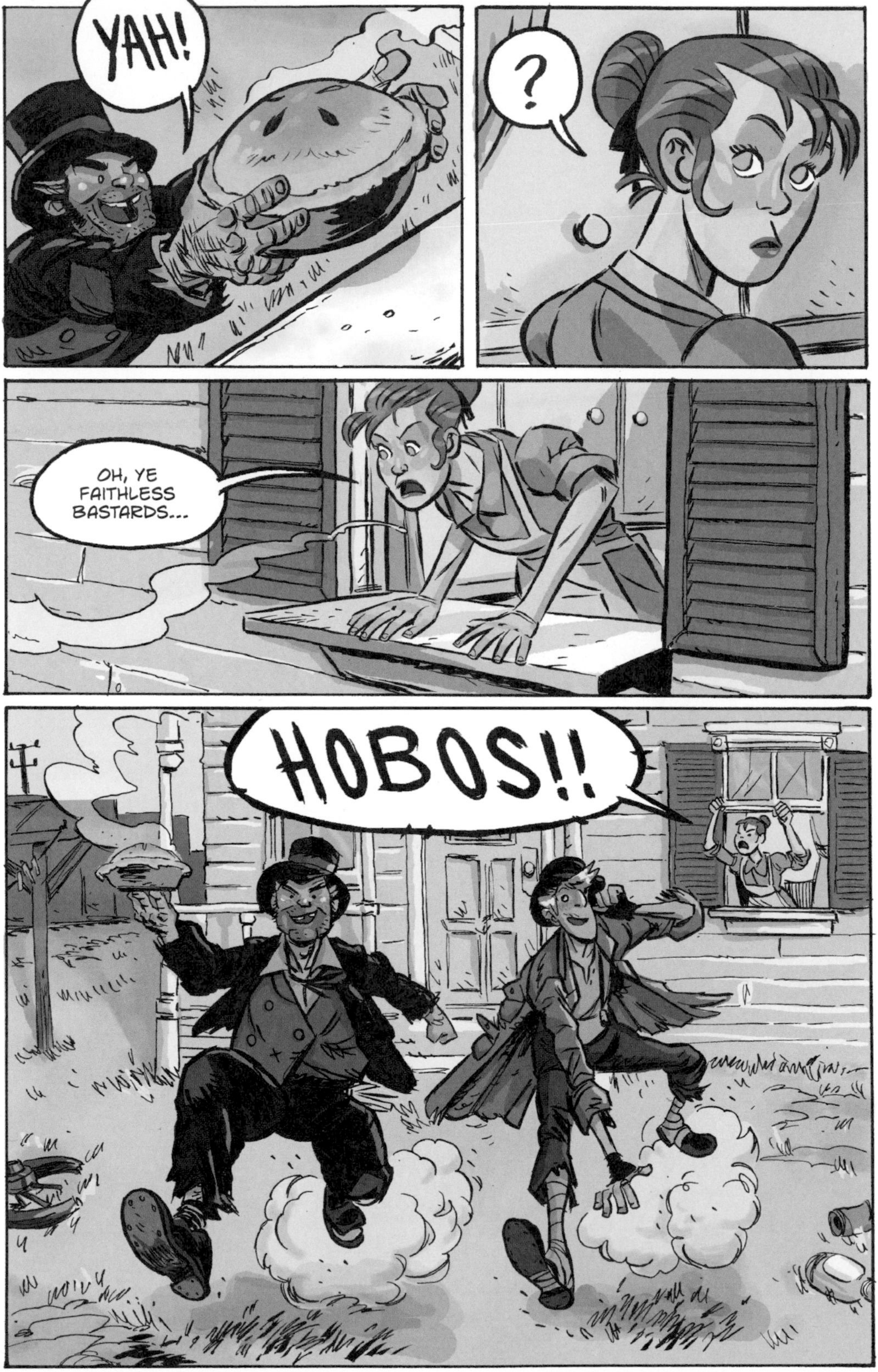
YAH!
?
OH, YE FAITHLESS BASTARDS...
HOBOS!!

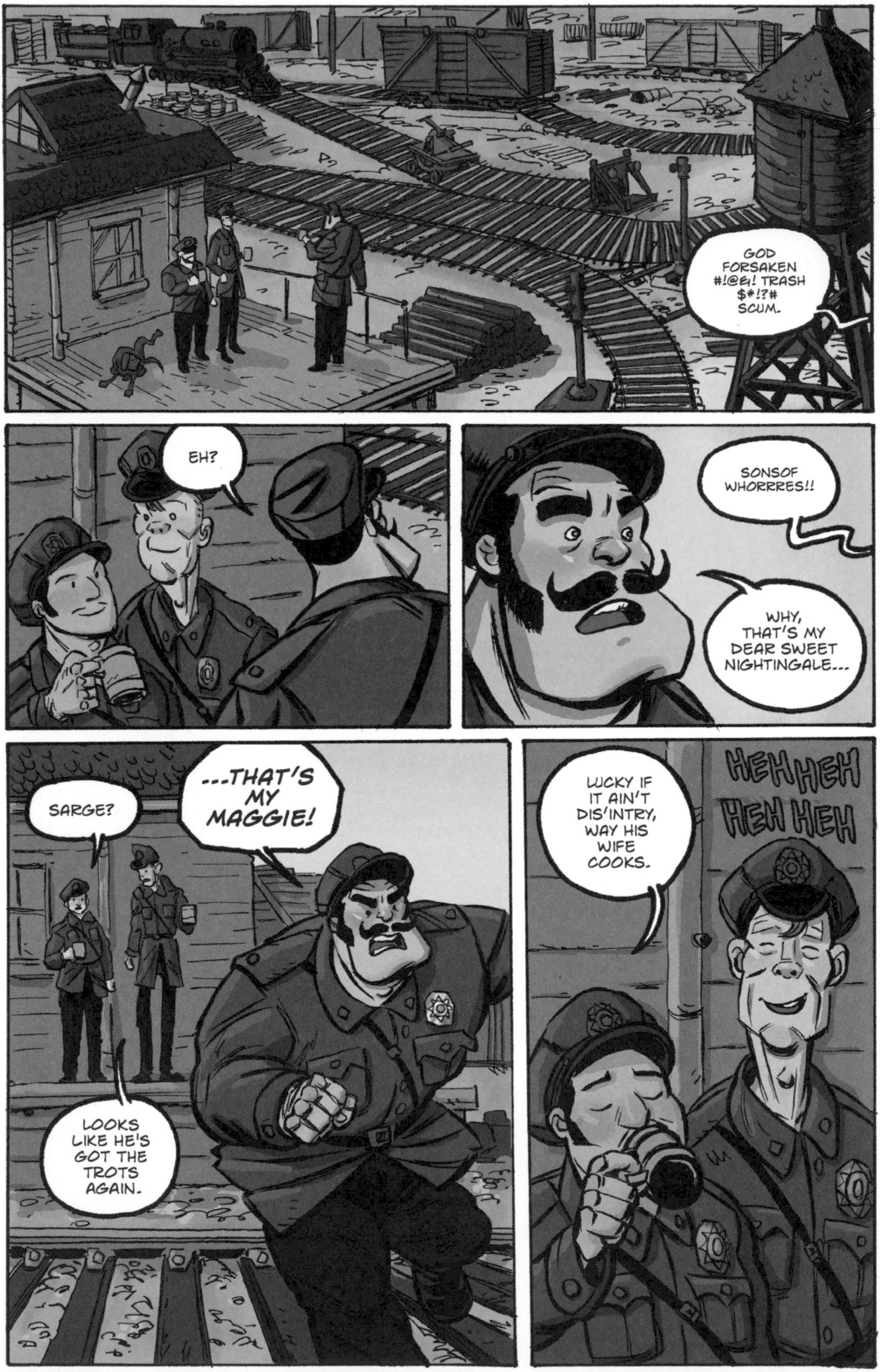
GOD FORSAKEN #!@&! TRASH $*!?# SCUM.
EH?
SONSOF WHORRES!!
WHY, THAT'S MY DEAR SWEET NIGHTINGALE...
SARGE?
...THAT'S MY MAGGIE!
LOOKS LIKE HE'S GOT THE TROTS AGAIN.
LUCKY IF IT AIN'T DIS'INTRY, WAY HIS WIFE COOKS.
HEH HEH HEH HEH

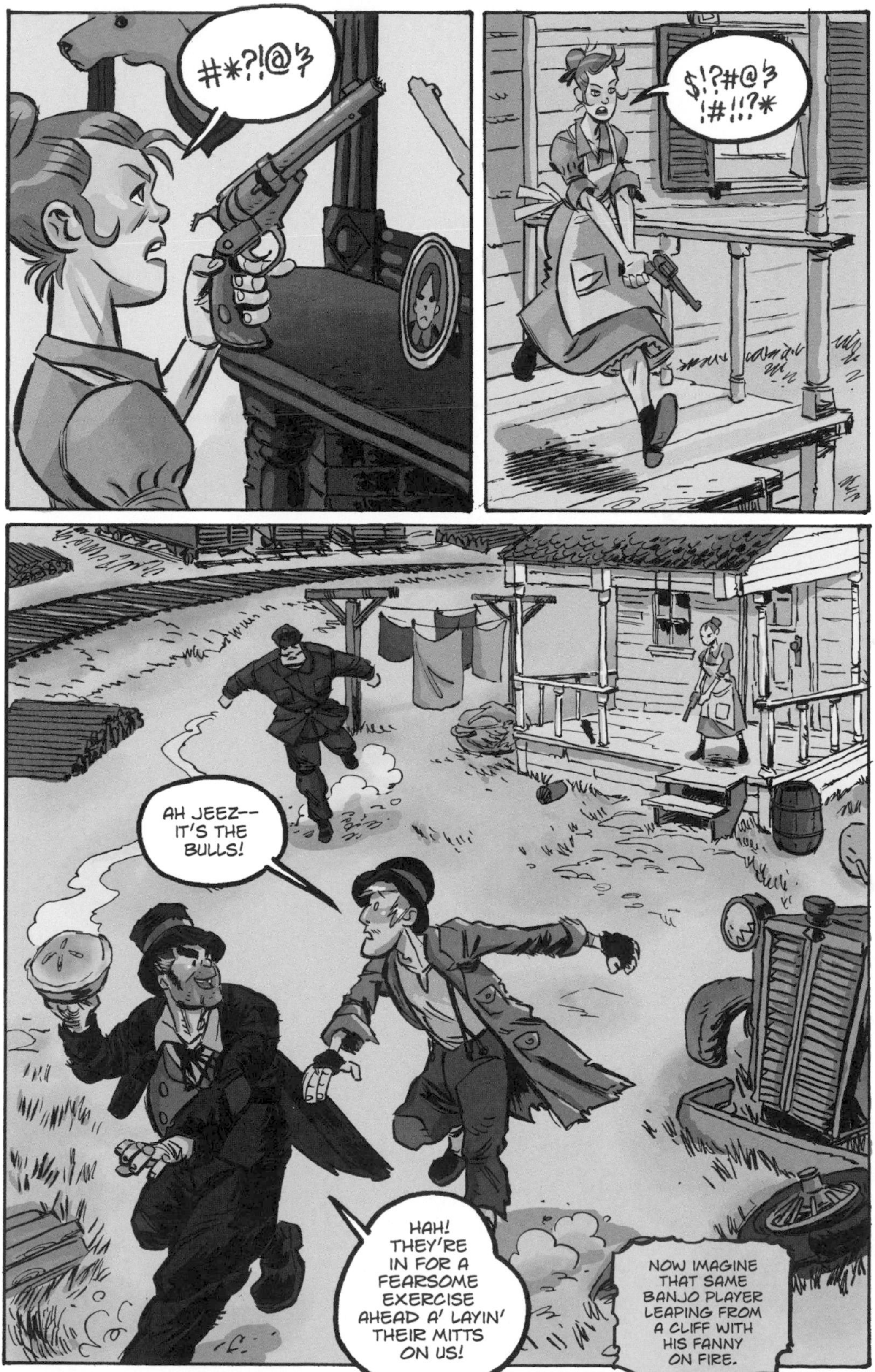
#*?!@≷
$!?#@≷ !#!!?*
AH JEEZ-- IT'S THE BULLS!
HAH! THEY'RE IN FOR A FEARSOME EXERCISE AHEAD A' LAYIN' THEIR MITTS ON US!
NOW IMAGINE THAT SAME BANJO PLAYER LEAPING FROM A CLIFF WITH HIS FANNY ON FIRE.

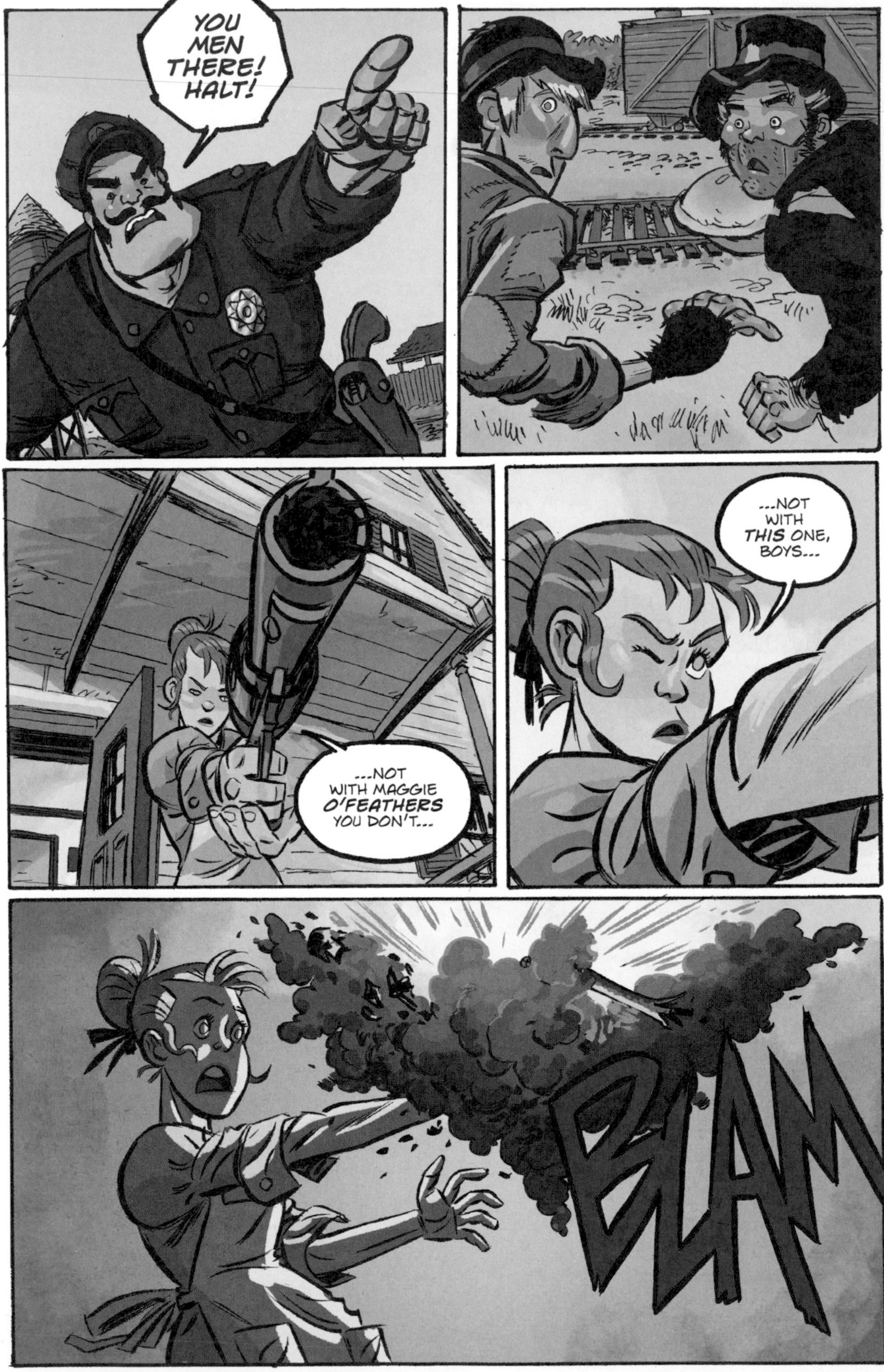
YOU MEN THERE! HALT!
...NOT WITH MAGGIE O'FEATHERS YOU DON'T...
...NOT WITH THIS ONE, BOYS...
BLAM

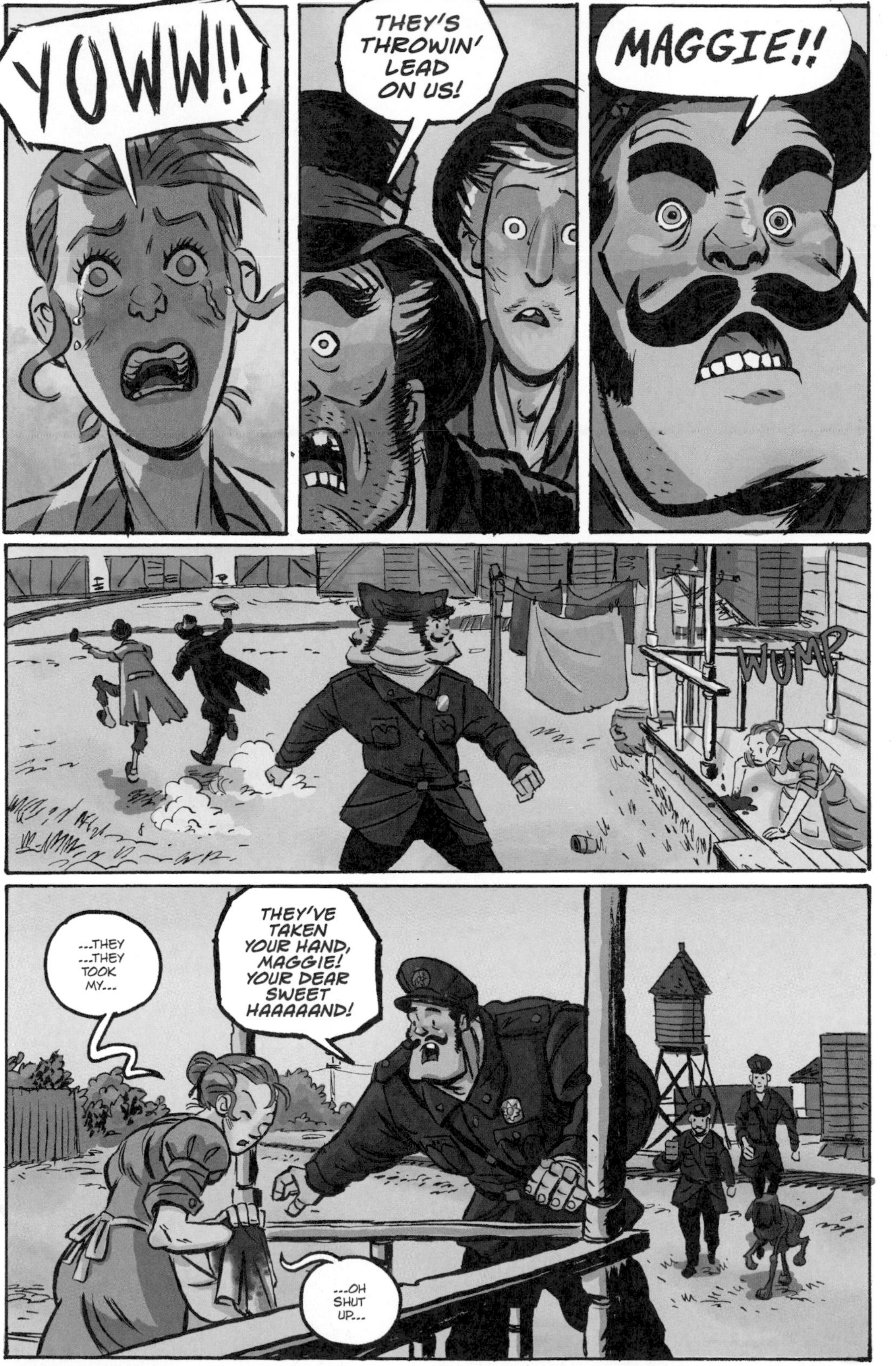
YOWW!!
THEY'S THROWIN' LEAD ON US!
MAGGIE!!
WUMP
...THEY ...THEY TOOK MY...
THEY'VE TAKEN YOUR HAND, MAGGIE! YOUR DEAR SWEET HAAAAAND!
...OH SHUT UP...

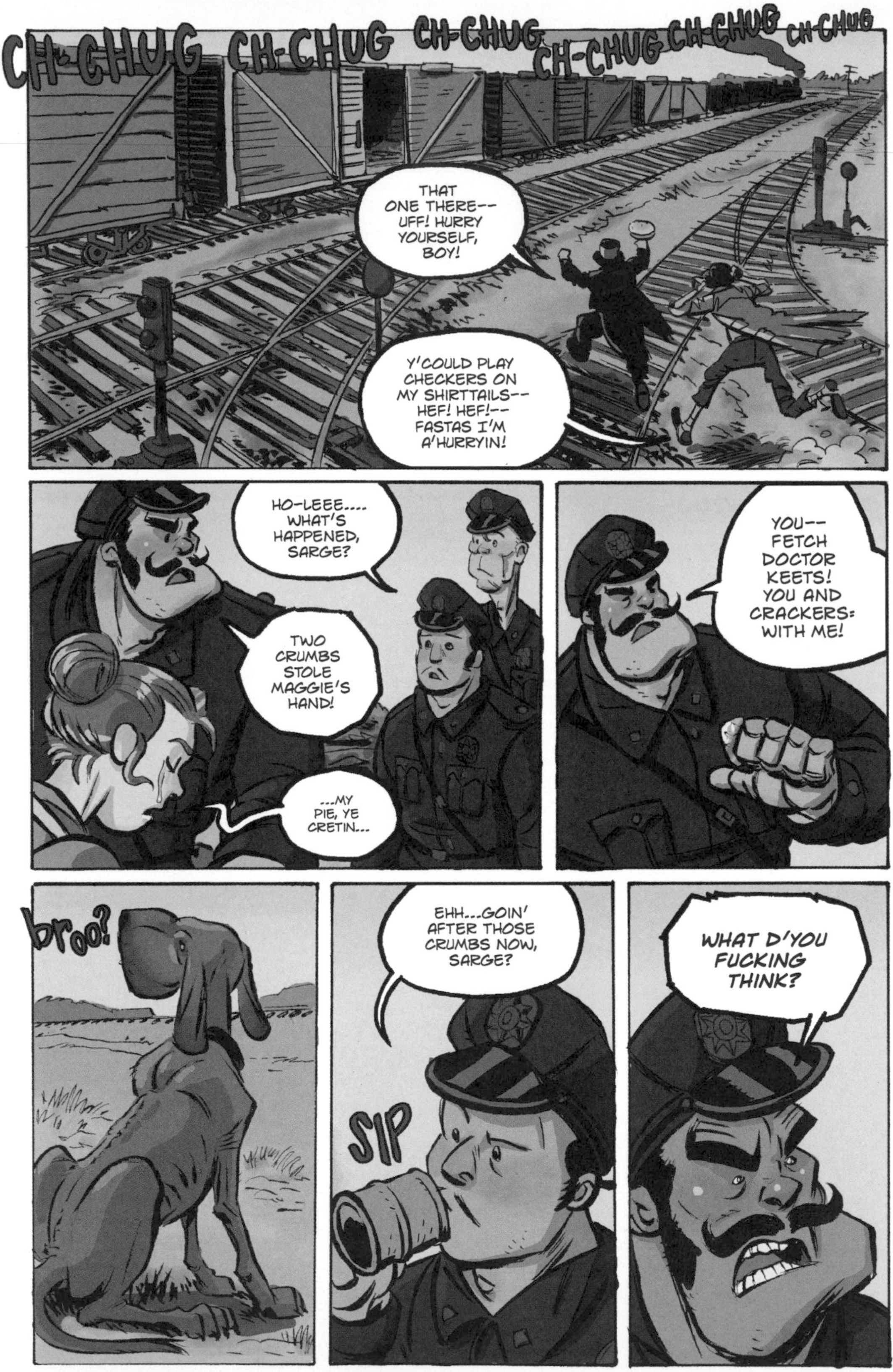
CH-CHUG CH-CHUG CH-CHUG CH-CHUG CH-CHUG CH-CHUG
THAT ONE THERE-- UFF! HURRY YOURSELF, BOY!
Y'COULD PLAY CHECKERS ON MY SHIRTTAILS-- HEF! HEF!-- FASTAS I'M A'HURRYIN!
HO-LEEE.... WHAT'S HAPPENED, SARGE?
TWO CRUMBS STOLE MAGGIE'S HAND!
...MY PIE, YE CRETIN...
YOU-- FETCH DOCTOR KEETS! YOU AND CRACKERS: WITH ME!
broo?
EHH...GOIN' AFTER THOSE CRUMBS NOW, SARGE?
SIP
WHAT D'YOU FUCKING THINK?

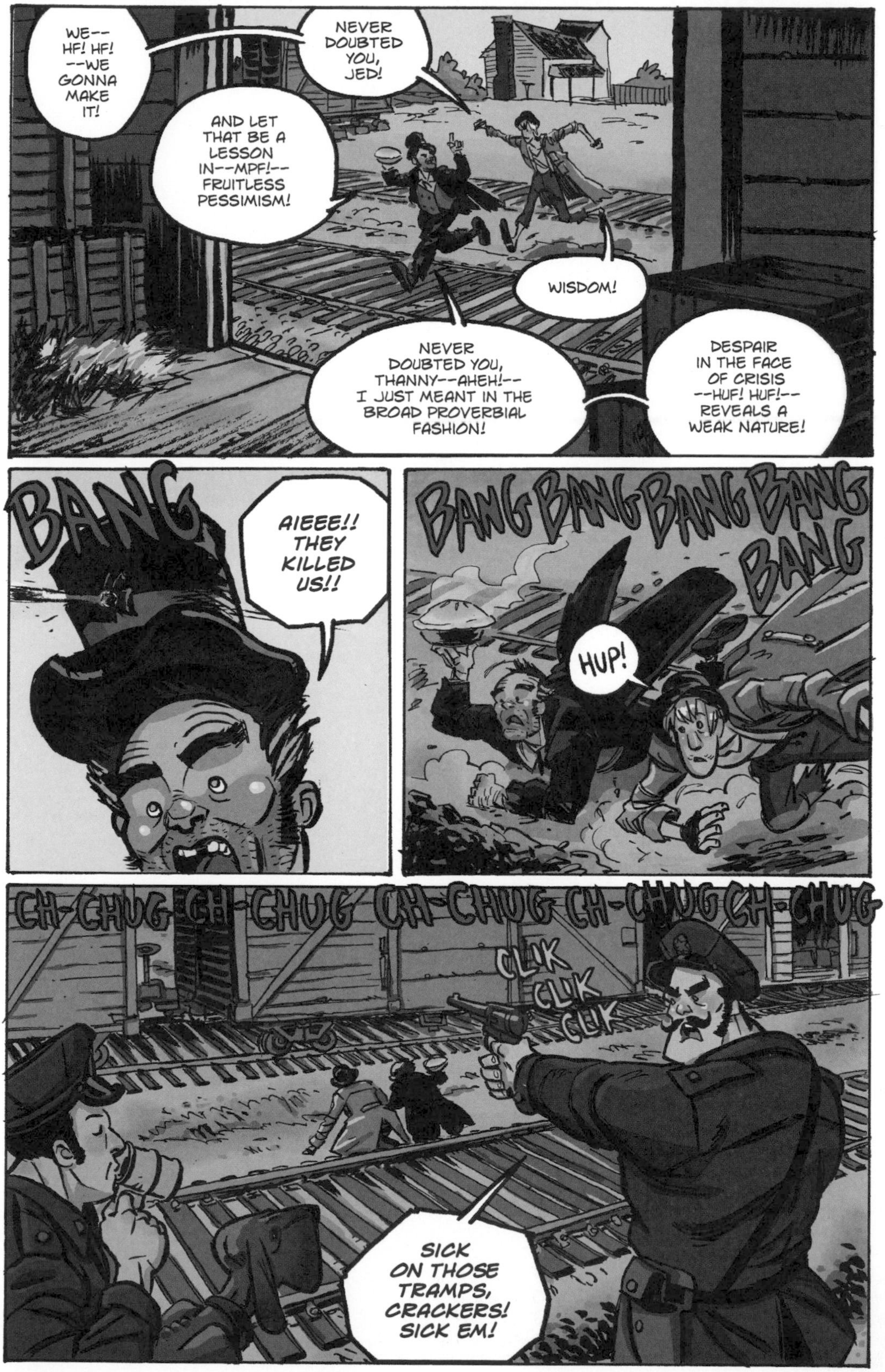
WE-- HF! HF! --WE GONNA MAKE IT!
NEVER DOUBTED YOU, JED!
AND LET THAT BE A LESSON IN--MPF!-- FRUITLESS PESSIMISM!
WISDOM!
NEVER DOUBTED YOU, THANNY--AHEH!-- I JUST MEANT IN THE BROAD PROVERBIAL FASHION!
DESPAIR IN THE FACE OF CRISIS --HUF! HUF!-- REVEALS A WEAK NATURE!
BANG
AIEEE!! THEY KILLED US!!
BANG BANG BANG BANG BANG
HUP!
CH-CHUG CH-CHUG CH-CHUG CH-CHUG CH-CHUG
CLIK CLIK CLIK
SICK ON THOSE TRAMPS, CRACKERS! SICK EM!

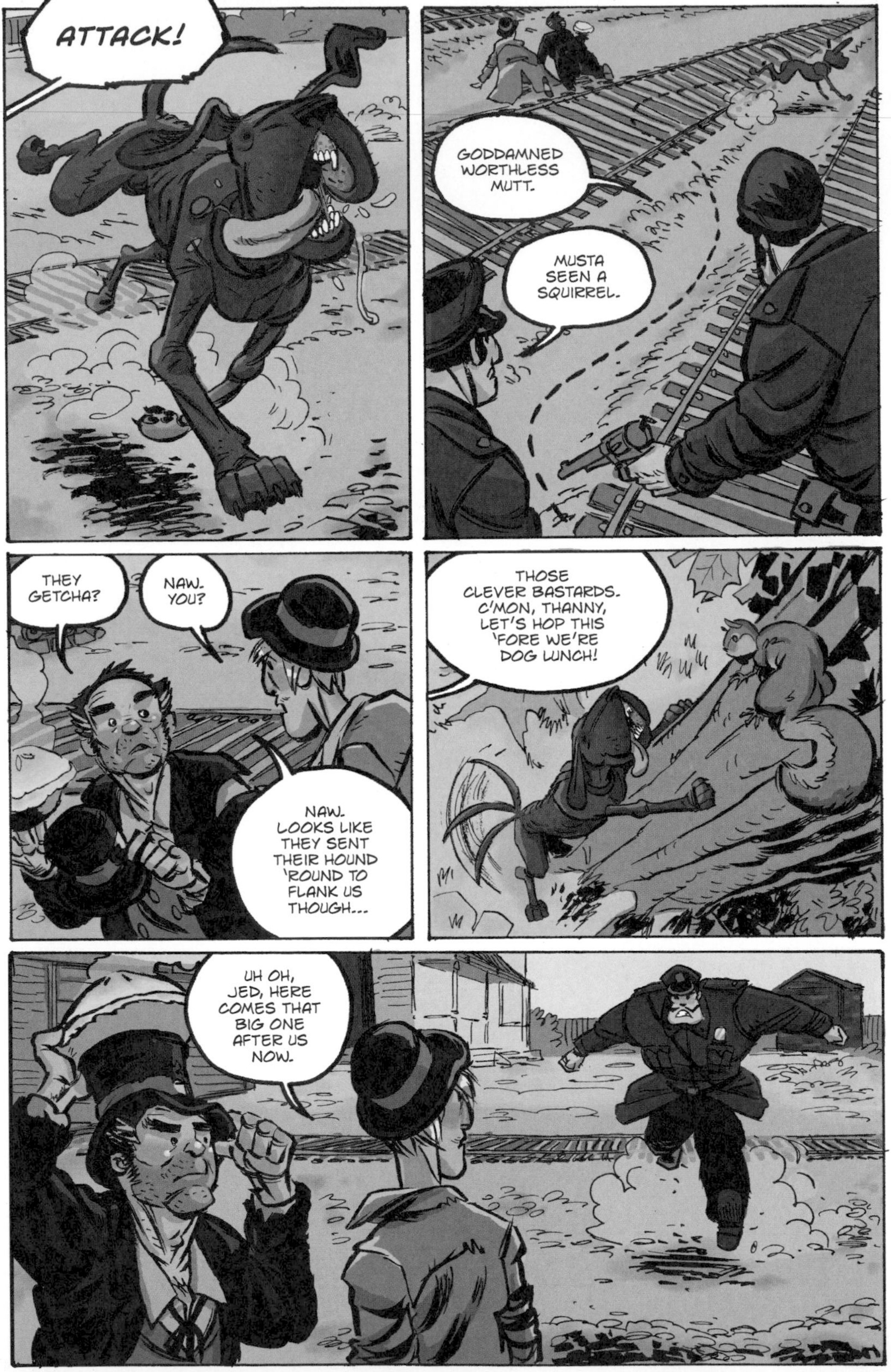
ATTACK!
GODDAMNED WORTHLESS MUTT.
MUSTA SEEN A SQUIRREL.
THEY GETCHA?
NAW. YOU?
NAW. LOOKS LIKE THEY SENT THEIR HOUND 'ROUND TO FLANK US THOUGH...
THOSE CLEVER BASTARDS. C'MON, THANNY, LET'S HOP THIS 'FORE WE'RE DOG LUNCH!
UH OH, JED, HERE COMES THAT BIG ONE AFTER US NOW.

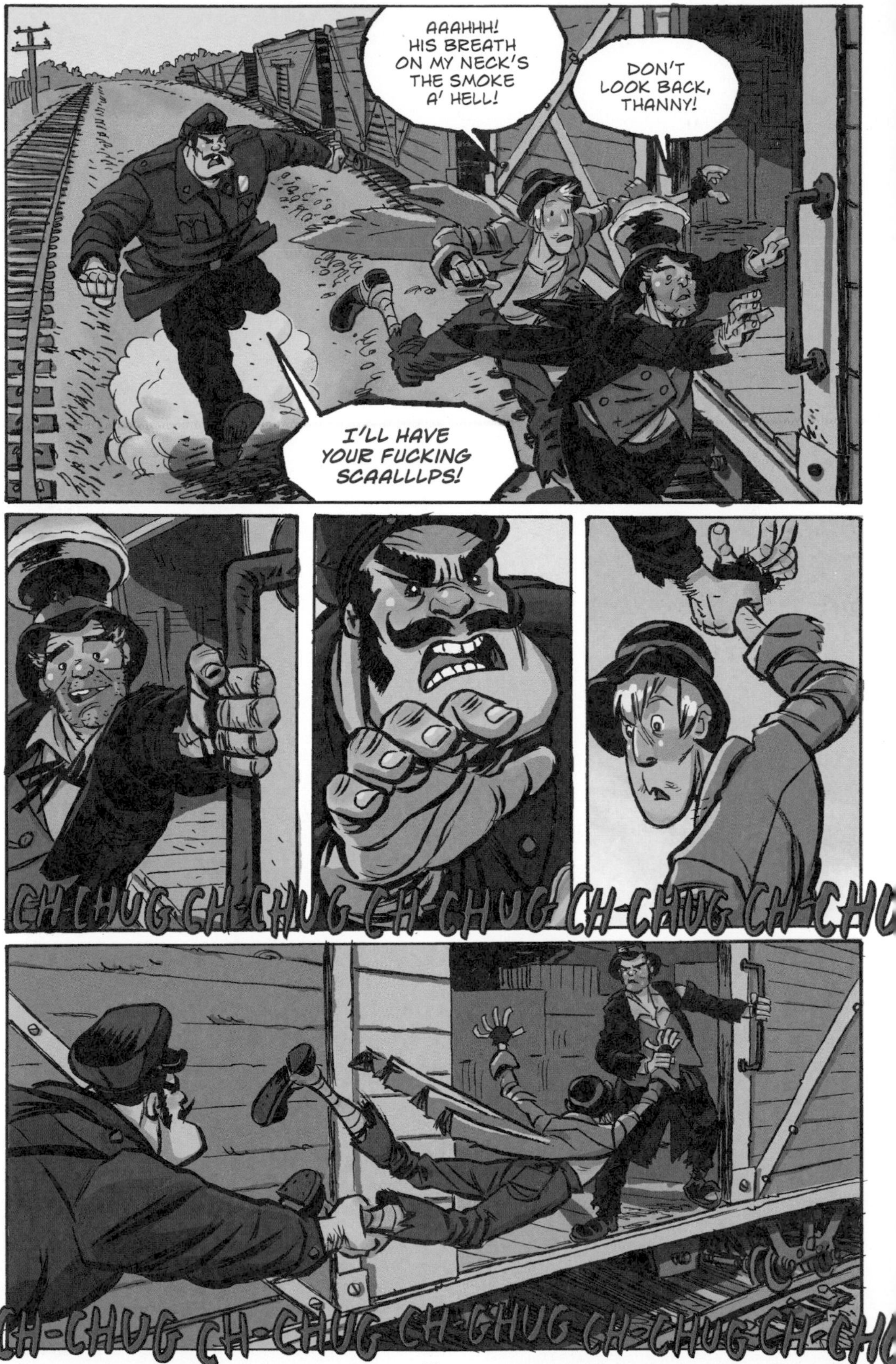
AAAHHH!
HIS BREATH ON MY NECK'S THE SMOKE A' HELL!
DON'T LOOK BACK, THANNY!
I'LL HAVE YOUR FUCKING SCAALLLPS!
CH-CHUG CH-CHUG CH-CHUG CH-CHUG CH-CHU
CH-CHUG CH-CHUG CH-CHUG CH-CHUG CH-CHU

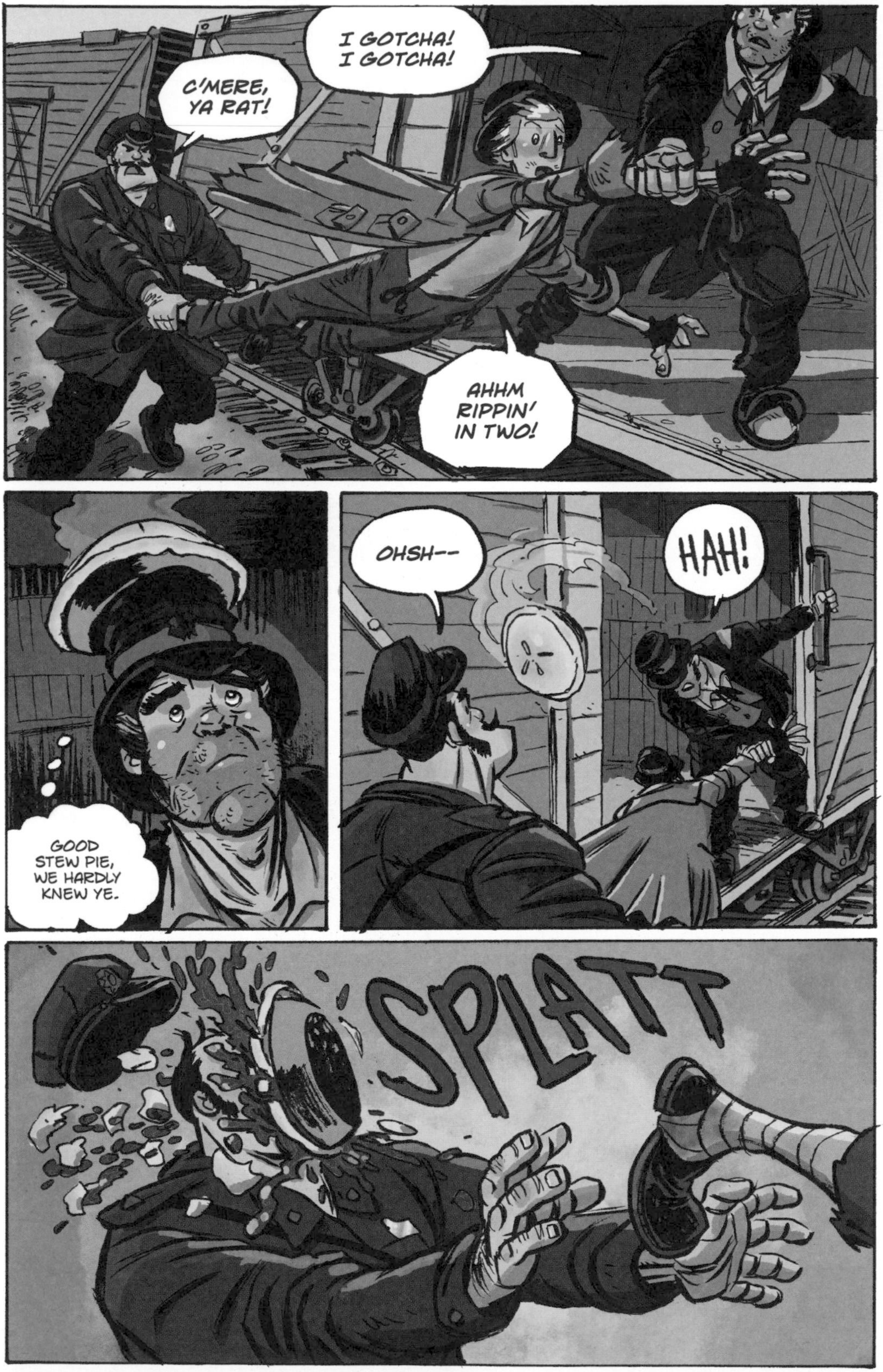
C'MERE, YA RAT!
I GOTCHA! I GOTCHA!
AHHM RIPPIN' IN TWO!
GOOD STEW PIE, WE HARDLY KNEW YE.
OHSH--
HAH!
SPLATT

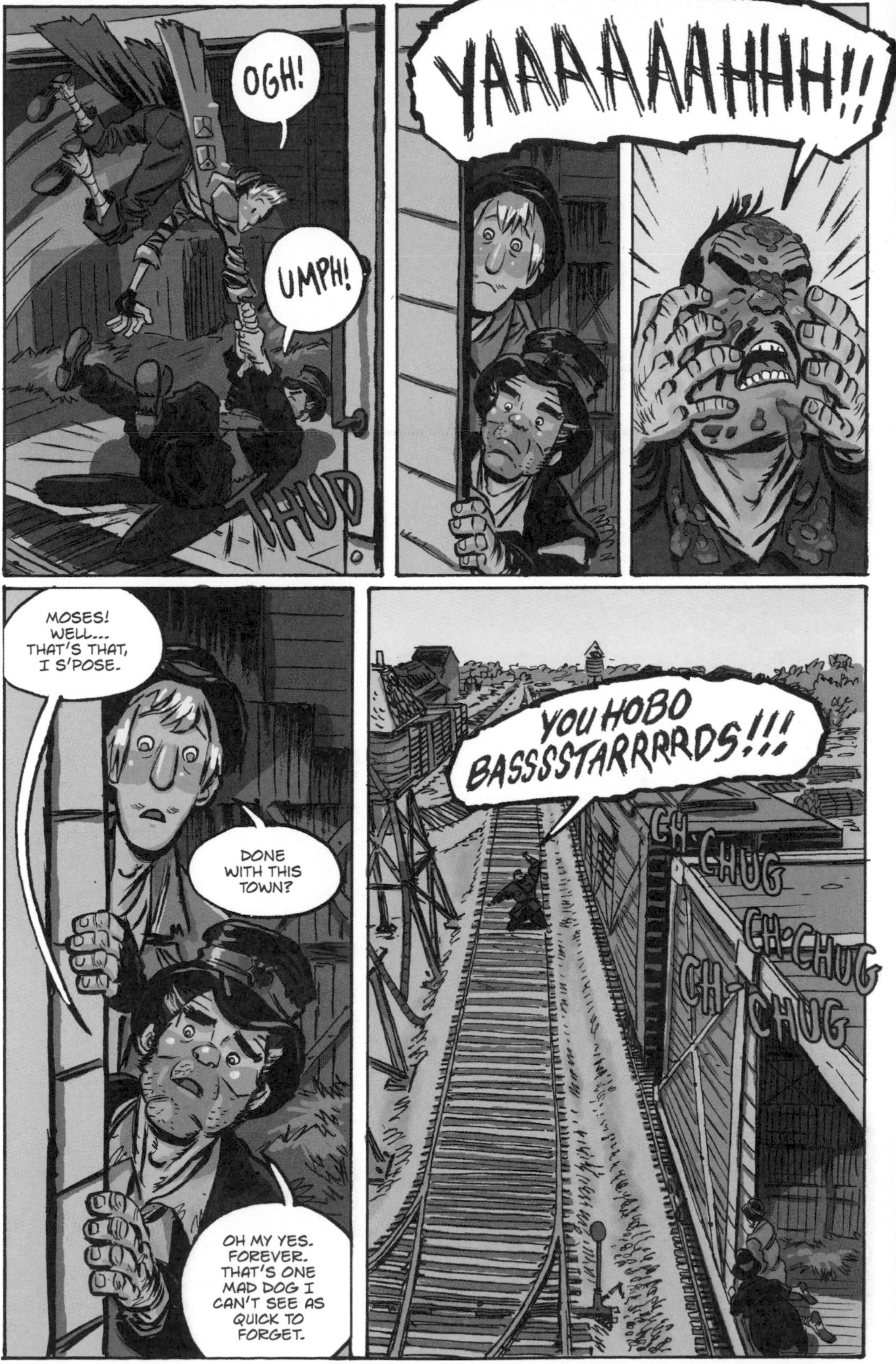
OGH!
UMPH!
THUD
YAAAAAAHHH!!
MOSES! WELL... THAT'S THAT, I S'POSE.
DONE WITH THIS TOWN?
OH MY YES. FOREVER. THAT'S ONE MAD DOG I CAN'T SEE AS QUICK TO FORGET.
YOU HOBO BASSSSTARRRRDS!!!
CH-CHUG
CH-CHUG
CH-CHUG

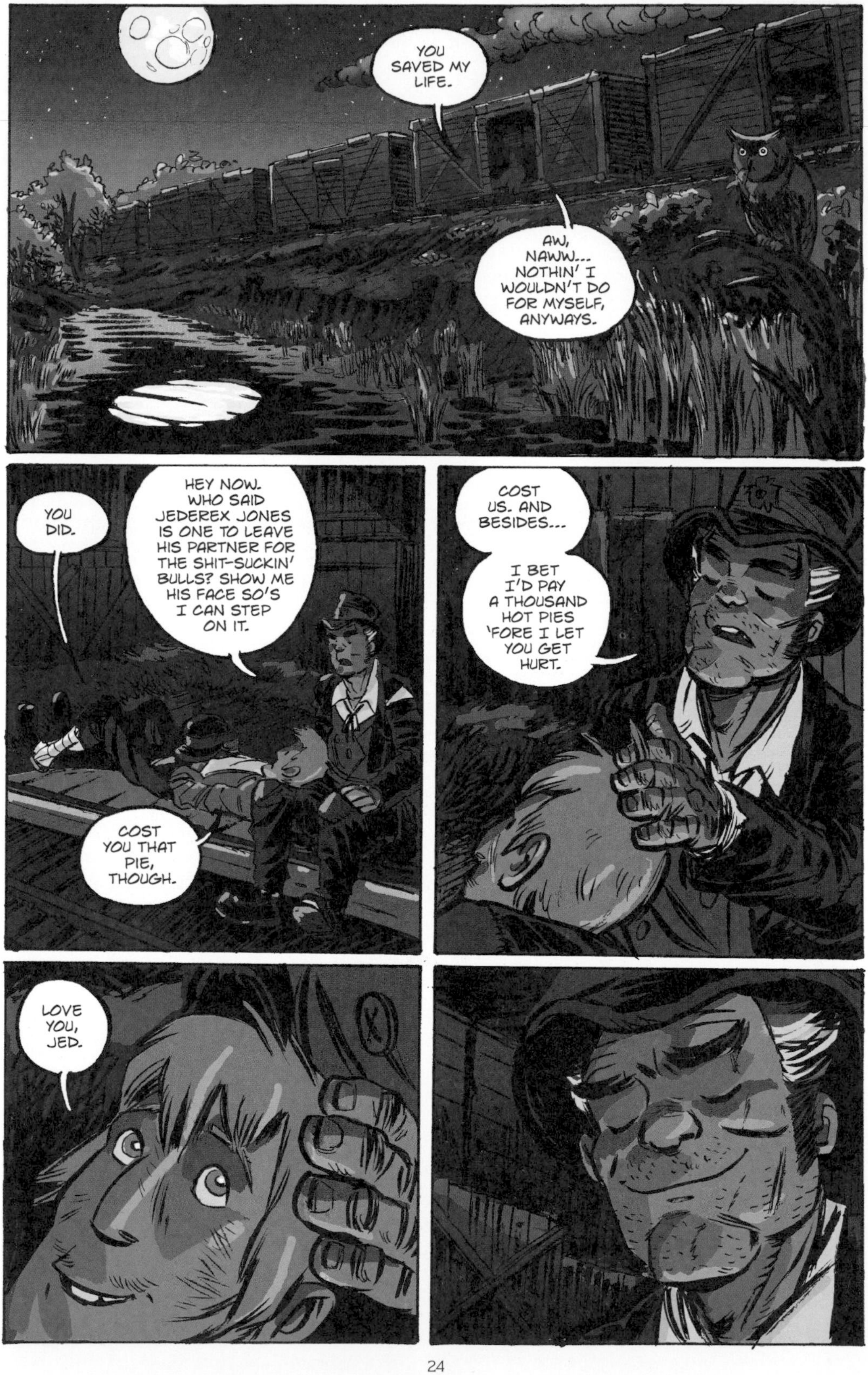
YOU SAVED MY LIFE.
AW, NAWW... NOTHIN' I WOULDN'T DO FOR MYSELF, ANYWAYS.
YOU DID.
HEY NOW. WHO SAID JEDEREX JONES IS ONE TO LEAVE HIS PARTNER FOR THE SHIT-SUCKIN' BULLS? SHOW ME HIS FACE SO'S I CAN STEP ON IT.
COST YOU THAT PIE, THOUGH.
COST US. AND BESIDES...
I BET I'D PAY A THOUSAND HOT PIES 'FORE I LET YOU GET HURT.
LOVE YOU, JED.

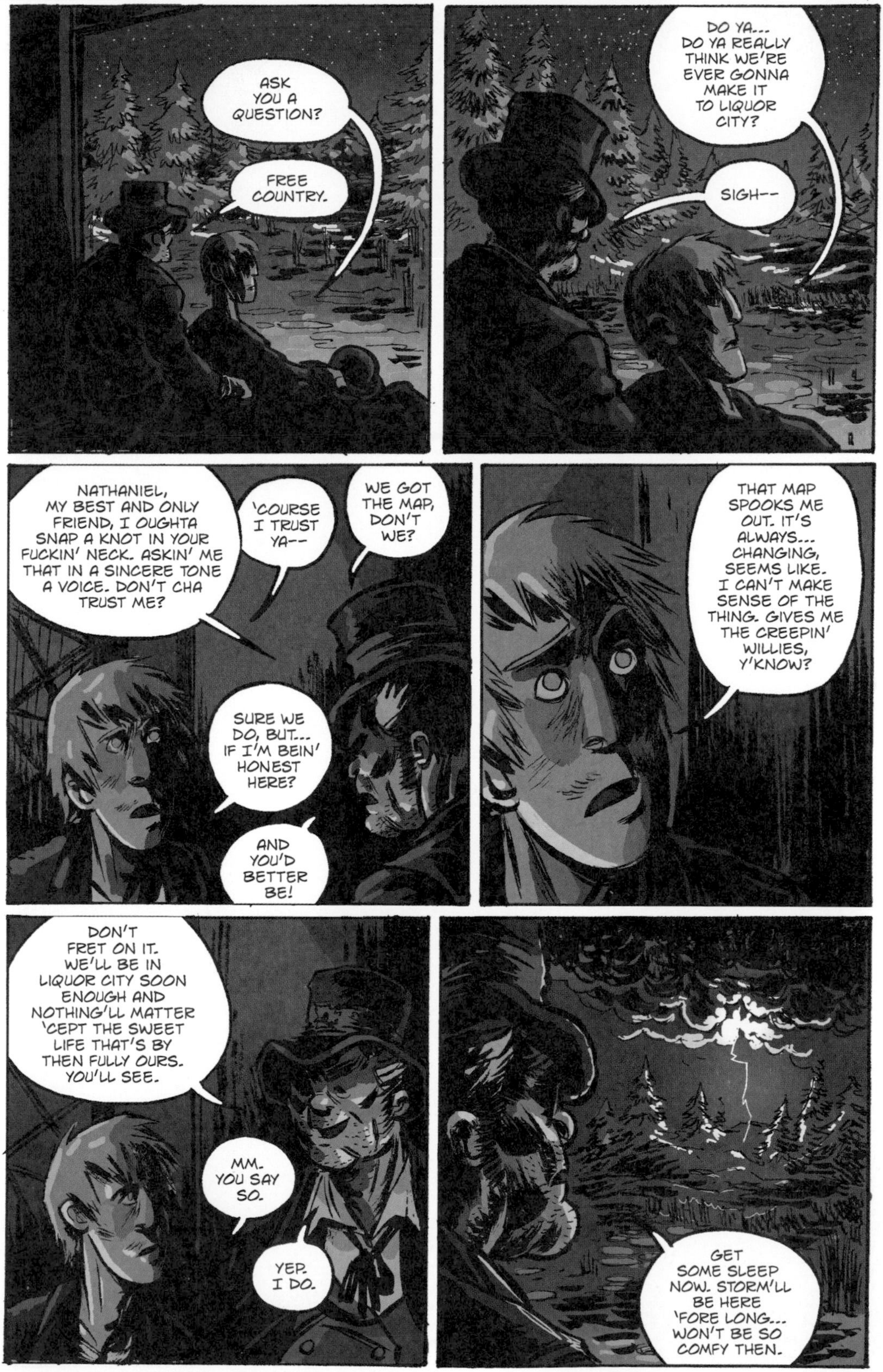
ASK YOU A QUESTION?
FREE COUNTRY.
DO YA... DO YA REALLY THINK WE'RE EVER GONNA MAKE IT TO LIQUOR CITY?
SIGH--
NATHANIEL, MY BEST AND ONLY FRIEND, I OUGHTA SNAP A KNOT IN YOUR FUCKIN' NECK. ASKIN' ME THAT IN A SINCERE TONE A VOICE. DON'T CHA TRUST ME?
'COURSE I TRUST YA--
WE GOT THE MAP, DON'T WE?
SURE WE DO, BUT... IF I'M BEIN' HONEST HERE?
AND YOU'D BETTER BE!
THAT MAP SPOOKS ME OUT. IT'S ALWAYS... CHANGING, SEEMS LIKE. I CAN'T MAKE SENSE OF THE THING. GIVES ME THE CREEPIN' WILLIES, Y'KNOW?
DON'T FRET ON IT. WE'LL BE IN LIQUOR CITY SOON ENOUGH AND NOTHING'LL MATTER 'CEPT THE SWEET LIFE THAT'S BY THEN FULLY OURS. YOU'LL SEE.
MM. YOU SAY SO.
YEP. I DO.
GET SOME SLEEP NOW. STORM'LL BE HERE 'FORE LONG... WON'T BE SO COMFY THEN.

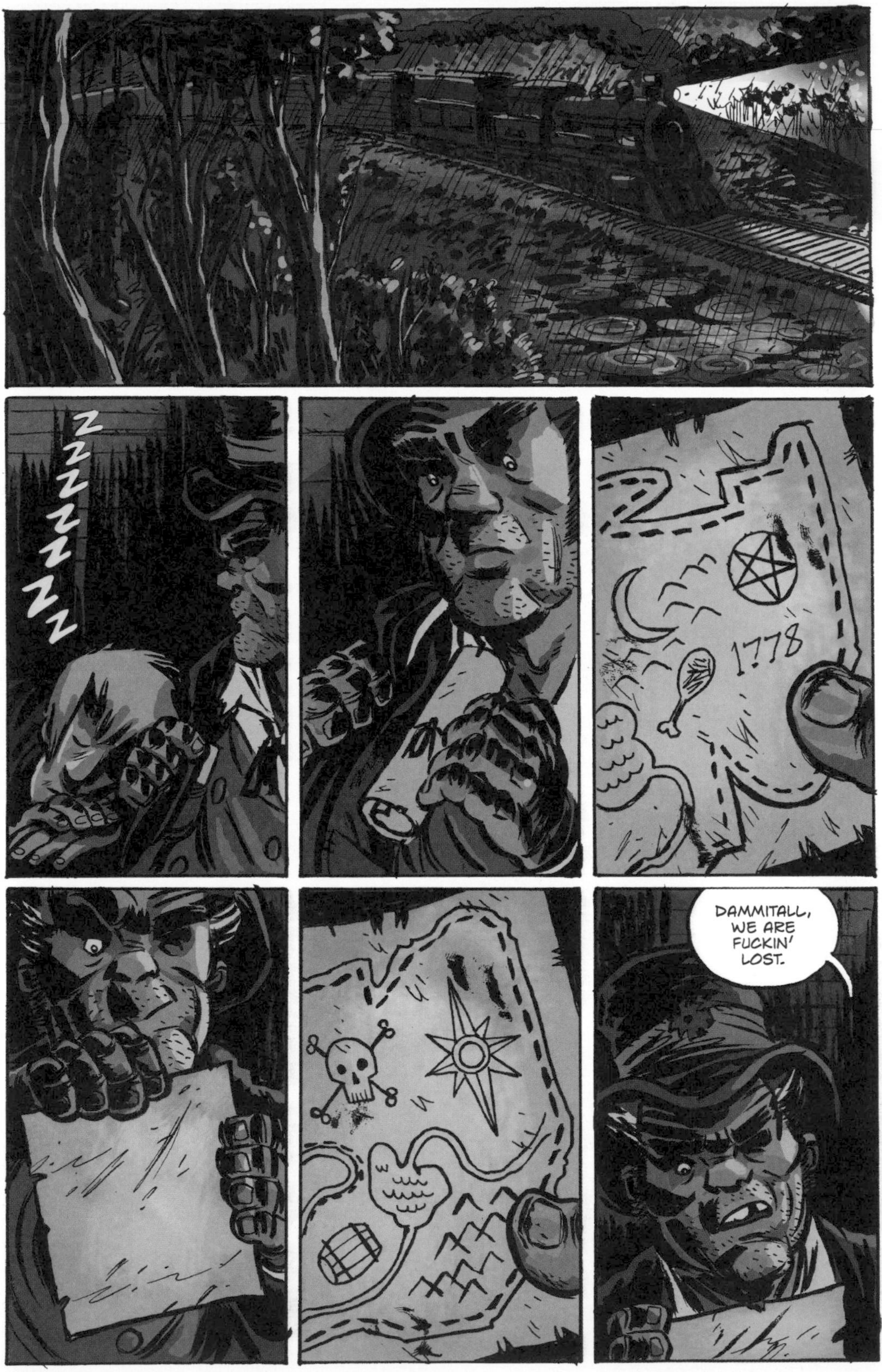
ZZZZZZZ
1778
DAMMITALL, WE ARE FUCKIN' LOST.

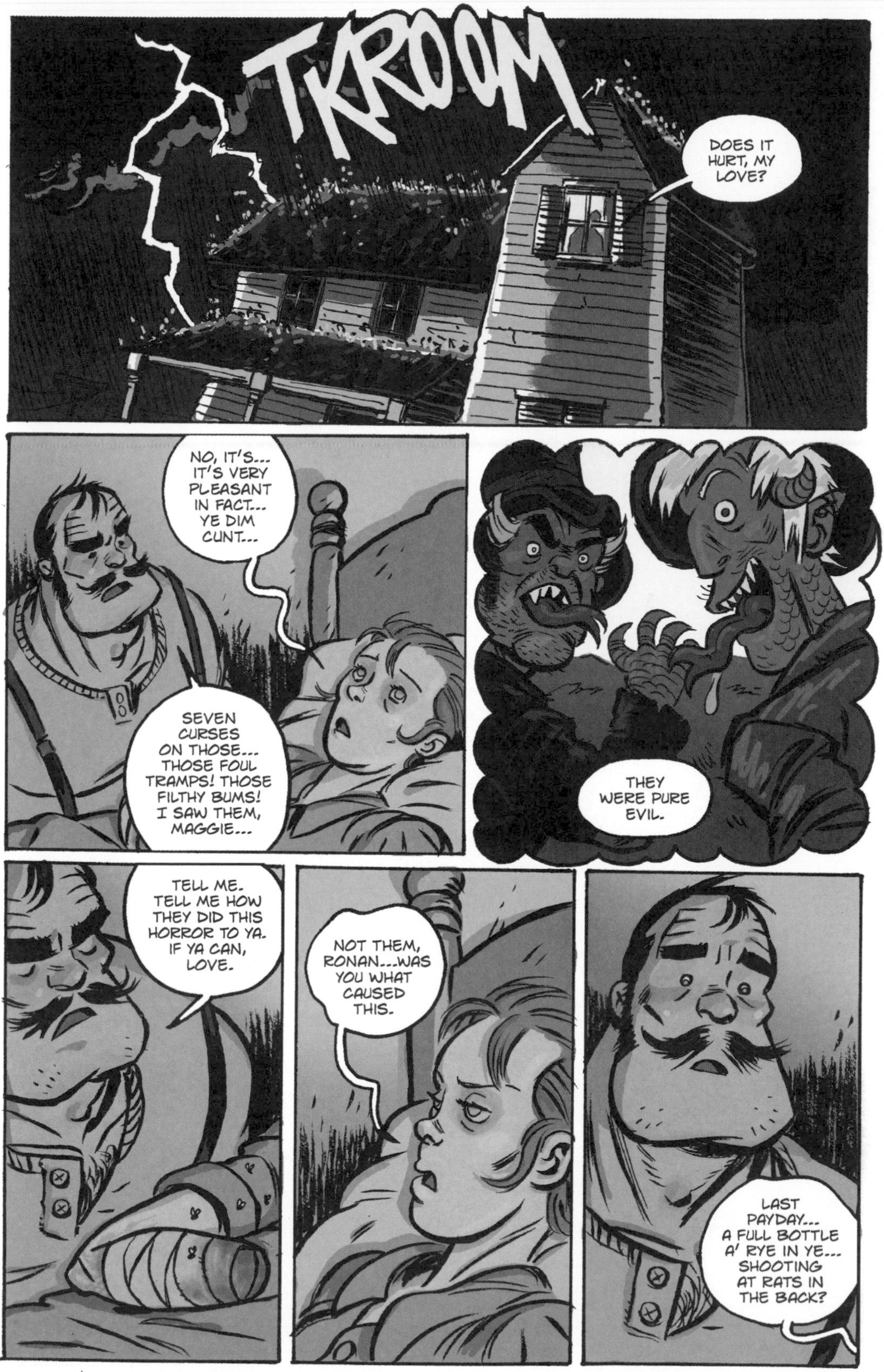
TKROOM
DOES IT HURT, MY LOVE?
NO, IT'S... IT'S VERY PLEASANT IN FACT... YE DIM CUNT...
SEVEN CURSES ON THOSE... THOSE FOUL TRAMPS! THOSE FILTHY BUMS! I SAW THEM, MAGGIE...
THEY WERE PURE EVIL.
TELL ME. TELL ME HOW THEY DID THIS HORROR TO YA. IF YA CAN, LOVE.
NOT THEM, RONAN...WAS YOU WHAT CAUSED THIS.
LAST PAYDAY... A FULL BOTTLE A' RYE IN YE... SHOOTING AT RATS IN THE BACK?

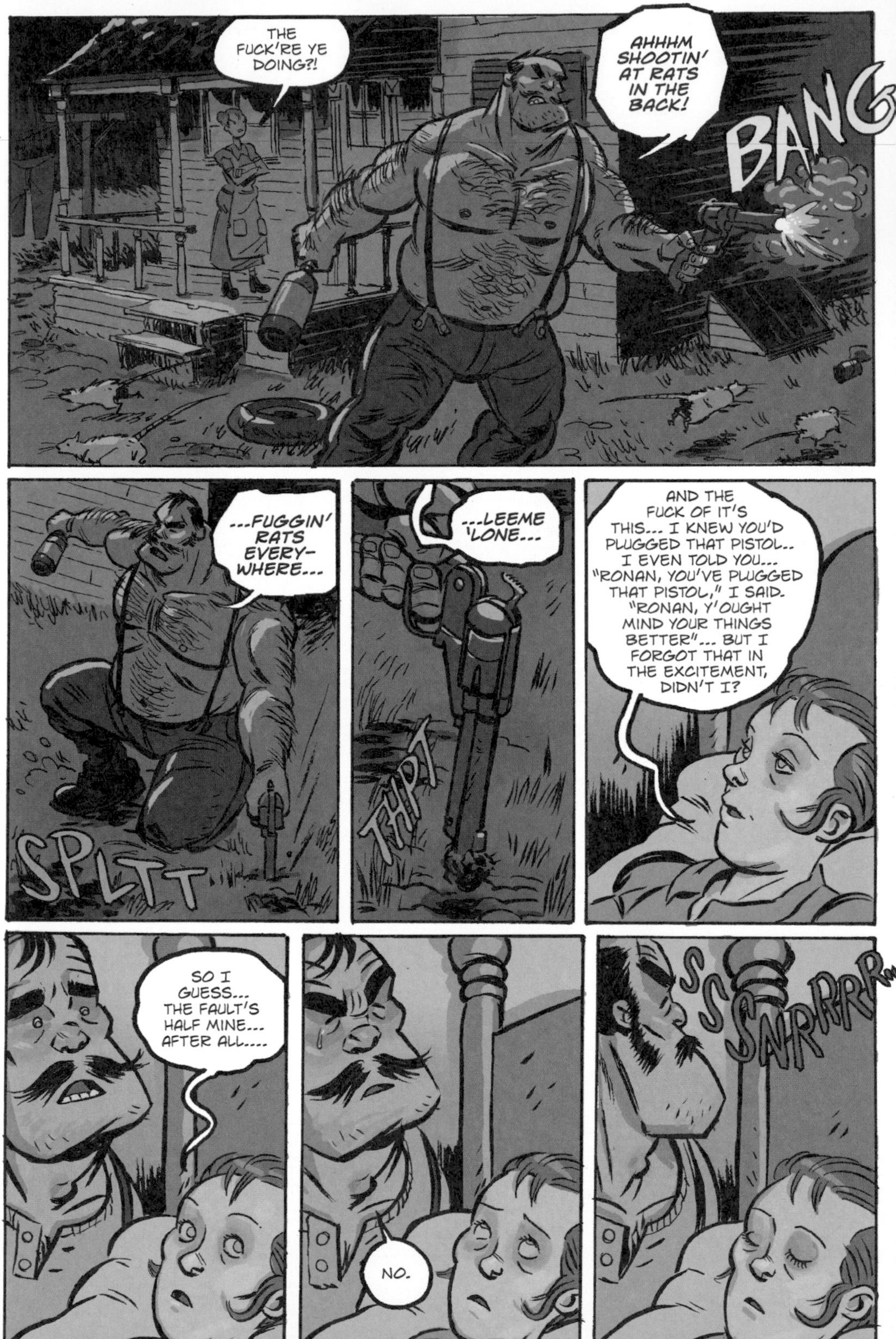
THE FUCK'RE YE DOING?!
AHHHM SHOOTIN' AT RATS IN THE BACK!
BANG
...FUGGIN' RATS EVERY-WHERE...
SPLTT
...LEEME 'LONE...
THPT
AND THE FUCK OF IT'S THIS... I KNEW YOU'D PLUGGED THAT PISTOL.. I EVEN TOLD YOU... "RONAN, YOU'VE PLUGGED THAT PISTOL," I SAID. "RONAN, Y'OUGHT MIND YOUR THINGS BETTER"... BUT I FORGOT THAT IN THE EXCITEMENT, DIDN'T I?
SO I GUESS... THE FAULT'S HALF MINE... AFTER ALL....
NO.
SSSNRRRRR

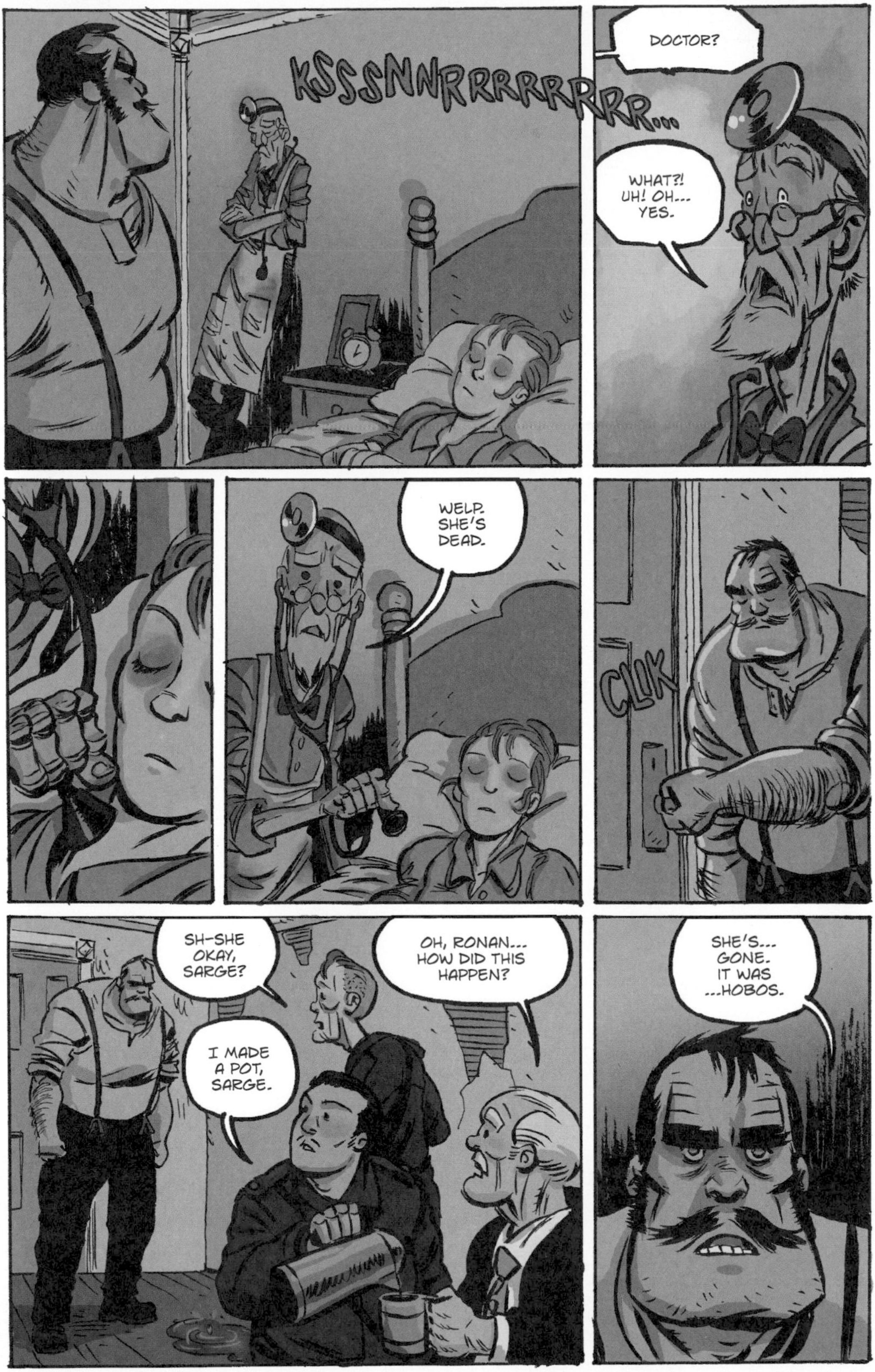
KSSSNNRRRRRRRRR...
DOCTOR?
WHAT?! UH! OH... YES.
WELP. SHE'S DEAD.
CLIK
SH-SHE OKAY, SARGE?
OH, RONAN... HOW DID THIS HAPPEN?
I MADE A POT, SARGE.
SHE'S... GONE. IT WAS ...HOBOS.

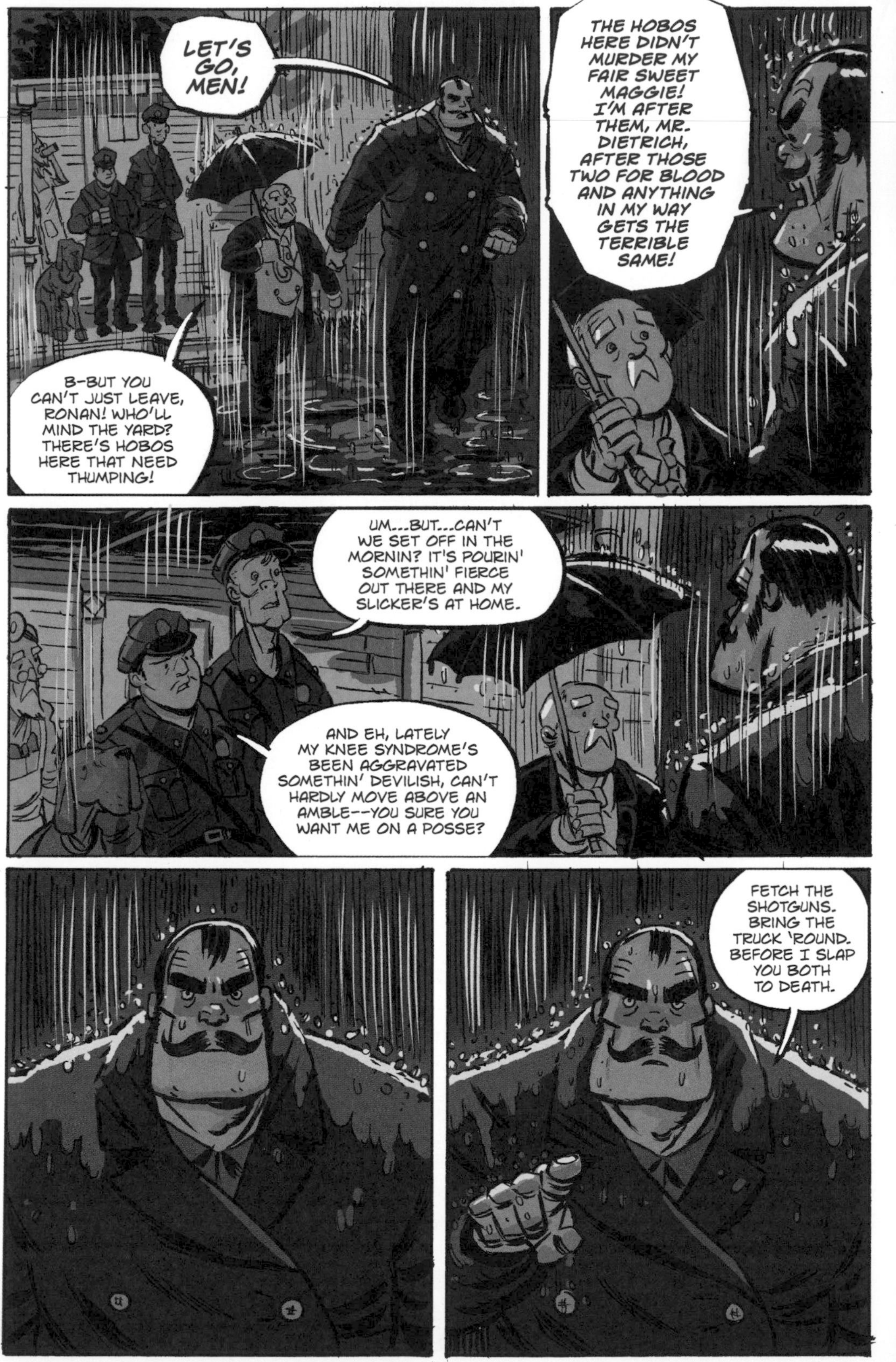
LET'S GO, MEN!
B-BUT YOU CAN'T JUST LEAVE, RONAN! WHO'LL MIND THE YARD? THERE'S HOBOS HERE THAT NEED THUMPING!
THE HOBOS HERE DIDN'T MURDER MY FAIR SWEET MAGGIE! I'M AFTER THEM, MR. DIETRICH, AFTER THOSE TWO FOR BLOOD AND ANYTHING IN MY WAY GETS THE TERRIBLE SAME!
UM...BUT...CAN'T WE SET OFF IN THE MORNIN? IT'S POURIN' SOMETHIN' FIERCE OUT THERE AND MY SLICKER'S AT HOME.
AND EH, LATELY MY KNEE SYNDROME'S BEEN AGGRAVATED SOMETHIN' DEVILISH, CAN'T HARDLY MOVE ABOVE AN AMBLE--YOU SURE YOU WANT ME ON A POSSE?
FETCH THE SHOTGUNS. BRING THE TRUCK 'ROUND. BEFORE I SLAP YOU BOTH TO DEATH.

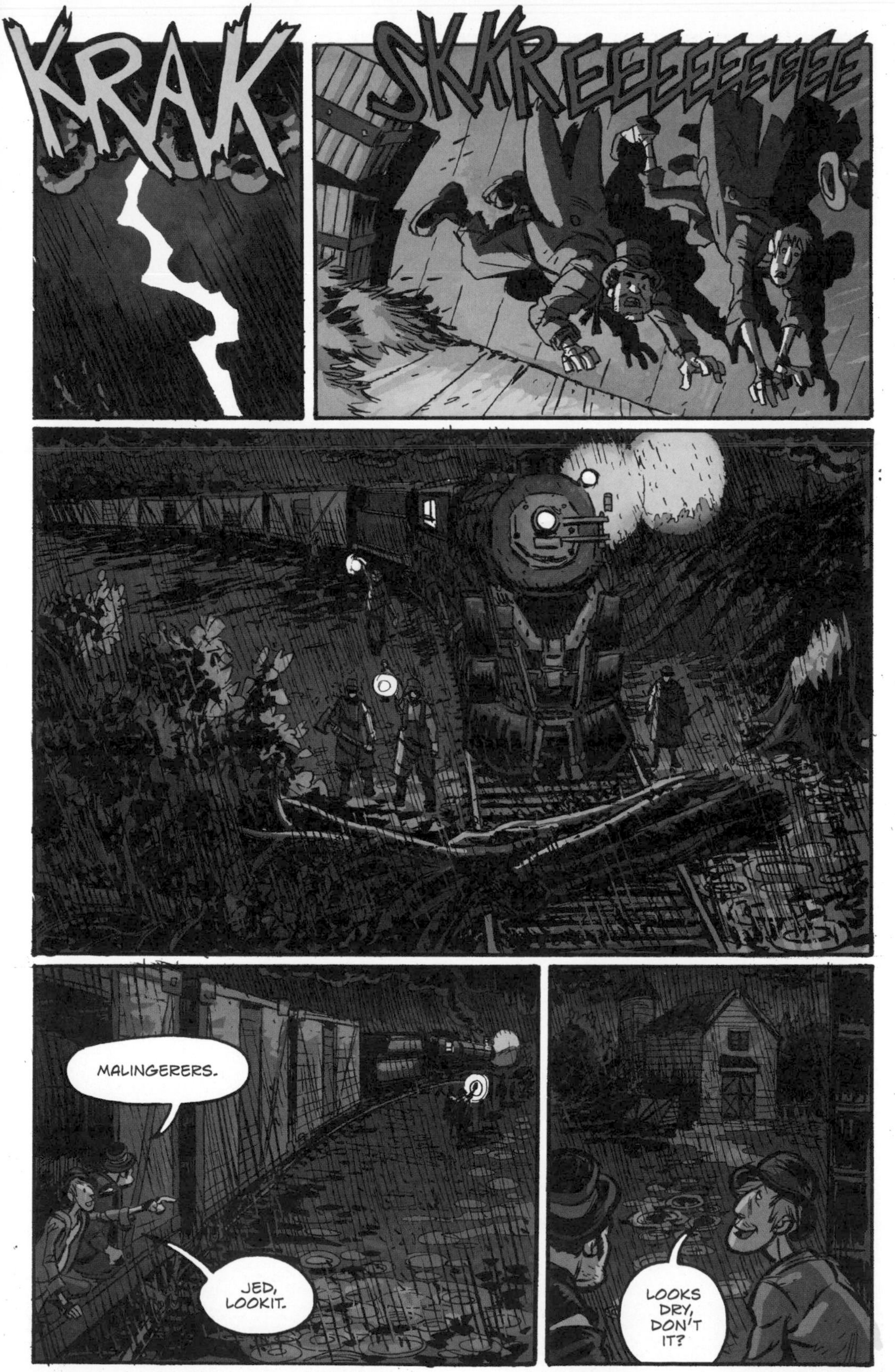
KRAK
SKKREEEEEEEEE
MALINGERERS.
JED, LOOKIT.
LOOKS DRY, DON'T IT?

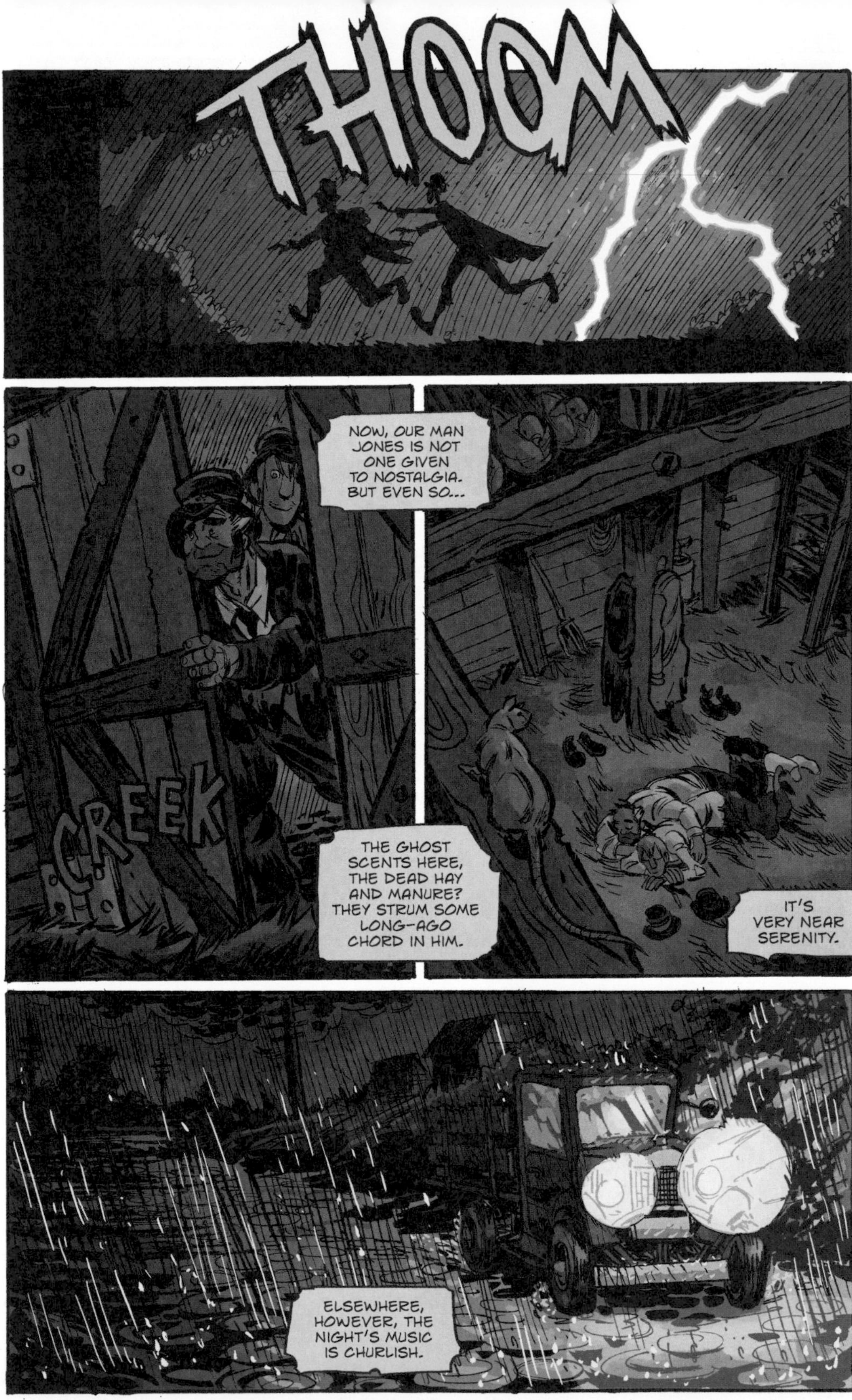
THOOM
NOW, OUR MAN JONES IS NOT ONE GIVEN TO NOSTALGIA. BUT EVEN SO...
CREEK
THE GHOST SCENTS HERE, THE DEAD HAY AND MANURE? THEY STRUM SOME LONG-AGO CHORD IN HIM.
IT'S VERY NEAR SERENITY.
ELSEWHERE, HOWEVER, THE NIGHT'S MUSIC IS CHURLISH.

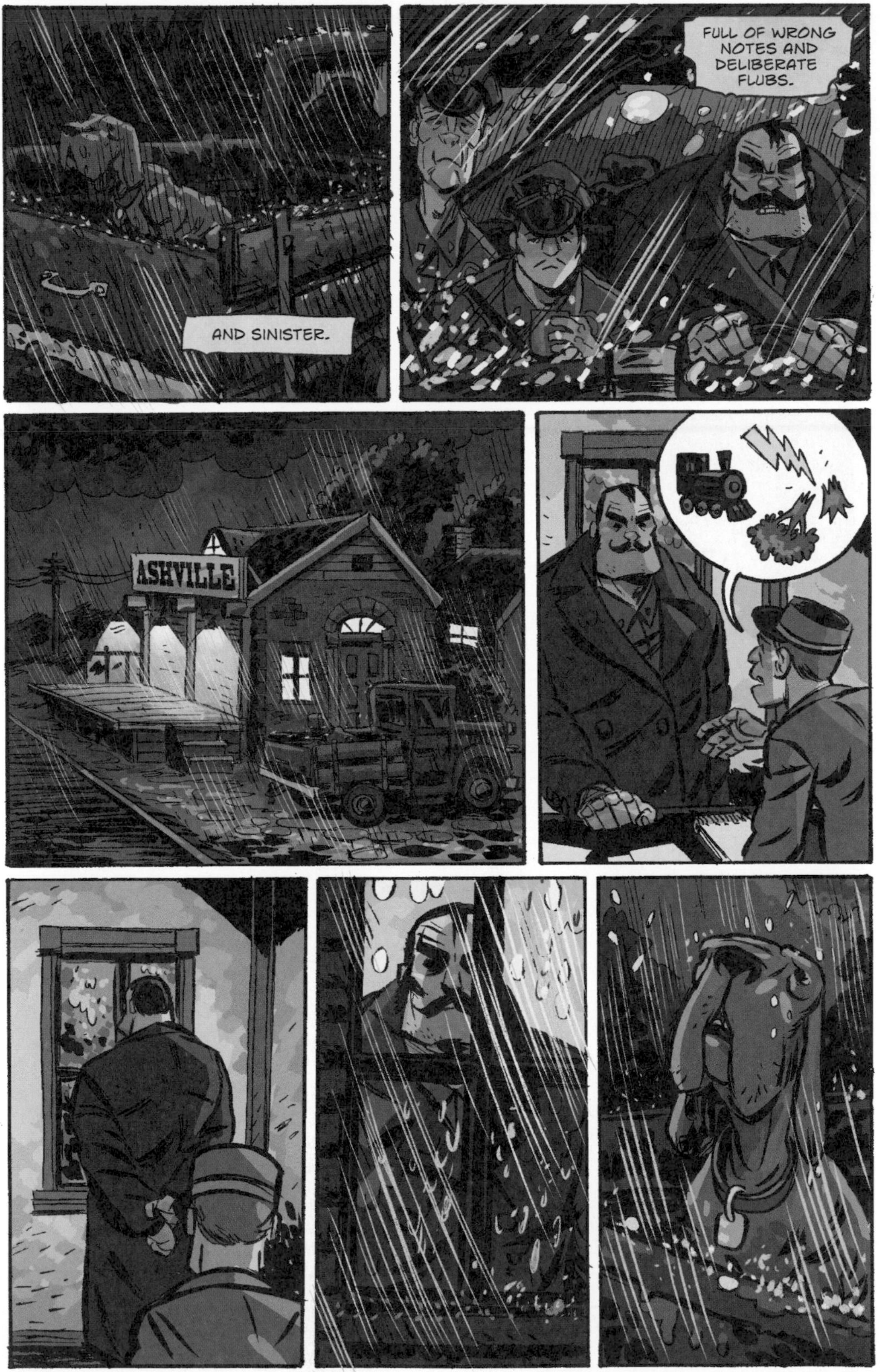
AND SINISTER.
FULL OF WRONG NOTES AND DELIBERATE FLUBS.
ASHVILLE

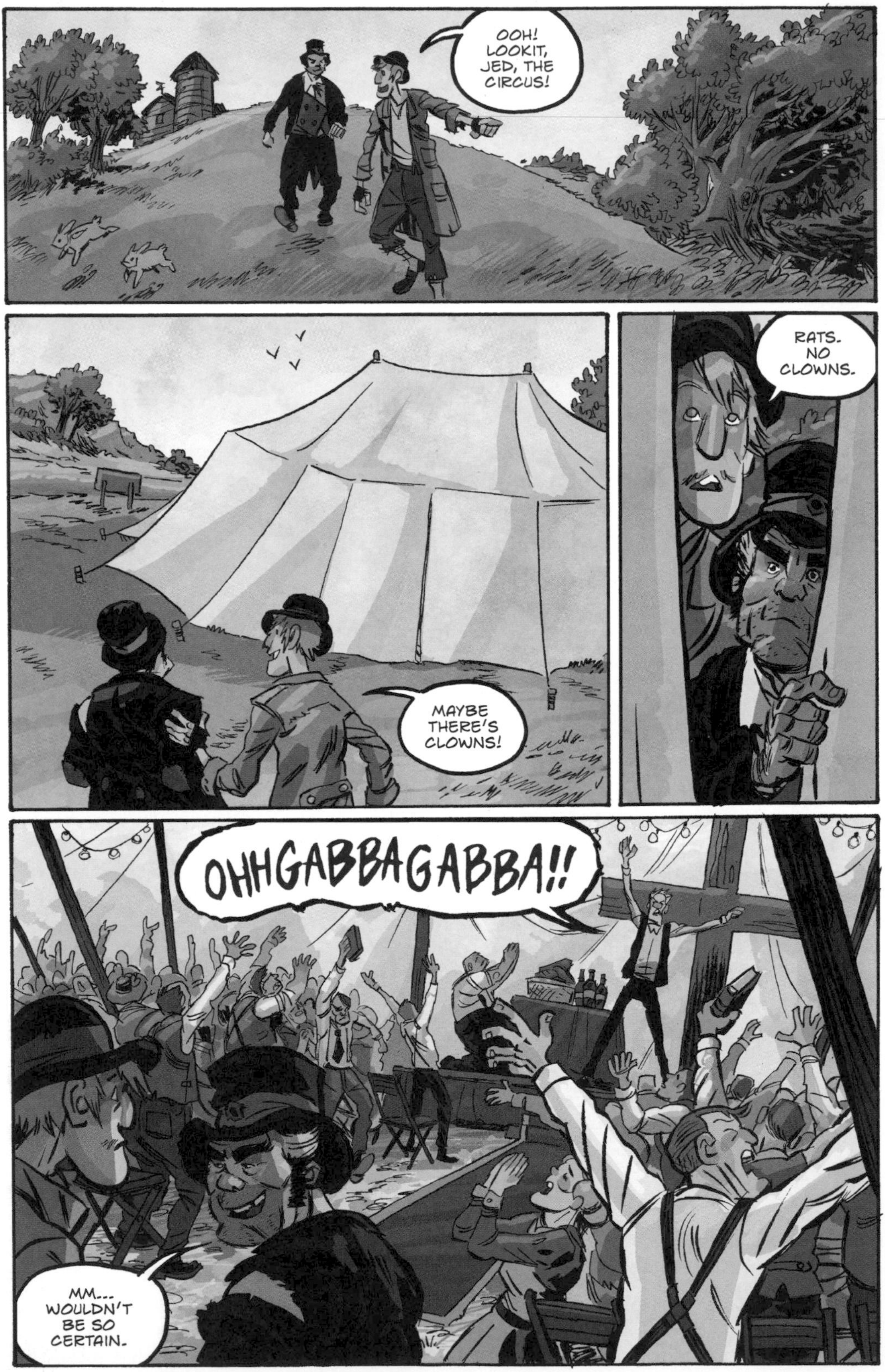
OOH! LOOKIT, JED, THE CIRCUS!
MAYBE THERE'S CLOWNS!
RATS. NO CLOWNS.
OHHGABBAGABBA!!
MM... WOULDN'T BE SO CERTAIN.

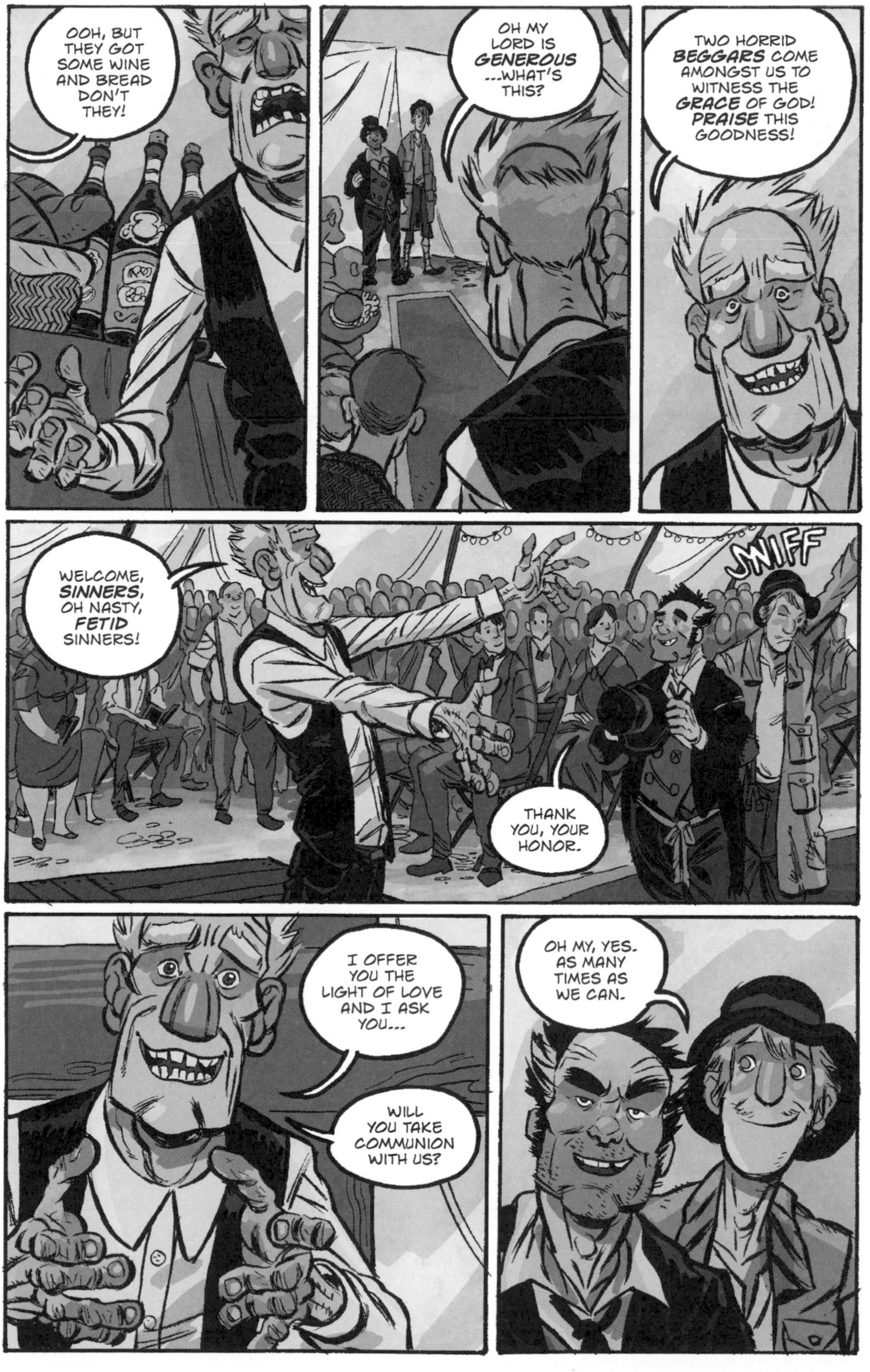

OOH, BUT THEY GOT SOME WINE AND BREAD DON'T THEY!
OH MY LORD IS **GENEROUS** ...WHAT'S THIS?
TWO HORRID **BEGGARS** COME AMONGST US TO WITNESS THE **GRACE** OF GOD! **PRAISE** THIS GOODNESS!
WELCOME, **SINNERS**, OH NASTY, **FETID** SINNERS!
SNIFF
THANK YOU, YOUR HONOR.
I OFFER YOU THE LIGHT OF LOVE AND I ASK YOU...
WILL YOU TAKE COMMUNION WITH US?
OH MY, YES. AS MANY TIMES AS WE CAN.

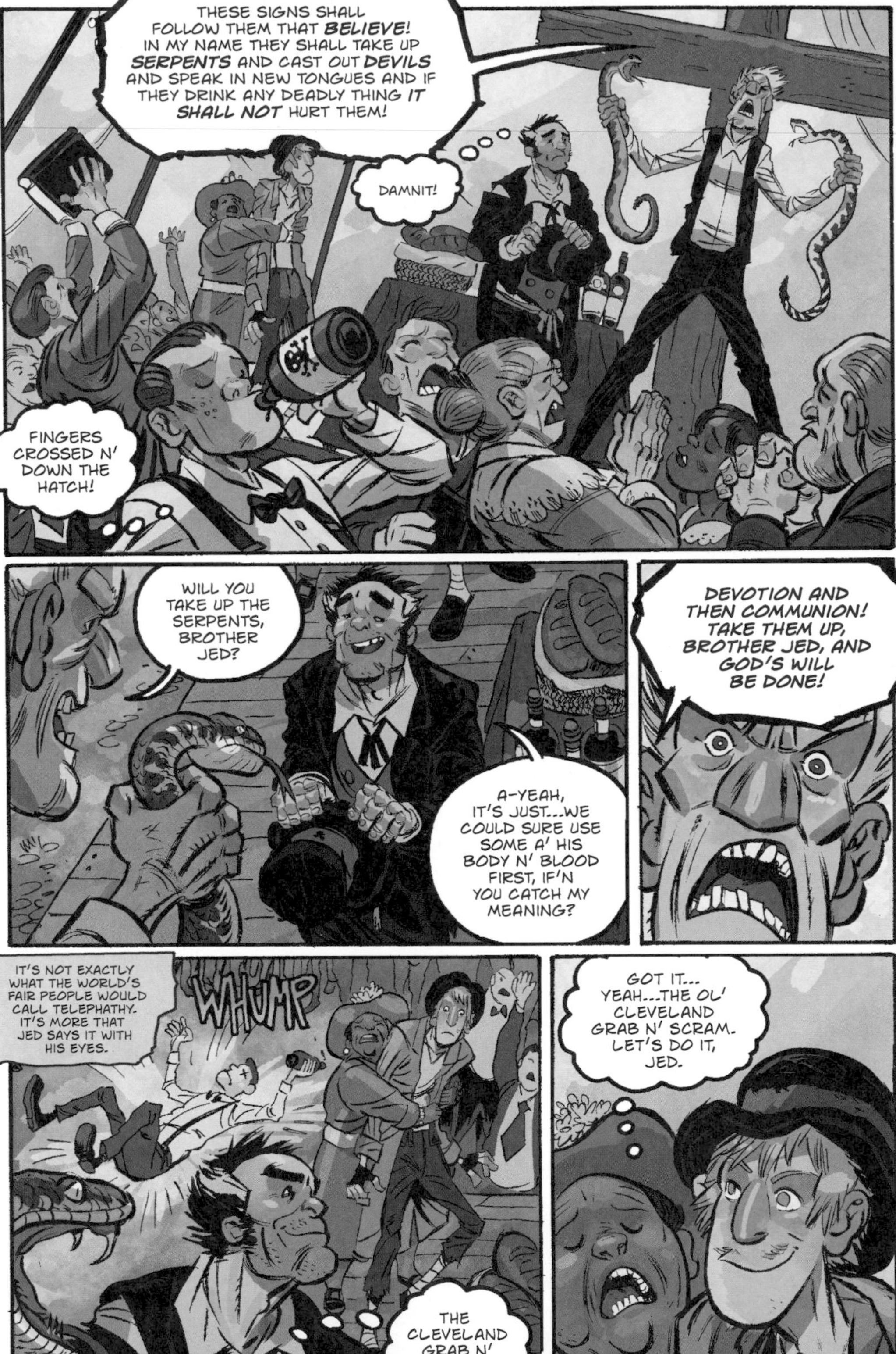
THESE SIGNS SHALL FOLLOW THEM THAT BELIEVE! IN MY NAME THEY SHALL TAKE UP SERPENTS AND CAST OUT DEVILS AND SPEAK IN NEW TONGUES AND IF THEY DRINK ANY DEADLY THING IT SHALL NOT HURT THEM!
DAMNIT!
FINGERS CROSSED N' DOWN THE HATCH!
WILL YOU TAKE UP THE SERPENTS, BROTHER JED?
A-YEAH, IT'S JUST...WE COULD SURE USE SOME A' HIS BODY N' BLOOD FIRST, IF'N YOU CATCH MY MEANING?
DEVOTION AND THEN COMMUNION! TAKE THEM UP, BROTHER JED, AND GOD'S WILL BE DONE!
IT'S NOT EXACTLY WHAT THE WORLD'S FAIR PEOPLE WOULD CALL TELEPHATHY. IT'S MORE THAT JED SAYS IT WITH HIS EYES.
WHUMP
THE CLEVELAND GRAB N' SCRAM!
GOT IT... YEAH...THE OL' CLEVELAND GRAB N' SCRAM. LET'S DO IT, JED.

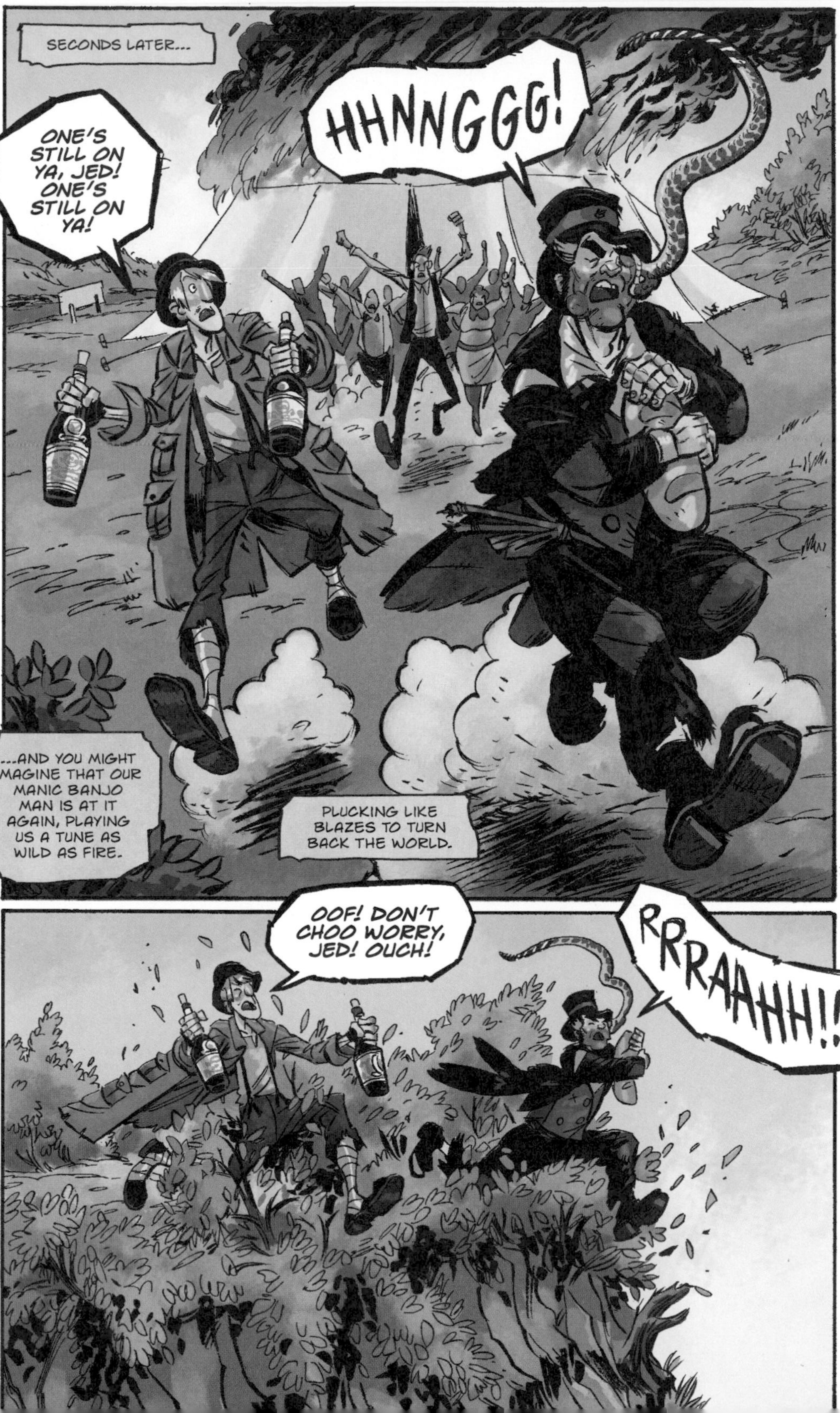
SECONDS LATER...
ONE'S STILL ON YA, JED! ONE'S STILL ON YA!
HHNNGGG!
...AND YOU MIGHT IMAGINE THAT OUR MANIC BANJO MAN IS AT IT AGAIN, PLAYING US A TUNE AS WILD AS FIRE.
PLUCKING LIKE BLAZES TO TURN BACK THE WORLD.
OOF! DON'T CHOO WORRY, JED! OUCH!
RRRAAHH!!

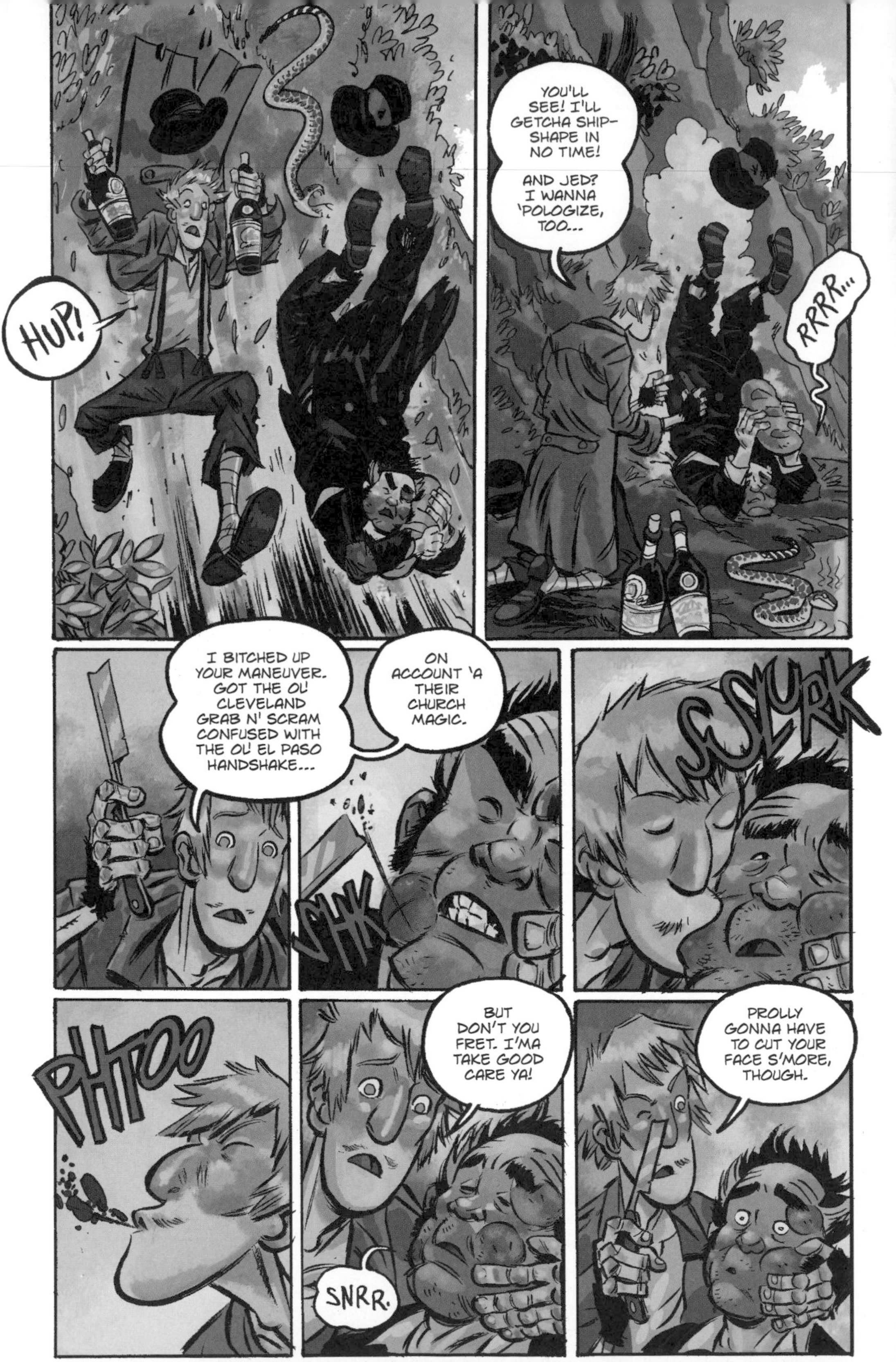
HUP!
YOU'LL SEE! I'LL GETCHA SHIP-SHAPE IN NO TIME!
AND JED? I WANNA 'POLOGIZE, TOO...
RRRR...
I BITCHED UP YOUR MANEUVER. GOT THE OL' CLEVELAND GRAB N' SCRAM CONFUSED WITH THE OL' EL PASO HANDSHAKE...
ON ACCOUNT 'A THEIR CHURCH MAGIC.
SHK
SSLURK
PHTOO
BUT DON'T YOU FRET. I'MA TAKE GOOD CARE YA!
SNRR.
PROLLY GONNA HAVE TO CUT YOUR FACE S'MORE, THOUGH.

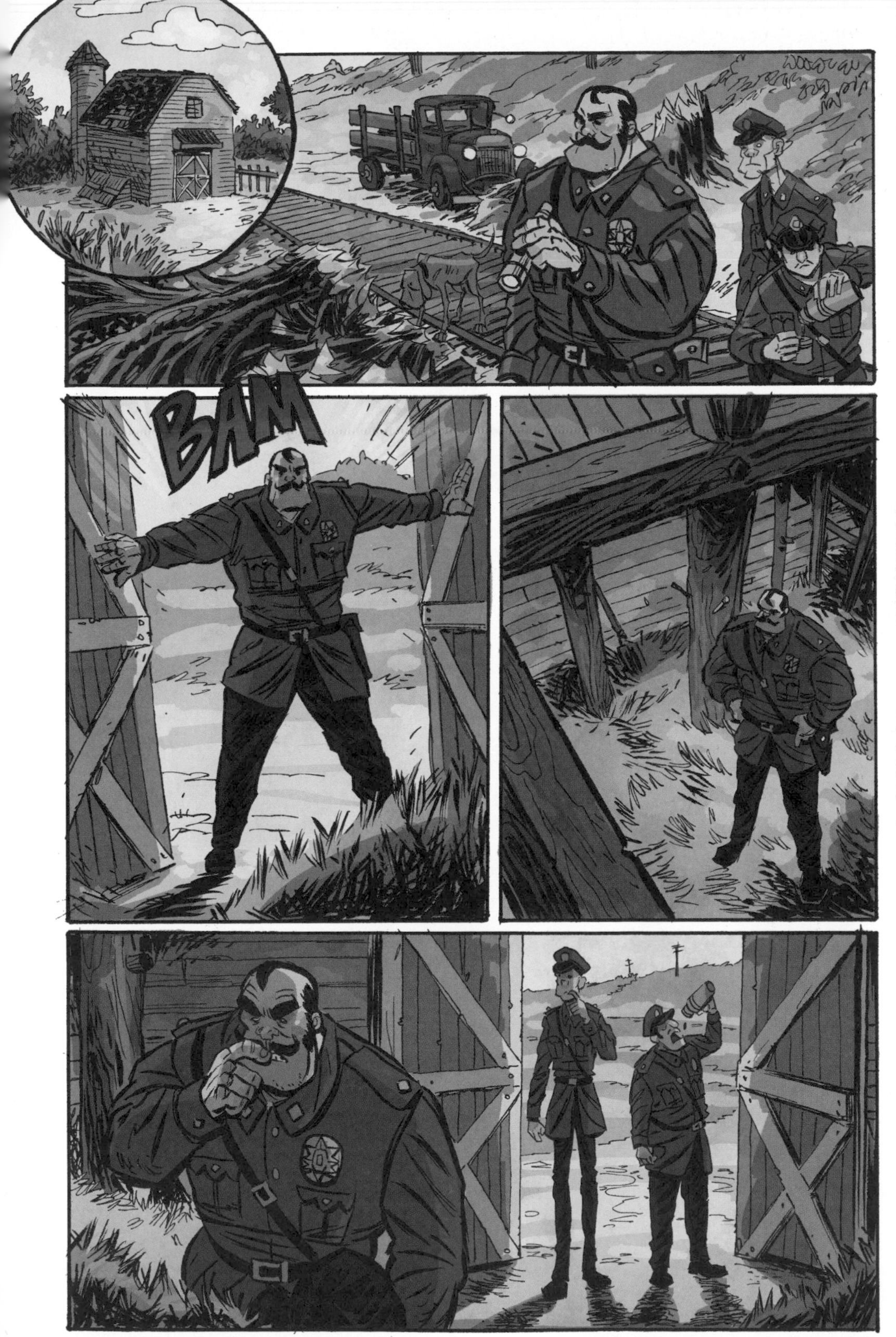
BAM

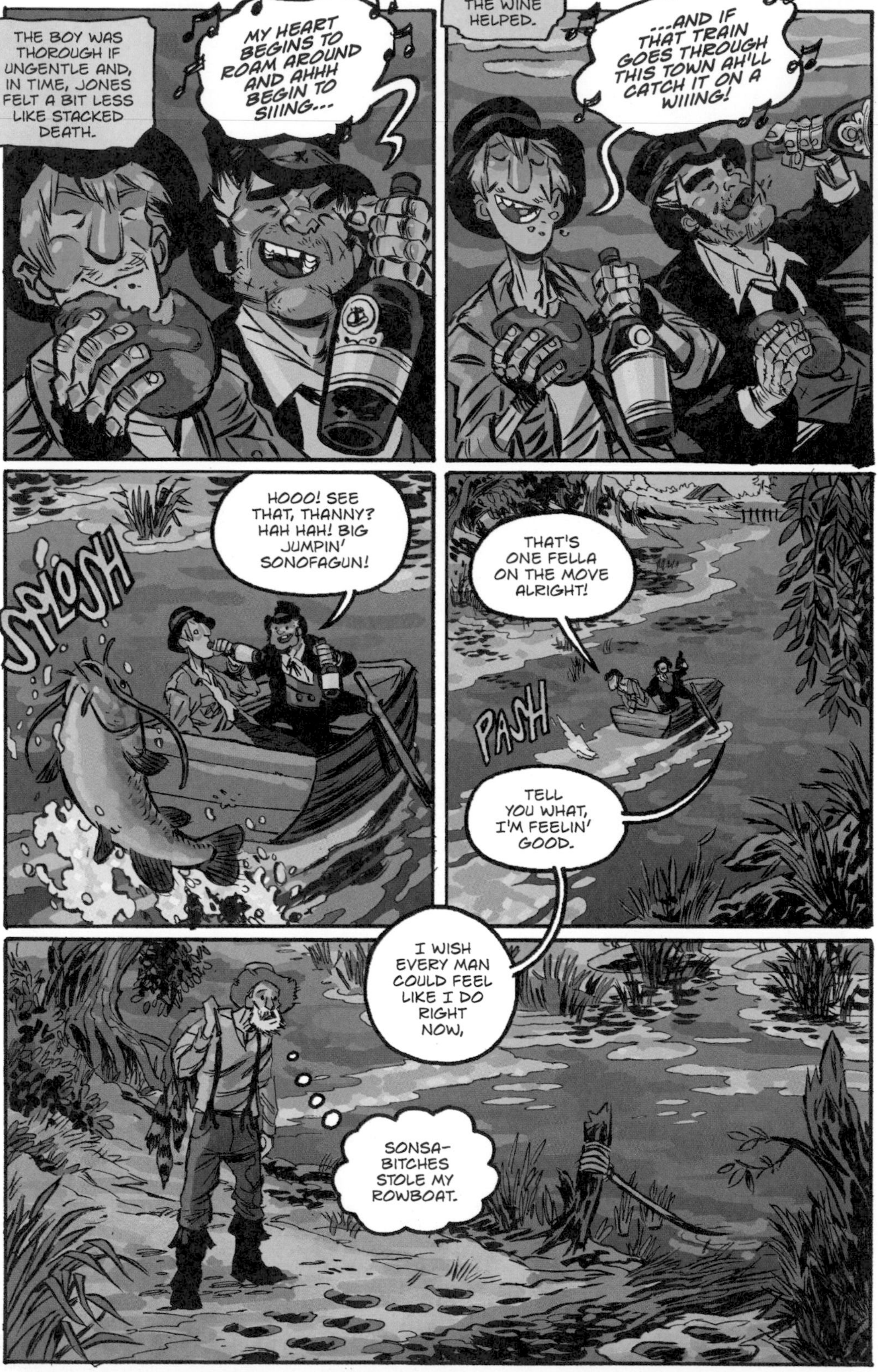

THE BOY WAS THOROUGH IF UNGENTLE AND, IN TIME, JONES FELT A BIT LESS LIKE STACKED DEATH.
MY HEART BEGINS TO ROAM AROUND AND AHHH BEGIN TO SIIING...
THE WINE HELPED.
...AND IF THAT TRAIN GOES THROUGH THIS TOWN AH'LL CATCH IT ON A WIIING!
SPLOSH
HOOO! SEE THAT, THANNY? HAH HAH! BIG JUMPIN' SONOFAGUN!
THAT'S ONE FELLA ON THE MOVE ALRIGHT!
PASH
TELL YOU WHAT, I'M FEELIN' GOOD.
I WISH EVERY MAN COULD FEEL LIKE I DO RIGHT NOW,
SONSA-BITCHES STOLE MY ROWBOAT.

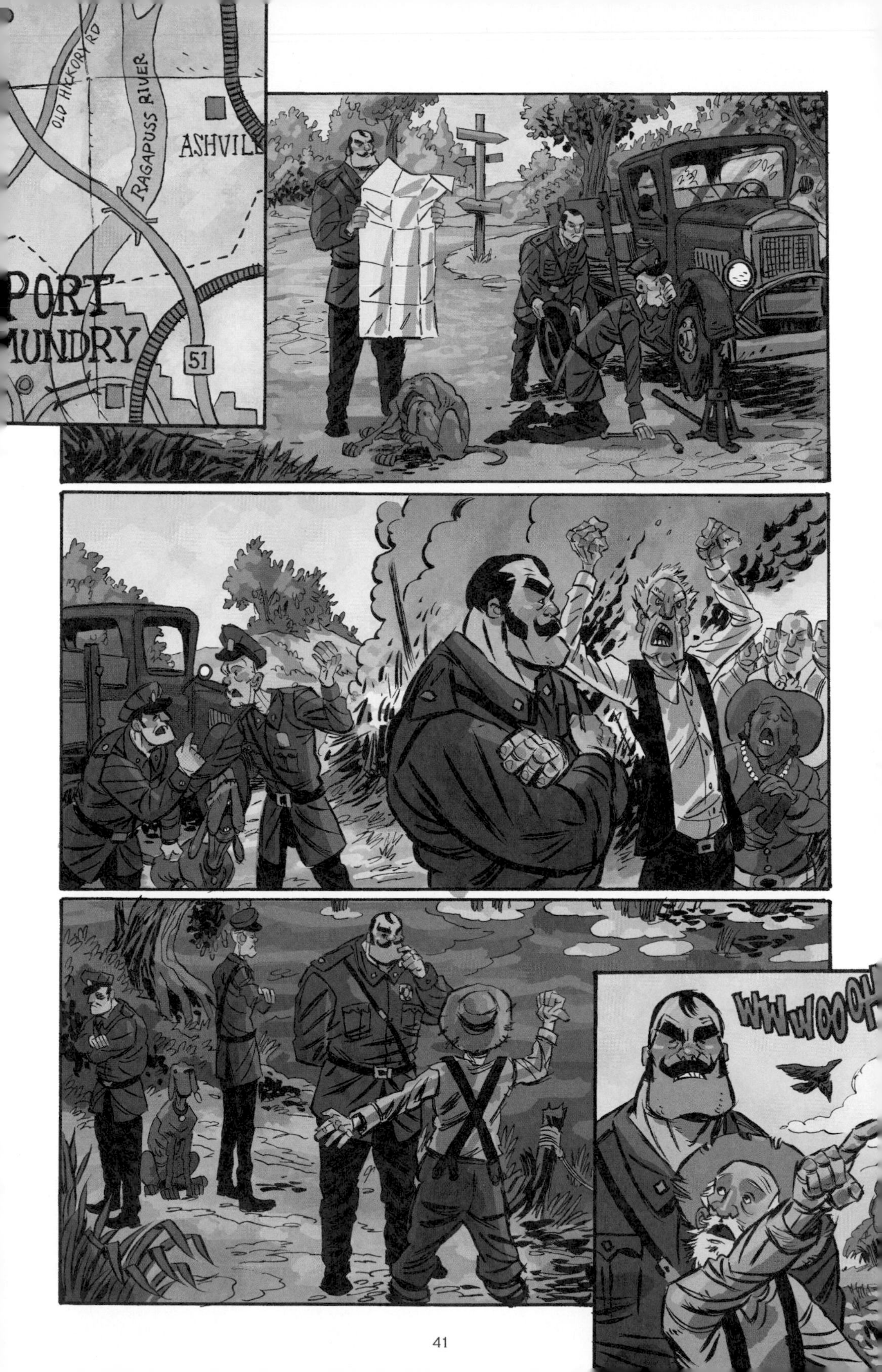
OLD HICKORY RD
RAGAPUSS RIVER
ASHVILL
PORT
MUNDRY
51
WWWOOOH

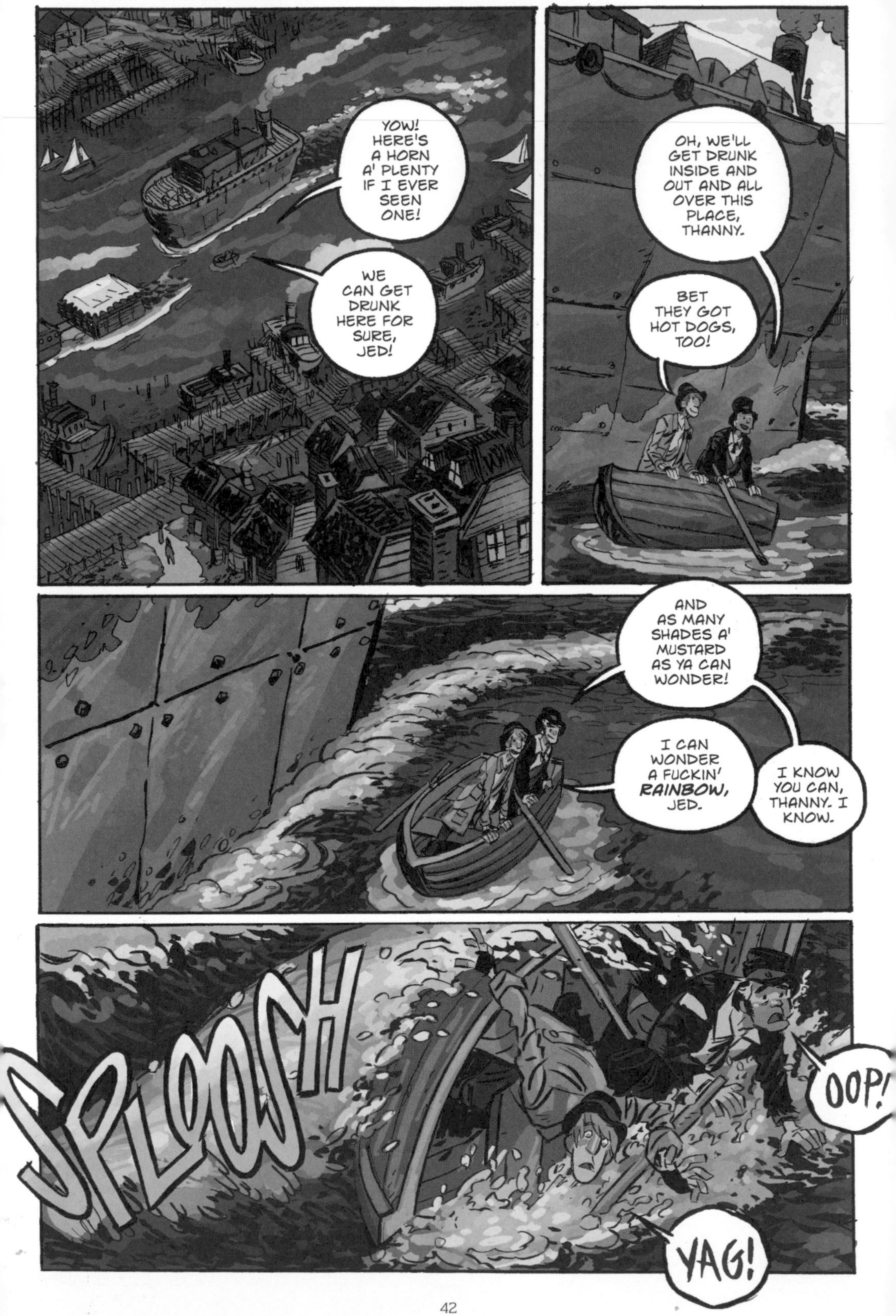
YOW! HERE'S A HORN A' PLENTY IF I EVER SEEN ONE!
WE CAN GET DRUNK HERE FOR SURE, JED!
OH, WE'LL GET DRUNK INSIDE AND OUT AND ALL OVER THIS PLACE, THANNY.
BET THEY GOT HOT DOGS, TOO!
AND AS MANY SHADES A' MUSTARD AS YA CAN WONDER!
I CAN WONDER A FUCKIN' RAINBOW, JED.
I KNOW YOU CAN, THANNY. I KNOW.
SPLOOSH
OOP!
YAG!

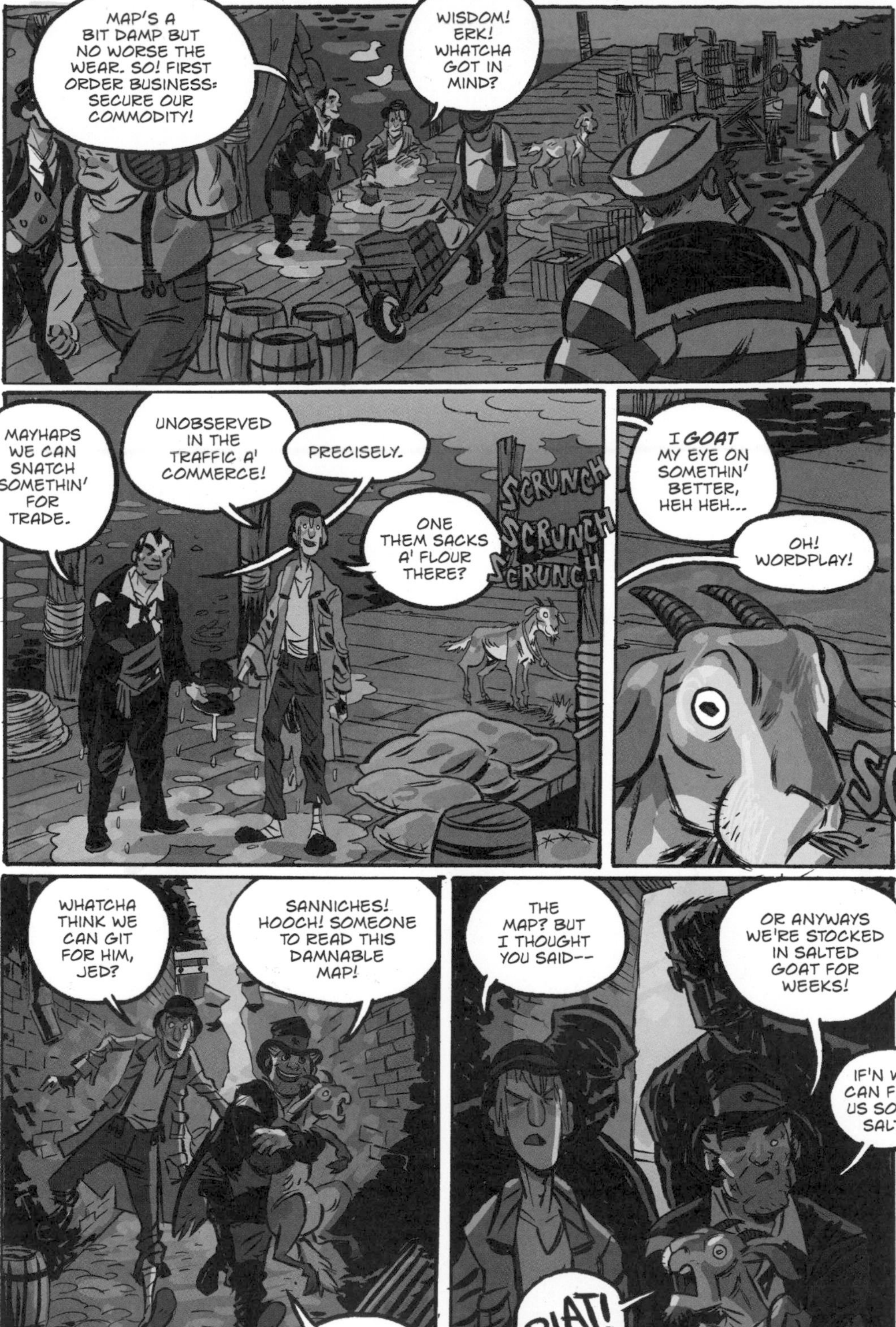
MAP'S A BIT DAMP BUT NO WORSE THE WEAR. SO! FIRST ORDER BUSINESS: SECURE OUR COMMODITY!
WISDOM! ERK! WHATCHA GOT IN MIND?
MAYHAPS WE CAN SNATCH SOMETHIN' FOR TRADE.
UNOBSERVED IN THE TRAFFIC A' COMMERCE!
PRECISELY.
ONE THEM SACKS A' FLOUR THERE?
SCRUNCH
SCRUNCH
SCRUNCH
I GOAT MY EYE ON SOMETHIN' BETTER, HEH HEH...
OH! WORDPLAY!
SCR
WHATCHA THINK WE CAN GIT FOR HIM, JED?
SANNICHES! HOOCH! SOMEONE TO READ THIS DAMNABLE MAP!
ANYTHING WE WANT, THANNY!
THE MAP? BUT I THOUGHT YOU SAID--
OR ANYWAYS WE'RE STOCKED IN SALTED GOAT FOR WEEKS!
IF'N WE CAN FIND US SOME SALT.
BLAT!

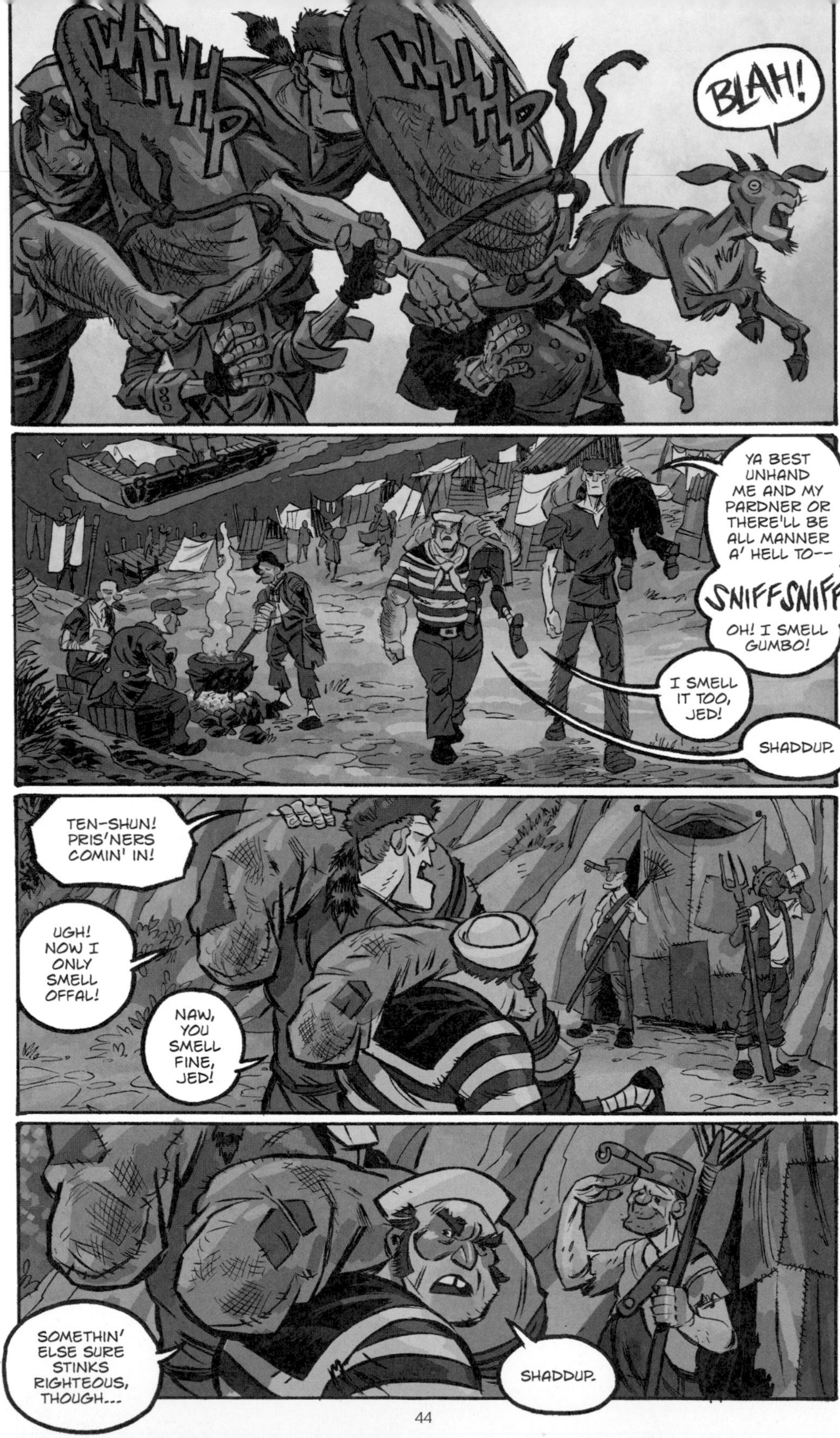

WHHP
WHHP
BLAH!
YA BEST UNHAND ME AND MY PARDNER OR THERE'LL BE ALL MANNER A' HELL TO--
SNIFFSNIFF
OH! I SMELL GUMBO!
I SMELL IT TOO, JED!
SHADDUP.
TEN-SHUN! PRIS'NERS COMIN' IN!
UGH! NOW I ONLY SMELL OFFAL!
NAW, YOU SMELL FINE, JED!
SOMETHIN' ELSE SURE STINKS RIGHTEOUS, THOUGH...
SHADDUP.

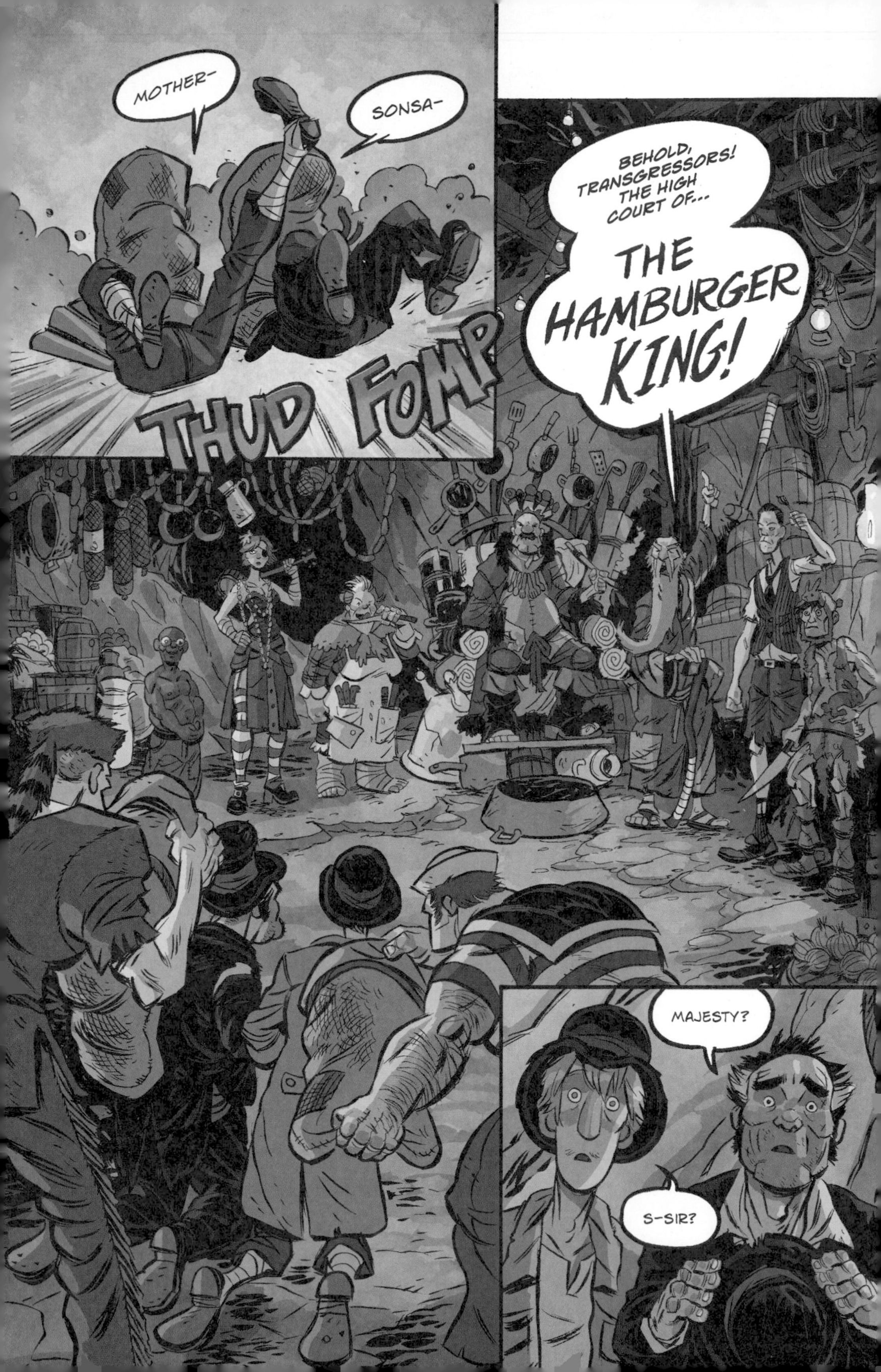
MOTHER-
SONSA-
THUD
FOMP
BEHOLD, TRANSGRESSORS! THE HIGH COURT OF...
THE HAMBURGER KING!
MAJESTY?
S-SIR?

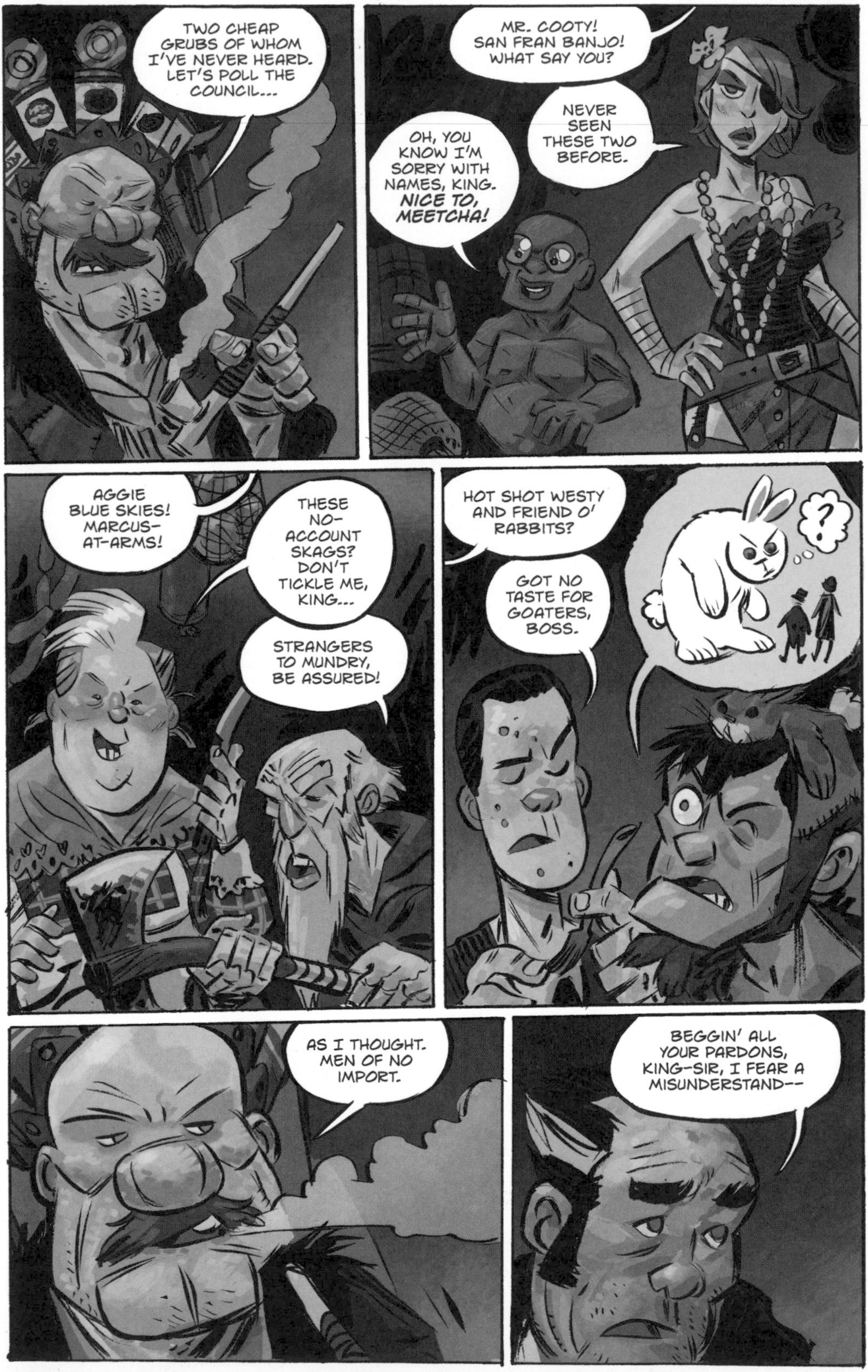

TWO CHEAP GRUBS OF WHOM I'VE NEVER HEARD. LET'S POLL THE COUNCIL...
MR. COOTY! SAN FRAN BANJO! WHAT SAY YOU?
OH, YOU KNOW I'M SORRY WITH NAMES, KING. *NICE TO, MEETCHA!*
NEVER SEEN THESE TWO BEFORE.
AGGIE BLUE SKIES! MARCUS-AT-ARMS!
THESE NO-ACCOUNT SKAGS? DON'T TICKLE ME, KING...
STRANGERS TO MUNDRY, BE ASSURED!
HOT SHOT WESTY AND FRIEND O' RABBITS?
GOT NO TASTE FOR GOATERS, BOSS.
?
AS I THOUGHT. MEN OF NO IMPORT.
BEGGIN' ALL YOUR PARDONS, KING-SIR, I FEAR A MISUNDERSTAND--

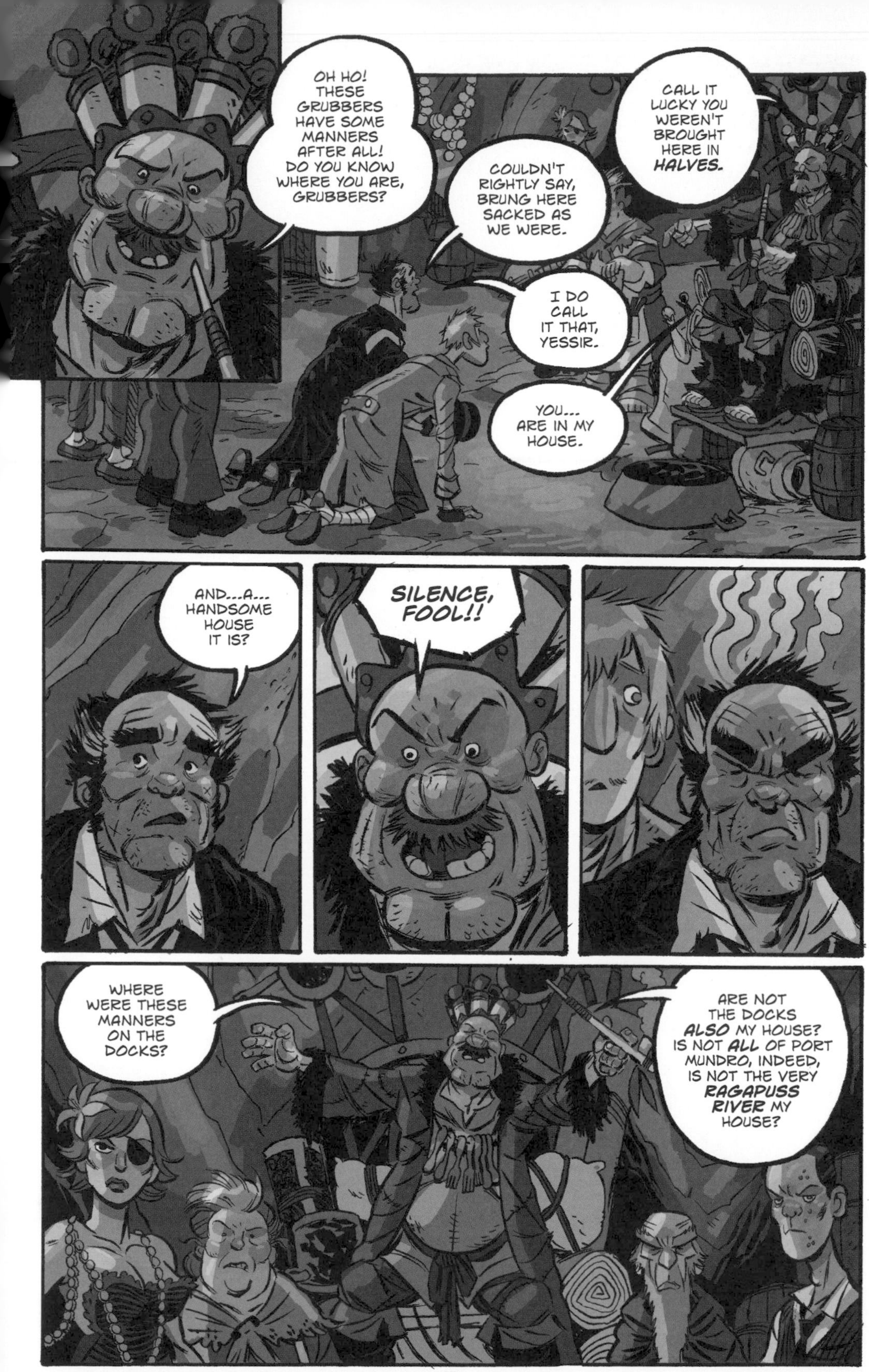
OH HO! THESE GRUBBERS HAVE SOME MANNERS AFTER ALL! DO YOU KNOW WHERE YOU ARE, GRUBBERS?
COULDN'T RIGHTLY SAY, BRUNG HERE SACKED AS WE WERE.
CALL IT LUCKY YOU WEREN'T BROUGHT HERE IN *HALVES.*
I DO CALL IT THAT, YESSIR.
YOU... ARE IN MY HOUSE.
AND...A... HANDSOME HOUSE IT IS?
SILENCE, FOOL!!
WHERE WERE THESE MANNERS ON THE DOCKS?
ARE NOT THE DOCKS *ALSO* MY HOUSE? IS NOT *ALL* OF PORT MUNDRO, INDEED, IS NOT THE VERY *RAGAPUSS RIVER* MY HOUSE?

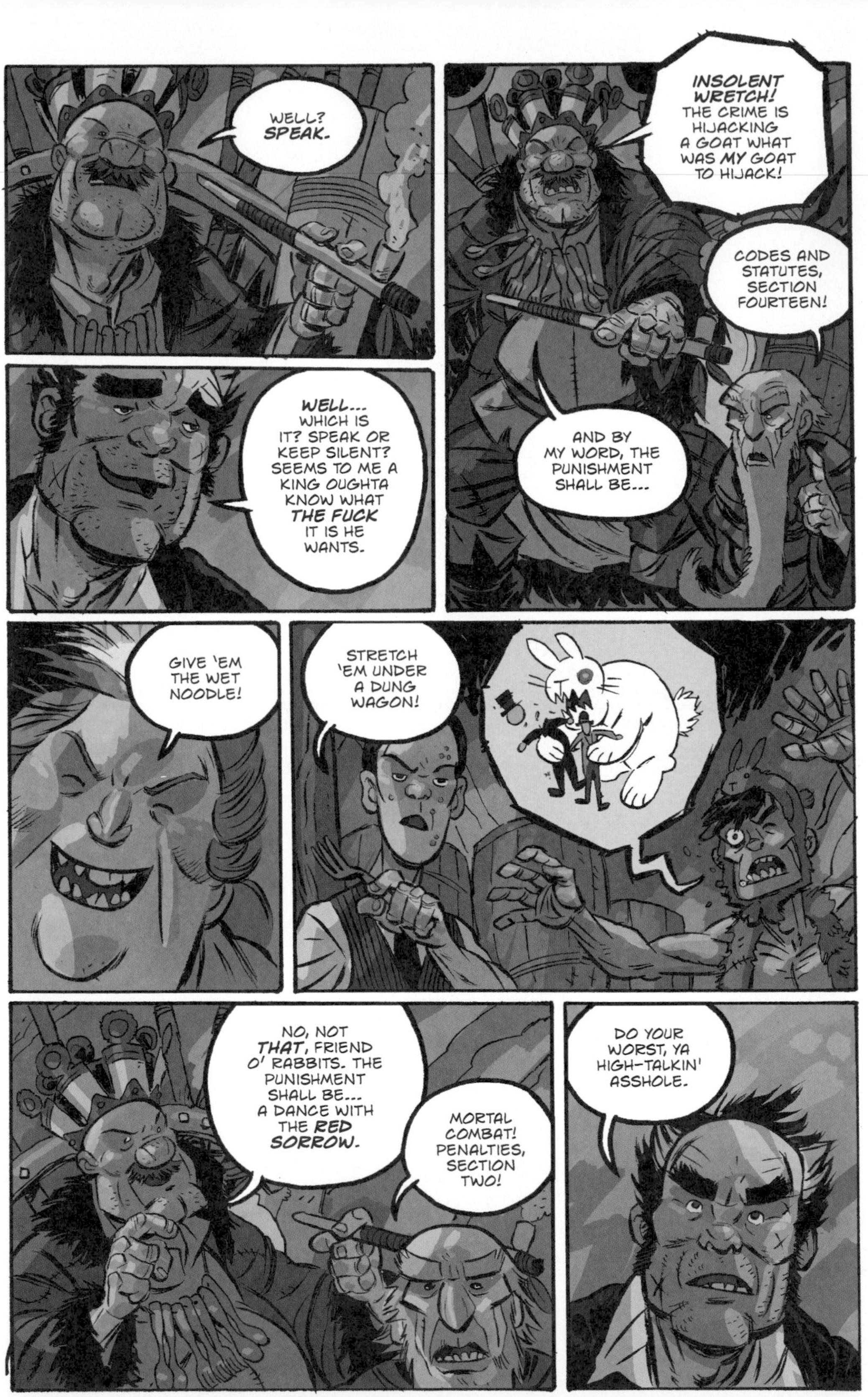
WELL? SPEAK.
INSOLENT WRETCH! THE CRIME IS HIJACKING A GOAT WHAT WAS MY GOAT TO HIJACK!
CODES AND STATUTES, SECTION FOURTEEN!
WELL... WHICH IS IT? SPEAK OR KEEP SILENT? SEEMS TO ME A KING OUGHTA KNOW WHAT THE FUCK IT IS HE WANTS.
AND BY MY WORD, THE PUNISHMENT SHALL BE...
GIVE 'EM THE WET NOODLE!
STRETCH 'EM UNDER A DUNG WAGON!
NO, NOT THAT, FRIEND O' RABBITS. THE PUNISHMENT SHALL BE... A DANCE WITH THE RED SORROW.
MORTAL COMBAT! PENALTIES, SECTION TWO!
DO YOUR WORST, YA HIGH-TALKIN' ASSHOLE.

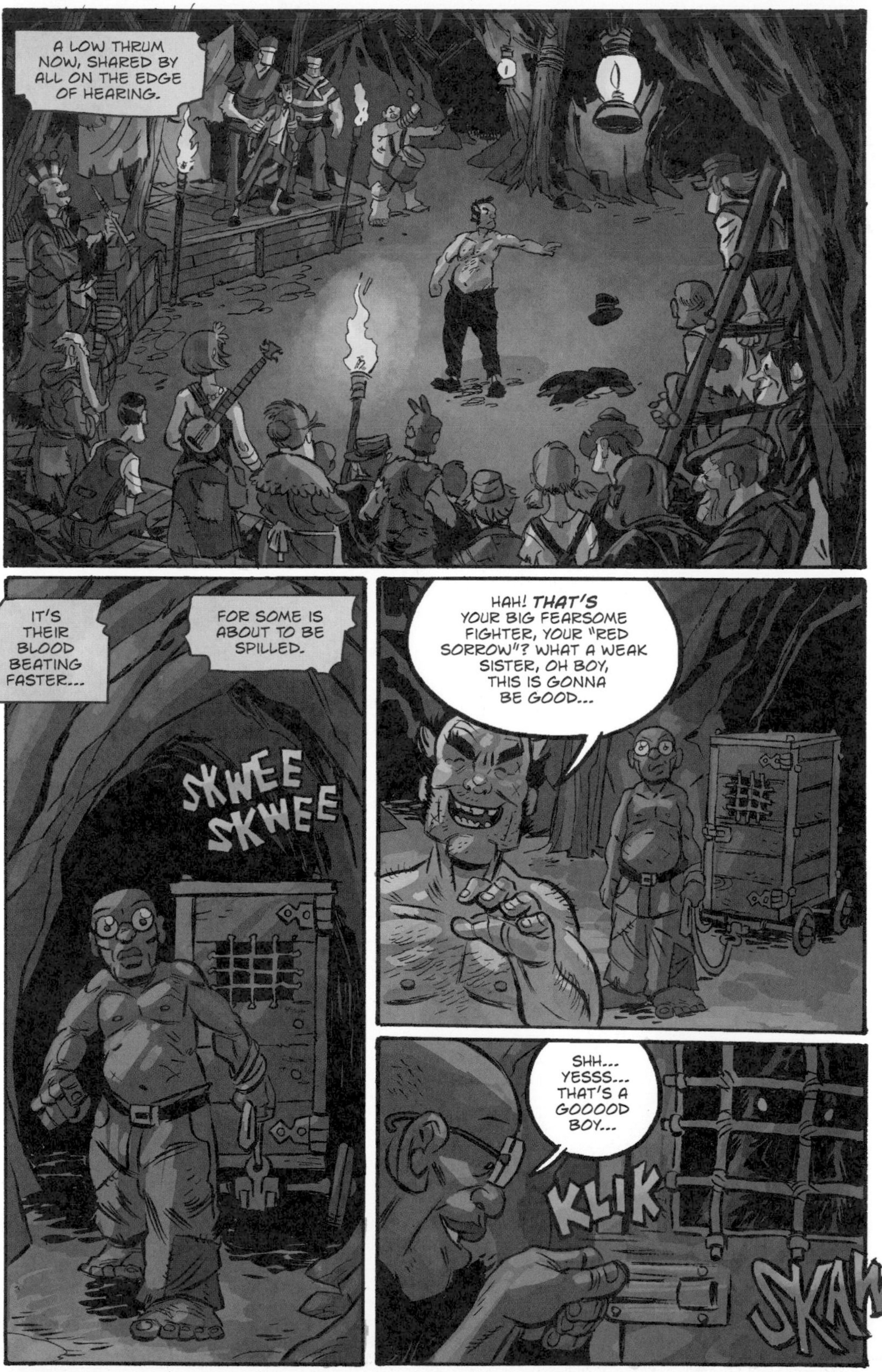
A LOW THRUM NOW, SHARED BY ALL ON THE EDGE OF HEARING.
IT'S THEIR BLOOD BEATING FASTER...
FOR SOME IS ABOUT TO BE SPILLED.
SKWEE SKWEE
HAH! THAT'S YOUR BIG FEARSOME FIGHTER, YOUR "RED SORROW"? WHAT A WEAK SISTER, OH BOY, THIS IS GONNA BE GOOD...
SHH... YESSS... THAT'S A GOOOOD BOY...
KLIK
SKAW

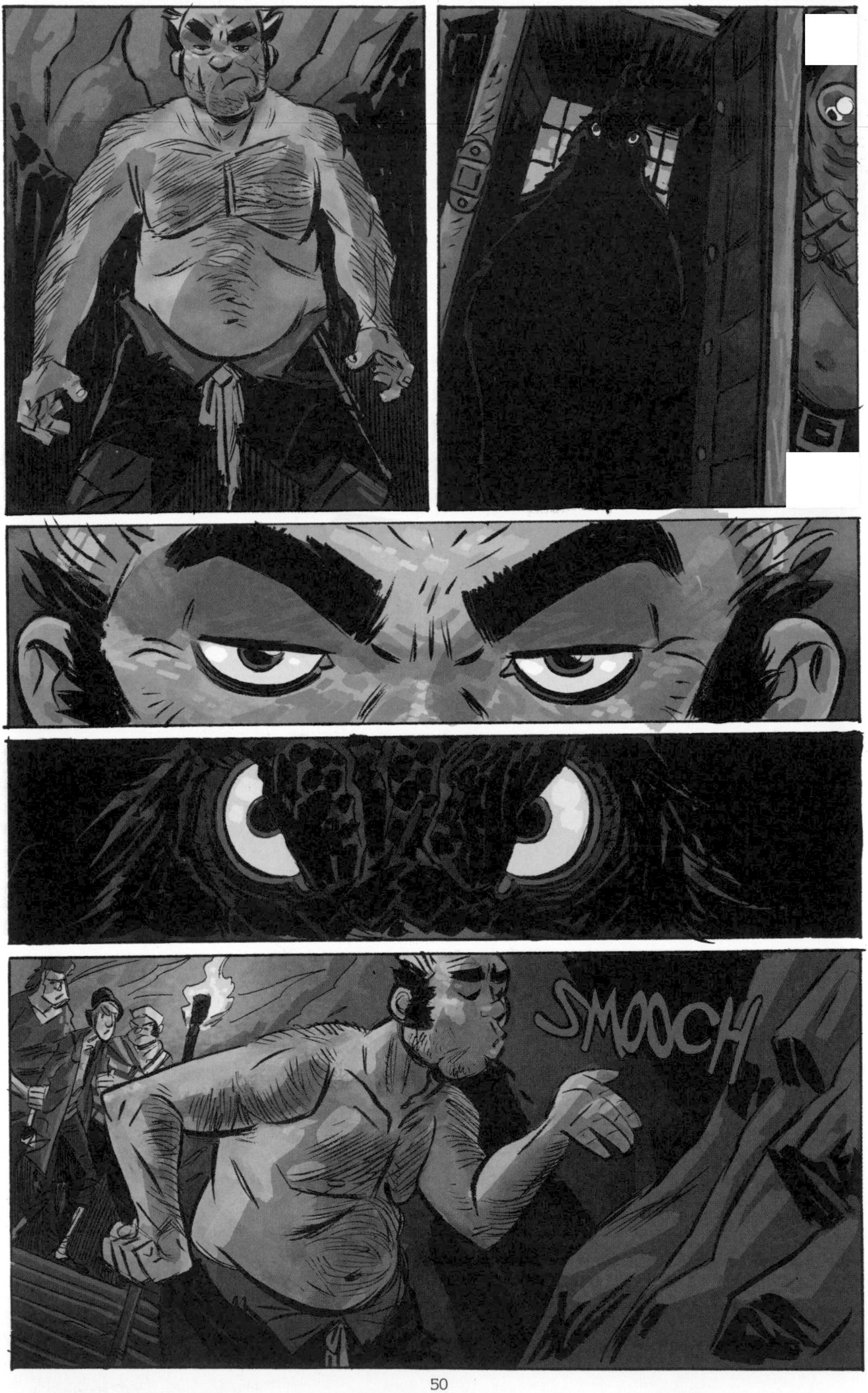
SMOOCH

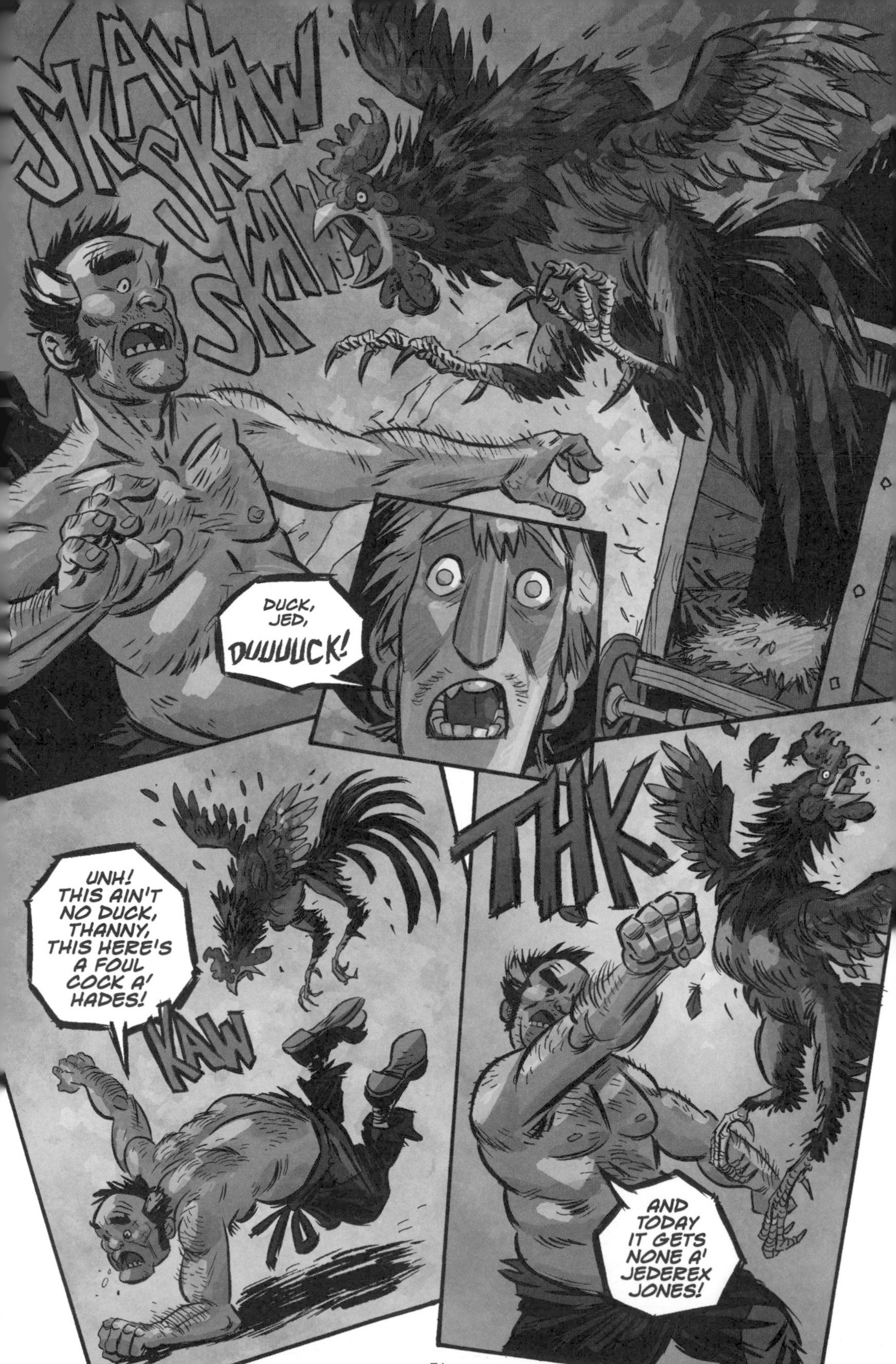
SKAW SKAW
SKAW SKAW
DUCK, JED, DUUUUCK!
UNH! THIS AIN'T NO DUCK, THANNY, THIS HERE'S A FOUL COCK A' HADES!
KAW
THK
AND TODAY IT GETS NONE A' JEDEREX JONES!

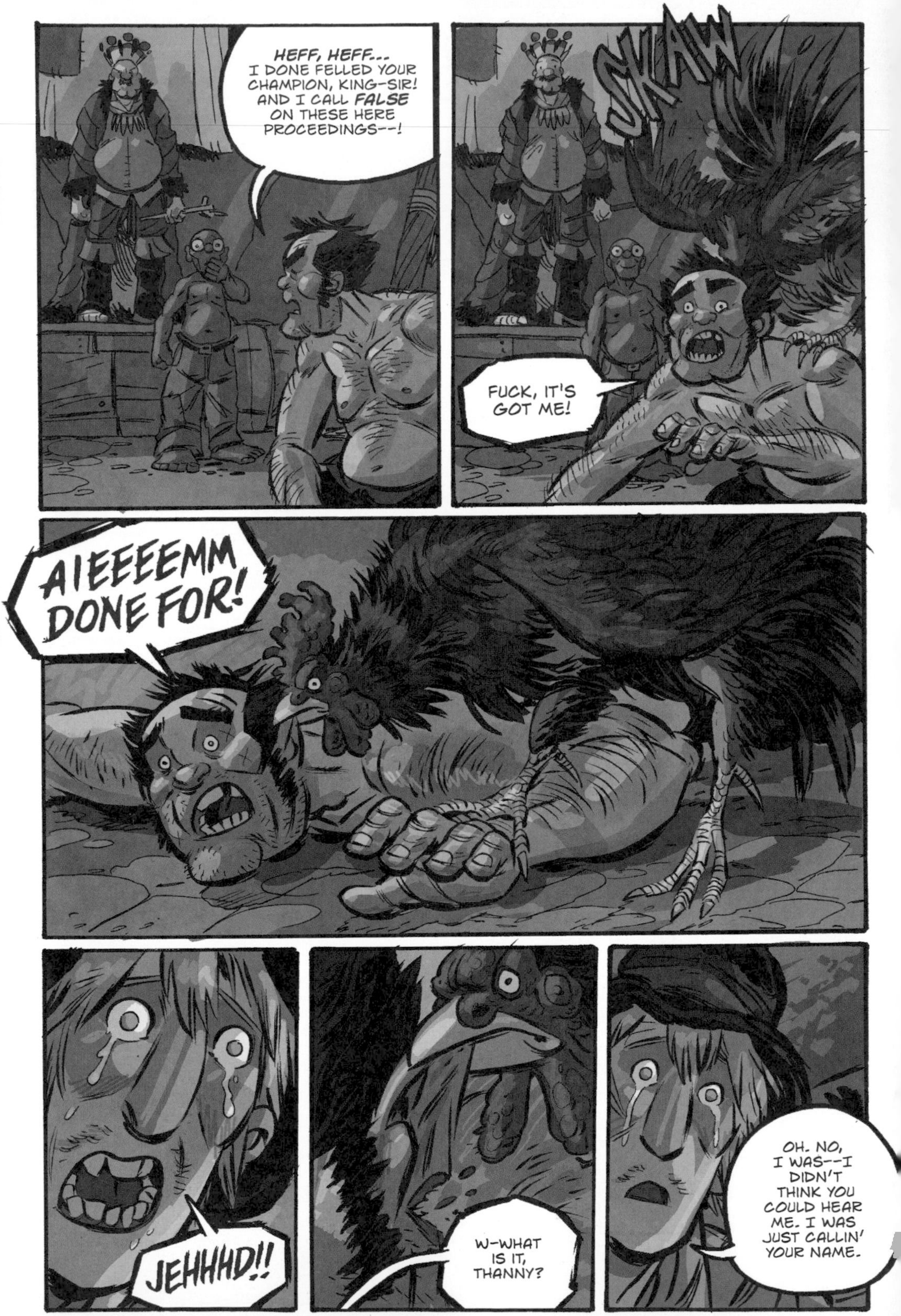
HEFF, HEFF... I DONE FELLED YOUR CHAMPION, KING-SIR! AND I CALL FALSE ON THESE HERE PROCEEDINGS--!
SKAW
FUCK, IT'S GOT ME!
AIEEEEMM DONE FOR!
JEHHHD!!
W-WHAT IS IT, THANNY?
OH. NO, I WAS--I DIDN'T THINK YOU COULD HEAR ME. I WAS JUST CALLIN' YOUR NAME.

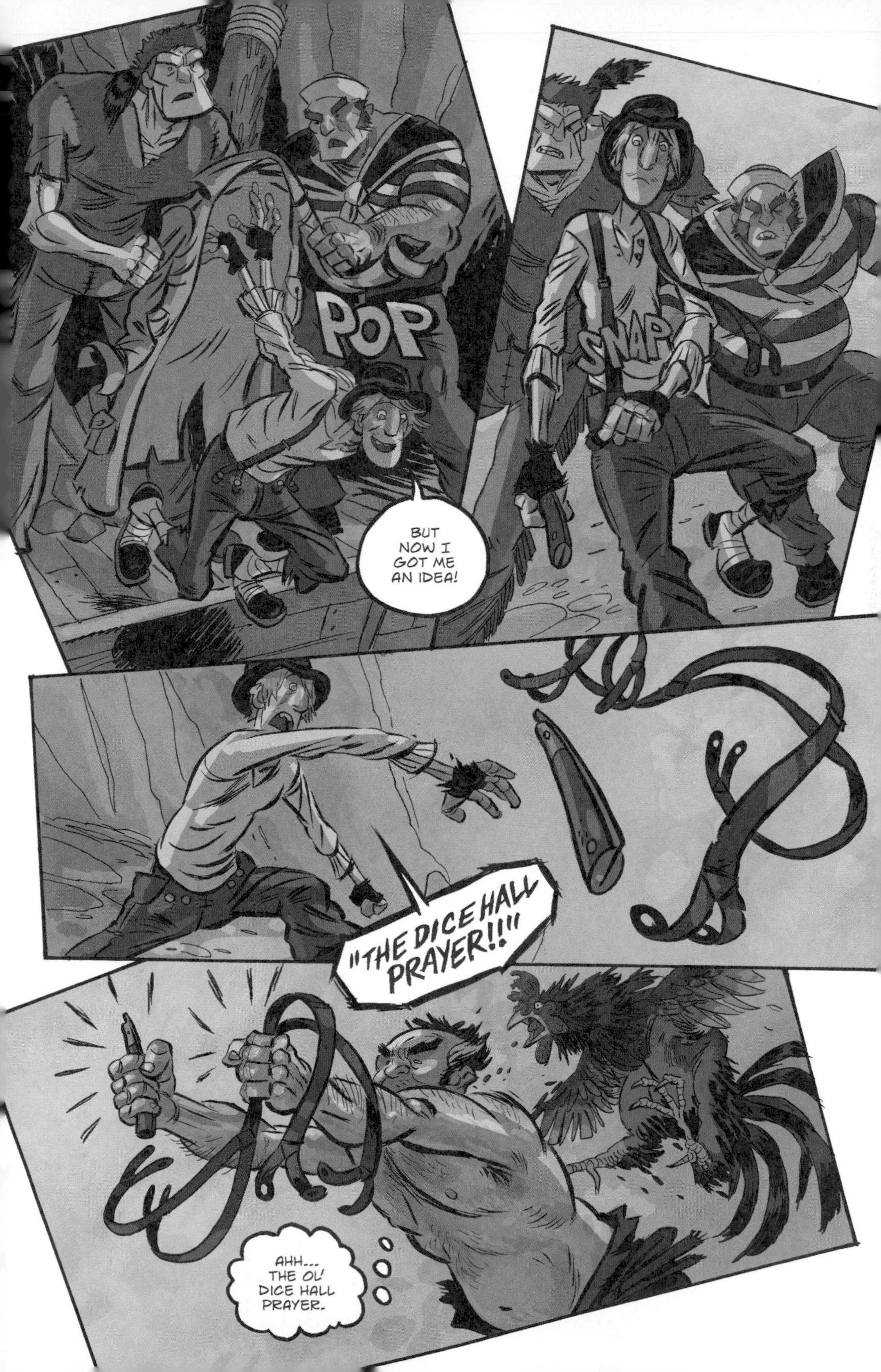
POP
BUT NOW I GOT ME AN IDEA!
SNAP
"THE DICE HALL PRAYER!!"
AHH... THE OL' DICE HALL PRAYER.

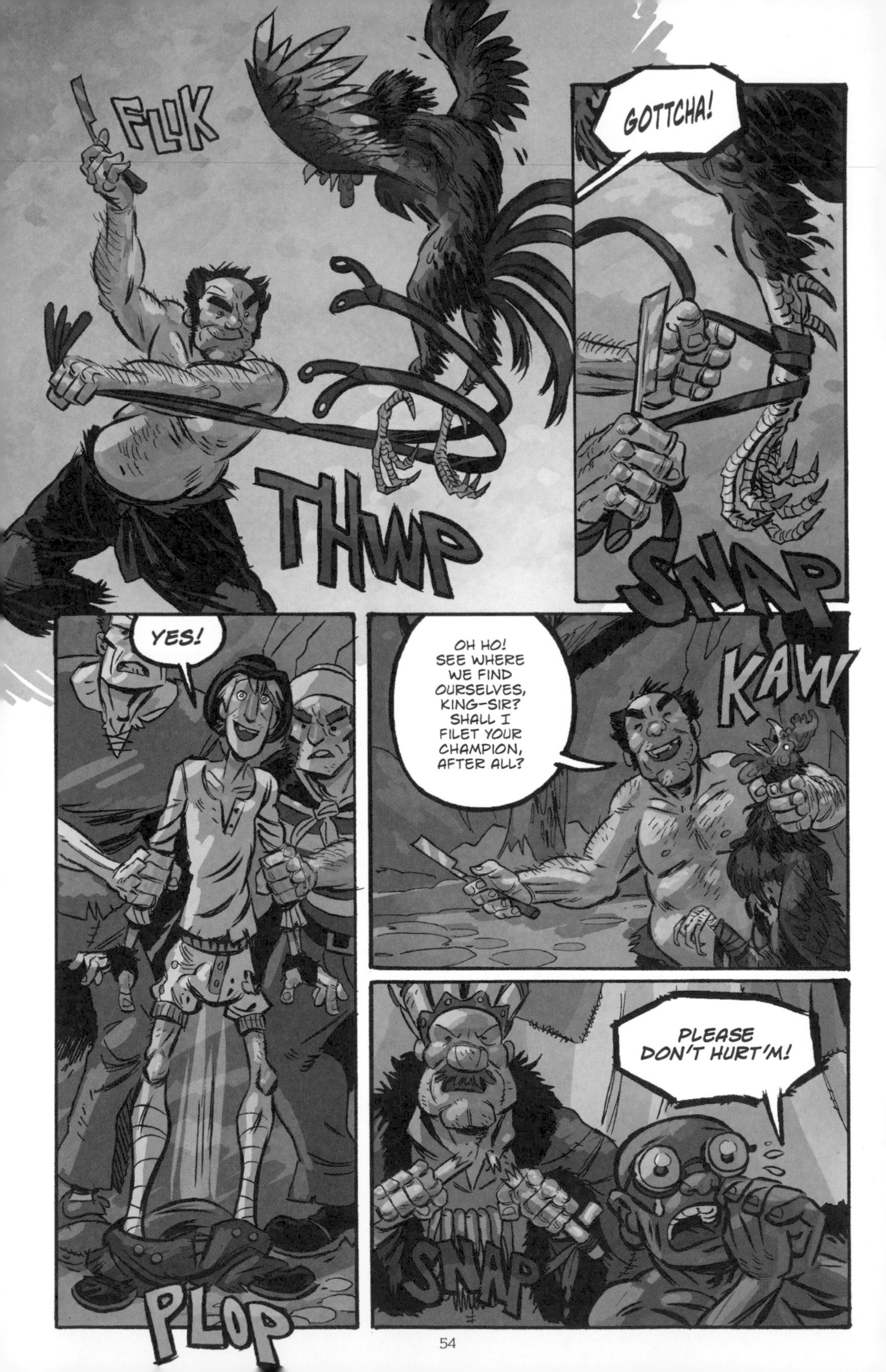
FLIK
THWP
GOTTCHA!
SNAP
YES!
PLOP
OH HO! SEE WHERE WE FIND OURSELVES, KING-SIR? SHALL I FILET YOUR CHAMPION, AFTER ALL?
KAW
PLEASE DON'T HURT'M!
SNAP

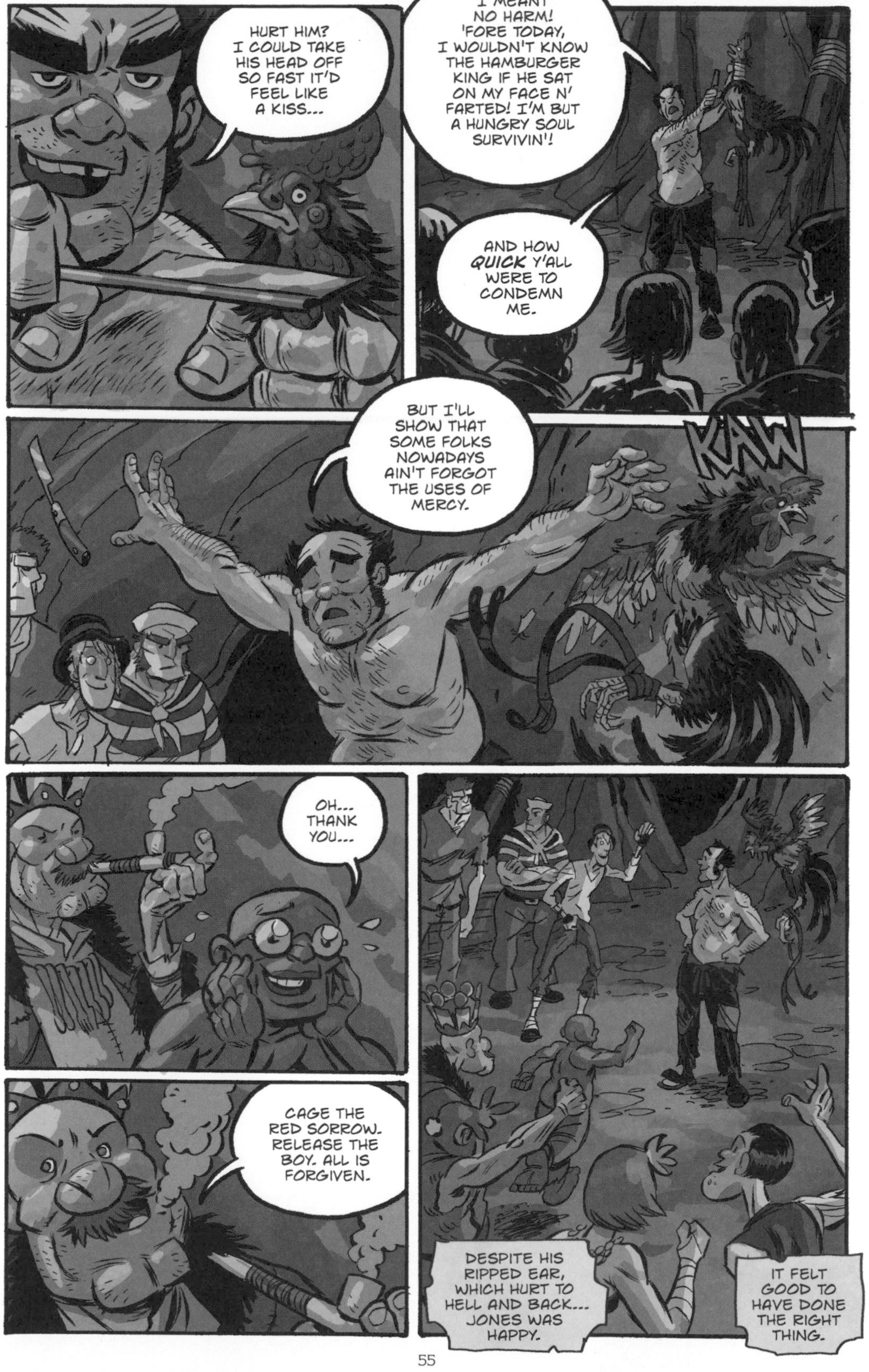
HURT HIM? I COULD TAKE HIS HEAD OFF SO FAST IT'D FEEL LIKE A KISS...
I MEANT NO HARM! 'FORE TODAY, I WOULDN'T KNOW THE HAMBURGER KING IF HE SAT ON MY FACE N' FARTED! I'M BUT A HUNGRY SOUL SURVIVIN'!
AND HOW QUICK Y'ALL WERE TO CONDEMN ME.
BUT I'LL SHOW THAT SOME FOLKS NOWADAYS AIN'T FORGOT THE USES OF MERCY.
KAW
OH... THANK YOU...
CAGE THE RED SORROW. RELEASE THE BOY. ALL IS FORGIVEN.
DESPITE HIS RIPPED EAR, WHICH HURT TO HELL AND BACK... JONES WAS HAPPY.
IT FELT GOOD TO HAVE DONE THE RIGHT THING.

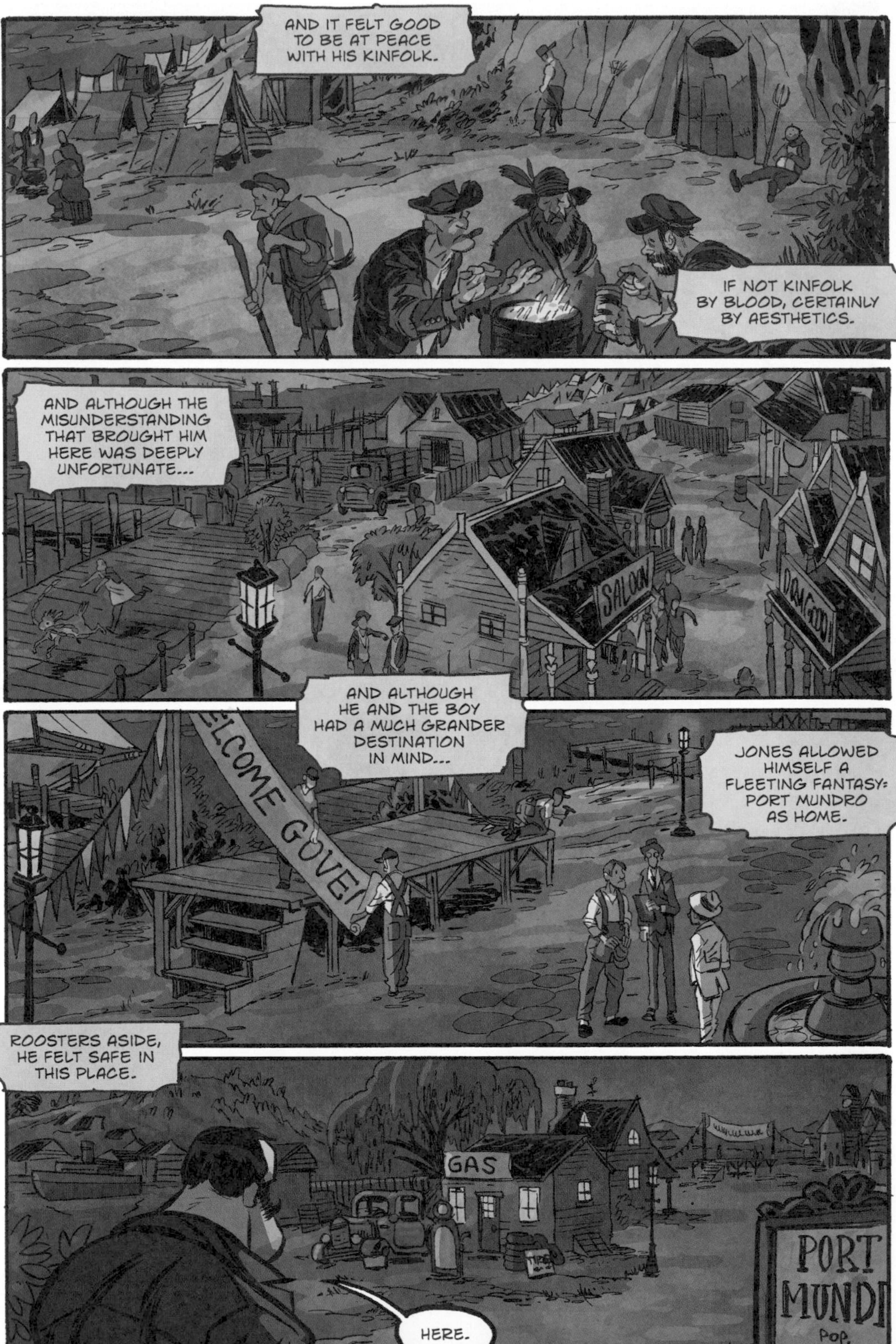
AND IT FELT GOOD TO BE AT PEACE WITH HIS KINFOLK.
IF NOT KINFOLK BY BLOOD, CERTAINLY BY AESTHETICS.
AND ALTHOUGH THE MISUNDERSTANDING THAT BROUGHT HIM HERE WAS DEEPLY UNFORTUNATE...
SALOON
AND ALTHOUGH HE AND THE BOY HAD A MUCH GRANDER DESTINATION IN MIND...
JONES ALLOWED HIMSELF A FLEETING FANTASY: PORT MUNDRO AS HOME.
ELCOME GOVE
ROOSTERS ASIDE, HE FELT SAFE IN THIS PLACE.
GAS
HERE.
PORT MUNDI
POP. 1578

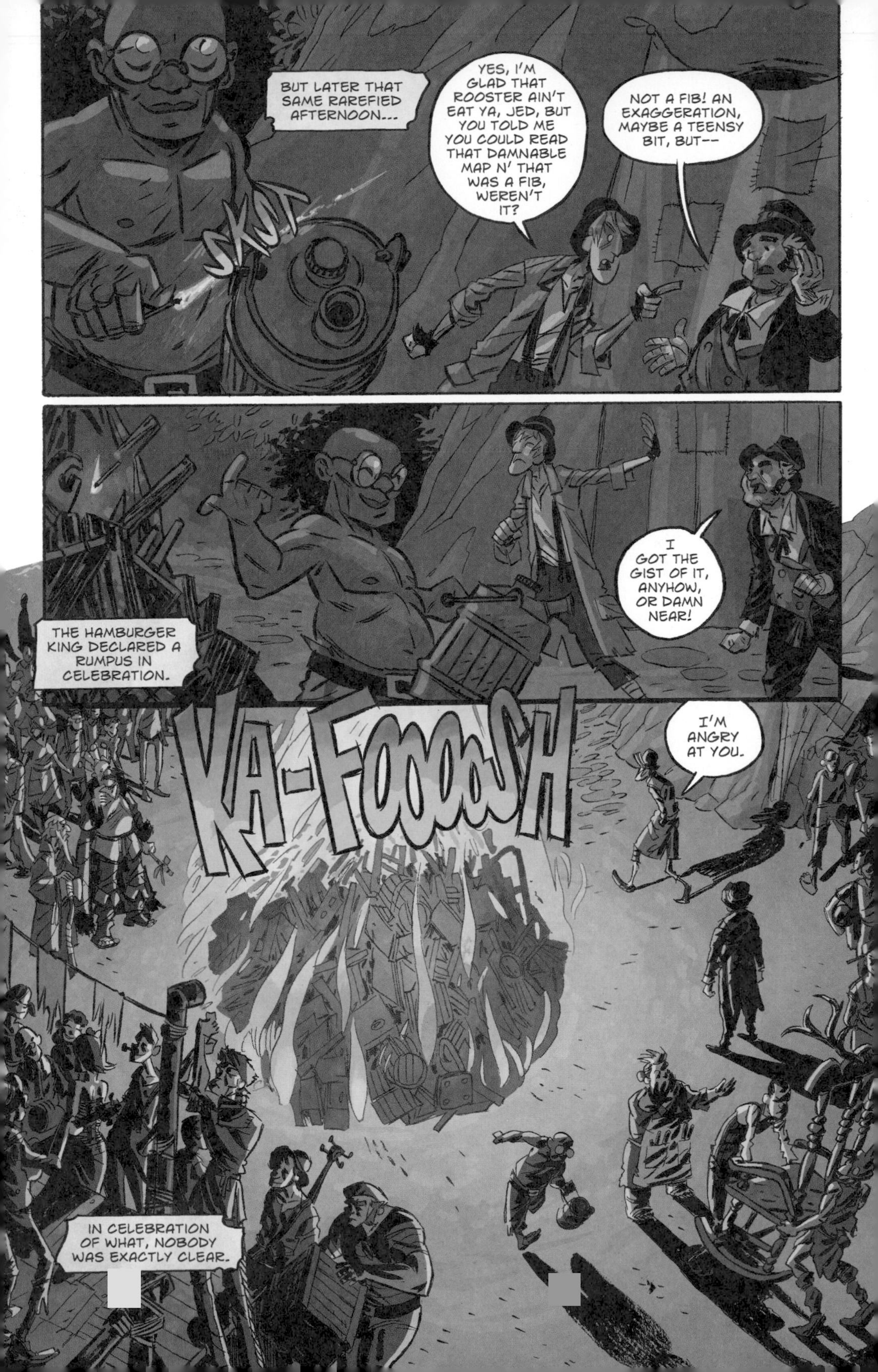

BUT LATER THAT SAME RAREFIED AFTERNOON...
SKST
YES, I'M GLAD THAT ROOSTER AIN'T EAT YA, JED, BUT YOU TOLD ME YOU COULD READ THAT DAMNABLE MAP N' THAT WAS A FIB, WEREN'T IT?
NOT A FIB! AN EXAGGERATION, MAYBE A TEENSY BIT, BUT--
I GOT THE GIST OF IT, ANYHOW, OR DAMN NEAR!
THE HAMBURGER KING DECLARED A RUMPUS IN CELEBRATION.
KA-FOOOOSH
I'M ANGRY AT YOU.
IN CELEBRATION OF WHAT, NOBODY WAS EXACTLY CLEAR.

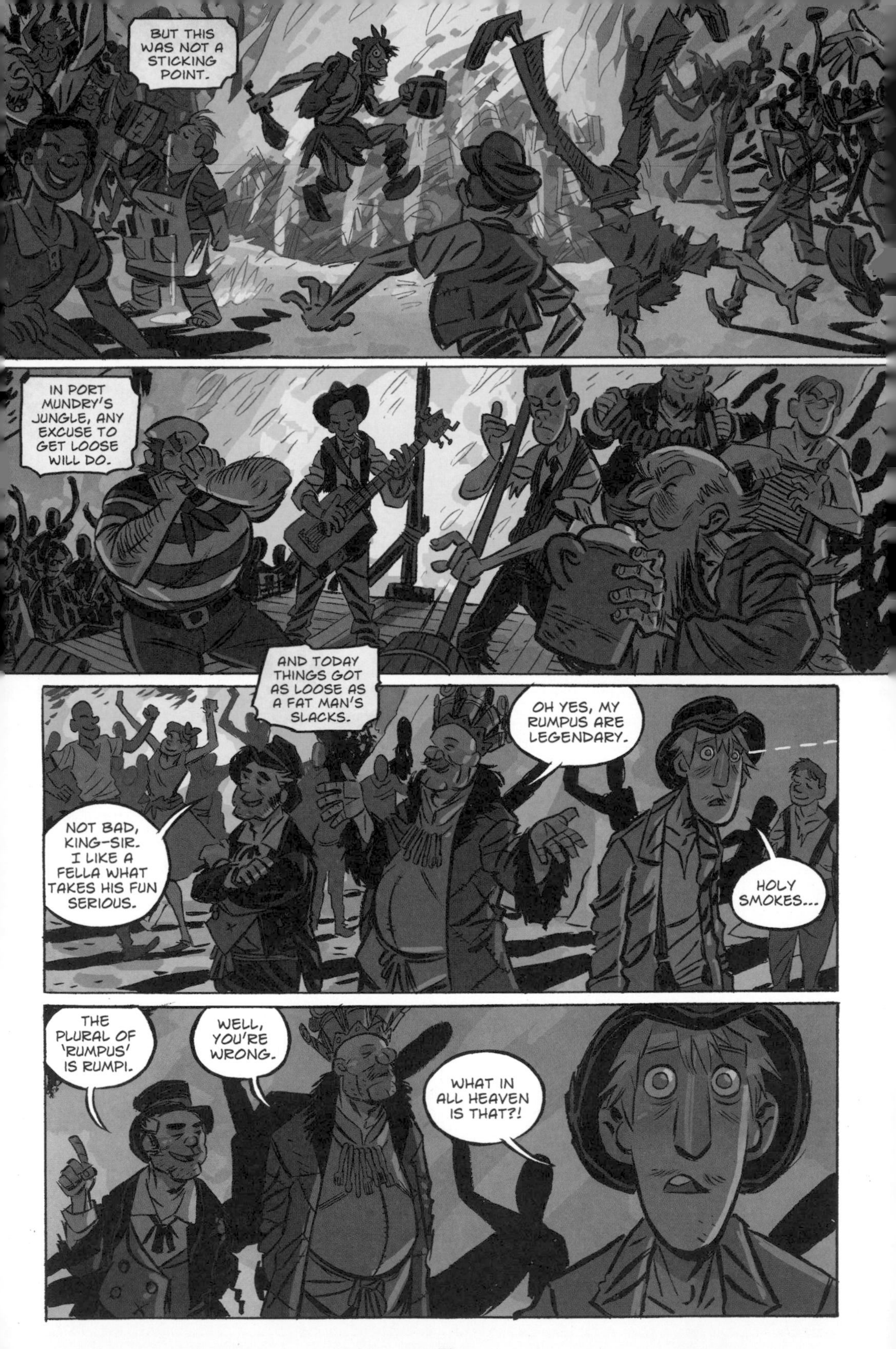
BUT THIS WAS NOT A STICKING POINT.
IN PORT MUNDRY'S JUNGLE, ANY EXCUSE TO GET LOOSE WILL DO.
AND TODAY THINGS GOT AS LOOSE AS A FAT MAN'S SLACKS.
OH YES, MY RUMPUS ARE LEGENDARY.
NOT BAD, KING-SIR. I LIKE A FELLA WHAT TAKES HIS FUN SERIOUS.
HOLY SMOKES...
THE PLURAL OF 'RUMPUS' IS RUMPI.
WELL, YOU'RE WRONG.
WHAT IN ALL HEAVEN IS THAT?!

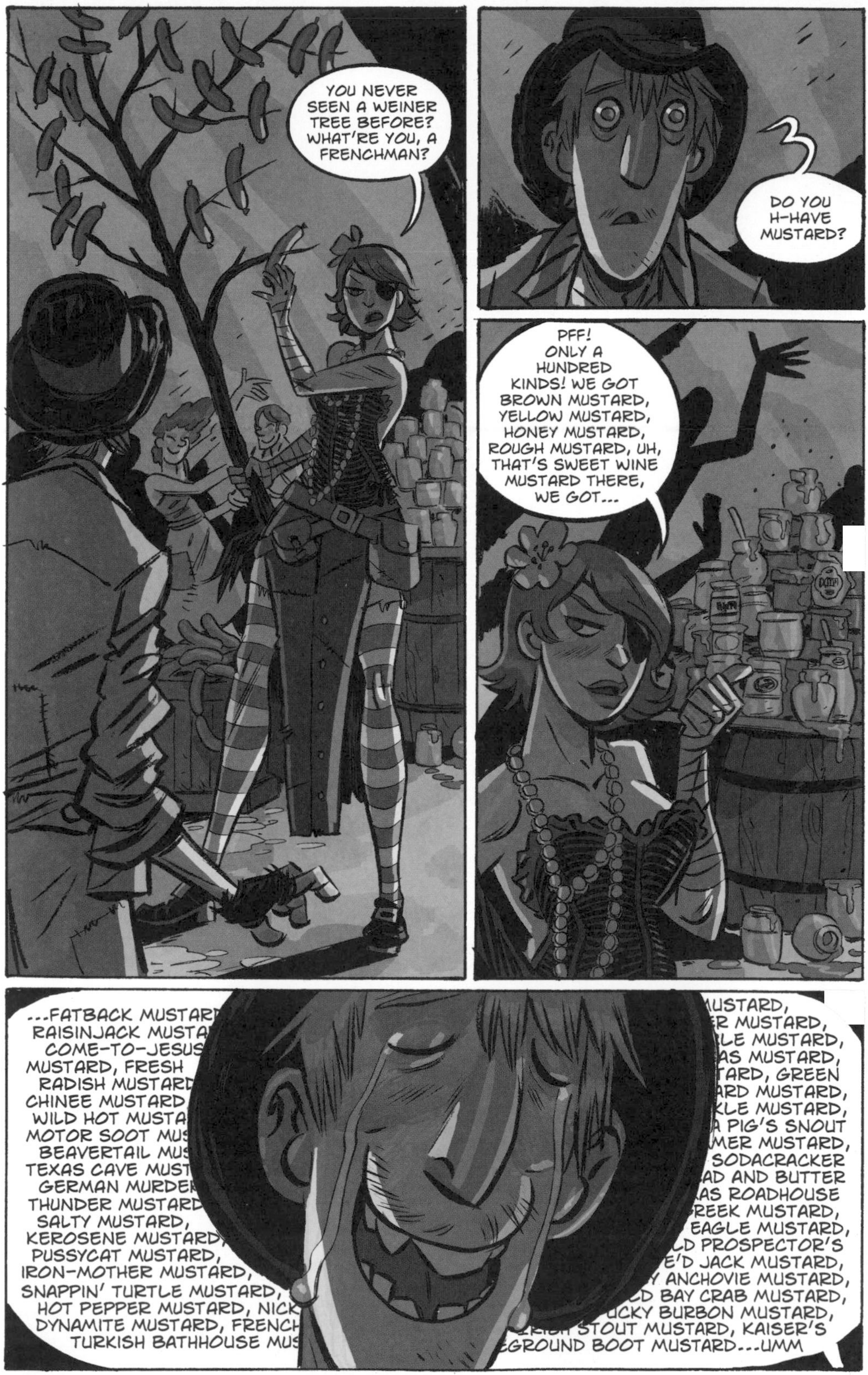
YOU NEVER SEEN A WEINER TREE BEFORE? WHAT'RE YOU, A FRENCHMAN?
DO YOU H-HAVE MUSTARD?
PFF! ONLY A HUNDRED KINDS! WE GOT BROWN MUSTARD, YELLOW MUSTARD, HONEY MUSTARD, ROUGH MUSTARD, UH, THAT'S SWEET WINE MUSTARD THERE, WE GOT...
...FATBACK MUSTARD
RAISINJACK MUSTA
COME-TO-JESUS
MUSTARD, FRESH
RADISH MUSTARD
CHINEE MUSTARD
WILD HOT MUSTA
MOTOR SOOT MUS
BEAVERTAIL MUS
TEXAS CAVE MUST
GERMAN MURDER
THUNDER MUSTARD
SALTY MUSTARD,
KEROSENE MUSTARD,
PUSSYCAT MUSTARD,
IRON-MOTHER MUSTARD,
SNAPPIN' TURTLE MUSTARD,
HOT PEPPER MUSTARD, NICK
DYNAMITE MUSTARD, FRENCH
TURKISH BATHHOUSE MUS
MUSTARD,
ER MUSTARD,
LE MUSTARD,
AS MUSTARD,
TARD, GREEN
ARD MUSTARD,
KLE MUSTARD,
A PIG'S SNOUT
MER MUSTARD,
SODACRACKER
AD AND BUTTER
AS ROADHOUSE
REEK MUSTARD,
EAGLE MUSTARD,
LD PROSPECTOR'S
E'D JACK MUSTARD,
Y ANCHOVIE MUSTARD,
D BAY CRAB MUSTARD,
UCKY BURBON MUSTARD,
IRISH STOUT MUSTARD, KAISER'S
EGROUND BOOT MUSTARD...UMM

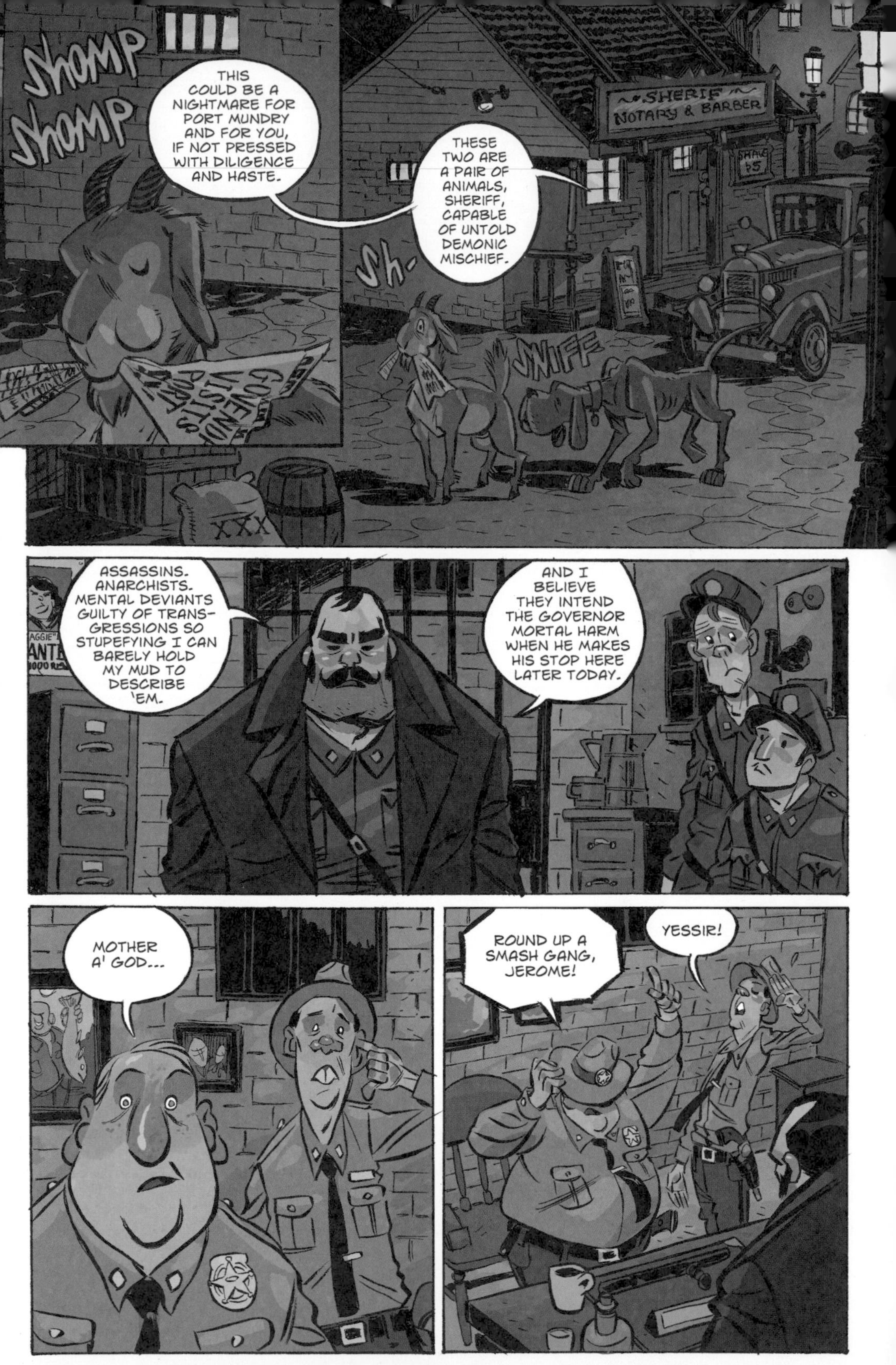
SHOMP SHOMP
THIS COULD BE A NIGHTMARE FOR PORT MUNDRY AND FOR YOU, IF NOT PRESSED WITH DILIGENCE AND HASTE.
THESE TWO ARE A PAIR OF ANIMALS, SHERIFF, CAPABLE OF UNTOLD DEMONIC MISCHIEF.
SH-
SHERIF
NOTARY & BARBER
SNIFF
ASSASSINS. ANARCHISTS. MENTAL DEVIANTS GUILTY OF TRANS-GRESSIONS SO STUPEFYING I CAN BARELY HOLD MY MUD TO DESCRIBE 'EM.
AND I BELIEVE THEY INTEND THE GOVERNOR MORTAL HARM WHEN HE MAKES HIS STOP HERE LATER TODAY.
MOTHER A' GOD...
ROUND UP A SMASH GANG, JEROME!
YESSIR!

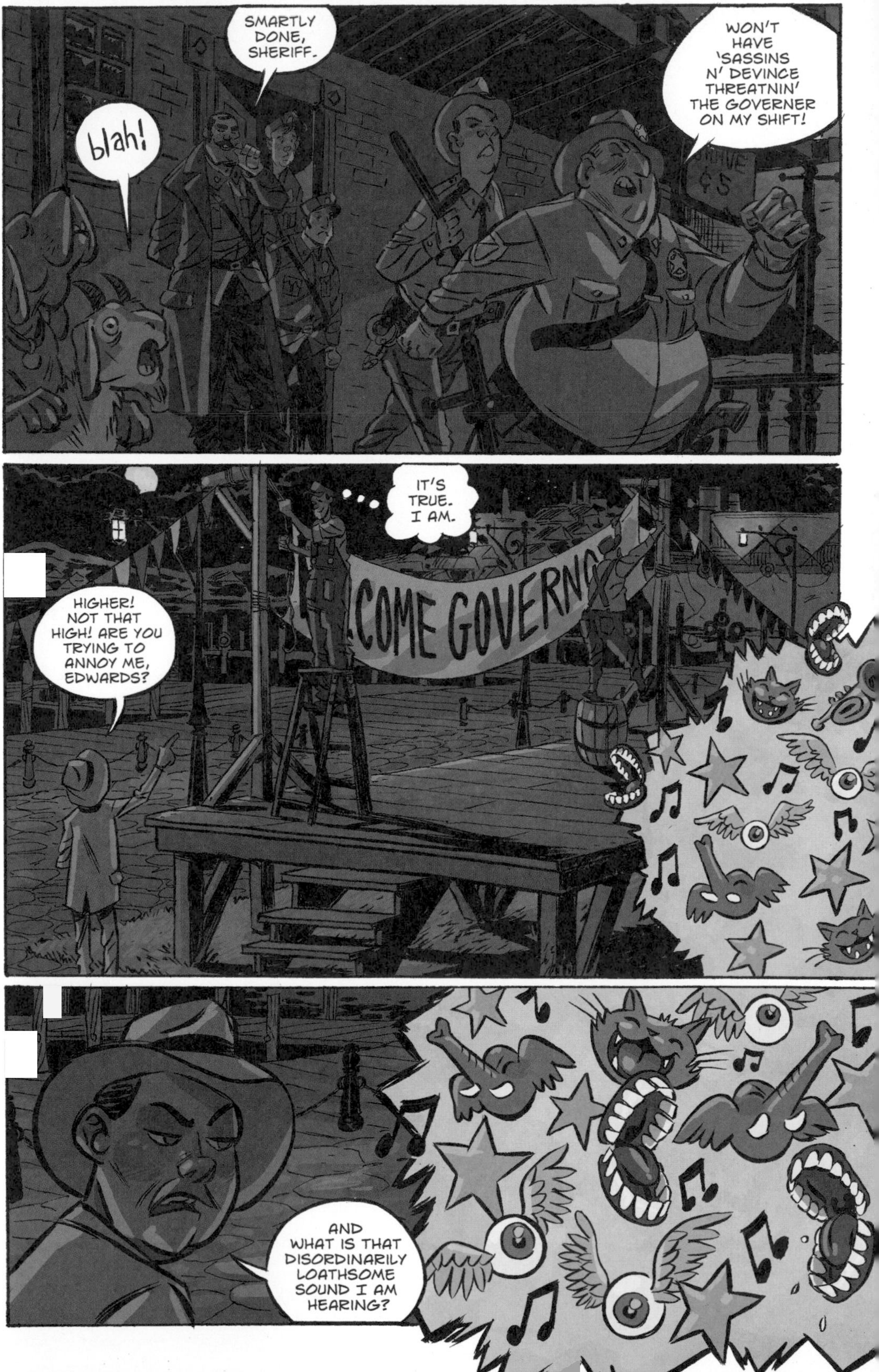
SMARTLY DONE, SHERIFF.
WON'T HAVE 'SASSINS N' DEVINCE THREATNIN' THE GOVERNER ON MY SHIFT!
blah!
IT'S TRUE. I AM.
COME GOVERN
HIGHER! NOT THAT HIGH! ARE YOU TRYING TO ANNOY ME, EDWARDS?
AND WHAT IS THAT DISORDINARILY LOATHSOME SOUND I AM HEARING?

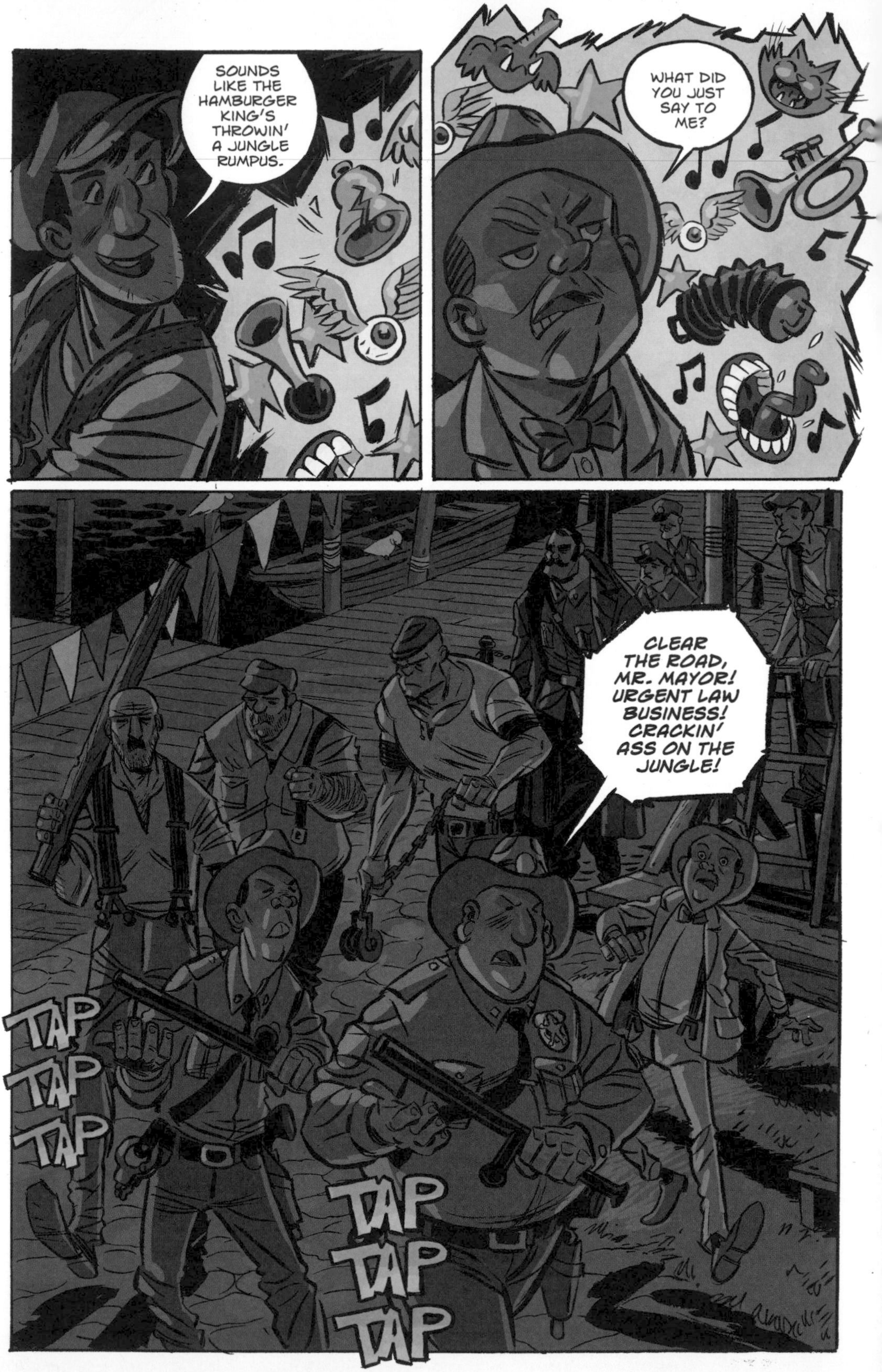
SOUNDS LIKE THE HAMBURGER KING'S THROWIN' A JUNGLE RUMPUS.
WHAT DID YOU JUST SAY TO ME?
CLEAR THE ROAD, MR. MAYOR! URGENT LAW BUSINESS! CRACKIN' ASS ON THE JUNGLE!
TAP TAP TAP
TAP TAP TAP

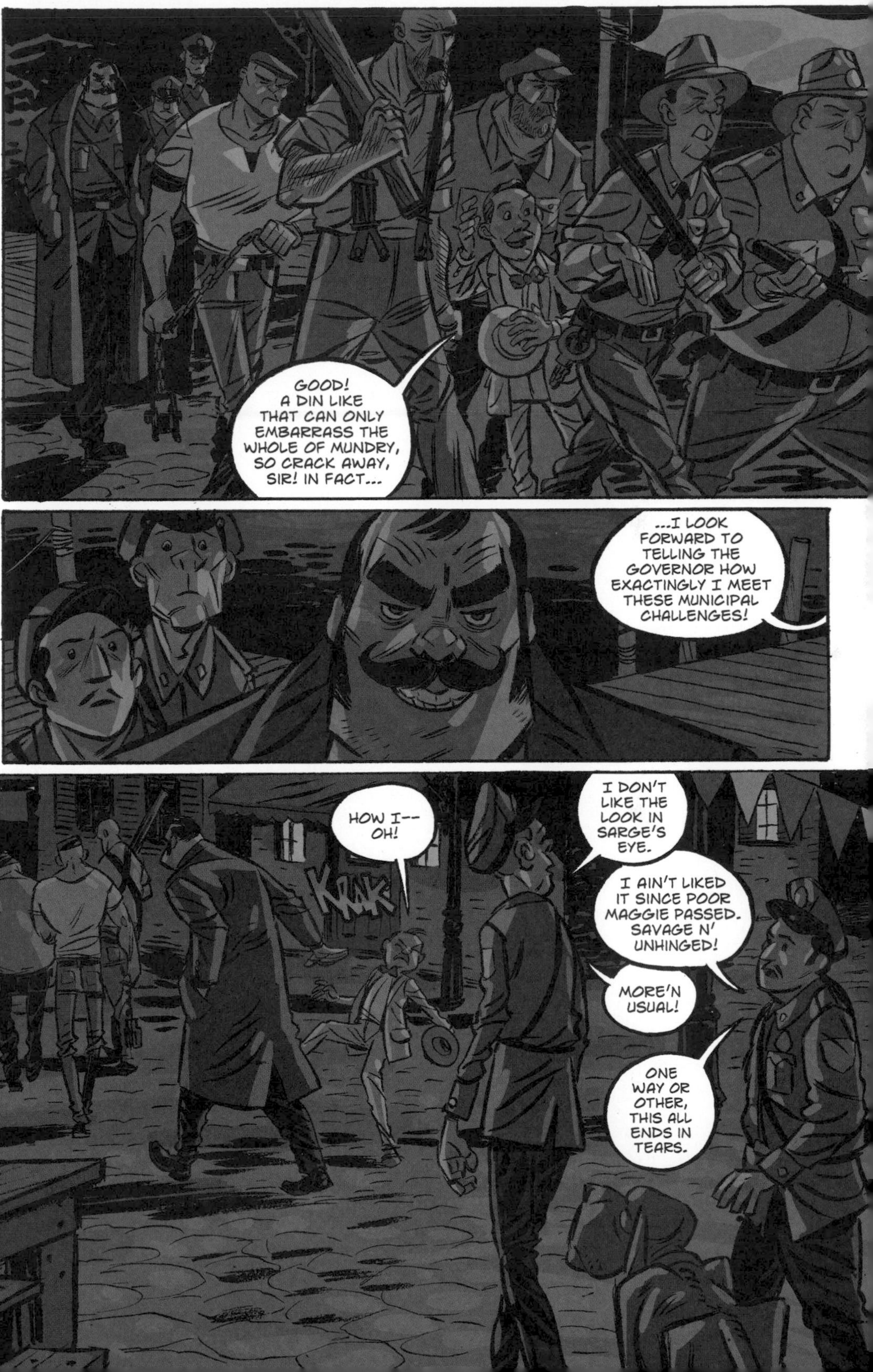
GOOD! A DIN LIKE THAT CAN ONLY EMBARRASS THE WHOLE OF MUNDRY, SO CRACK AWAY, SIR! IN FACT...
...I LOOK FORWARD TO TELLING THE GOVERNOR HOW EXACTINGLY I MEET THESE MUNICIPAL CHALLENGES!
KRAK
HOW I-- OH!
I DON'T LIKE THE LOOK IN SARGE'S EYE.
I AIN'T LIKED IT SINCE POOR MAGGIE PASSED. SAVAGE N' UNHINGED!
MORE'N USUAL!
ONE WAY OR OTHER, THIS ALL ENDS IN TEARS.

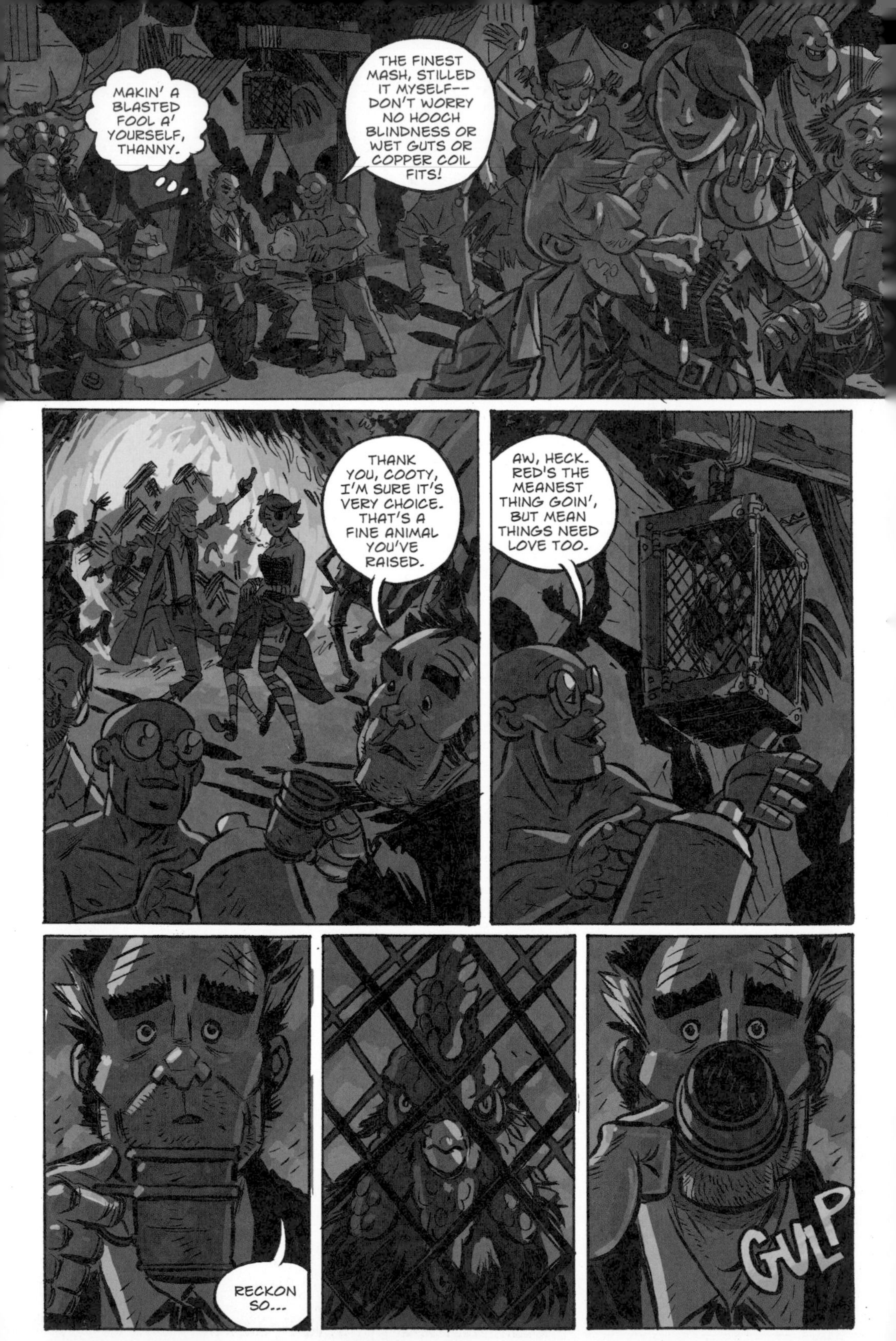
MAKIN' A BLASTED FOOL A' YOURSELF, THANNY.
THE FINEST MASH, STILLED IT MYSELF-- DON'T WORRY NO HOOCH BLINDNESS OR WET GUTS OR COPPER COIL FITS!
THANK YOU, COOTY, I'M SURE IT'S VERY CHOICE. THAT'S A FINE ANIMAL YOU'VE RAISED.
AW, HECK. RED'S THE MEANEST THING GOIN', BUT MEAN THINGS NEED LOVE TOO.
RECKON SO...
GULP

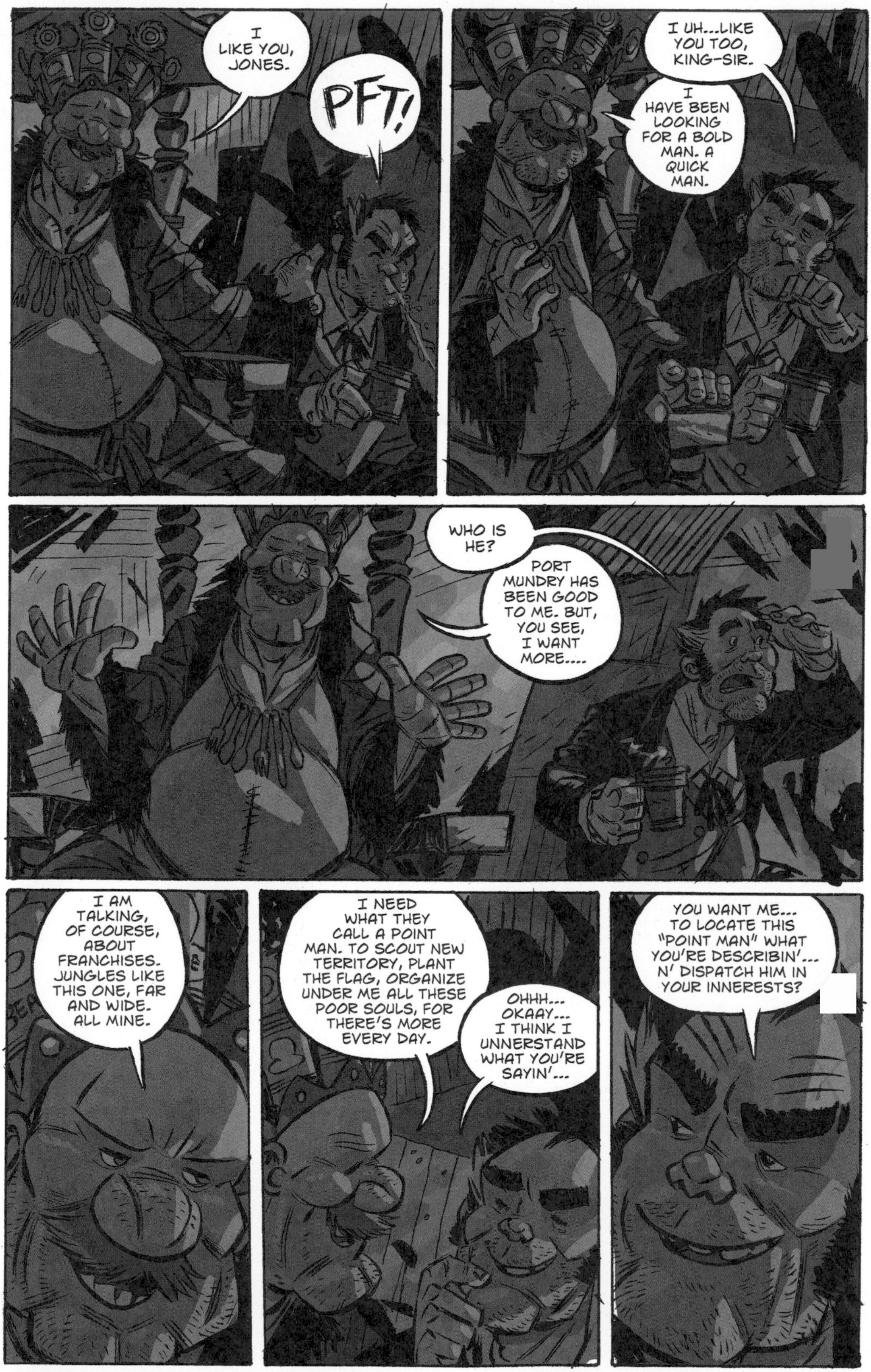
I LIKE YOU, JONES.
PFT!
I UH...LIKE YOU TOO, KING-SIR.
I HAVE BEEN LOOKING FOR A BOLD MAN. A QUICK MAN.
WHO IS HE?
PORT MUNDRY HAS BEEN GOOD TO ME. BUT, YOU SEE, I WANT MORE....
I AM TALKING, OF COURSE, ABOUT FRANCHISES. JUNGLES LIKE THIS ONE, FAR AND WIDE. ALL MINE.
I NEED WHAT THEY CALL A POINT MAN. TO SCOUT NEW TERRITORY, PLANT THE FLAG, ORGANIZE UNDER ME ALL THESE POOR SOULS, FOR THERE'S MORE EVERY DAY.
OHHH... OKAAY... I THINK I UNNERSTAND WHAT YOU'RE SAYIN'...
YOU WANT ME... TO LOCATE THIS "POINT MAN" WHAT YOU'RE DESCRIBIN'... N' DISPATCH HIM IN YOUR INNERESTS?

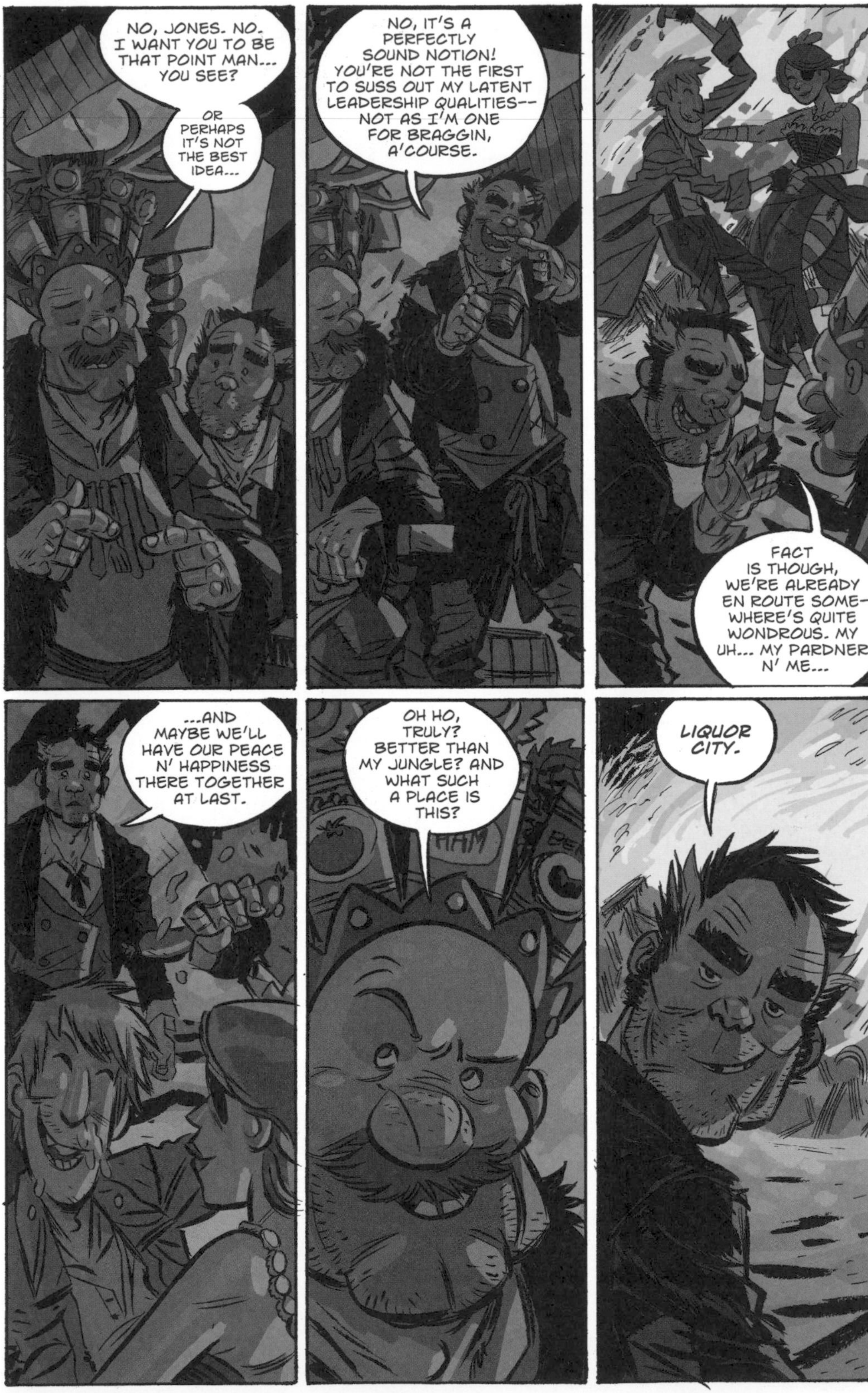
NO, JONES. NO. I WANT YOU TO BE THAT POINT MAN... YOU SEE?
OR PERHAPS IT'S NOT THE BEST IDEA...
NO, IT'S A PERFECTLY SOUND NOTION! YOU'RE NOT THE FIRST TO SUSS OUT MY LATENT LEADERSHIP QUALITIES-- NOT AS I'M ONE FOR BRAGGIN, A'COURSE.
FACT IS THOUGH, WE'RE ALREADY EN ROUTE SOME-WHERE'S QUITE WONDROUS. MY UH... MY PARDNER N' ME...
...AND MAYBE WE'LL HAVE OUR PEACE N' HAPPINESS THERE TOGETHER AT LAST.
OH HO, TRULY? BETTER THAN MY JUNGLE? AND WHAT SUCH A PLACE IS THIS?
HAM
LIQUOR CITY.

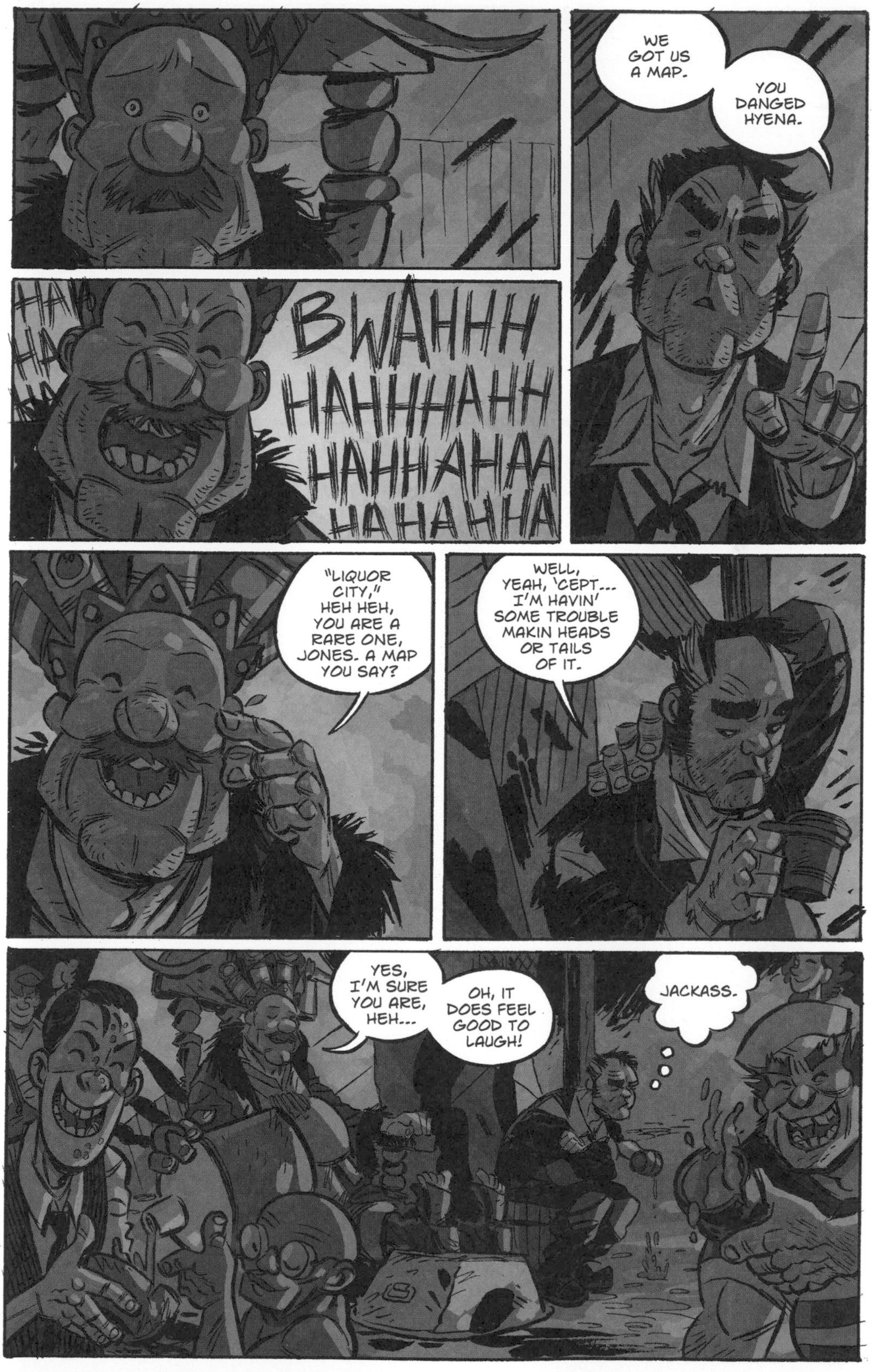
WE GOT US A MAP.
YOU DANGED HYENA.
BWAHHH HAHHHAHH HAHHAHAA HAHAHHA
HAHA HA
"LIQUOR CITY," HEH HEH, YOU ARE A RARE ONE, JONES. A MAP YOU SAY?
WELL, YEAH, 'CEPT... I'M HAVIN' SOME TROUBLE MAKIN HEADS OR TAILS OF IT.
YES, I'M SURE YOU ARE, HEH...
OH, IT DOES FEEL GOOD TO LAUGH!
JACKASS.

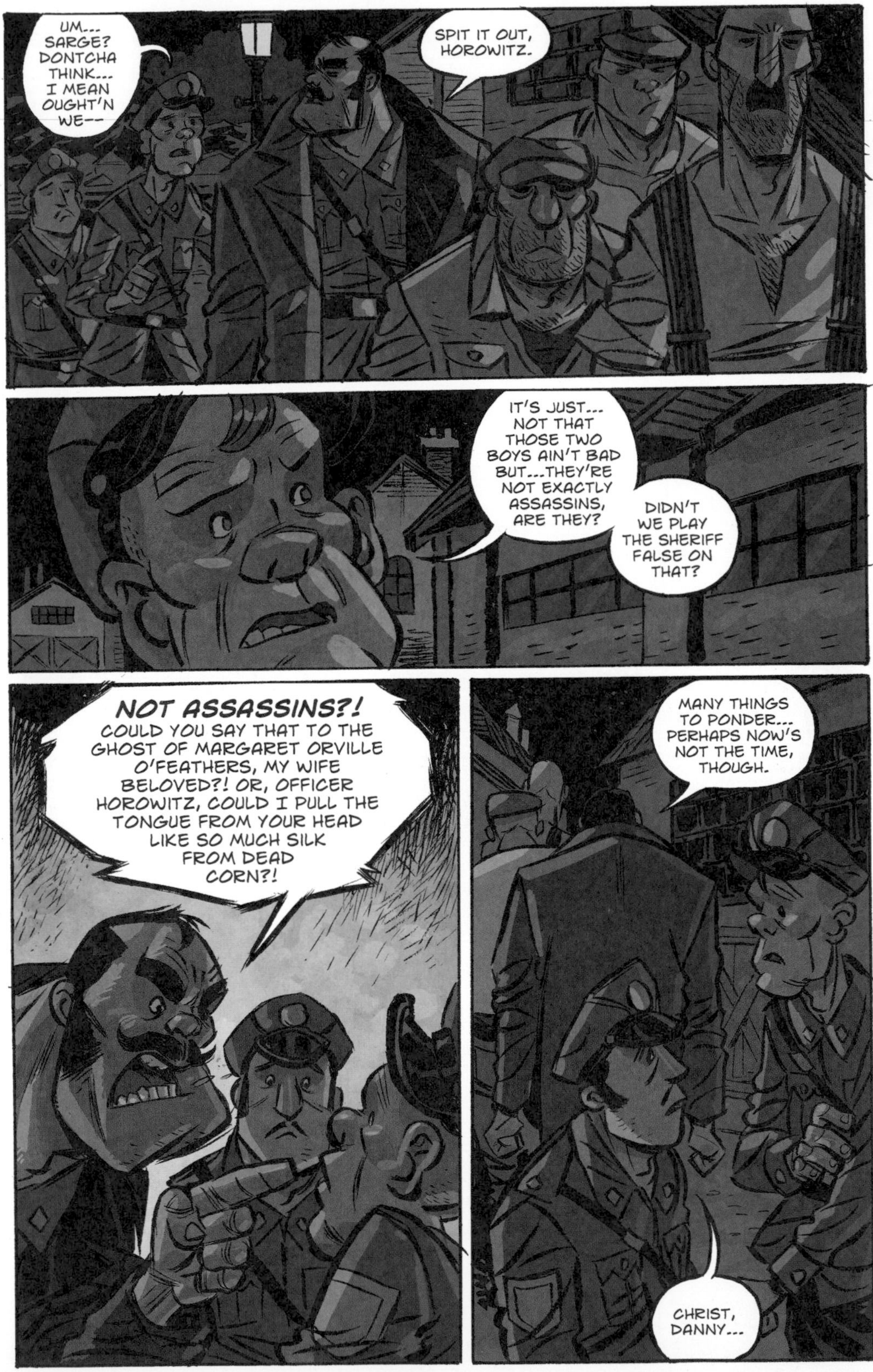
UM... SARGE? DONTCHA THINK... I MEAN OUGHT'N WE--
SPIT IT OUT, HOROWITZ.
IT'S JUST... NOT THAT THOSE TWO BOYS AIN'T BAD BUT... THEY'RE NOT EXACTLY ASSASSINS, ARE THEY?
DIDN'T WE PLAY THE SHERIFF FALSE ON THAT?
NOT ASSASSINS?! COULD YOU SAY THAT TO THE GHOST OF MARGARET ORVILLE O'FEATHERS, MY WIFE BELOVED?! OR, OFFICER HOROWITZ, COULD I PULL THE TONGUE FROM YOUR HEAD LIKE SO MUCH SILK FROM DEAD CORN?!
MANY THINGS TO PONDER... PERHAPS NOW'S NOT THE TIME, THOUGH.
CHRIST, DANNY...

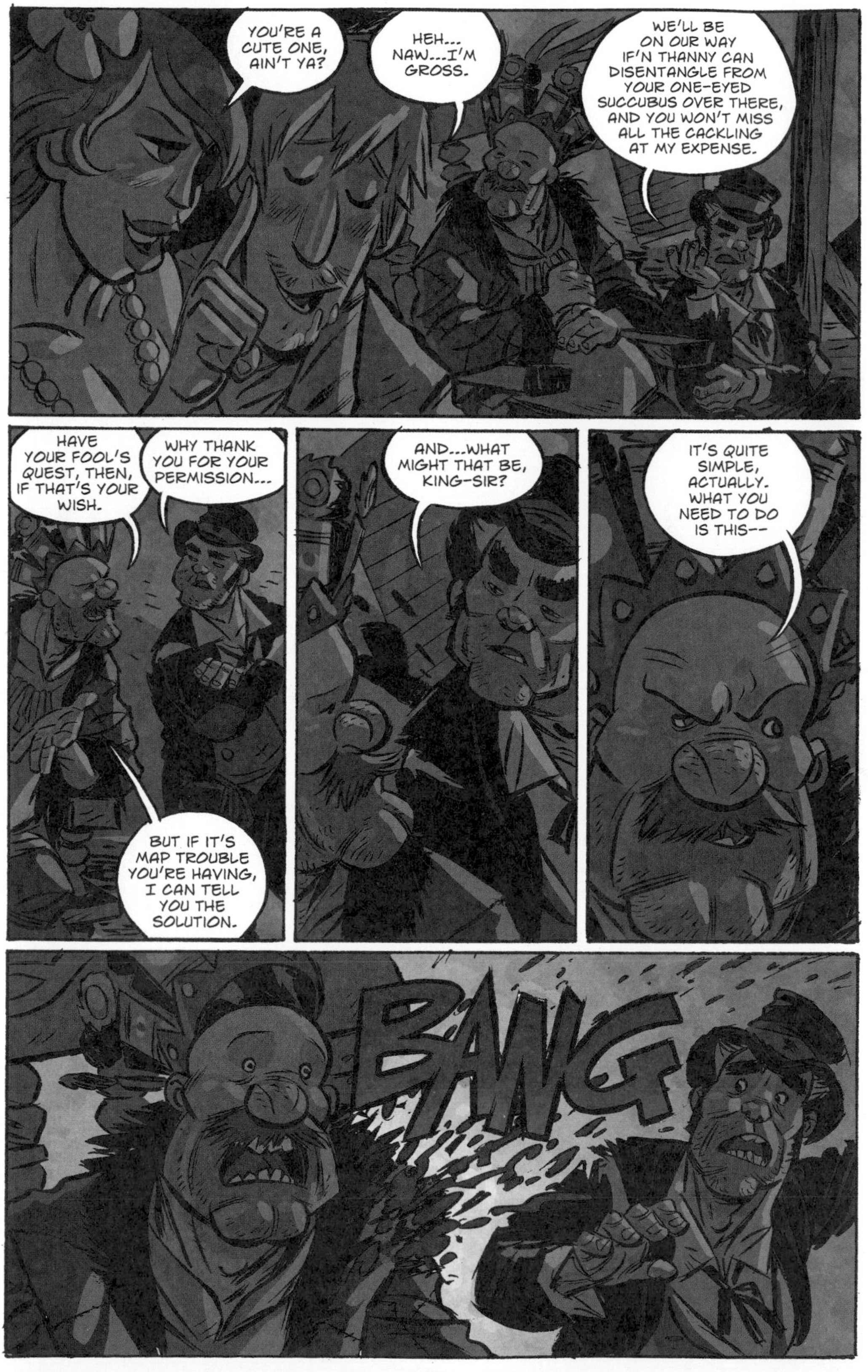
YOU'RE A CUTE ONE, AIN'T YA?
HEH... NAW...I'M GROSS.
WE'LL BE ON OUR WAY IF'N THANNY CAN DISENTANGLE FROM YOUR ONE-EYED SUCCUBUS OVER THERE, AND YOU WON'T MISS ALL THE CACKLING AT MY EXPENSE.
HAVE YOUR FOOL'S QUEST, THEN, IF THAT'S YOUR WISH.
WHY THANK YOU FOR YOUR PERMISSION...
BUT IF IT'S MAP TROUBLE YOU'RE HAVING, I CAN TELL YOU THE SOLUTION.
AND...WHAT MIGHT THAT BE, KING-SIR?
IT'S QUITE SIMPLE, ACTUALLY. WHAT YOU NEED TO DO IS THIS--
BANG

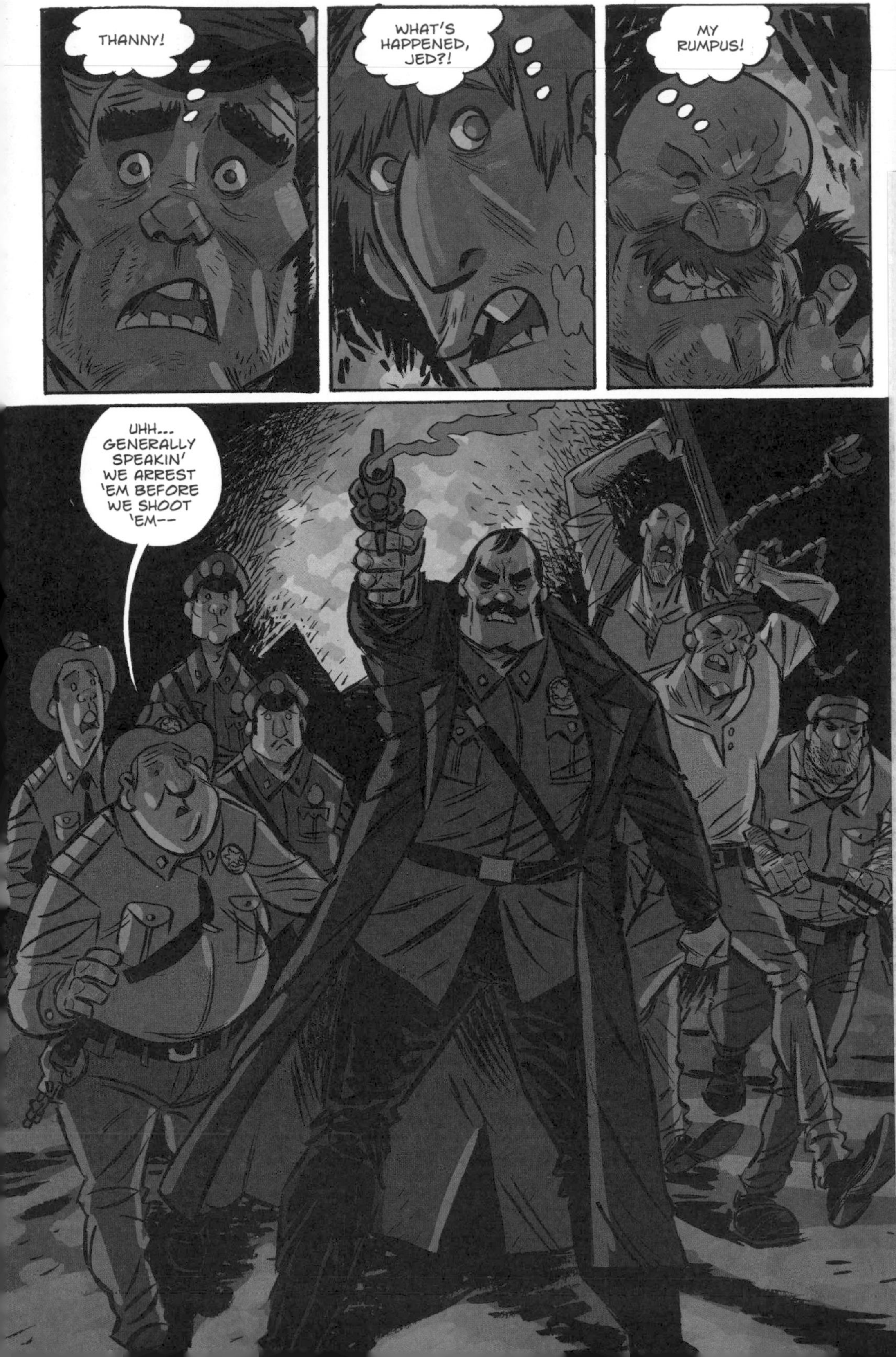
THANNY!
WHAT'S HAPPENED, JED?!
MY RUMPUS!
UHH... GENERALLY SPEAKIN' WE ARREST 'EM BEFORE WE SHOOT 'EM--

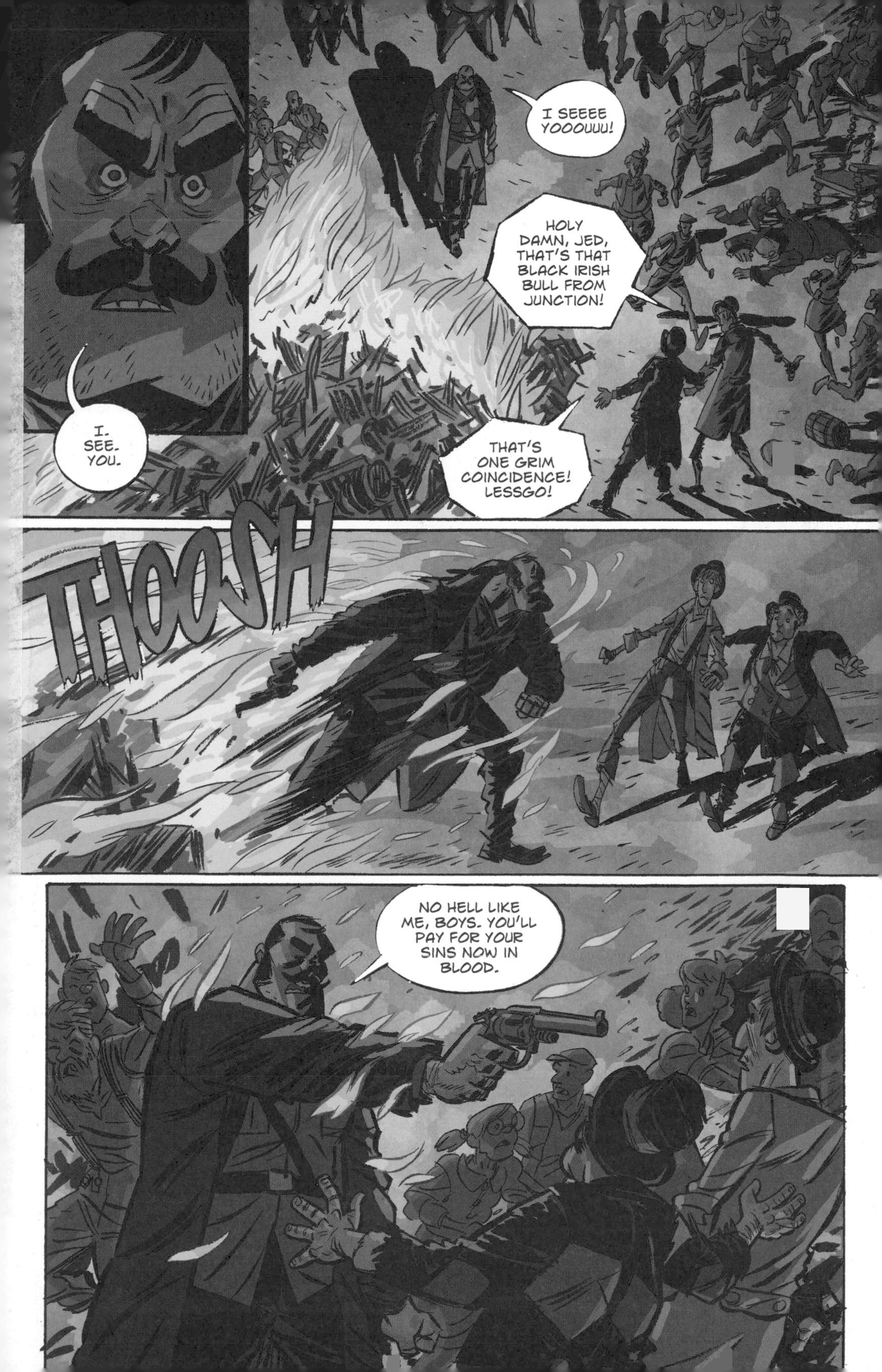
I SEEEE YOOOUUU!
HOLY DAMN, JED, THAT'S THAT BLACK IRISH BULL FROM JUNCTION!
I. SEE. YOU.
THAT'S ONE GRIM COINCIDENCE! LESSGO!
THOOSH
NO HELL LIKE ME, BOYS. YOU'LL PAY FOR YOUR SINS NOW IN BLOOD.

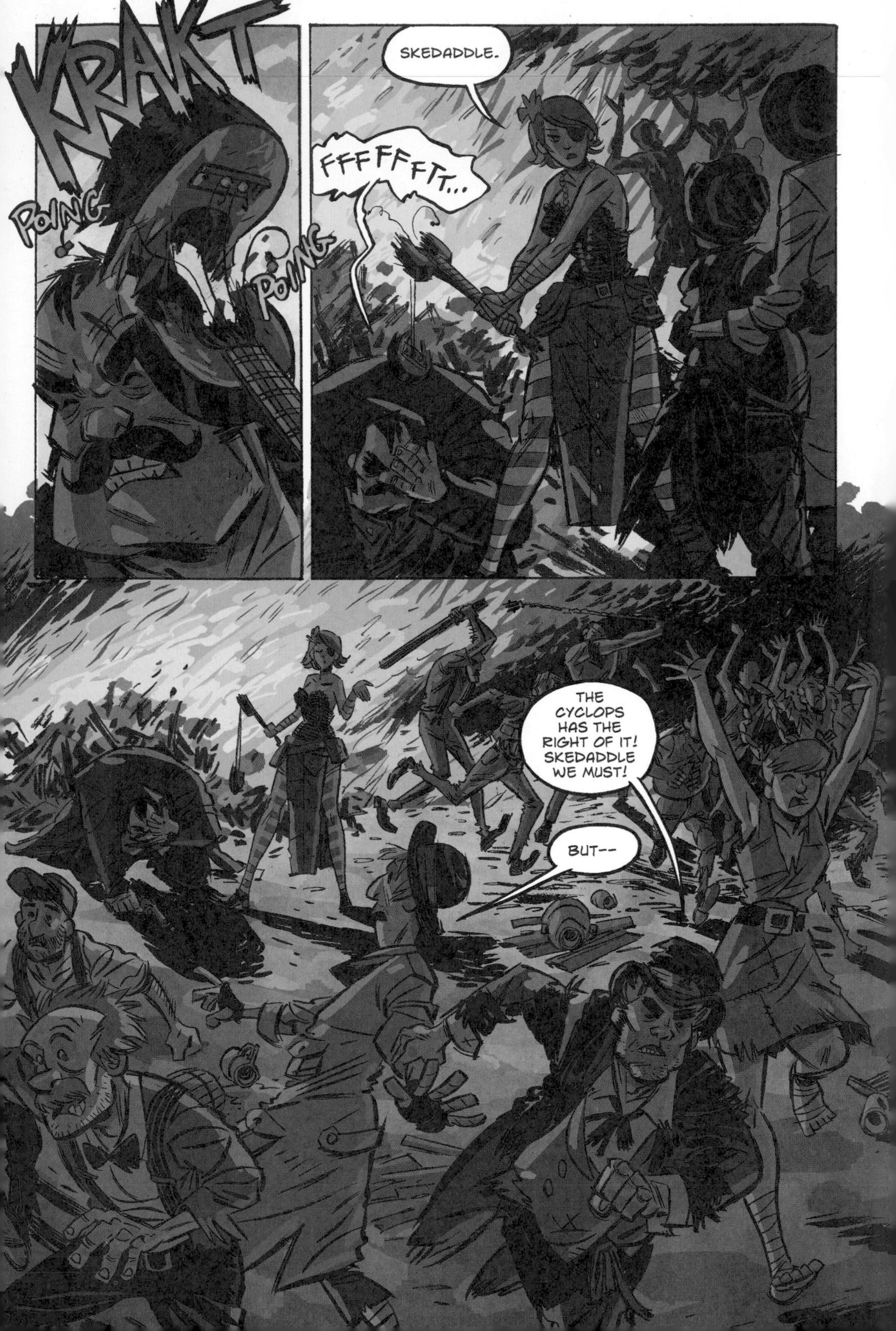
KRAKT
POING
POING
SKEDADDLE.
FFFFFFTT...
THE CYCLOPS HAS THE RIGHT OF IT! SKEDADDLE WE MUST!
BUT--

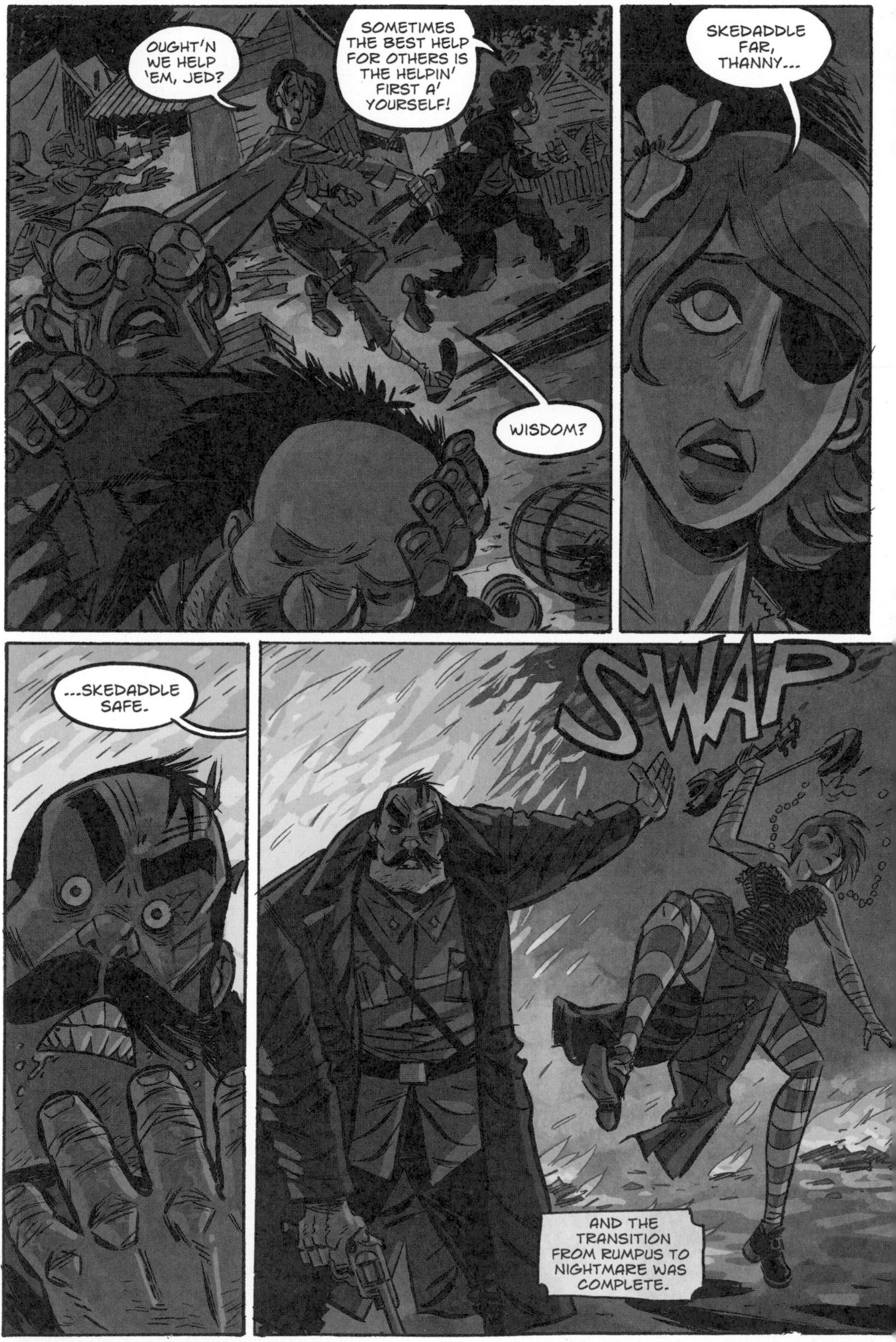
OUGHT'N WE HELP 'EM, JED?
SOMETIMES THE BEST HELP FOR OTHERS IS THE HELPIN' FIRST A' YOURSELF!
WISDOM?
SKEDADDLE FAR, THANNY...
...SKEDADDLE SAFE.
SWAP
AND THE TRANSITION FROM RUMPUS TO NIGHTMARE WAS COMPLETE.

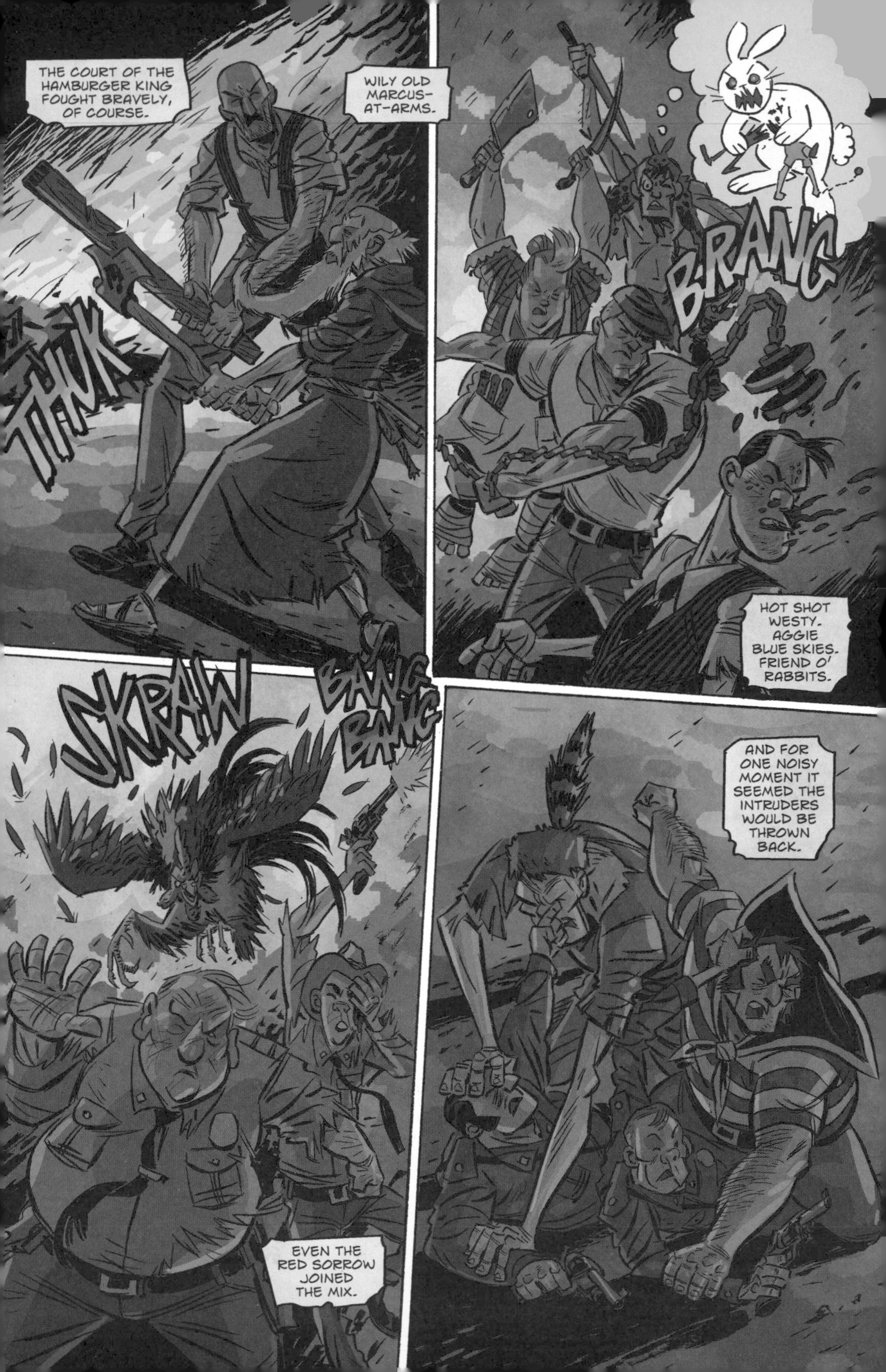
THE COURT OF THE HAMBURGER KING FOUGHT BRAVELY, OF COURSE.
WILY OLD MARCUS-AT-ARMS.
THUK
BRANG
HOT SHOT WESTY. AGGIE BLUE SKIES. FRIEND O' RABBITS.
SKRAW
BANG BANG
EVEN THE RED SORROW JOINED THE MIX.
AND FOR ONE NOISY MOMENT IT SEEMED THE INTRUDERS WOULD BE THROWN BACK.

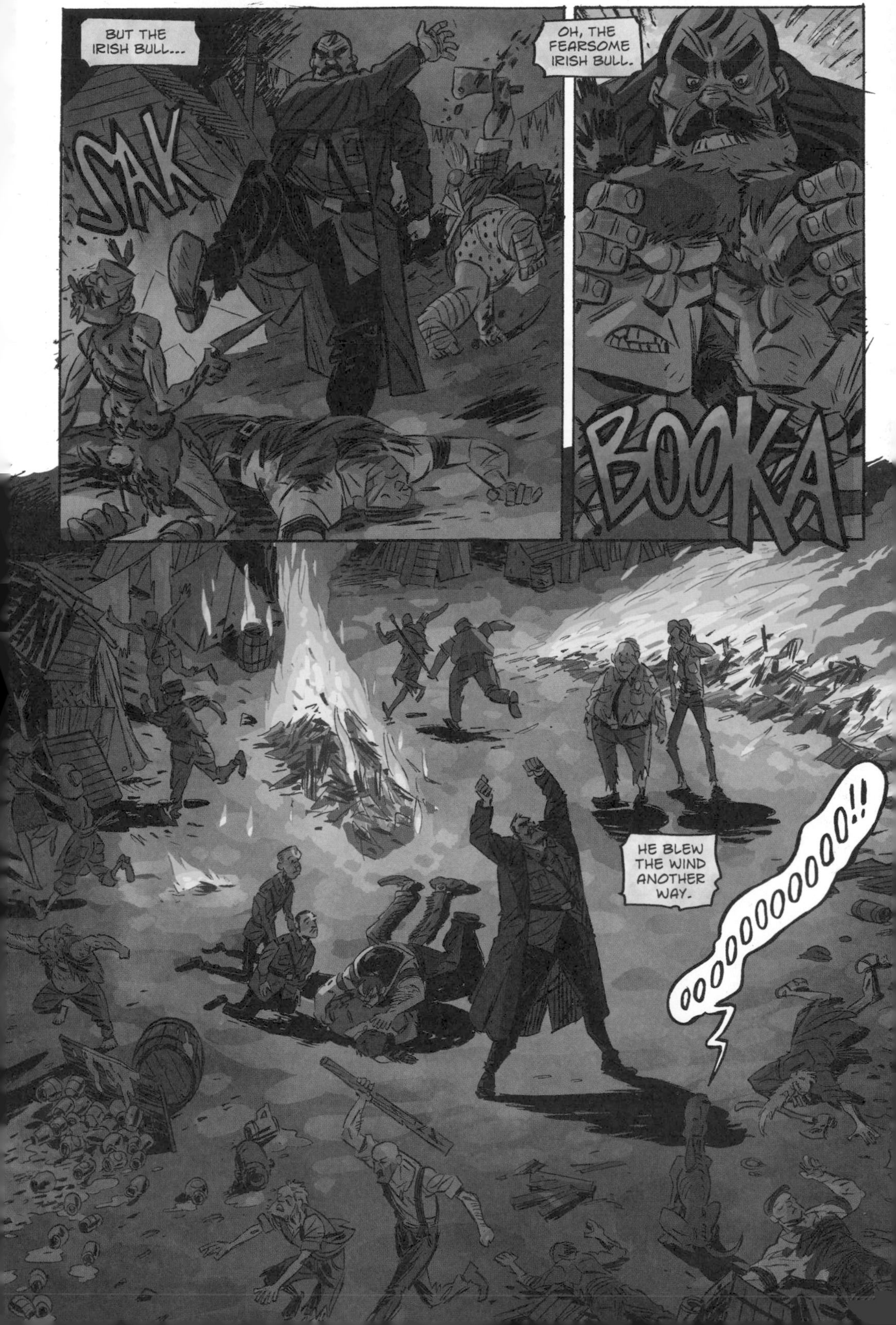

BUT THE IRISH BULL...
SAK
OH, THE FEARSOME IRISH BULL.
BOOKA
HE BLEW THE WIND ANOTHER WAY.
OOOOOOOOOOOO!!

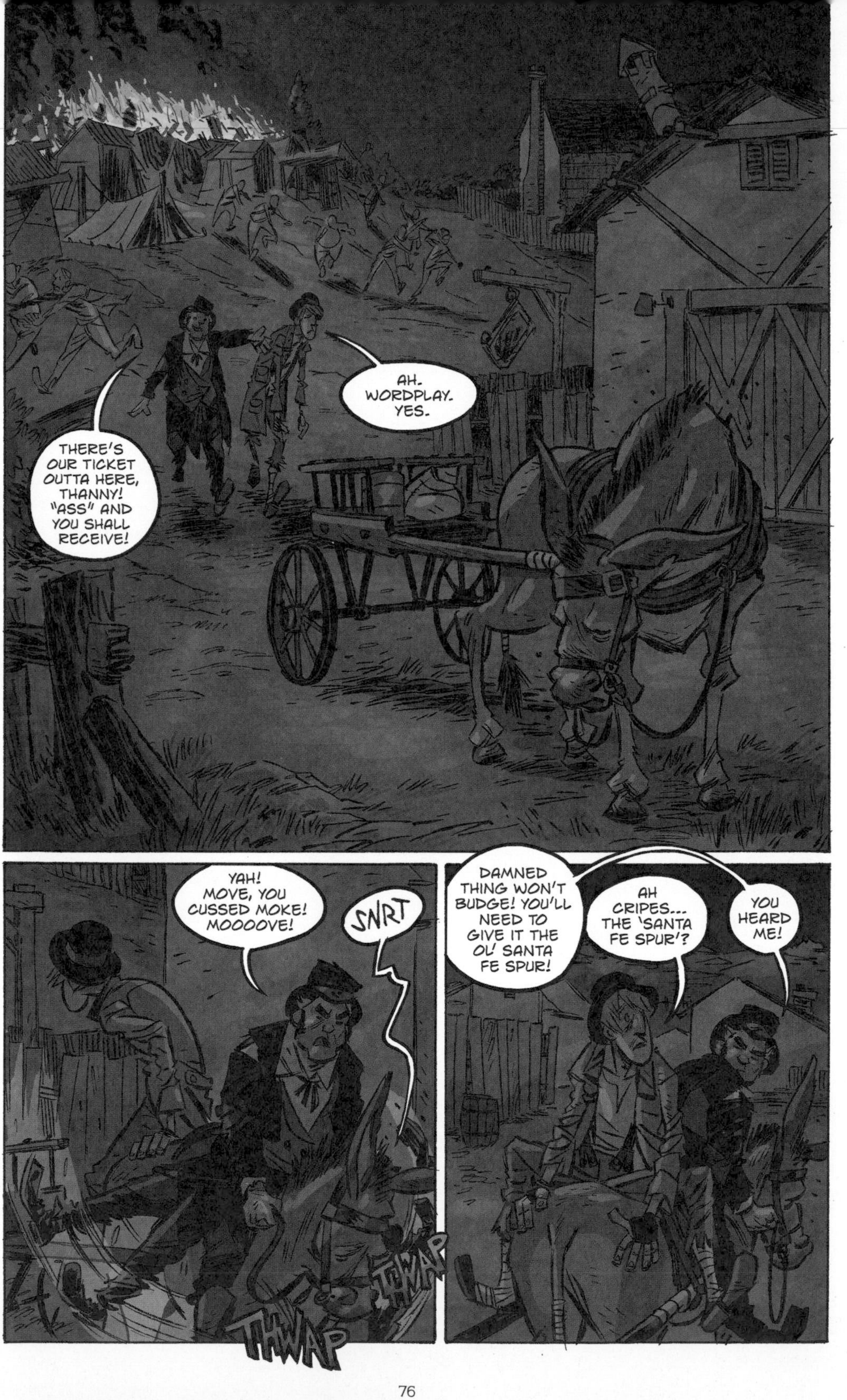
AH. WORDPLAY. YES.
THERE'S OUR TICKET OUTTA HERE, THANNY! "ASS" AND YOU SHALL RECEIVE!
YAH! MOVE, YOU CUSSED MOKE! MOOOOVE!
SNRT
THWAP
THWAP
DAMNED THING WON'T BUDGE! YOU'LL NEED TO GIVE IT THE OL' SANTA FE SPUR!
AH CRIPES... THE 'SANTA FE SPUR'?
YOU HEARD ME!

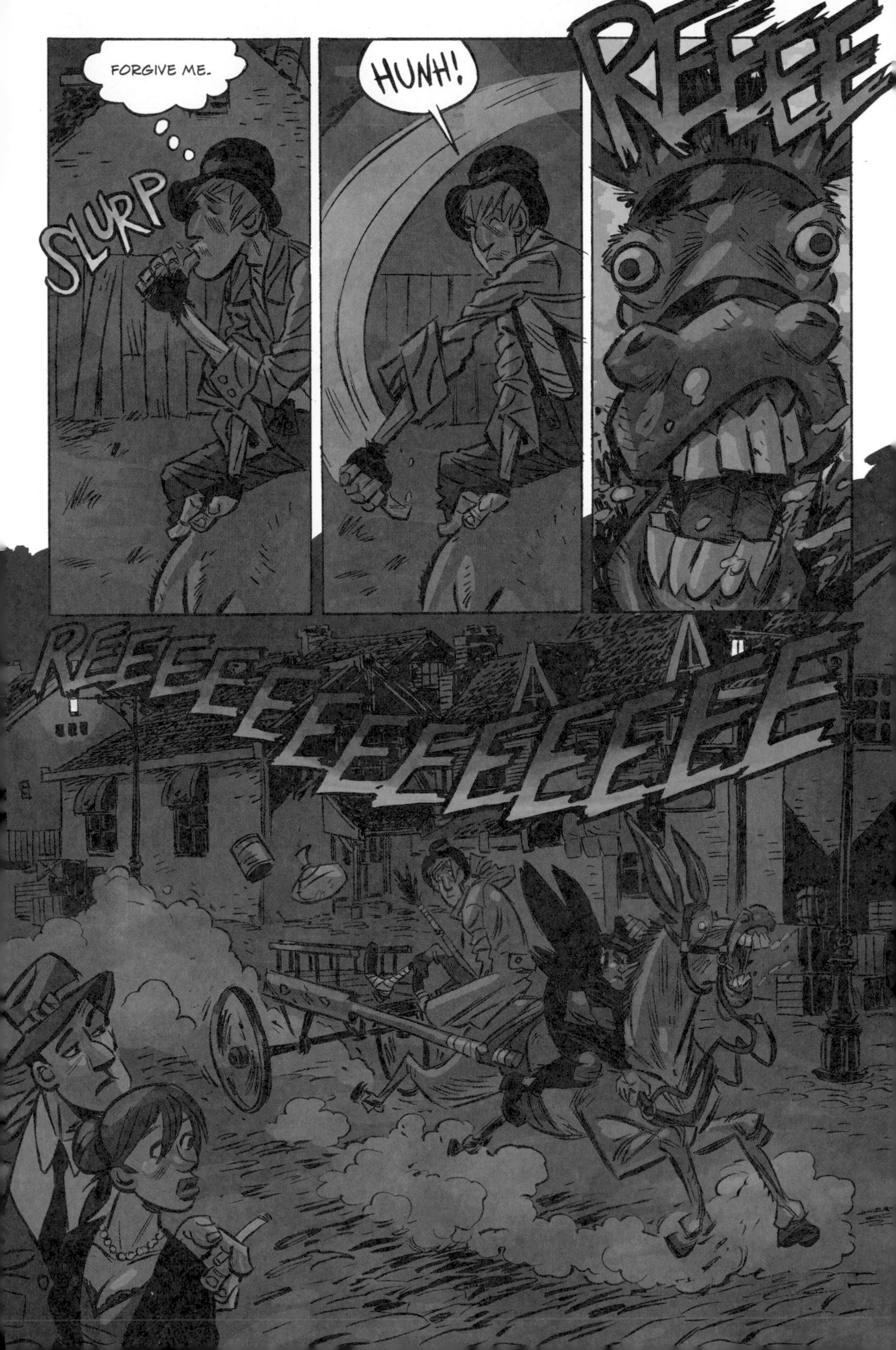
FORGIVE ME.
SLURP
HUNH!
REEEEE
REEEEEEEEEEEEEEEEE

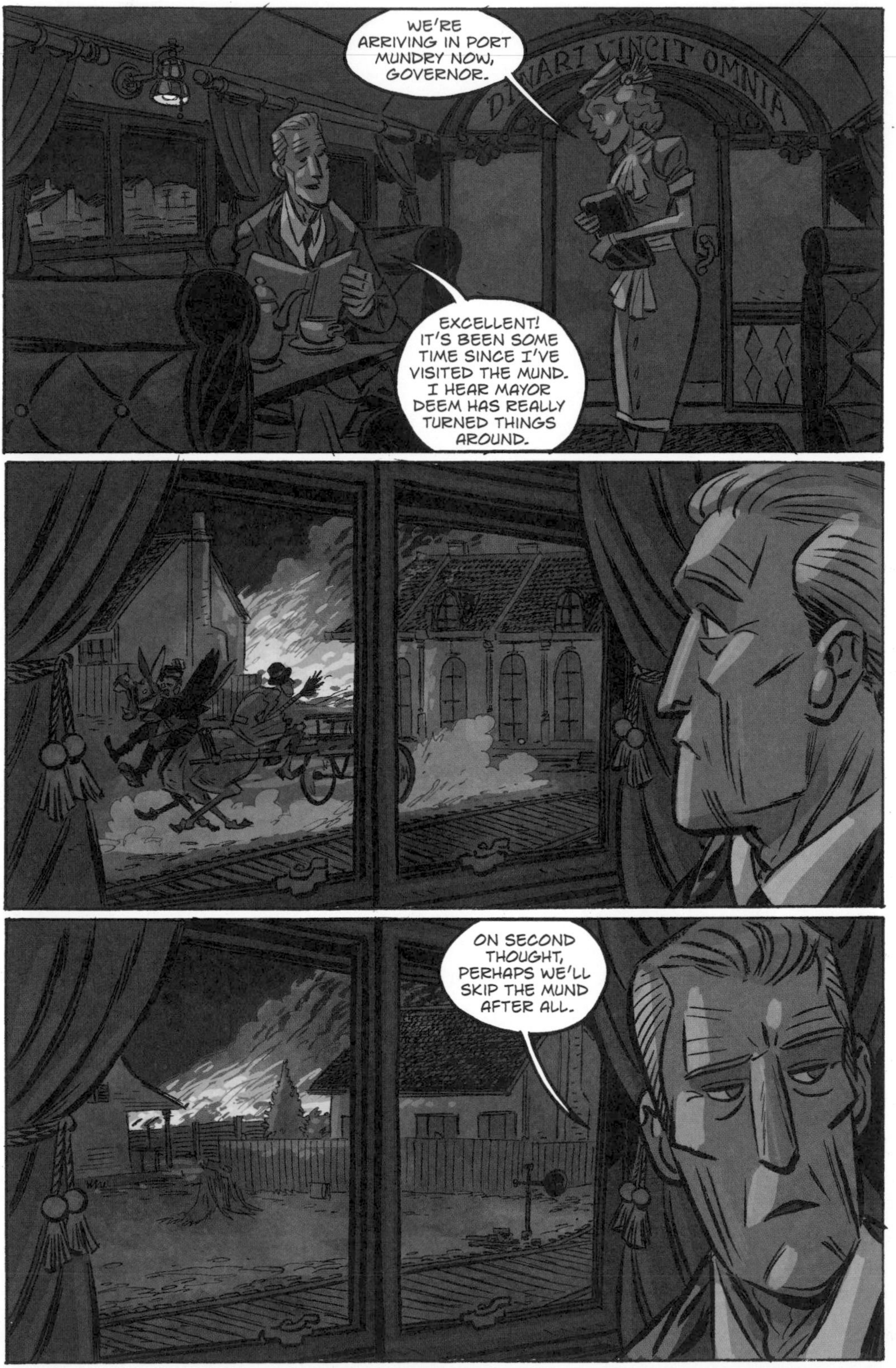

DINARI VINCIT OMNIA
WE'RE ARRIVING IN PORT MUNDRY NOW, GOVERNOR.
EXCELLENT! IT'S BEEN SOME TIME SINCE I'VE VISITED THE MUND. I HEAR MAYOR DEEM HAS REALLY TURNED THINGS AROUND.
ON SECOND THOUGHT, PERHAPS WE'LL SKIP THE MUND AFTER ALL.

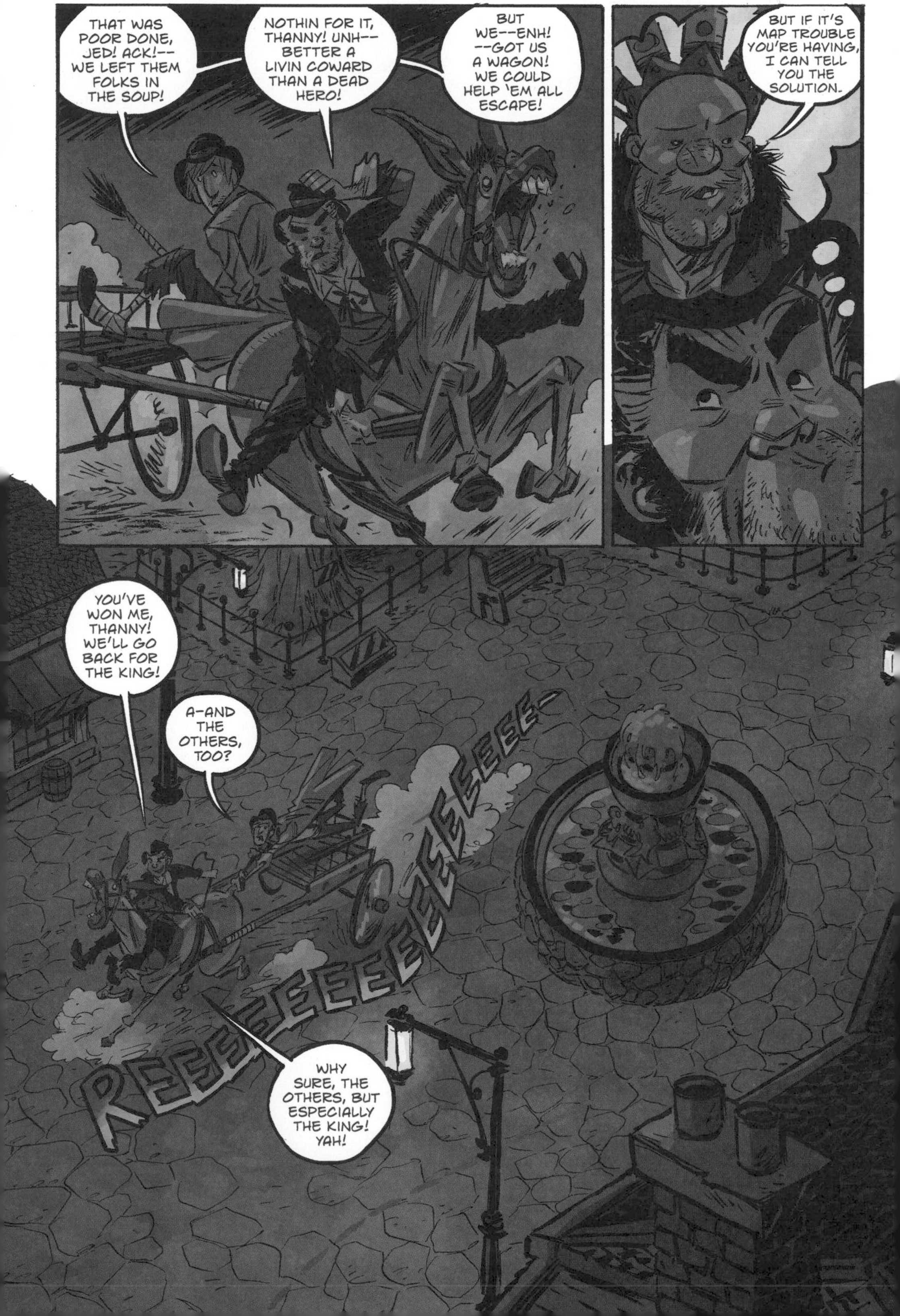
THAT WAS POOR DONE, JED! ACK!-- WE LEFT THEM FOLKS IN THE SOUP!
NOTHIN FOR IT, THANNY! UNH-- BETTER A LIVIN COWARD THAN A DEAD HERO!
BUT WE--ENH! --GOT US A WAGON! WE COULD HELP 'EM ALL ESCAPE!
BUT IF IT'S MAP TROUBLE YOU'RE HAVING, I CAN TELL YOU THE SOLUTION.
YOU'VE WON ME, THANNY! WE'LL GO BACK FOR THE KING!
A-AND THE OTHERS, TOO?
REEEEEEEEEEEEEE-
WHY SURE, THE OTHERS, BUT ESPECIALLY THE KING! YAH!

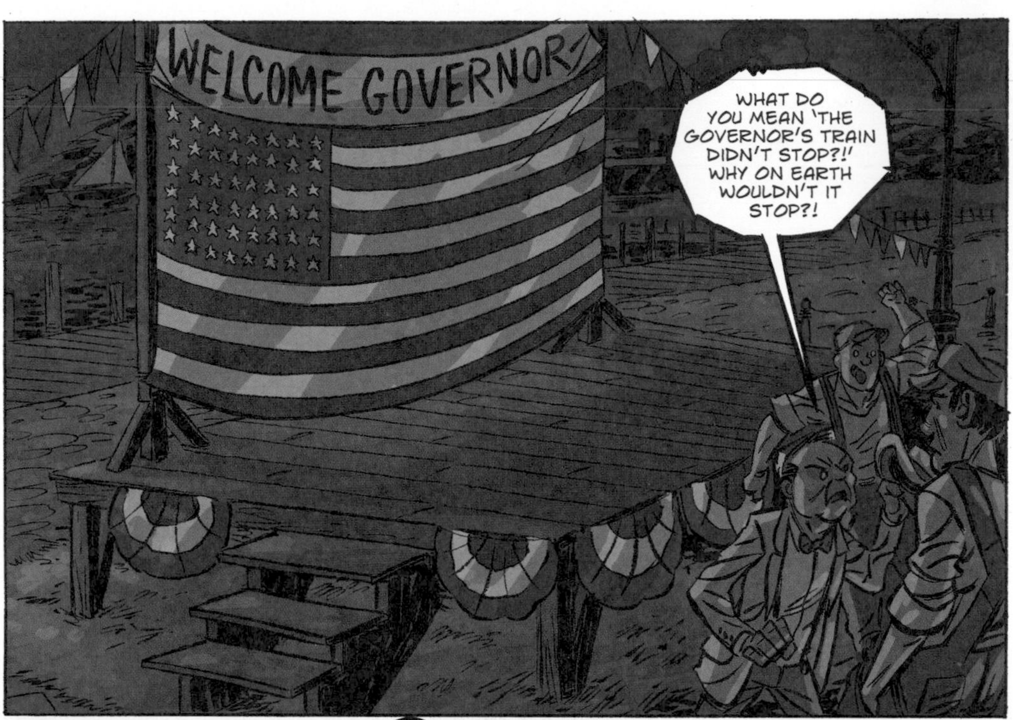
WELCOME GOVERNOR
WHAT DO YOU MEAN 'THE GOVERNOR'S TRAIN DIDN'T STOP?!' WHY ON EARTH WOULDN'T IT STOP?!

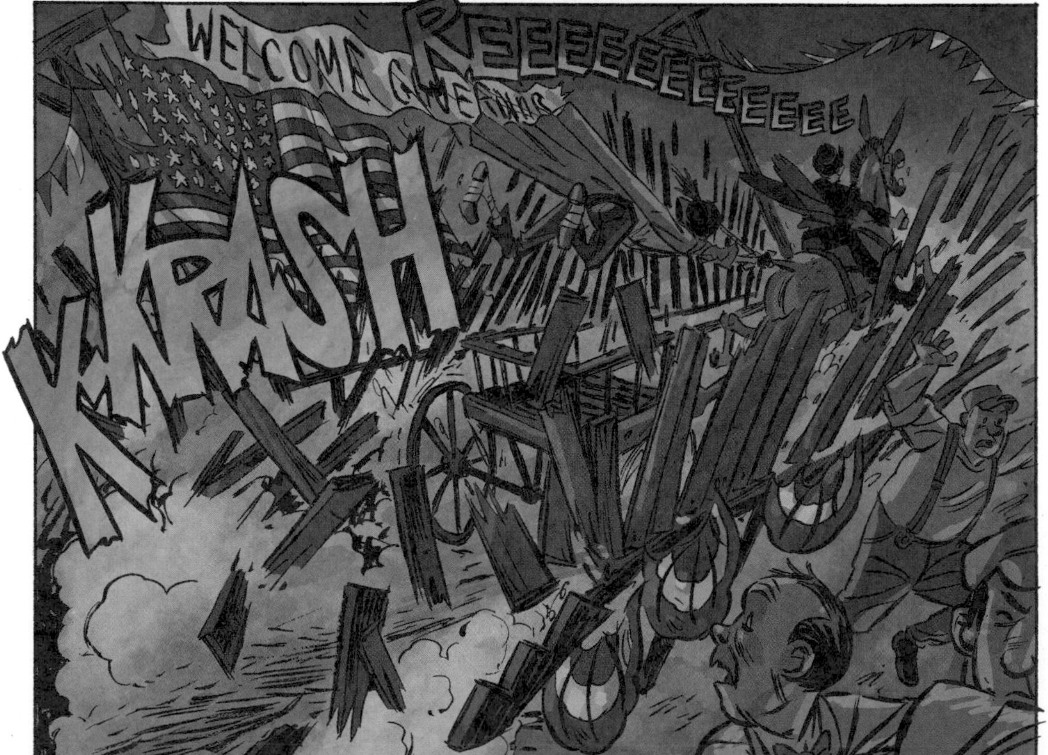
WELCOME
REEEEEEEEEEEEE
KRASH

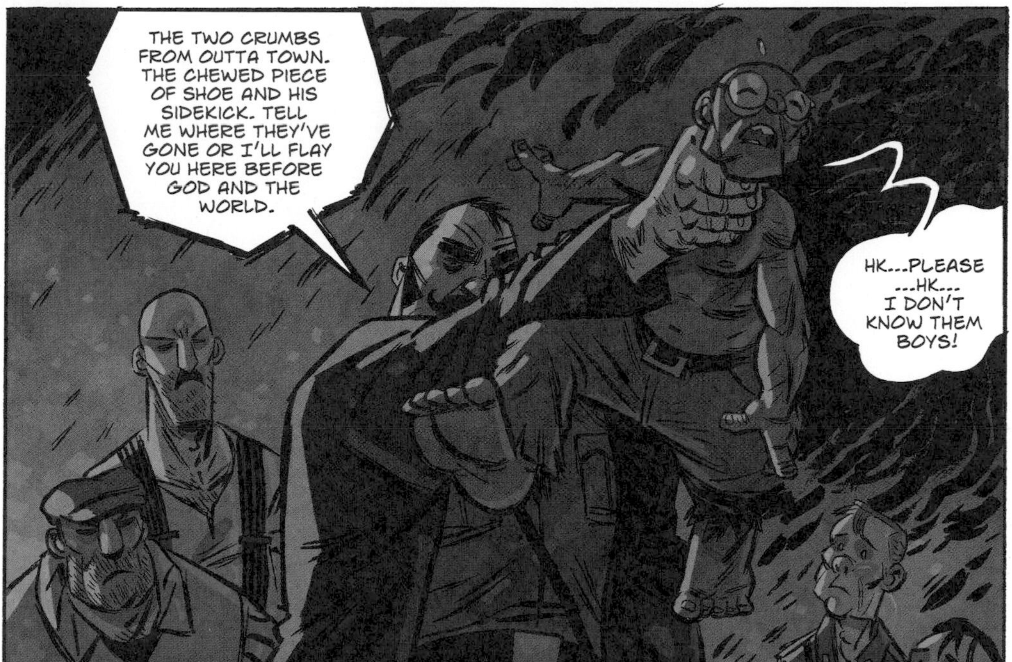
THE TWO CRUMBS FROM OUTTA TOWN. THE CHEWED PIECE OF SHOE AND HIS SIDEKICK. TELL ME WHERE THEY'VE GONE OR I'LL FLAY YOU HERE BEFORE GOD AND THE WORLD.
HK...PLEASE ...HK... I DON'T KNOW THEM BOYS!
WORF! WORF! WORF!

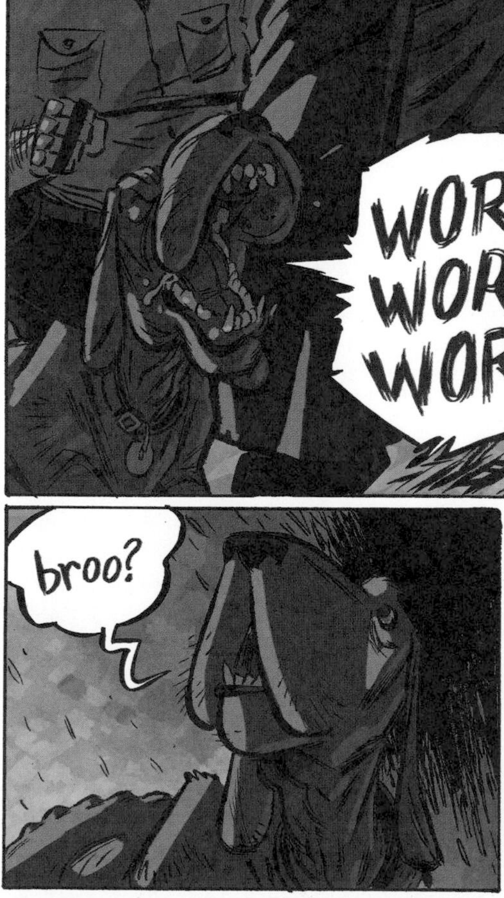
broo?

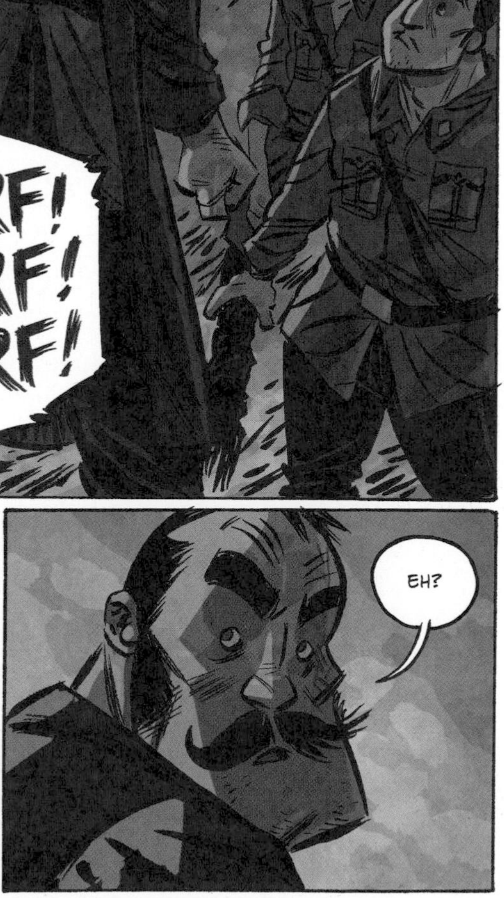
EH?

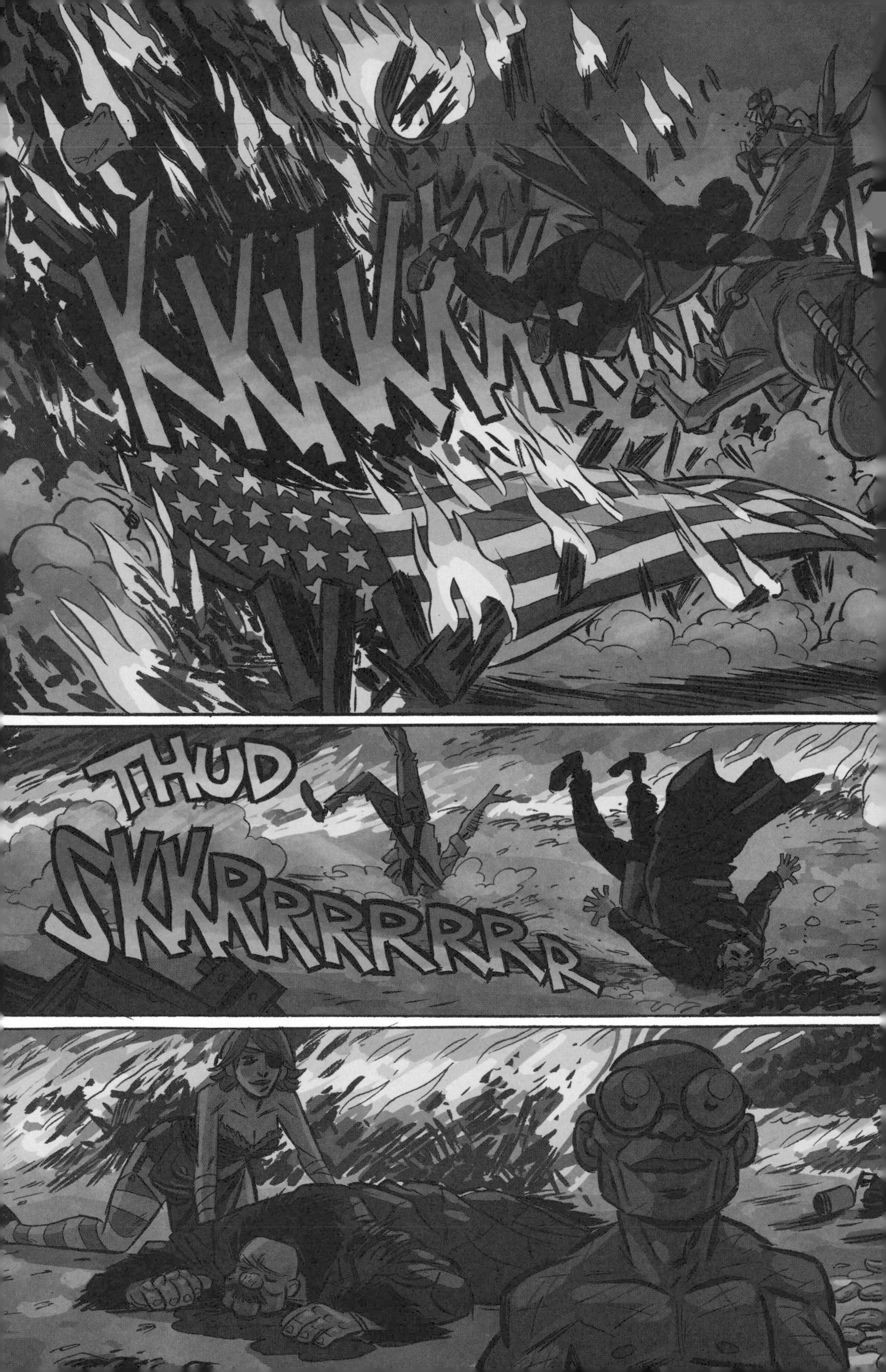
THUD
SKKRRRRRRRR

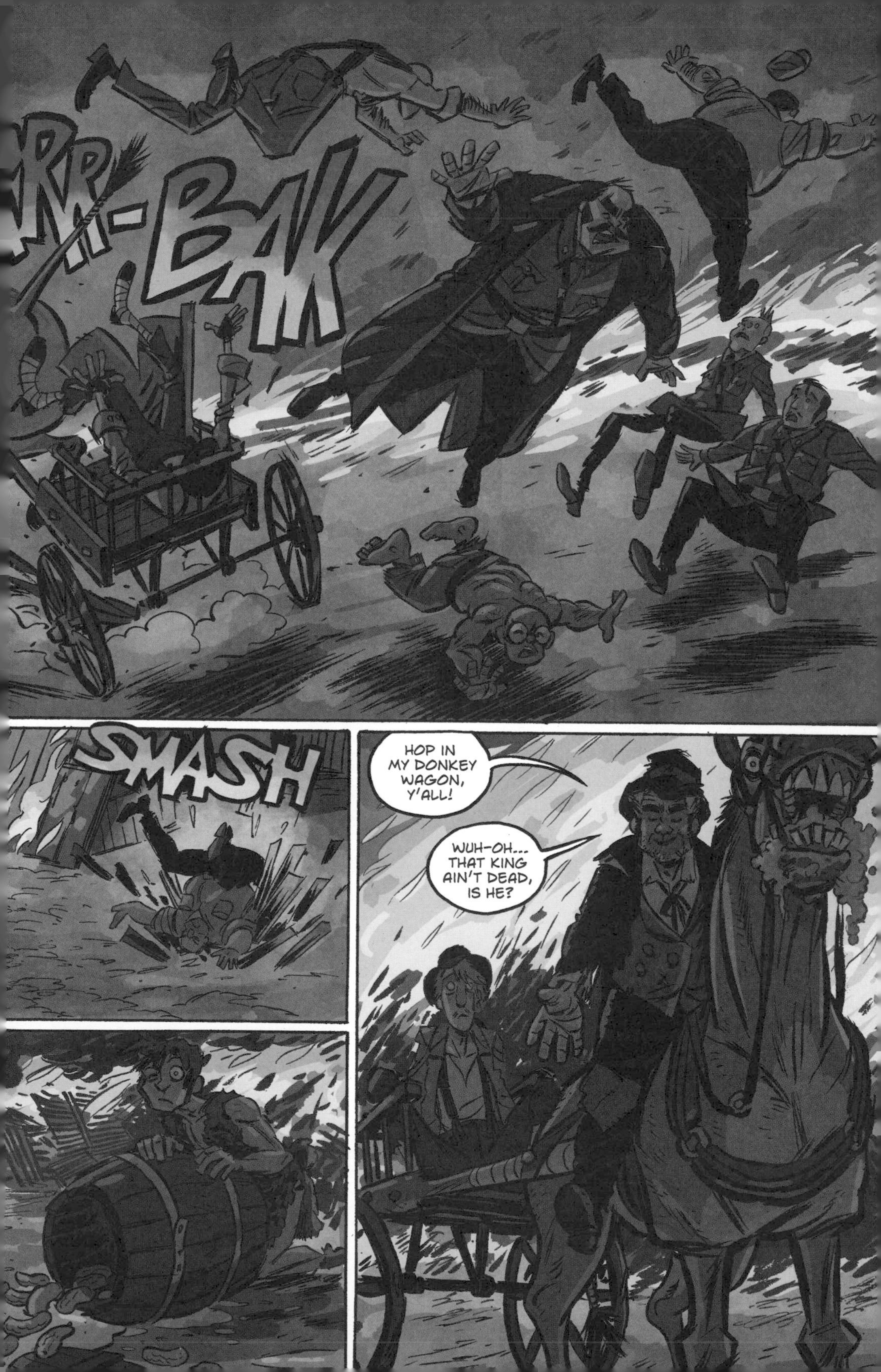

KRRP-BAK
SMASH
HOP IN MY DONKEY WAGON, Y'ALL!
WUH-OH... THAT KING AIN'T DEAD, IS HE?

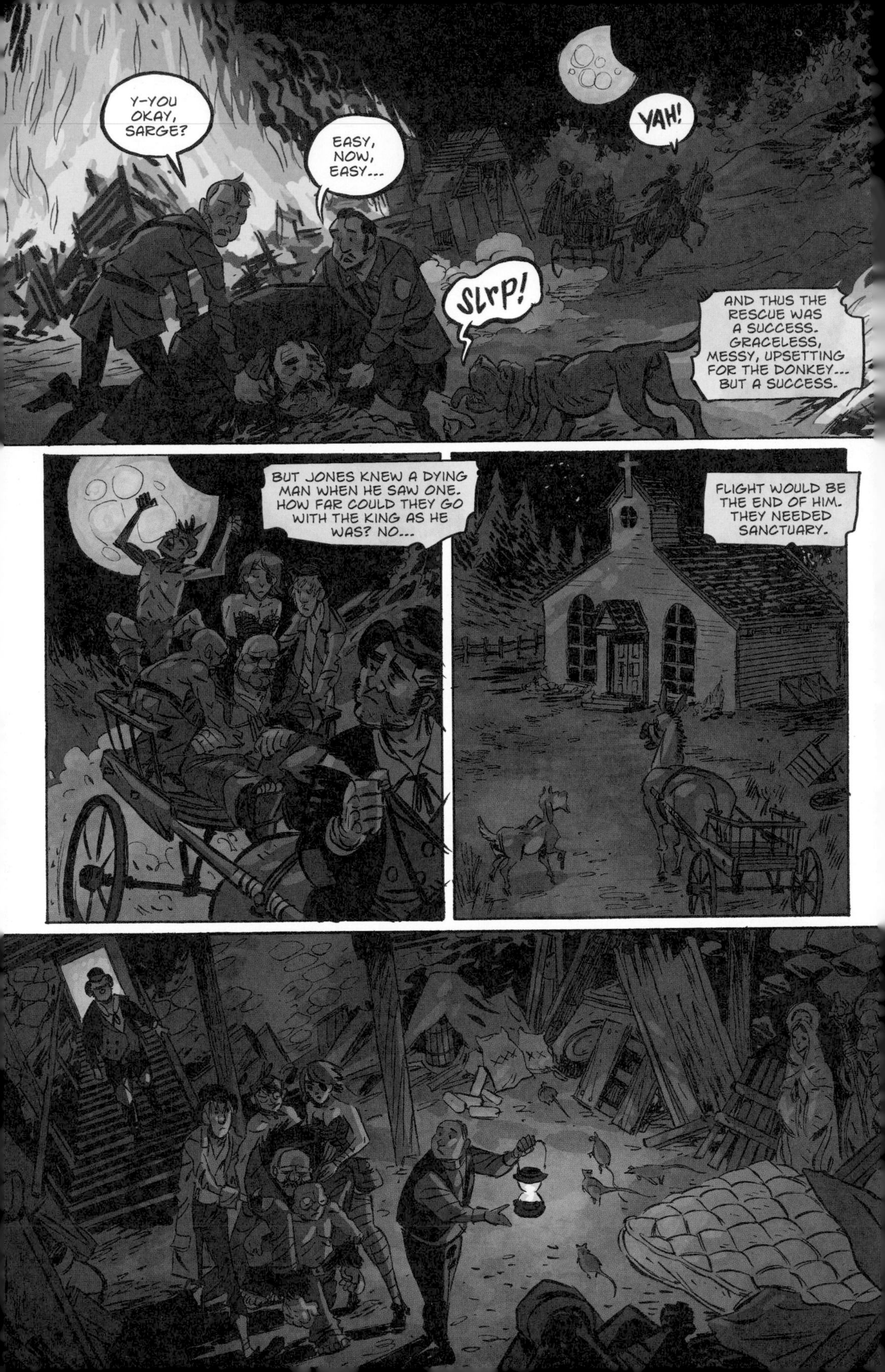
Y-YOU OKAY, SARGE?
EASY, NOW, EASY...
YAH!
SLRP!
AND THUS THE RESCUE WAS A SUCCESS. GRACELESS, MESSY, UPSETTING FOR THE DONKEY... BUT A SUCCESS.
BUT JONES KNEW A DYING MAN WHEN HE SAW ONE. HOW FAR COULD THEY GO WITH THE KING AS HE WAS? NO...
FLIGHT WOULD BE THE END OF HIM. THEY NEEDED SANCTUARY.

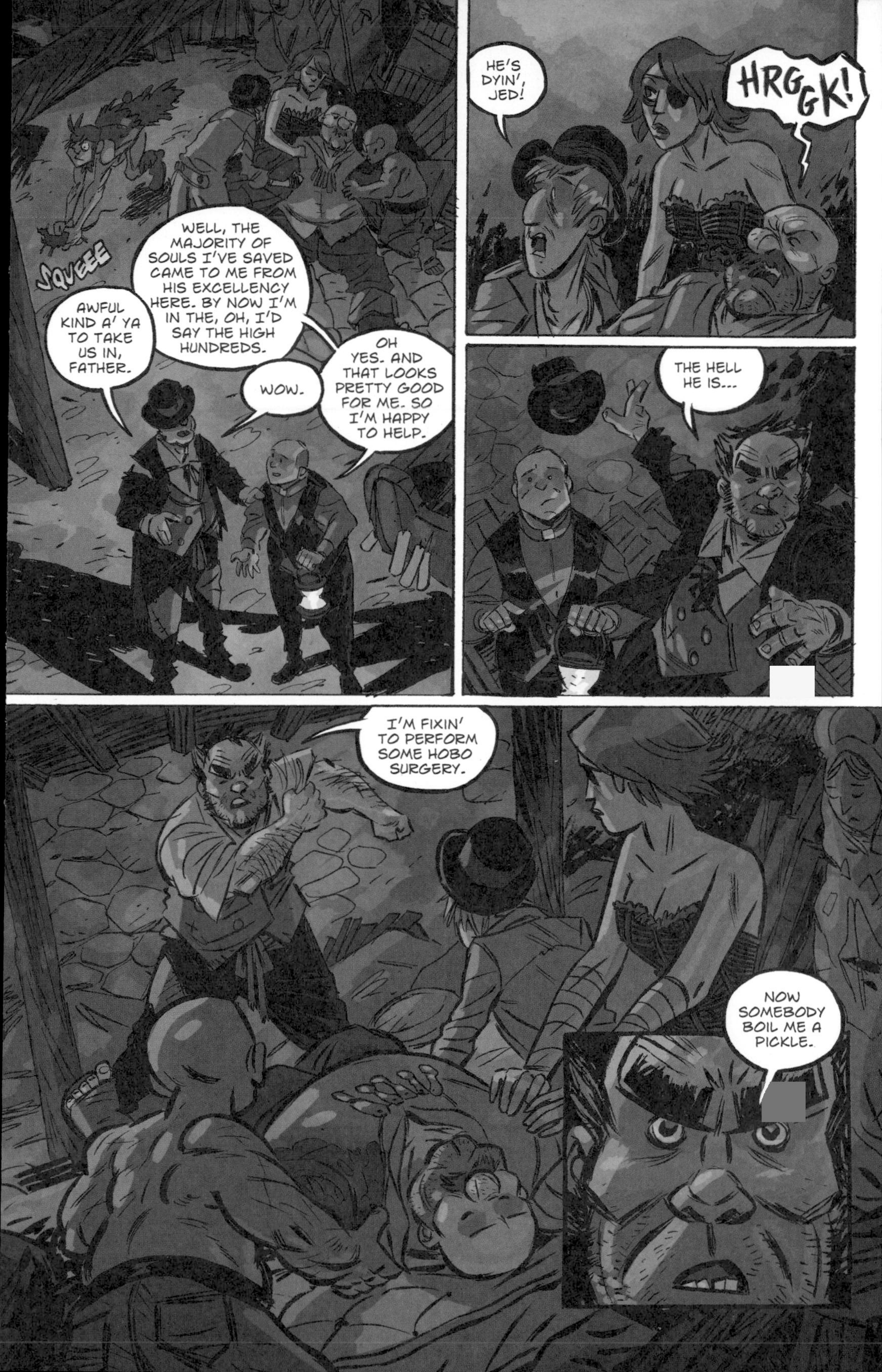
SQUEEE
AWFUL KIND A' YA TO TAKE US IN, FATHER.
WELL, THE MAJORITY OF SOULS I'VE SAVED CAME TO ME FROM HIS EXCELLENCY HERE. BY NOW I'M IN THE, OH, I'D SAY THE HIGH HUNDREDS.
WOW.
OH YES. AND THAT LOOKS PRETTY GOOD FOR ME. SO I'M HAPPY TO HELP.
HE'S DYIN', JED!
HRGGK!
THE HELL HE IS...
I'M FIXIN' TO PERFORM SOME HOBO SURGERY.
NOW SOMEBODY BOIL ME A PICKLE.

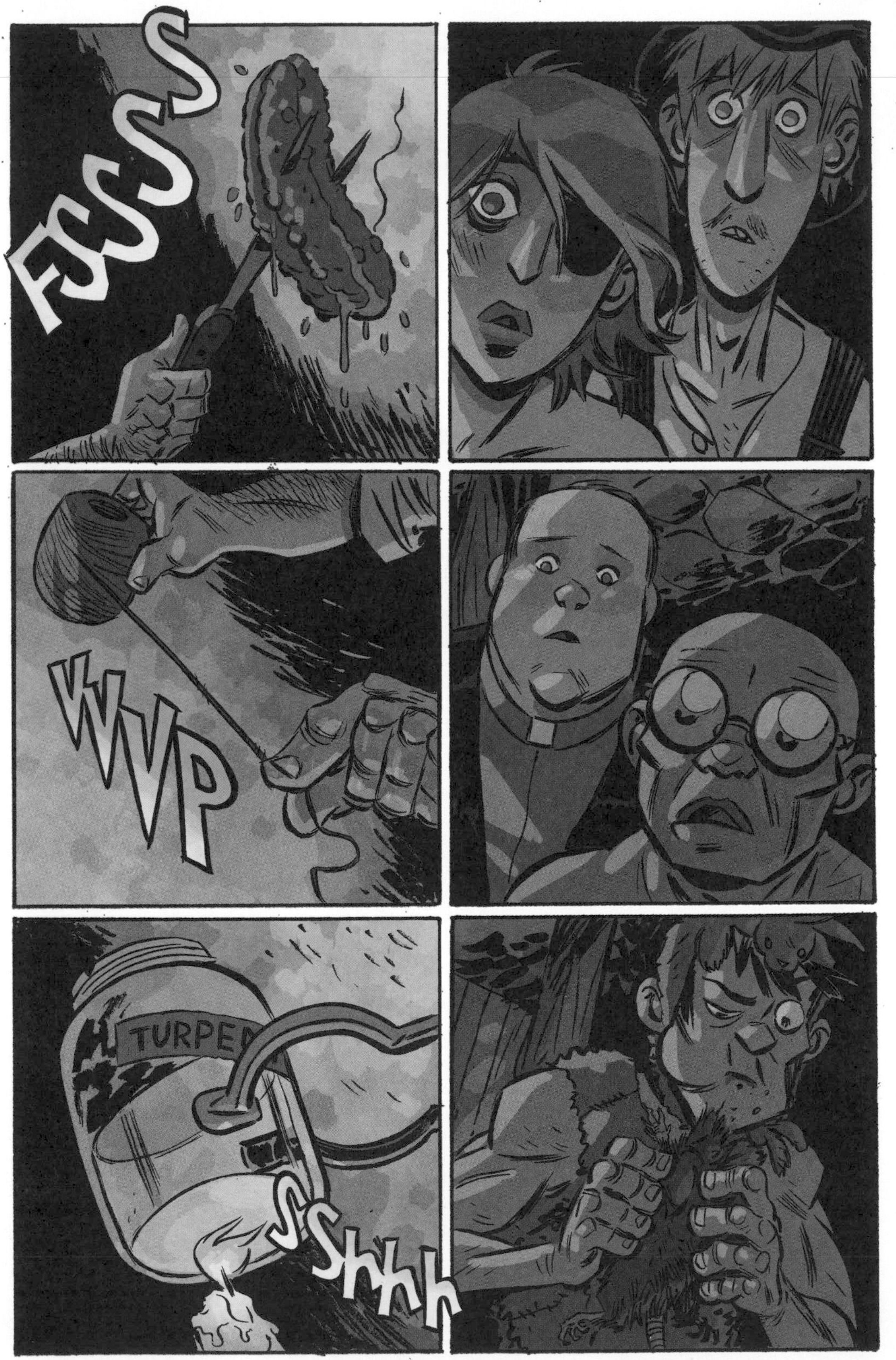
FSSSS
VVVP
TURPEN
SSHHH

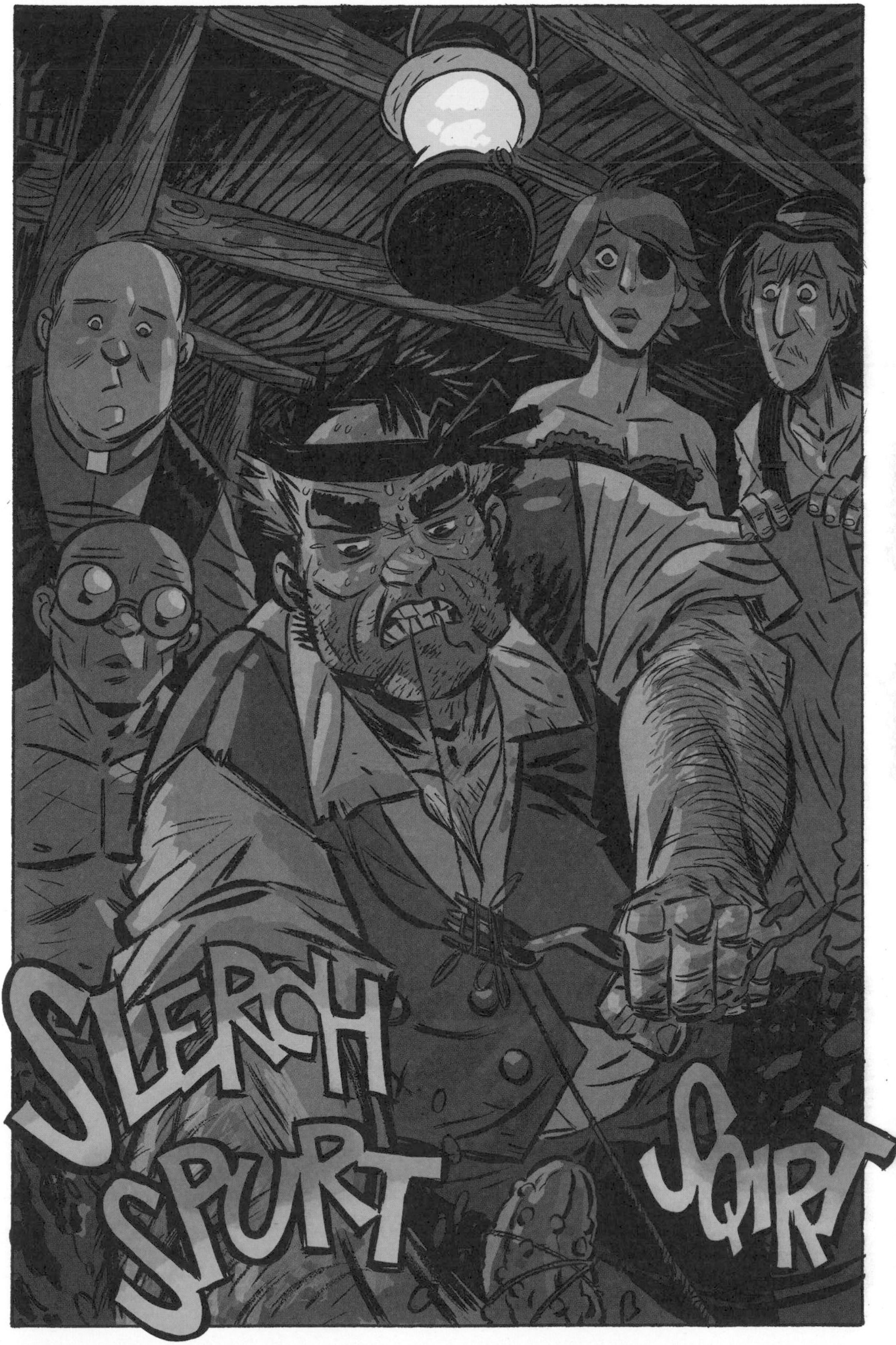
SLERCH
SPURT
SQIRT

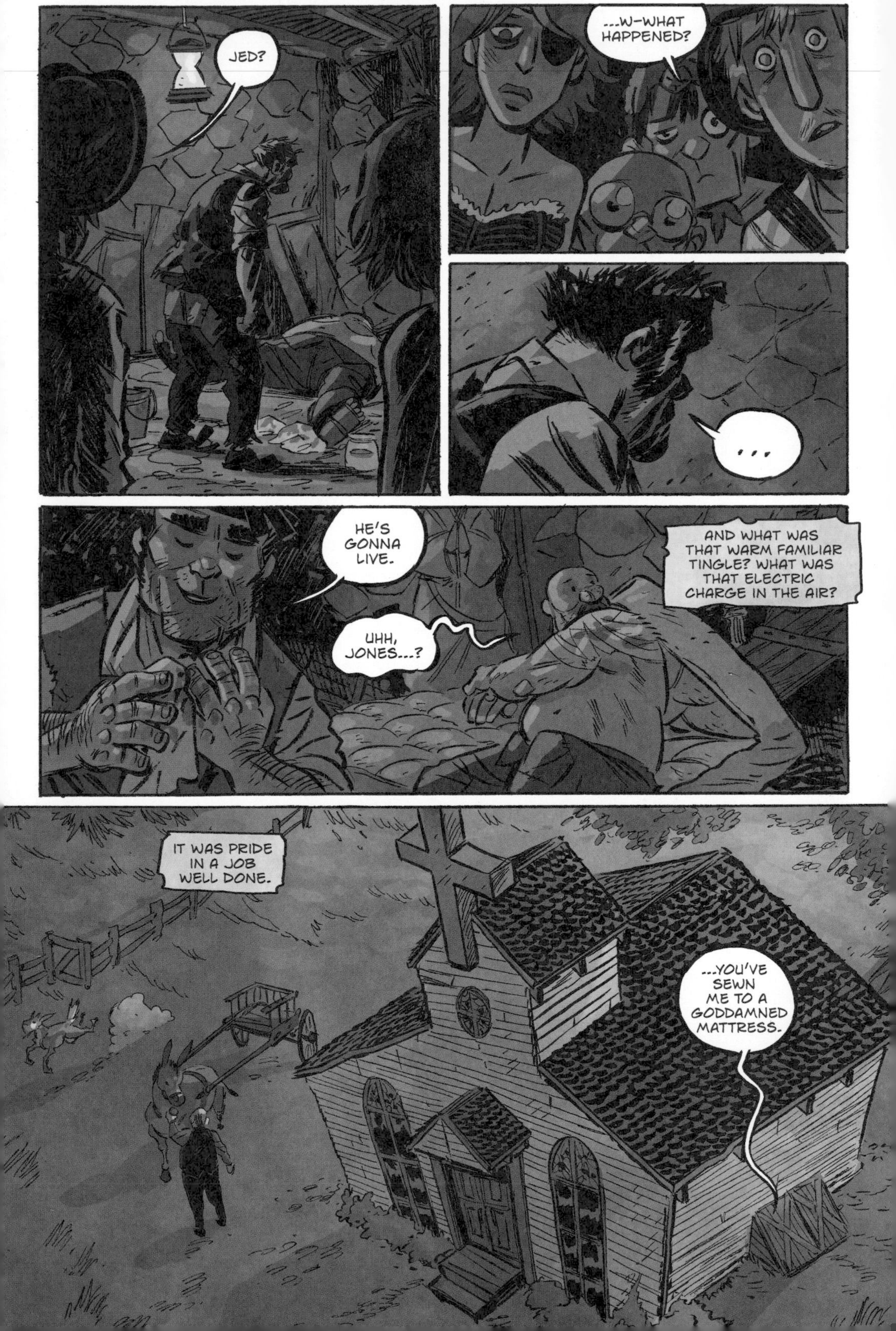

JED?
...W-WHAT HAPPENED?
...
HE'S GONNA LIVE.
AND WHAT WAS THAT WARM FAMILIAR TINGLE? WHAT WAS THAT ELECTRIC CHARGE IN THE AIR?
UHH, JONES...?
IT WAS PRIDE IN A JOB WELL DONE.
...YOU'VE SEWN ME TO A GODDAMNED MATTRESS.

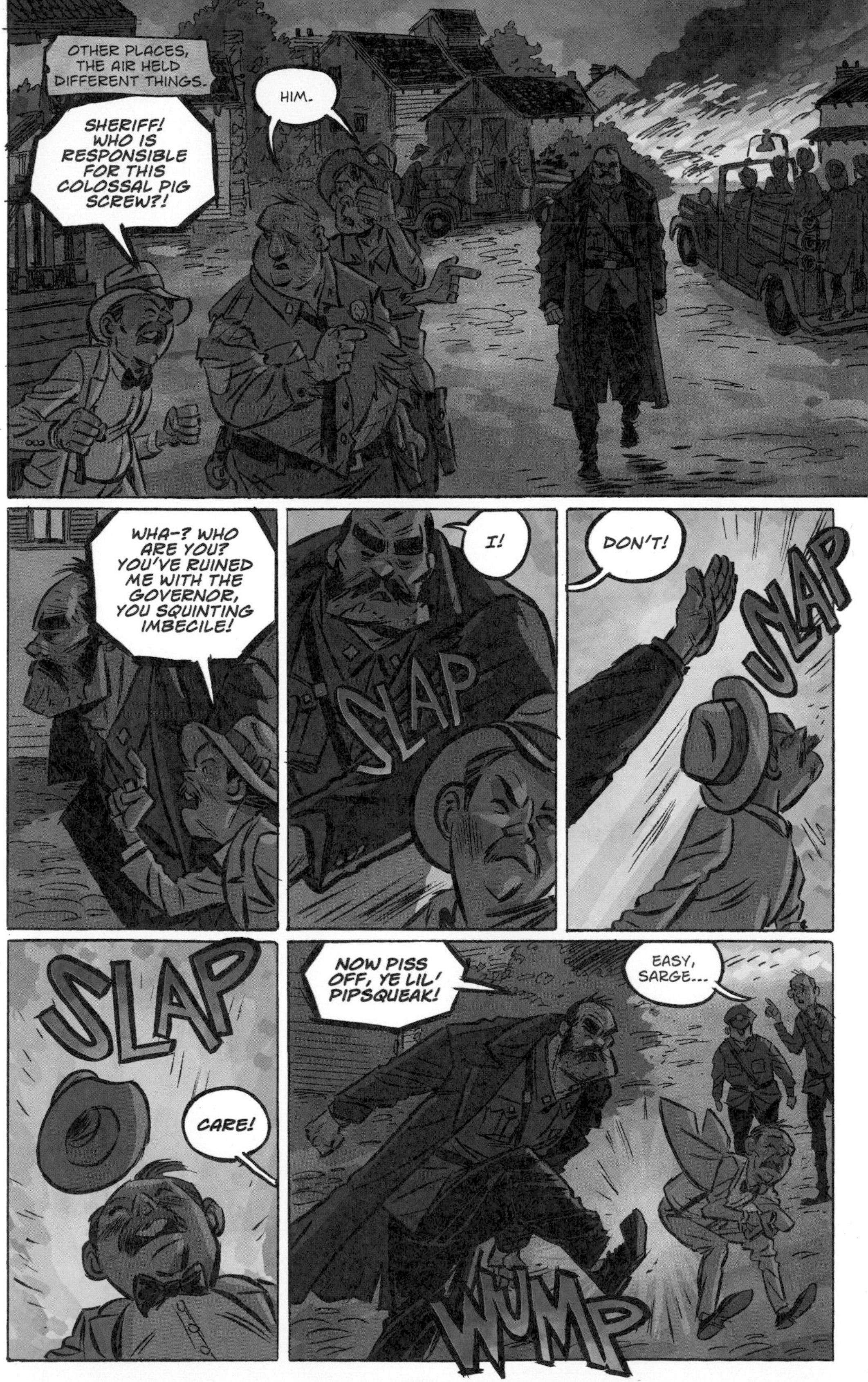
OTHER PLACES, THE AIR HELD DIFFERENT THINGS.
SHERIFF! WHO IS RESPONSIBLE FOR THIS COLOSSAL PIG SCREW?!
HIM.
WHA-? WHO ARE YOU? YOU'VE RUINED ME WITH THE GOVERNOR, YOU SQUINTING IMBECILE!
I!
SLAP
DON'T!
SLAP
SLAP
CARE!
NOW PISS OFF, YE LIL' PIPSQUEAK!
EASY, SARGE...
WUMP

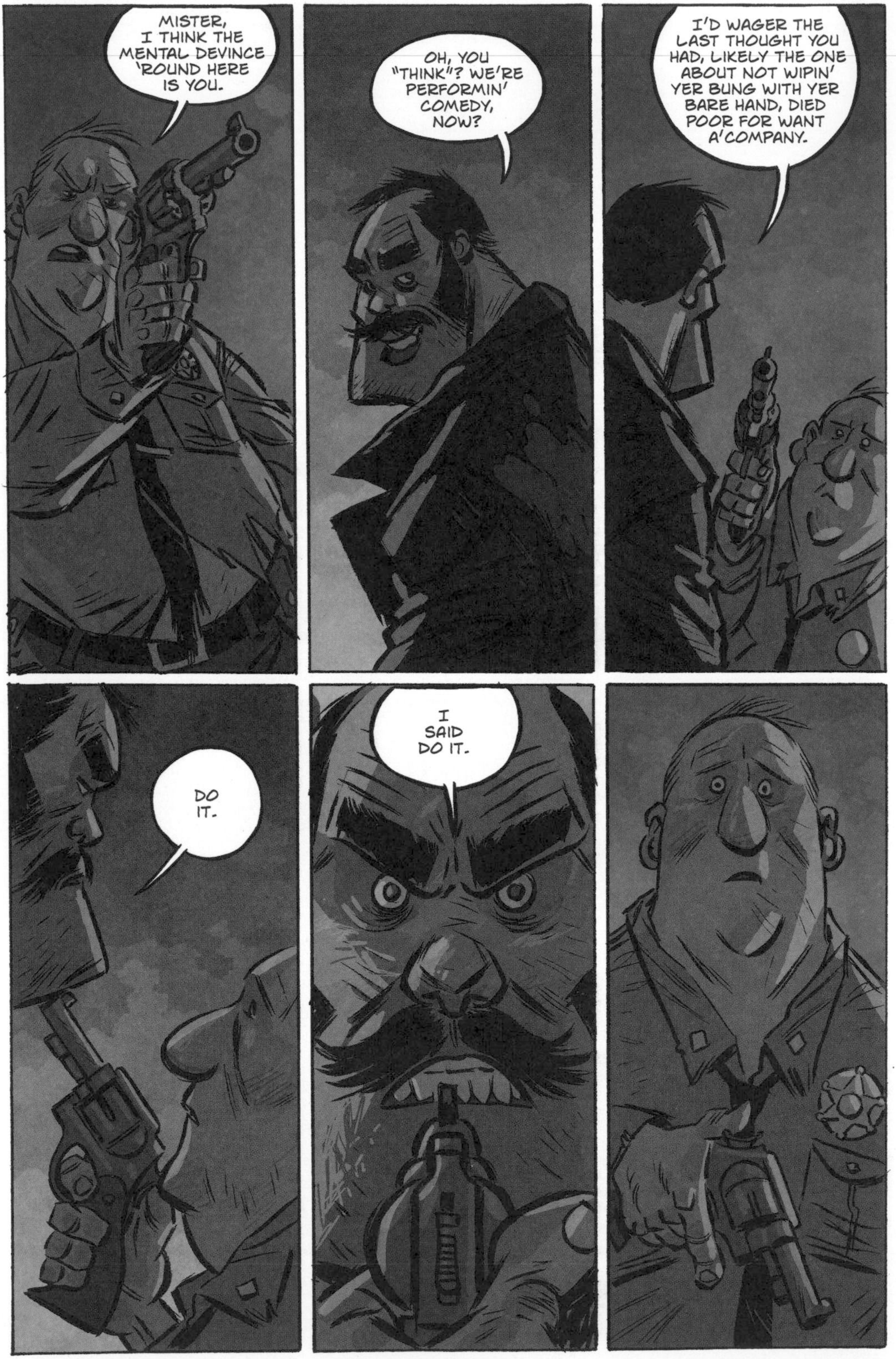
MISTER, I THINK THE MENTAL DEVINCE 'ROUND HERE IS YOU.
OH, YOU "THINK"? WE'RE PERFORMIN' COMEDY, NOW?
I'D WAGER THE LAST THOUGHT YOU HAD, LIKELY THE ONE ABOUT NOT WIPIN' YER BUNG WITH YER BARE HAND, DIED POOR FOR WANT A'COMPANY.
DO IT.
I SAID DO IT.

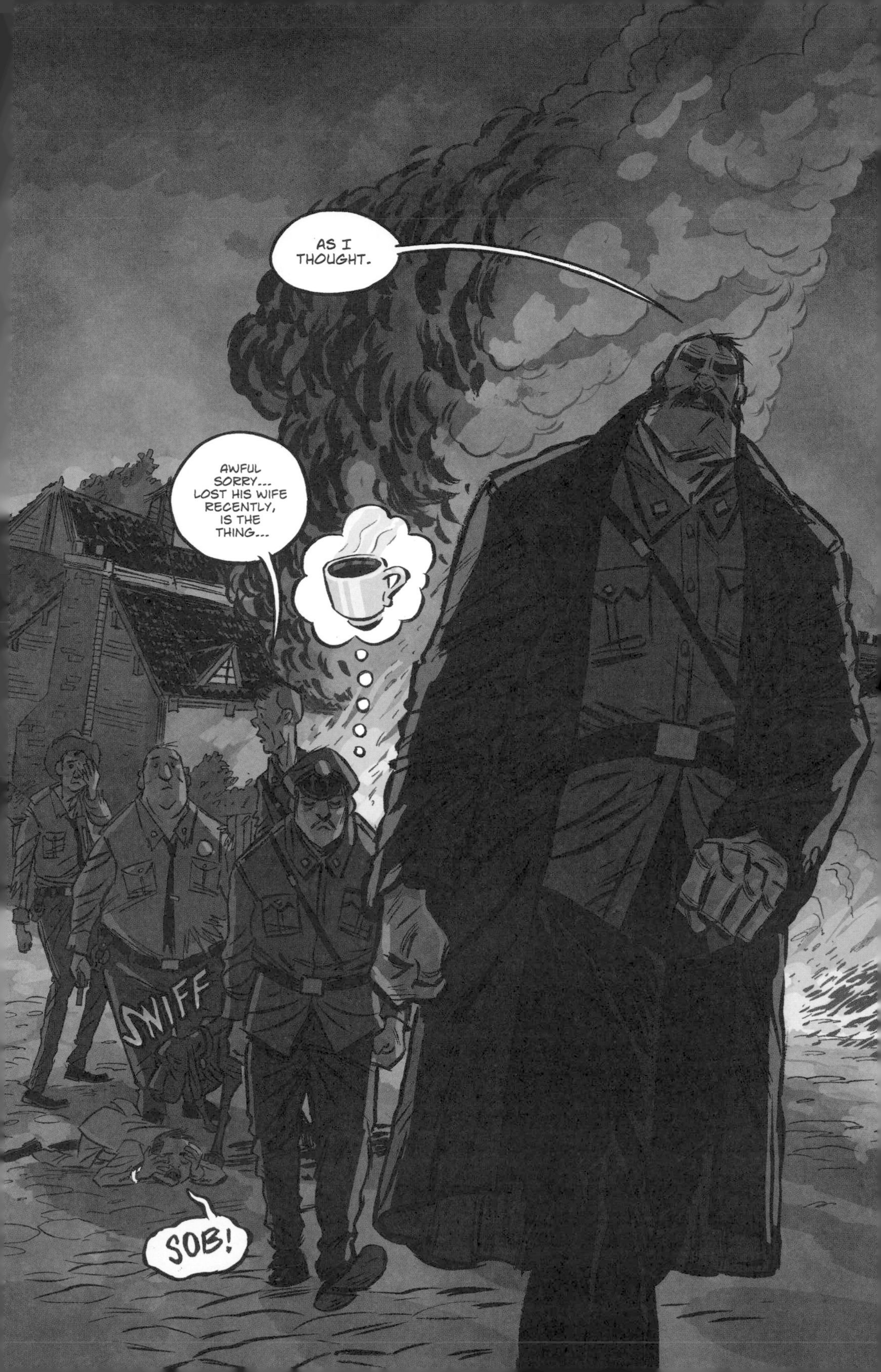
AS I THOUGHT.
AWFUL SORRY... LOST HIS WIFE RECENTLY, IS THE THING...
SNIFF
SOB!

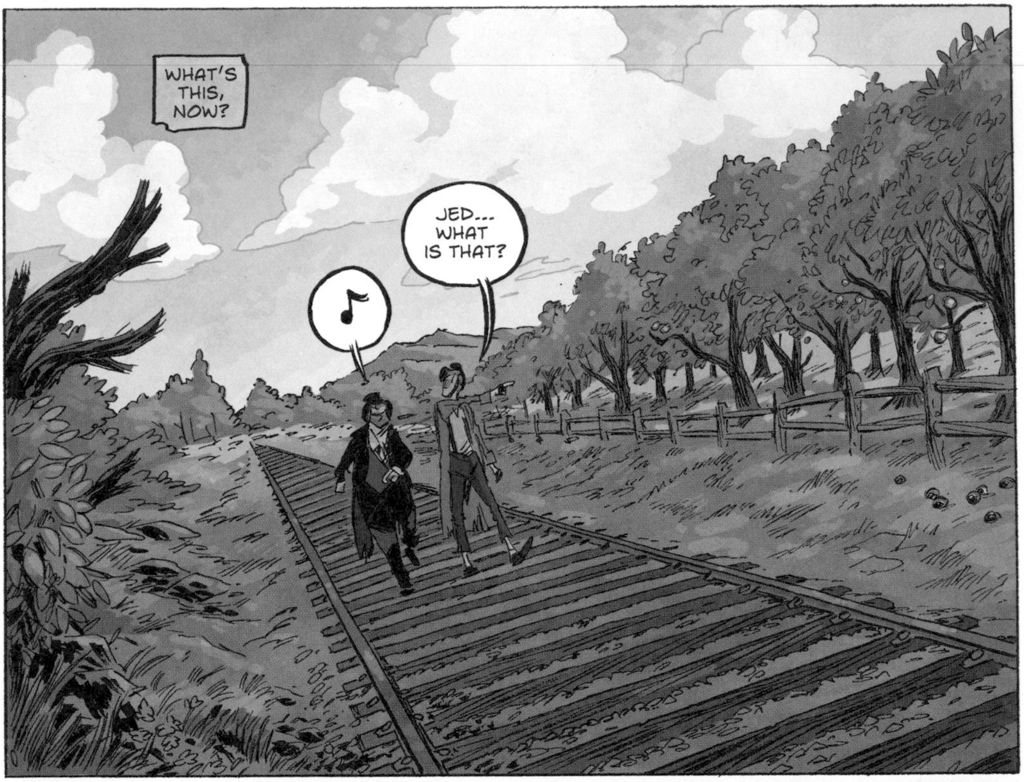
WHAT'S THIS, NOW?
♪
JED... WHAT IS THAT?

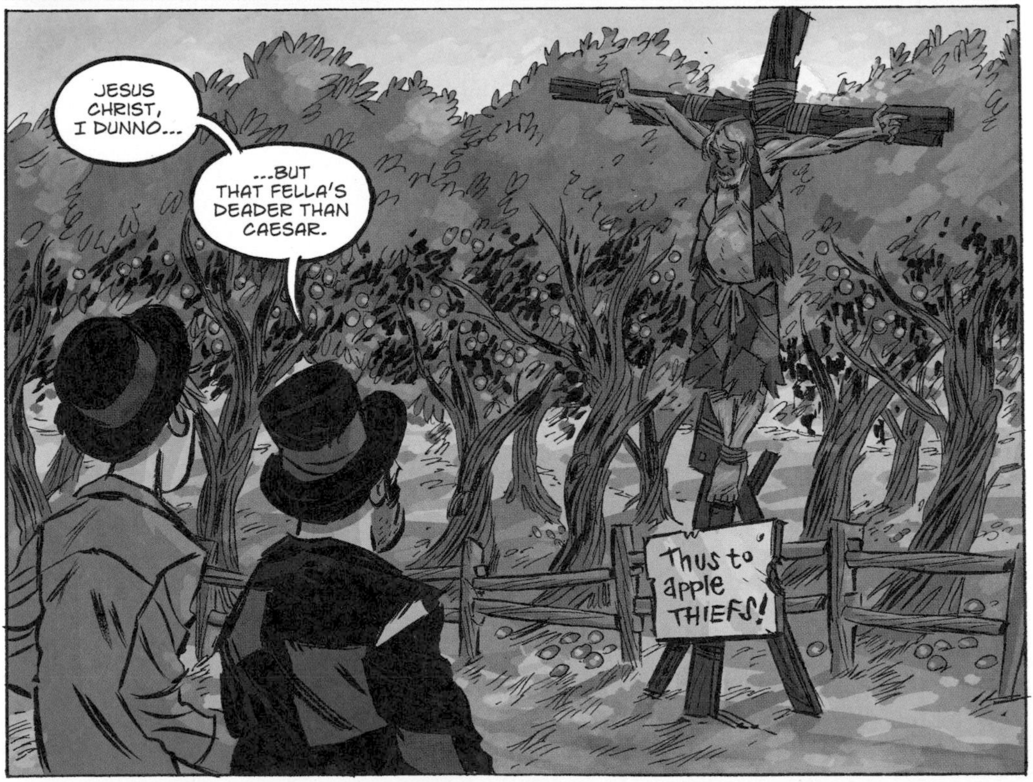
JESUS CHRIST, I DUNNO...
...BUT THAT FELLA'S DEADER THAN CAESAR.
Thus to apple THIEFS!

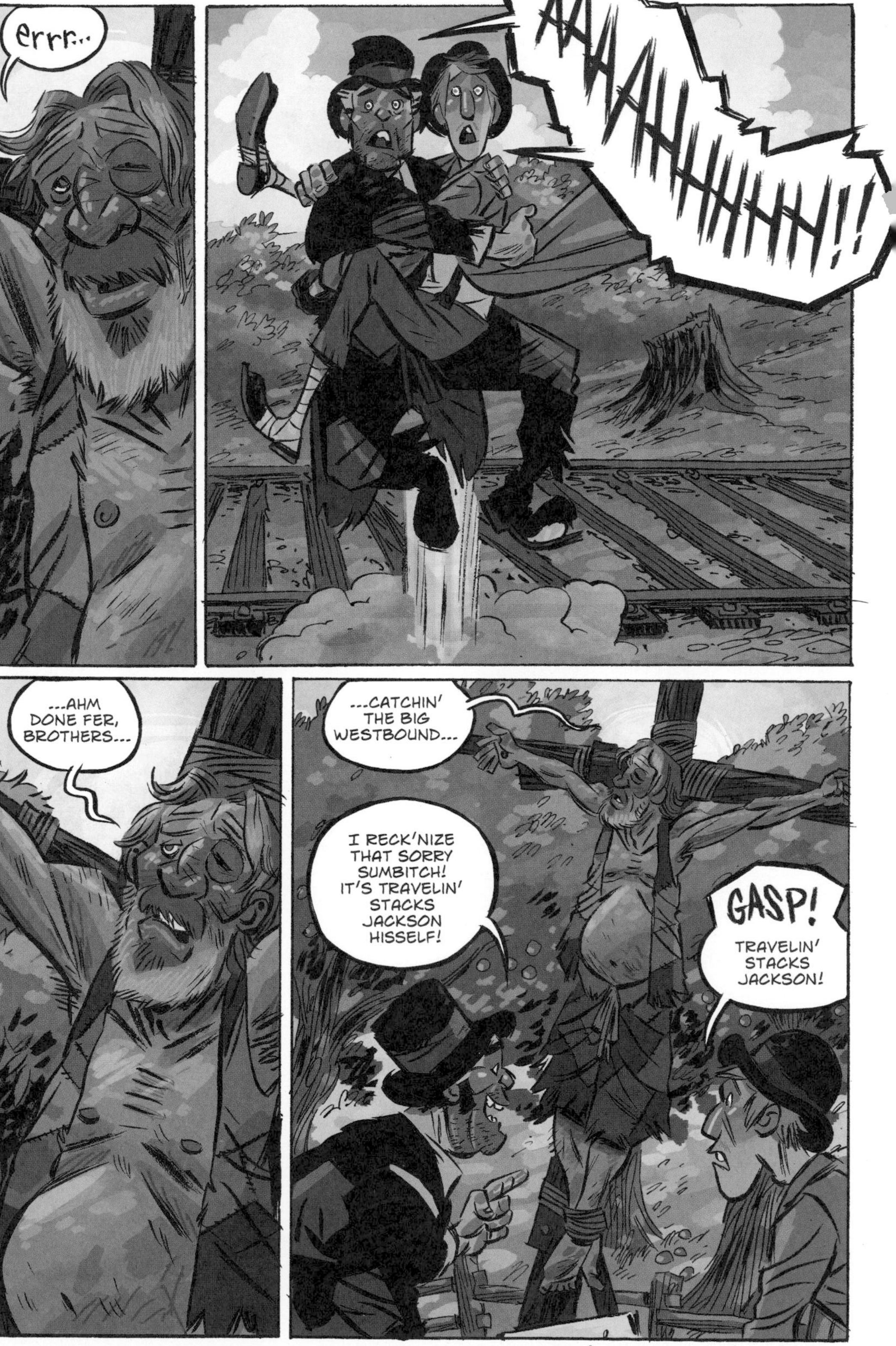
errr...
AAAAHHHHHHH!!
...AHM DONE FER, BROTHERS...
...CATCHIN' THE BIG WESTBOUND...
I RECK'NIZE THAT SORRY SUMBITCH! IT'S TRAVELIN' STACKS JACKSON HISSELF!
GASP!
TRAVELIN' STACKS JACKSON!

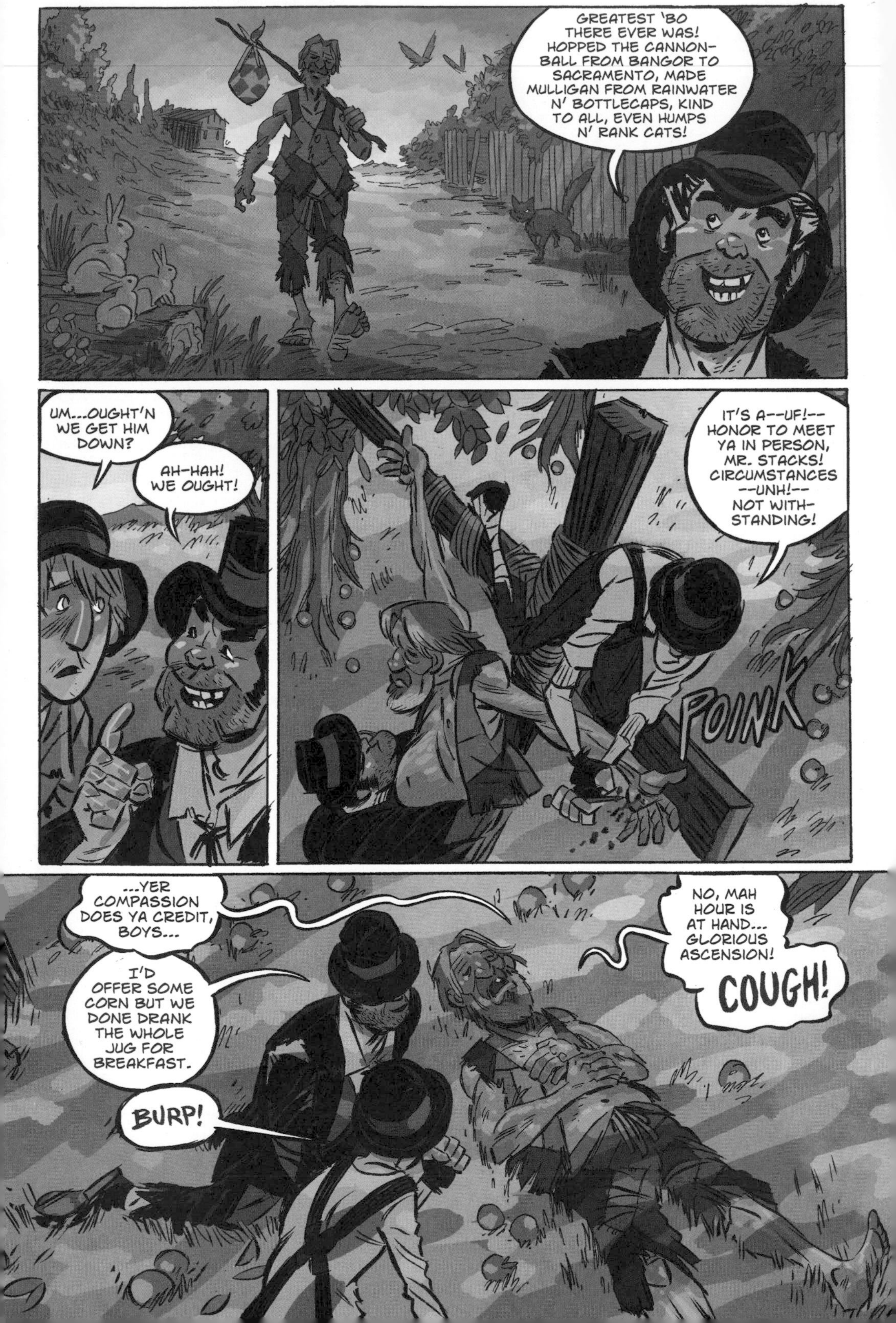
GREATEST 'BO THERE EVER WAS! HOPPED THE CANNON-BALL FROM BANGOR TO SACRAMENTO, MADE MULLIGAN FROM RAINWATER N' BOTTLECAPS, KIND TO ALL, EVEN HUMPS N' RANK CATS!
UM...OUGHT'N WE GET HIM DOWN?
AH-HAH! WE OUGHT!
IT'S A--UF!--HONOR TO MEET YA IN PERSON, MR. STACKS! CIRCUMSTANCES --UNH!-- NOT WITH-STANDING!
POINK
...YER COMPASSION DOES YA CREDIT, BOYS...
I'D OFFER SOME CORN BUT WE DONE DRANK THE WHOLE JUG FOR BREAKFAST.
BURP!
NO, MAH HOUR IS AT HAND... GLORIOUS ASCENSION!
COUGH!

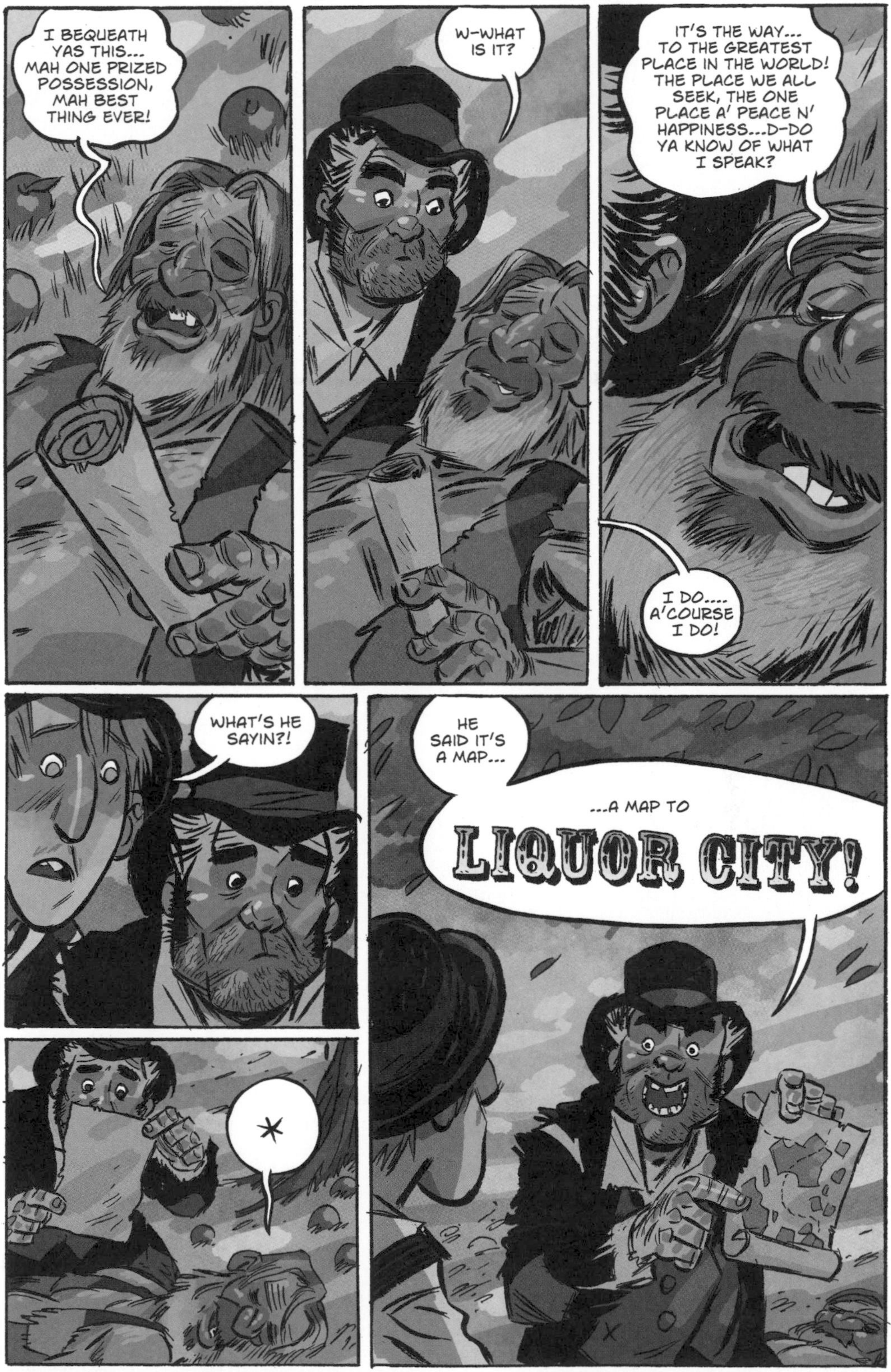
I BEQUEATH YAS THIS... MAH ONE PRIZED POSSESSION, MAH BEST THING EVER!
W-WHAT IS IT?
IT'S THE WAY... TO THE GREATEST PLACE IN THE WORLD! THE PLACE WE ALL SEEK, THE ONE PLACE A' PEACE N' HAPPINESS...D-DO YA KNOW OF WHAT I SPEAK?
I DO.... A'COURSE I DO!
WHAT'S HE SAYIN?!
HE SAID IT'S A MAP...
...A MAP TO LIQUOR CITY!
*

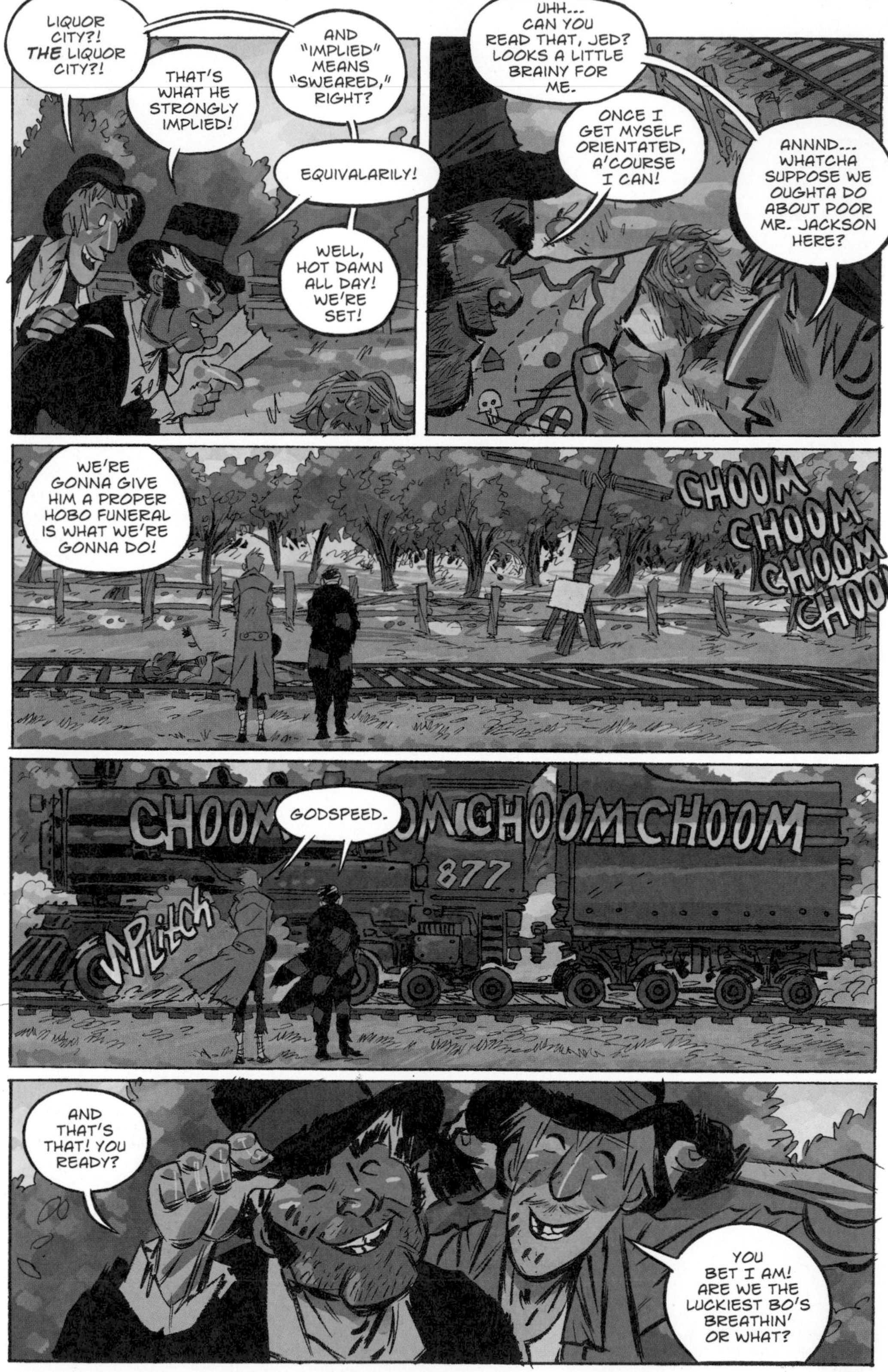
LIQUOR CITY?! THE LIQUOR CITY?!
THAT'S WHAT HE STRONGLY IMPLIED!
AND "IMPLIED" MEANS "SWEARED," RIGHT?
EQUIVALARILY!
WELL, HOT DAMN ALL DAY! WE'RE SET!
UHH... CAN YOU READ THAT, JED? LOOKS A LITTLE BRAINY FOR ME.
ONCE I GET MYSELF ORIENTATED, A'COURSE I CAN!
ANNND... WHATCHA SUPPOSE WE OUGHTA DO ABOUT POOR MR. JACKSON HERE?
WE'RE GONNA GIVE HIM A PROPER HOBO FUNERAL IS WHAT WE'RE GONNA DO!
CHOOM CHOOM CHOOM CHOOM
CHOOMCHOOMCHOOMCHOOM
GODSPEED.
877
SPLITCH
AND THAT'S THAT! YOU READY?
YOU BET I AM! ARE WE THE LUCKIEST BO'S BREATHIN' OR WHAT?

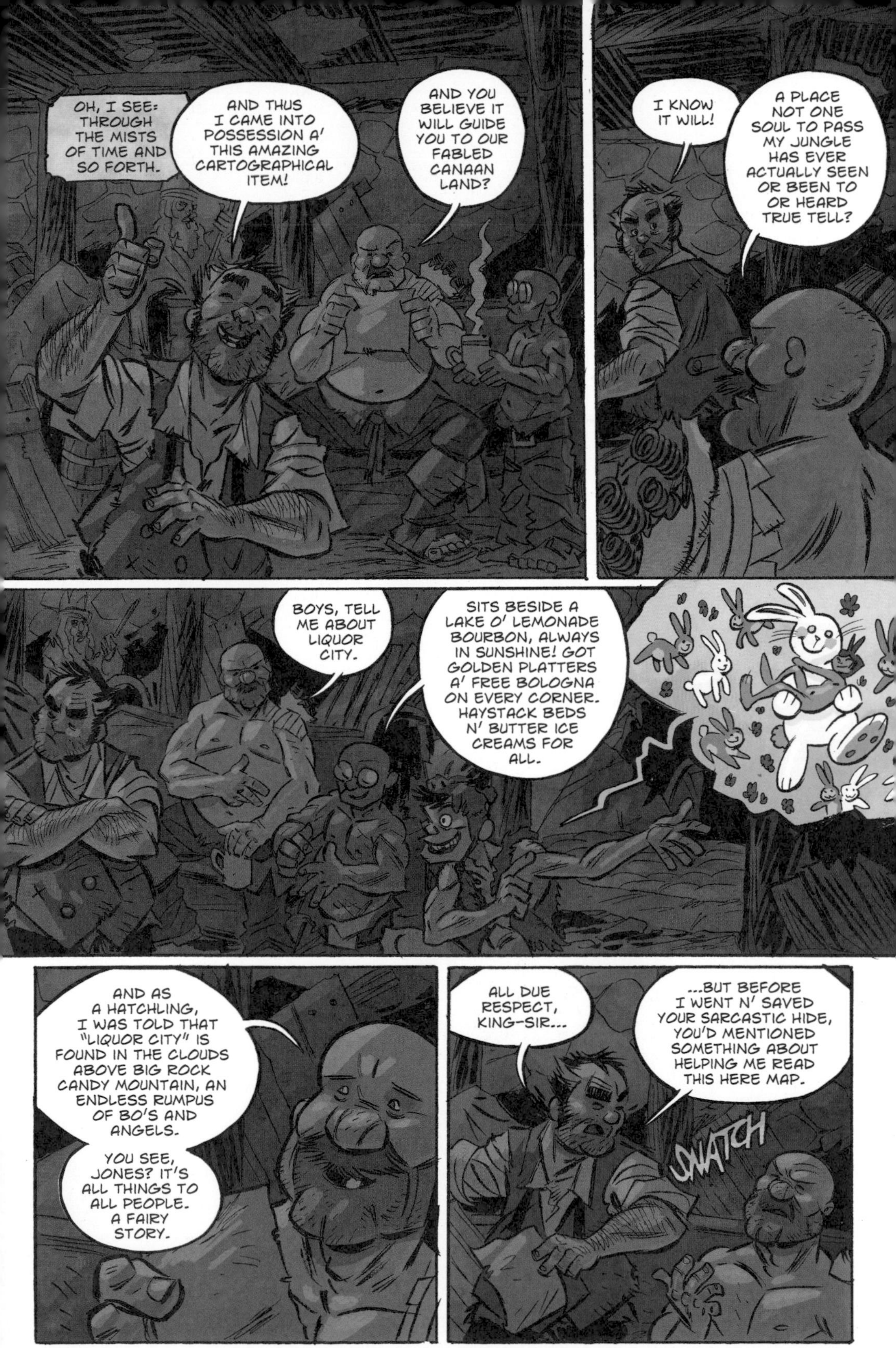

OH, I SEE: THROUGH THE MISTS OF TIME AND SO FORTH.
AND THUS I CAME INTO POSSESSION A' THIS AMAZING CARTOGRAPHICAL ITEM!
AND YOU BELIEVE IT WILL GUIDE YOU TO OUR FABLED CANAAN LAND?
I KNOW IT WILL!
A PLACE NOT ONE SOUL TO PASS MY JUNGLE HAS EVER ACTUALLY SEEN OR BEEN TO OR HEARD TRUE TELL?
BOYS, TELL ME ABOUT LIQUOR CITY.
SITS BESIDE A LAKE O' LEMONADE BOURBON, ALWAYS IN SUNSHINE! GOT GOLDEN PLATTERS A' FREE BOLOGNA ON EVERY CORNER. HAYSTACK BEDS N' BUTTER ICE CREAMS FOR ALL.
AND AS A HATCHLING, I WAS TOLD THAT "LIQUOR CITY" IS FOUND IN THE CLOUDS ABOVE BIG ROCK CANDY MOUNTAIN, AN ENDLESS RUMPUS OF BO'S AND ANGELS.
YOU SEE, JONES? IT'S ALL THINGS TO ALL PEOPLE. A FAIRY STORY.
ALL DUE RESPECT, KING-SIR...
...BUT BEFORE I WENT N' SAVED YOUR SARCASTIC HIDE, YOU'D MENTIONED SOMETHING ABOUT HELPING ME READ THIS HERE MAP.
SNATCH

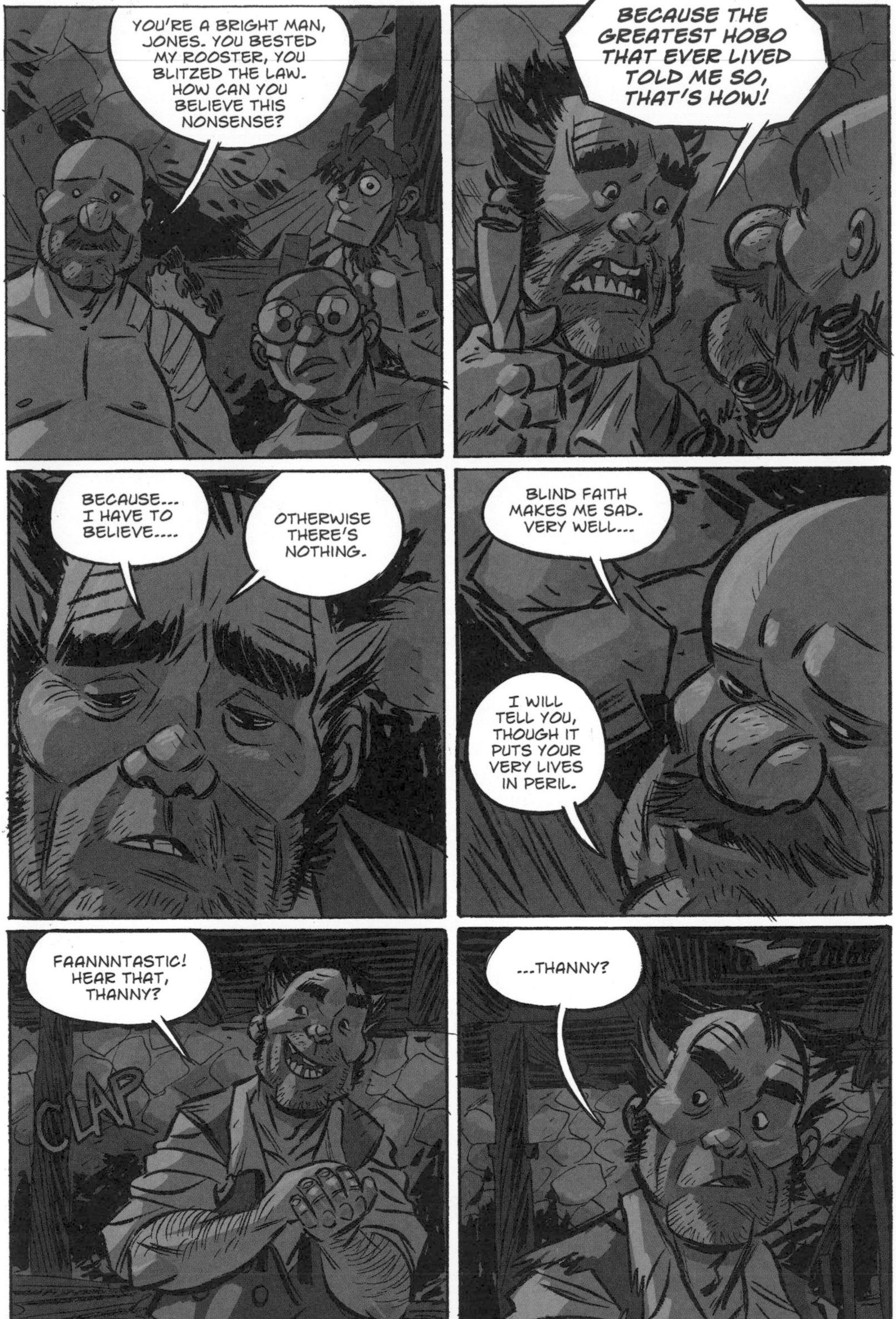
YOU'RE A BRIGHT MAN, JONES. YOU BESTED MY ROOSTER, YOU BLITZED THE LAW. HOW CAN YOU BELIEVE THIS NONSENSE?
BECAUSE THE GREATEST HOBO THAT EVER LIVED TOLD ME SO, THAT'S HOW!
BECAUSE... I HAVE TO BELIEVE....
OTHERWISE THERE'S NOTHING.
BLIND FAITH MAKES ME SAD. VERY WELL...
I WILL TELL YOU, THOUGH IT PUTS YOUR VERY LIVES IN PERIL.
FAANNNTASTIC! HEAR THAT, THANNY?
CLAP
...THANNY?

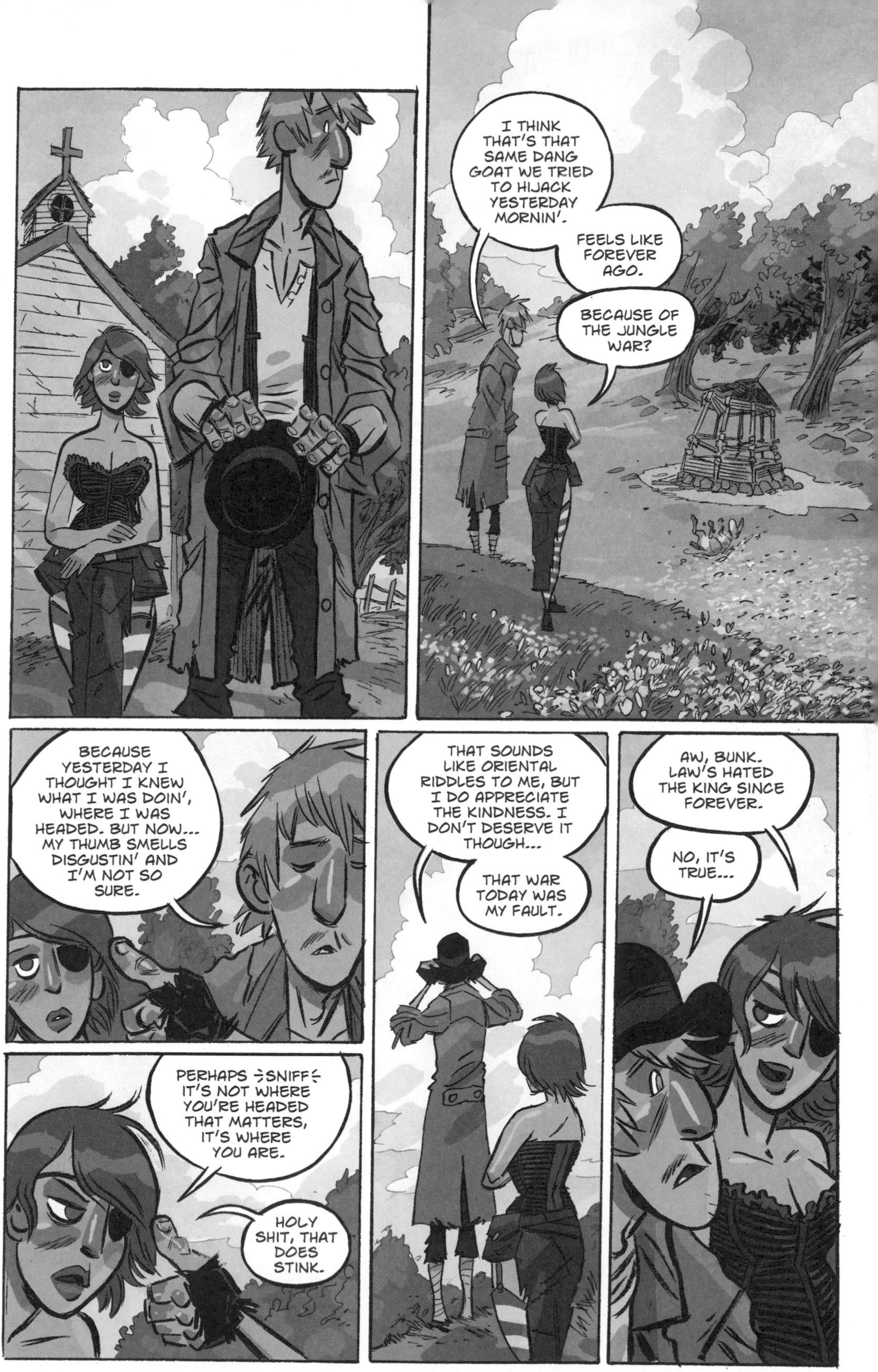
I THINK THAT'S THAT SAME DANG GOAT WE TRIED TO HIJACK YESTERDAY MORNIN'.
FEELS LIKE FOREVER AGO.
BECAUSE OF THE JUNGLE WAR?
BECAUSE YESTERDAY I THOUGHT I KNEW WHAT I WAS DOIN', WHERE I WAS HEADED. BUT NOW... MY THUMB SMELLS DISGUSTIN' AND I'M NOT SO SURE.
PERHAPS ÷SNIFF÷ IT'S NOT WHERE YOU'RE HEADED THAT MATTERS, IT'S WHERE YOU ARE.
HOLY SHIT, THAT DOES STINK.
THAT SOUNDS LIKE ORIENTAL RIDDLES TO ME, BUT I DO APPRECIATE THE KINDNESS. I DON'T DESERVE IT THOUGH...
THAT WAR TODAY WAS MY FAULT.
AW, BUNK. LAW'S HATED THE KING SINCE FOREVER.
NO, IT'S TRUE...

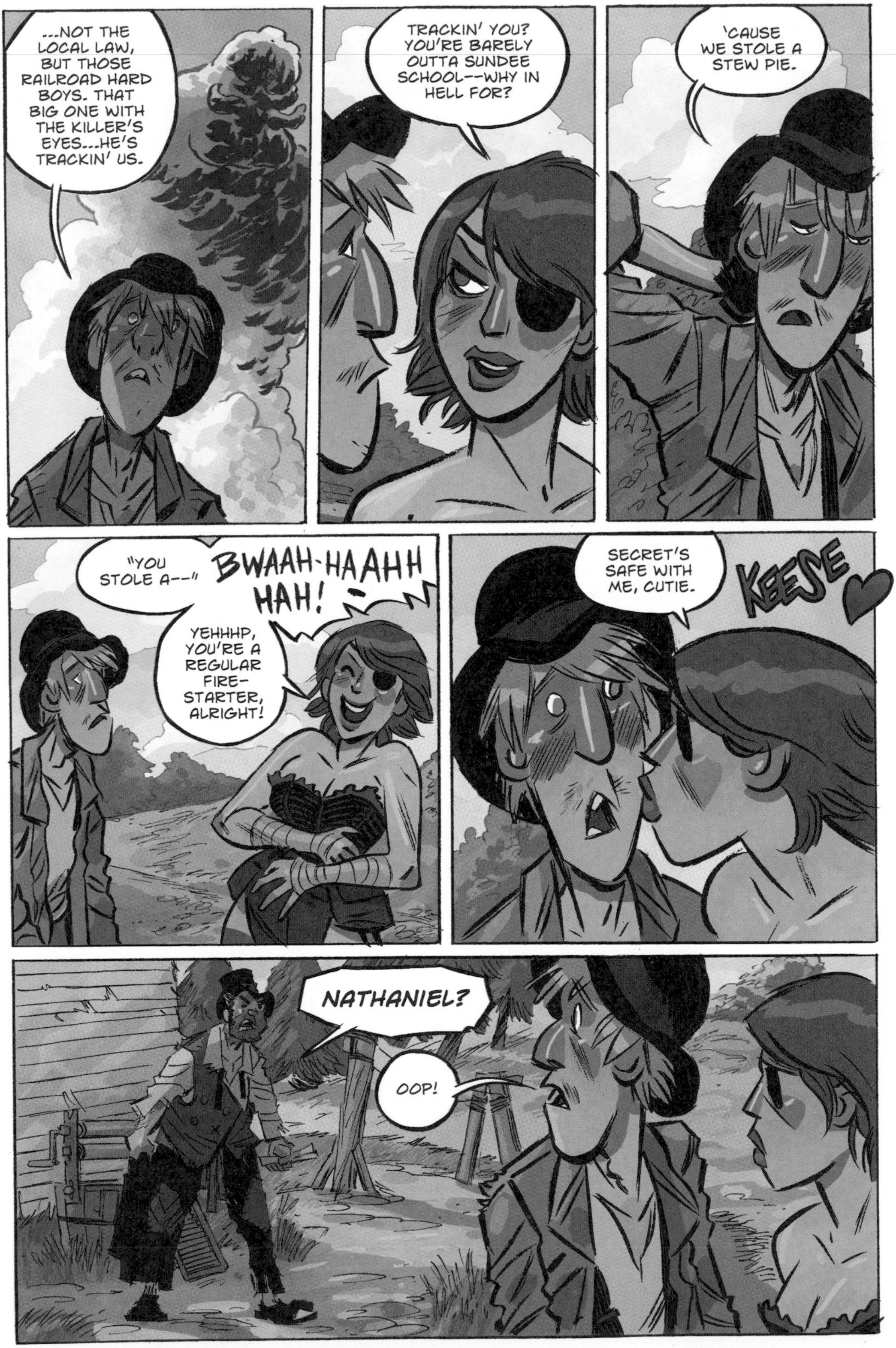
...NOT THE LOCAL LAW, BUT THOSE RAILROAD HARD BOYS. THAT BIG ONE WITH THE KILLER'S EYES...HE'S TRACKIN' US.
TRACKIN' YOU? YOU'RE BARELY OUTTA SUNDEE SCHOOL--WHY IN HELL FOR?
'CAUSE WE STOLE A STEW PIE.
"YOU STOLE A--"
BWAAH-HAAHH HAH!
YEHHHP, YOU'RE A REGULAR FIRE-STARTER, ALRIGHT!
SECRET'S SAFE WITH ME, CUTIE.
KEESE
NATHANIEL?
OOP!

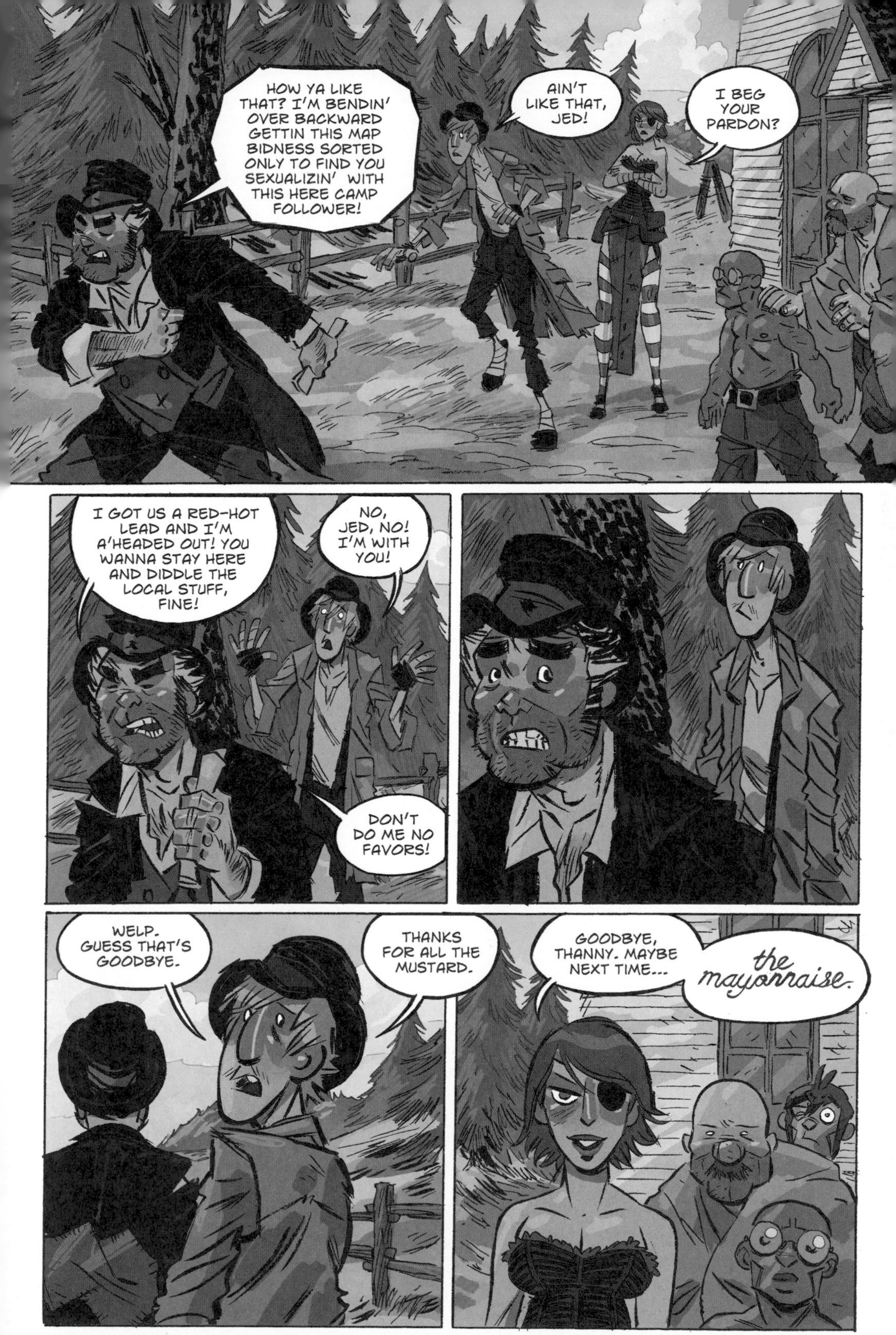
HOW YA LIKE THAT? I'M BENDIN' OVER BACKWARD GETTIN THIS MAP BIDNESS SORTED ONLY TO FIND YOU SEXUALIZIN' WITH THIS HERE CAMP FOLLOWER!
AIN'T LIKE THAT, JED!
I BEG YOUR PARDON?
I GOT US A RED-HOT LEAD AND I'M A'HEADED OUT! YOU WANNA STAY HERE AND DIDDLE THE LOCAL STUFF, FINE!
NO, JED, NO! I'M WITH YOU!
DON'T DO ME NO FAVORS!
WELP. GUESS THAT'S GOODBYE.
THANKS FOR ALL THE MUSTARD.
GOODBYE, THANNY. MAYBE NEXT TIME...
the mayonnaise.

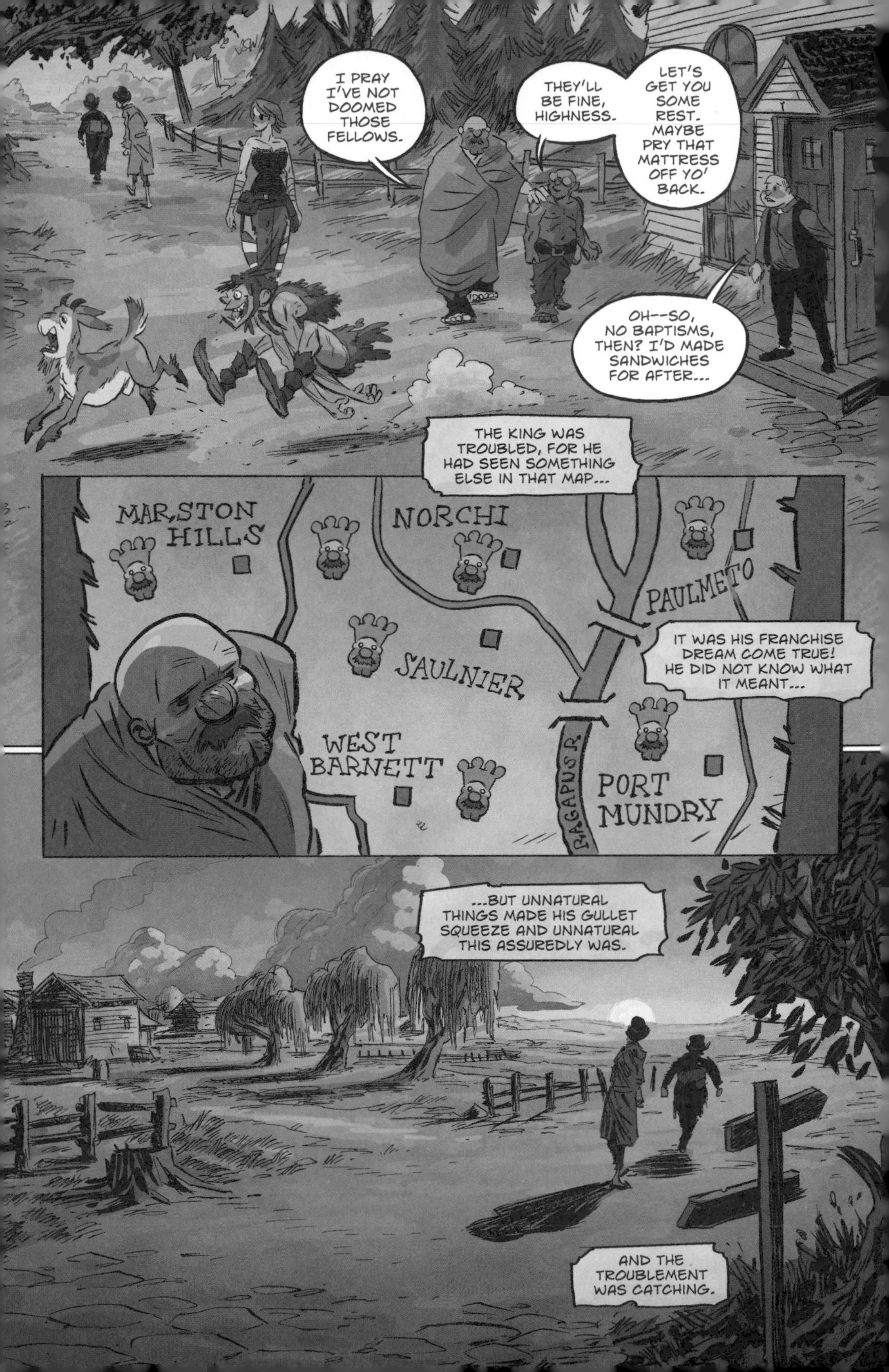
I PRAY I'VE NOT DOOMED THOSE FELLOWS.
THEY'LL BE FINE, HIGHNESS.
LET'S GET YOU SOME REST. MAYBE PRY THAT MATTRESS OFF YO' BACK.
OH--SO, NO BAPTISMS, THEN? I'D MADE SANDWICHES FOR AFTER...
THE KING WAS TROUBLED, FOR HE HAD SEEN SOMETHING ELSE IN THAT MAP...
MARSTON HILLS
NORCHI
PAULMETO
SAULNIER
WEST BARNETT
RAGAPUS R.
PORT MUNDRY
IT WAS HIS FRANCHISE DREAM COME TRUE! HE DID NOT KNOW WHAT IT MEANT...
...BUT UNNATURAL THINGS MADE HIS GULLET SQUEEZE AND UNNATURAL THIS ASSUREDLY WAS.
AND THE TROUBLEMENT WAS CATCHING.

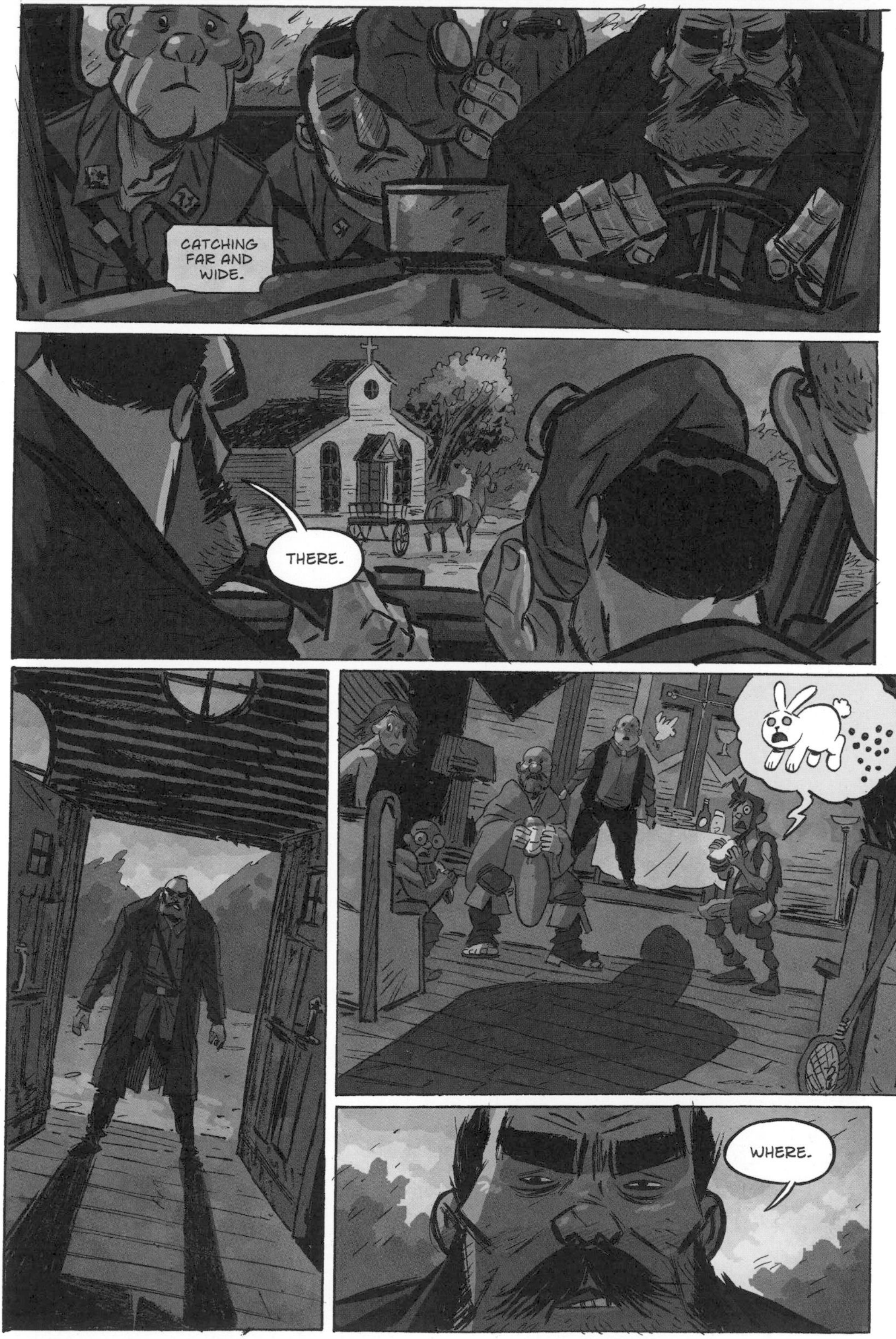
CATCHING FAR AND WIDE.
THERE.
WHERE.

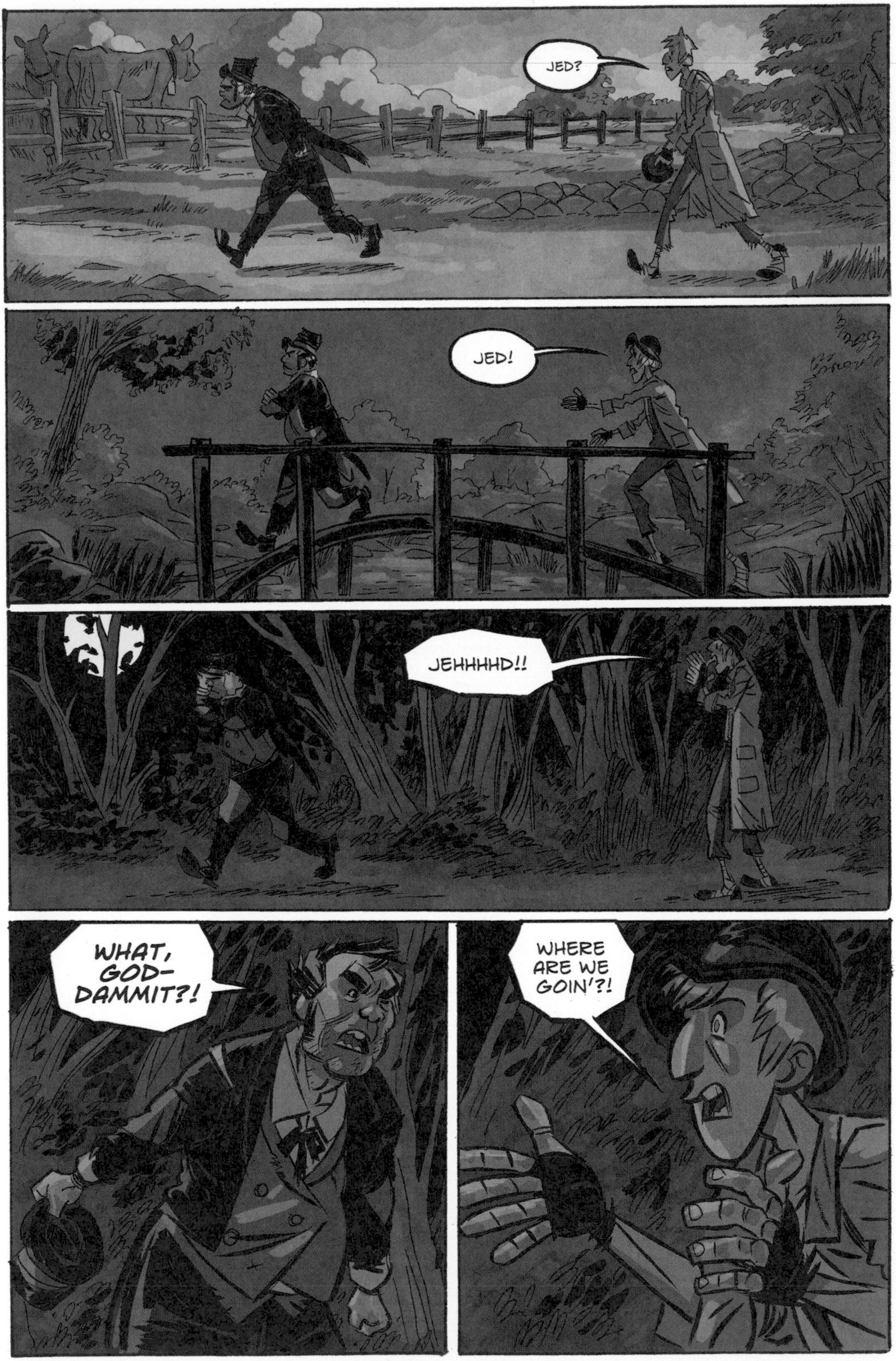
JED?
JED!
JEHHHHD!!
WHAT, GOD-DAMMIT?!
WHERE ARE WE GOIN'?!

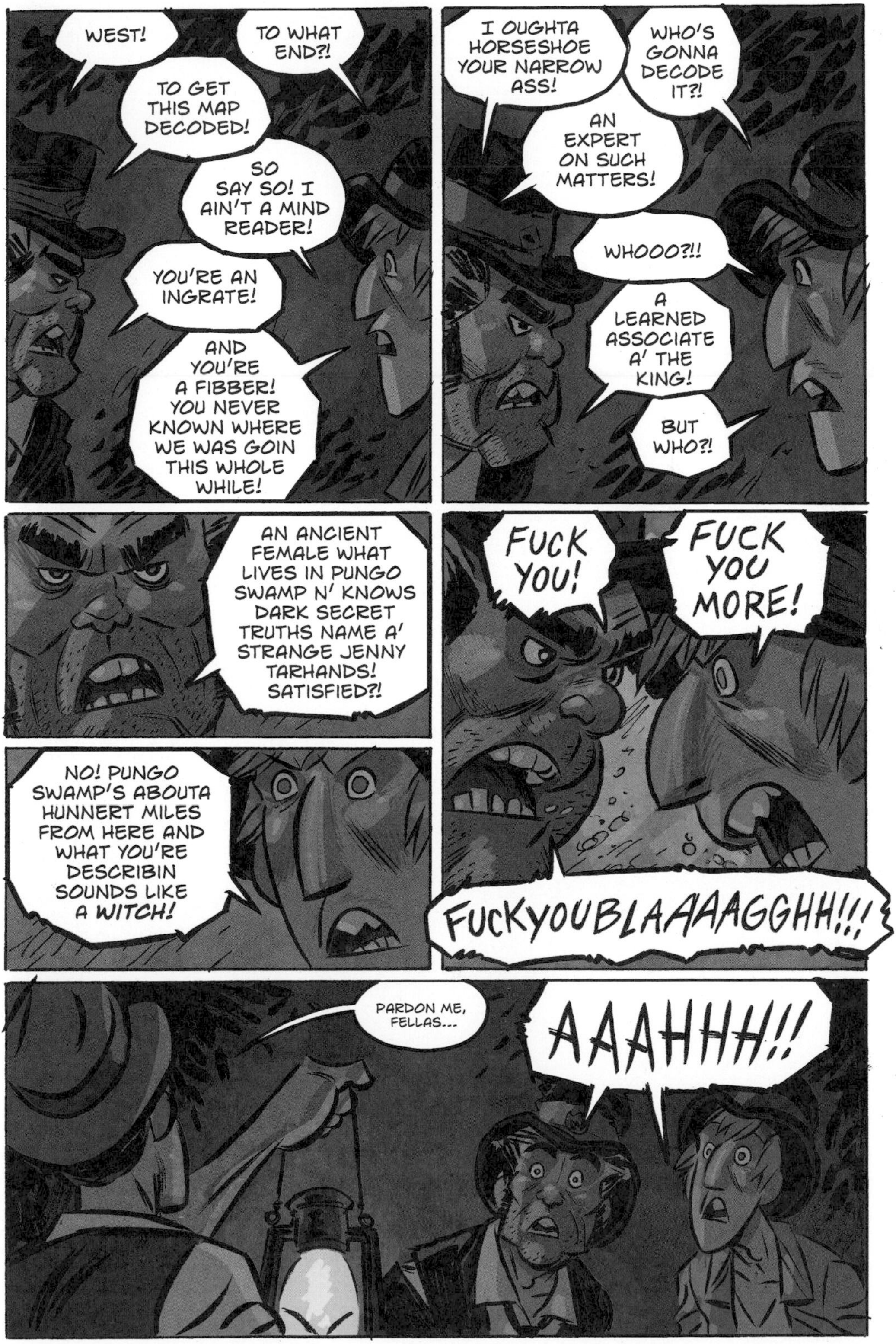
WEST!
TO WHAT END?!
TO GET THIS MAP DECODED!
SO SAY SO! I AIN'T A MIND READER!
YOU'RE AN INGRATE!
AND YOU'RE A FIBBER! YOU NEVER KNOWN WHERE WE WAS GOIN THIS WHOLE WHILE!
I OUGHTA HORSESHOE YOUR NARROW ASS!
WHO'S GONNA DECODE IT?!
AN EXPERT ON SUCH MATTERS!
WHOOO?!!
A LEARNED ASSOCIATE A' THE KING!
BUT WHO?!
AN ANCIENT FEMALE WHAT LIVES IN PUNGO SWAMP N' KNOWS DARK SECRET TRUTHS NAME A' STRANGE JENNY TARHANDS! SATISFIED?!
NO! PUNGO SWAMP'S ABOUTA HUNNERT MILES FROM HERE AND WHAT YOU'RE DESCRIBIN SOUNDS LIKE A WITCH!
FUCK YOU!
FUCK YOU MORE!
FUCKYOUBLAAAAGGHH!!!
PARDON ME, FELLAS...
AAAHHH!!

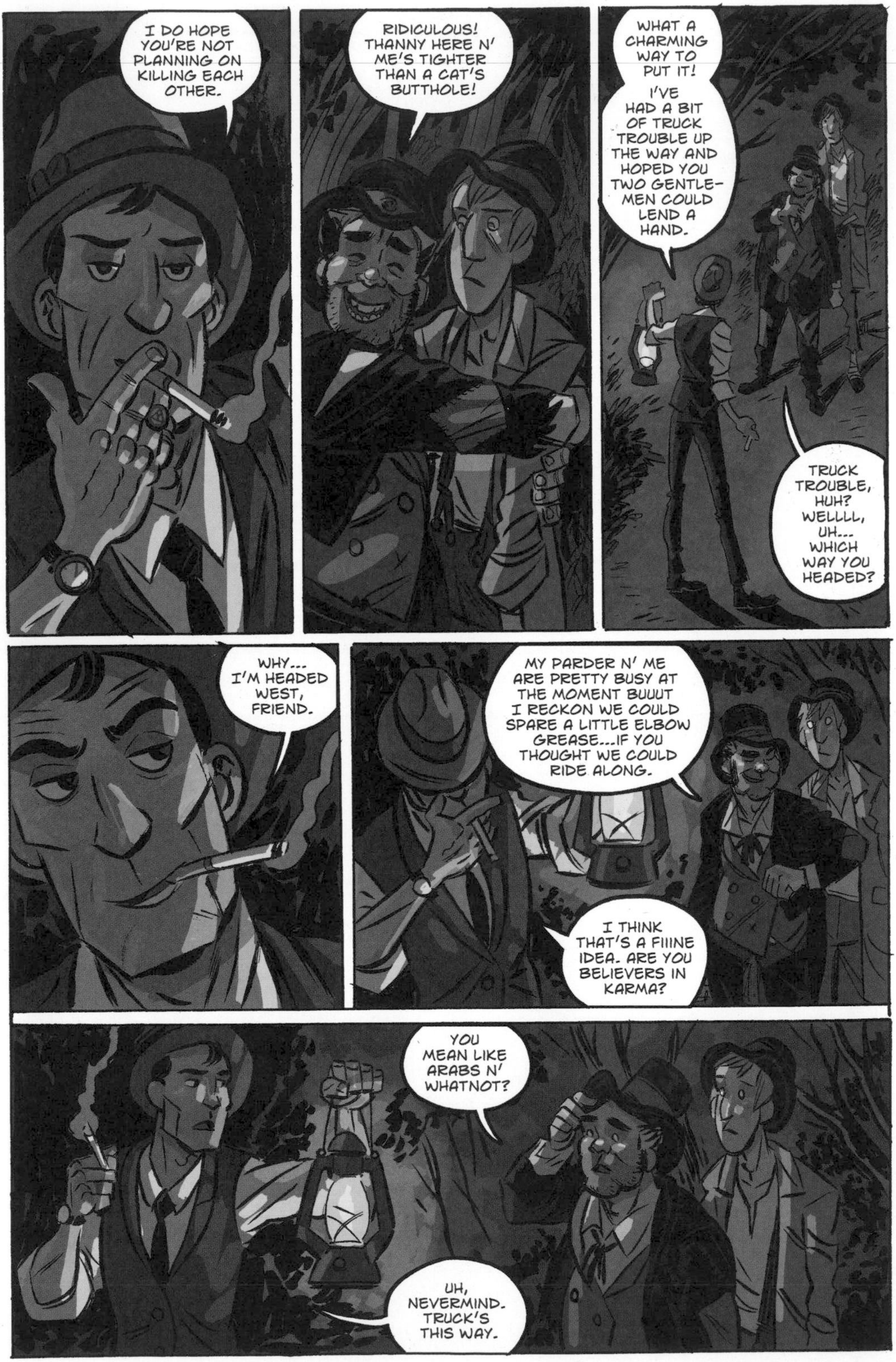
I DO HOPE YOU'RE NOT PLANNING ON KILLING EACH OTHER.
RIDICULOUS! THANNY HERE N' ME'S TIGHTER THAN A CAT'S BUTTHOLE!
WHAT A CHARMING WAY TO PUT IT!
I'VE HAD A BIT OF TRUCK TROUBLE UP THE WAY AND HOPED YOU TWO GENTLE-MEN COULD LEND A HAND.
TRUCK TROUBLE, HUH? WELLLL, UH... WHICH WAY YOU HEADED?
WHY... I'M HEADED WEST, FRIEND.
MY PARDER N' ME ARE PRETTY BUSY AT THE MOMENT BUUUT I RECKON WE COULD SPARE A LITTLE ELBOW GREASE...IF YOU THOUGHT WE COULD RIDE ALONG.
I THINK THAT'S A FIIINE IDEA. ARE YOU BELIEVERS IN KARMA?
YOU MEAN LIKE ARABS N' WHATNOT?
UH, NEVERMIND. TRUCK'S THIS WAY.

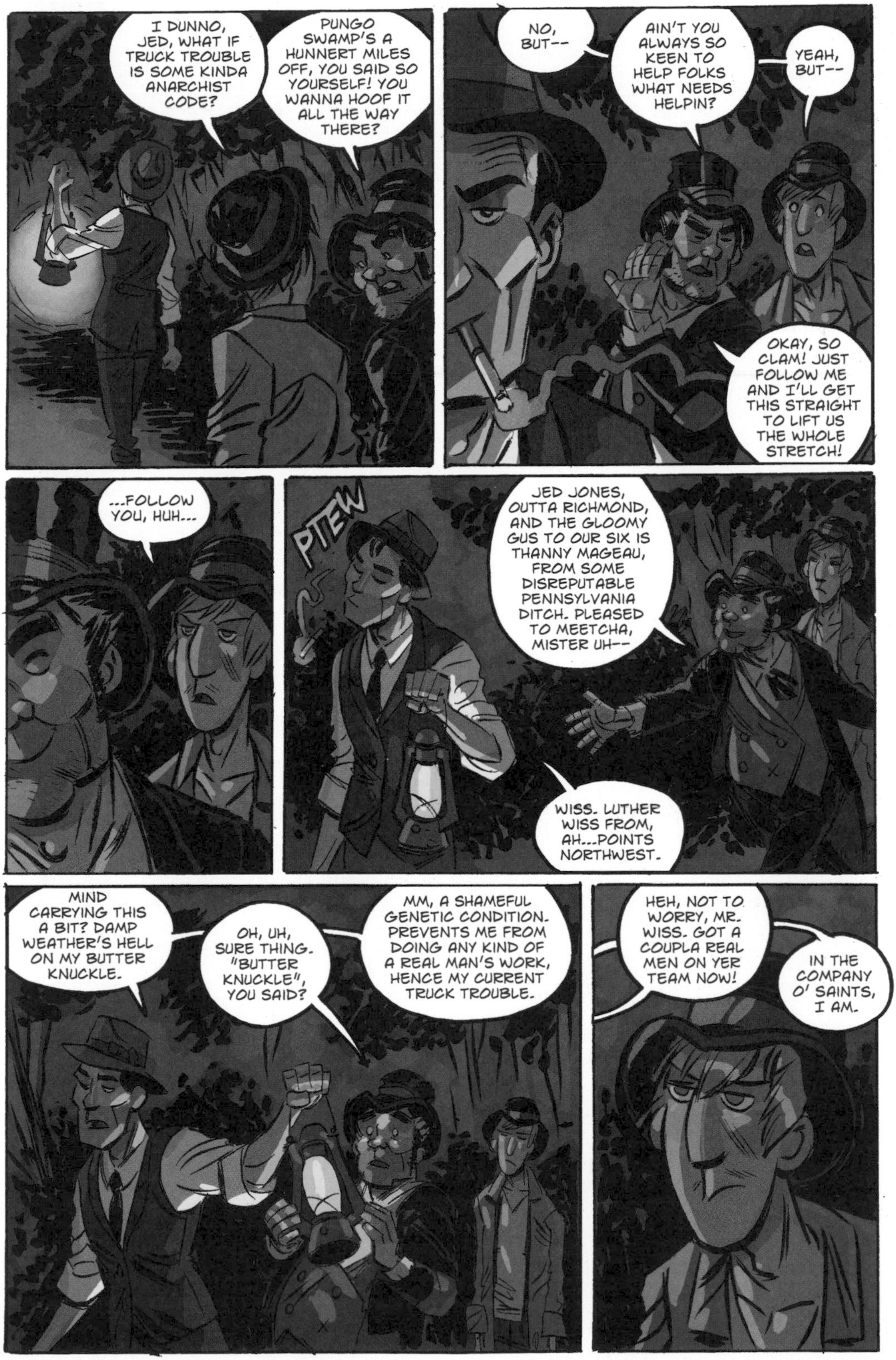
I DUNNO, JED, WHAT IF TRUCK TROUBLE IS SOME KINDA ANARCHIST CODE?
PUNGO SWAMP'S A HUNNERT MILES OFF, YOU SAID SO YOURSELF! YOU WANNA HOOF IT ALL THE WAY THERE?
NO, BUT--
AIN'T YOU ALWAYS SO KEEN TO HELP FOLKS WHAT NEEDS HELPIN?
YEAH, BUT--
OKAY, SO CLAM! JUST FOLLOW ME AND I'LL GET THIS STRAIGHT TO LIFT US THE WHOLE STRETCH!
...FOLLOW YOU, HUH...
PTEW
JED JONES, OUTTA RICHMOND, AND THE GLOOMY GUS TO OUR SIX IS THANNY MAGEAU, FROM SOME DISREPUTABLE PENNSYLVANIA DITCH. PLEASED TO MEETCHA, MISTER UH--
WISS. LUTHER WISS FROM, AH...POINTS NORTHWEST.
MIND CARRYING THIS A BIT? DAMP WEATHER'S HELL ON MY BUTTER KNUCKLE.
OH, UH, SURE THING. "BUTTER KNUCKLE", YOU SAID?
MM, A SHAMEFUL GENETIC CONDITION. PREVENTS ME FROM DOING ANY KIND OF A REAL MAN'S WORK, HENCE MY CURRENT TRUCK TROUBLE.
HEH, NOT TO WORRY, MR. WISS. GOT A COUPLA REAL MEN ON YER TEAM NOW!
IN THE COMPANY O' SAINTS, I AM.

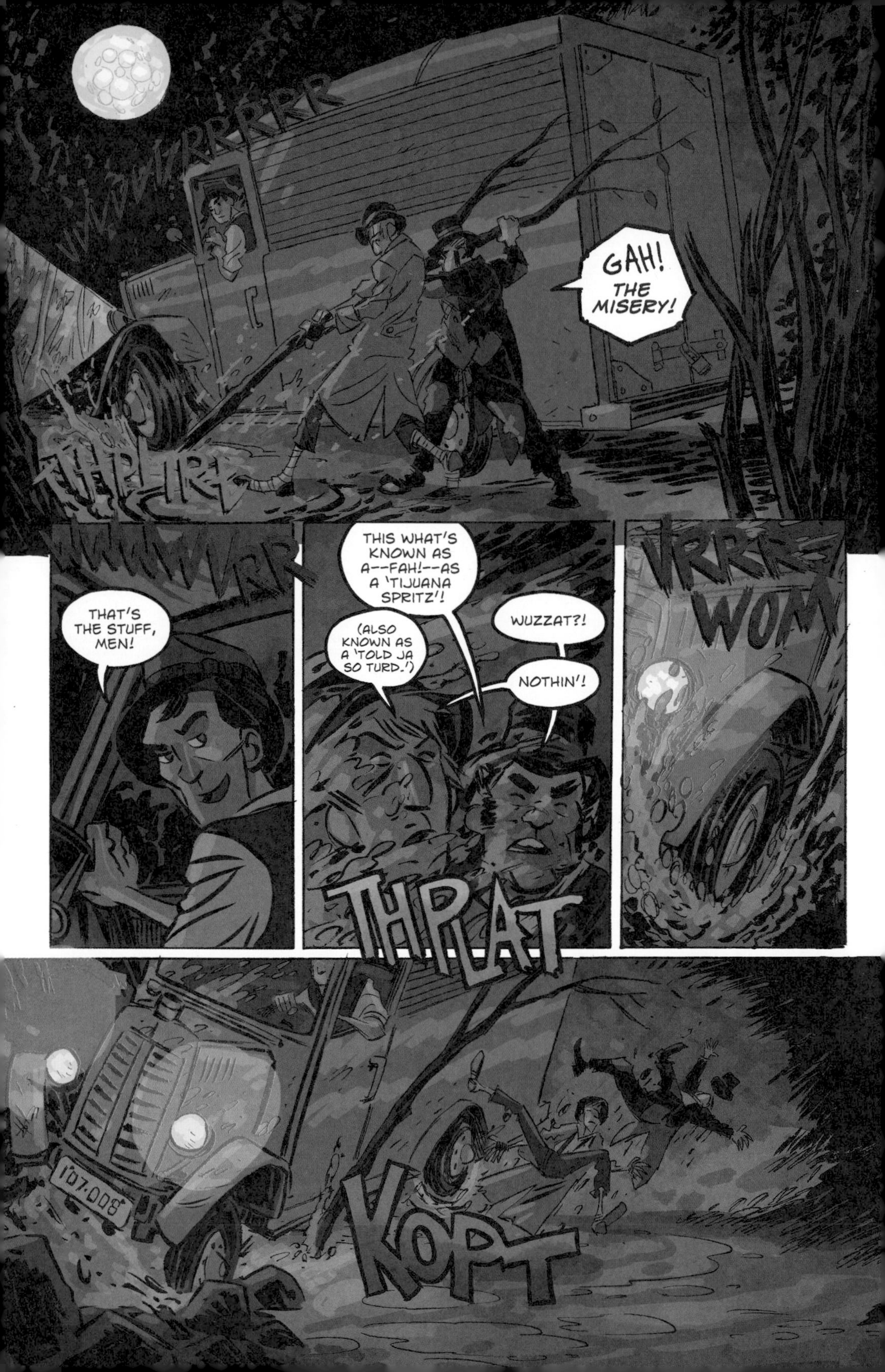
VWVVVVVVRRRRRRR
GAH! THE MISERY!
THPLIRR
WWWWRR
THAT'S THE STUFF, MEN!
THIS WHAT'S KNOWN AS A--FAH!--AS A 'TIJUANA SPRITZ'!
(ALSO KNOWN AS A 'TOLD JA SO TURD.')
WUZZAT?!
NOTHIN'!
THPLAT
VRRR
WOM
107-008
KOPT

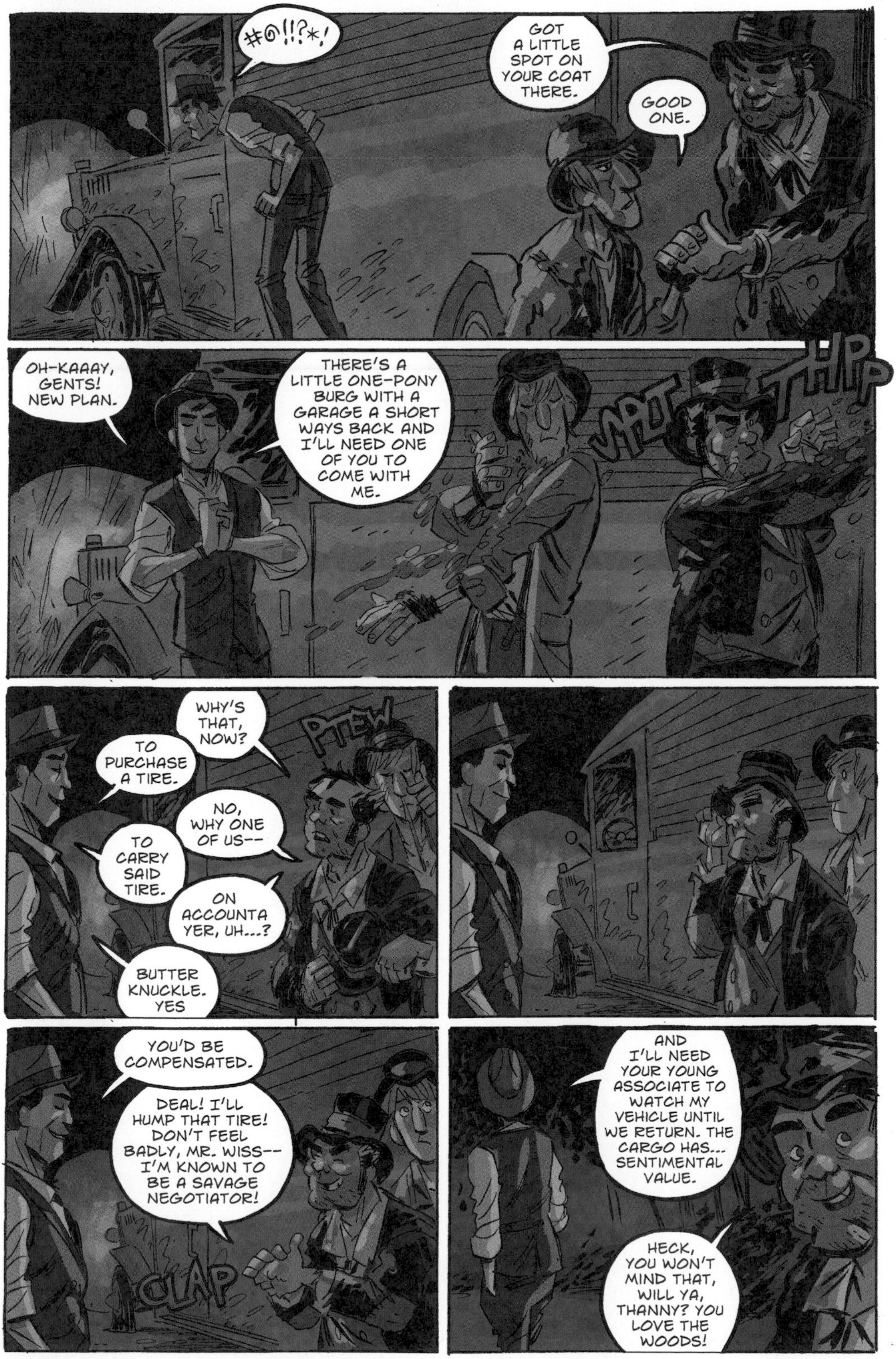
#@!!?*!
GOT A LITTLE SPOT ON YOUR COAT THERE.
GOOD ONE.
OH-KAAAY, GENTS! NEW PLAN.
THERE'S A LITTLE ONE-PONY BURG WITH A GARAGE A SHORT WAYS BACK AND I'LL NEED ONE OF YOU TO COME WITH ME.
SPIT
THPP
WHY'S THAT, NOW?
PTEW
TO PURCHASE A TIRE.
NO, WHY ONE OF US--
TO CARRY SAID TIRE.
ON ACCOUNTA YER, UH...?
BUTTER KNUCKLE. YES
YOU'D BE COMPENSATED.
DEAL! I'LL HUMP THAT TIRE! DON'T FEEL BADLY, MR. WISS-- I'M KNOWN TO BE A SAVAGE NEGOTIATOR!
CLAP
AND I'LL NEED YOUR YOUNG ASSOCIATE TO WATCH MY VEHICLE UNTIL WE RETURN. THE CARGO HAS... SENTIMENTAL VALUE.
HECK, YOU WON'T MIND THAT, WILL YA, THANNY? YOU LOVE THE WOODS!

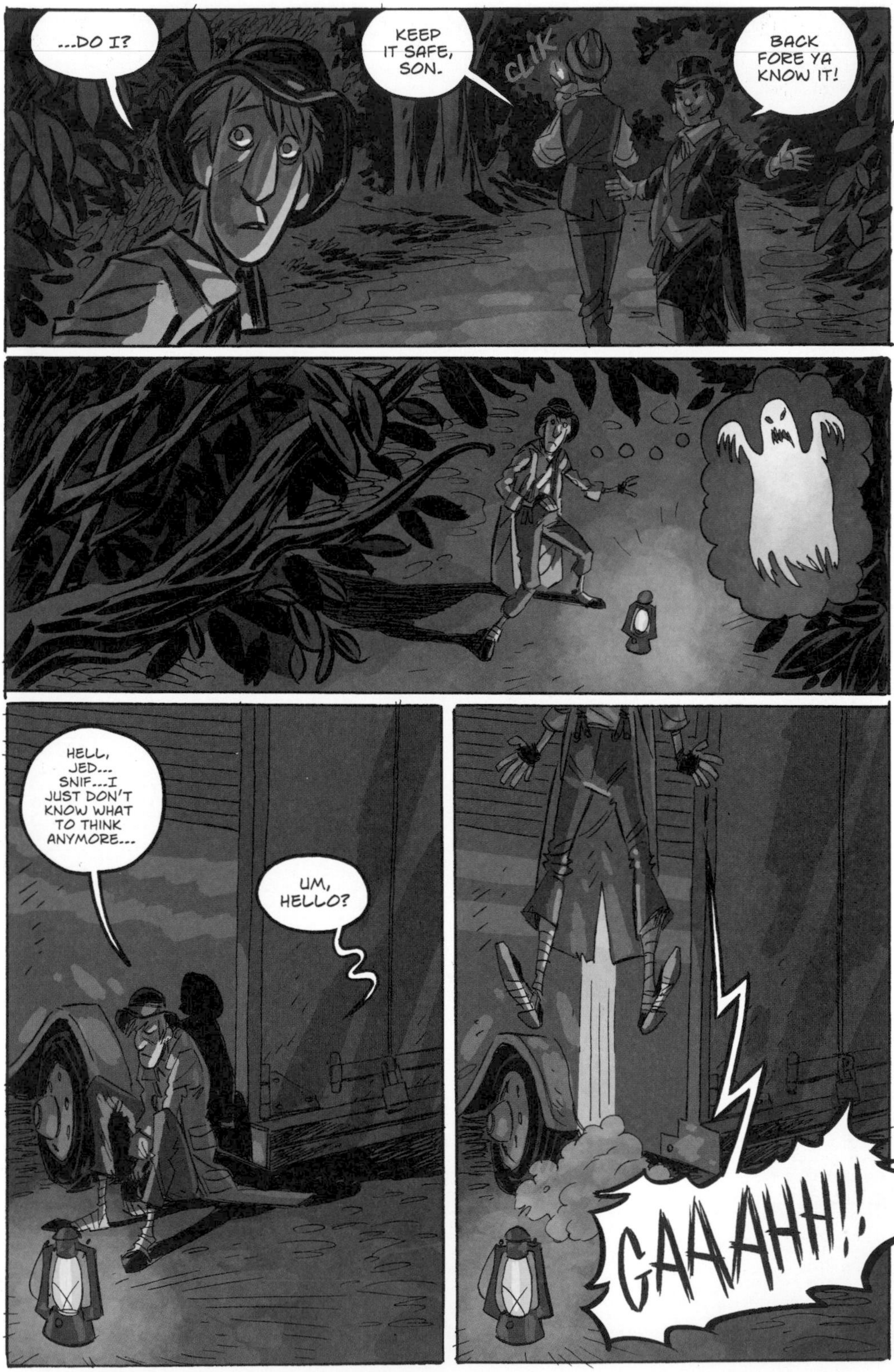
...DO I?
KEEP IT SAFE, SON.
CLIK
BACK FORE YA KNOW IT!
HELL, JED... SNIF...I JUST DON'T KNOW WHAT TO THINK ANYMORE...
UM, HELLO?
GAAAHH!!

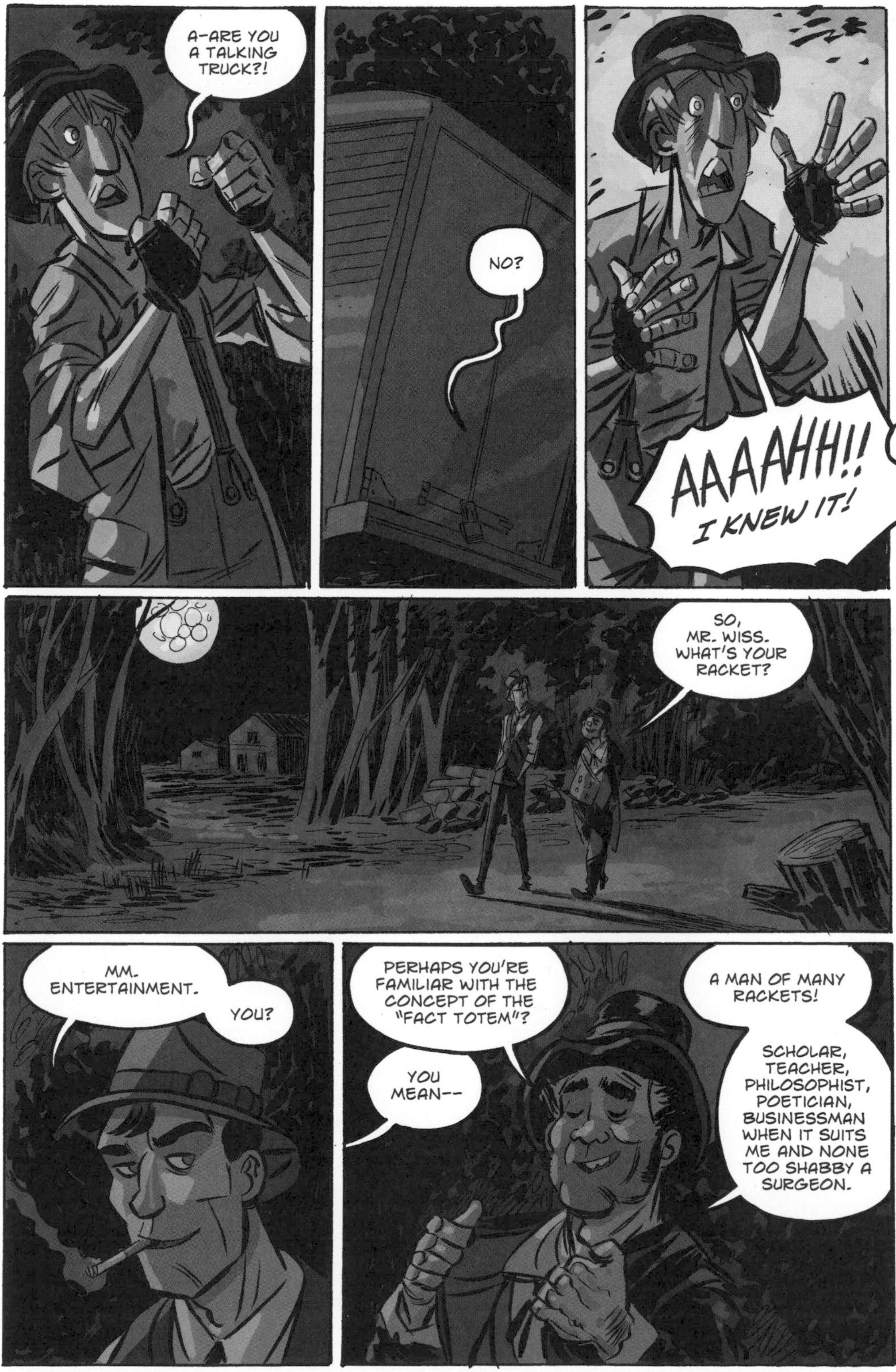
A-ARE YOU A TALKING TRUCK?!
NO?
AAAAHH!! I KNEW IT!
SO, MR. WISS. WHAT'S YOUR RACKET?
MM. ENTERTAINMENT.
YOU?
PERHAPS YOU'RE FAMILIAR WITH THE CONCEPT OF THE "FACT TOTEM"?
YOU MEAN--
A MAN OF MANY RACKETS!
SCHOLAR, TEACHER, PHILOSOPHIST, POETICIAN, BUSINESSMAN WHEN IT SUITS ME AND NONE TOO SHABBY A SURGEON.

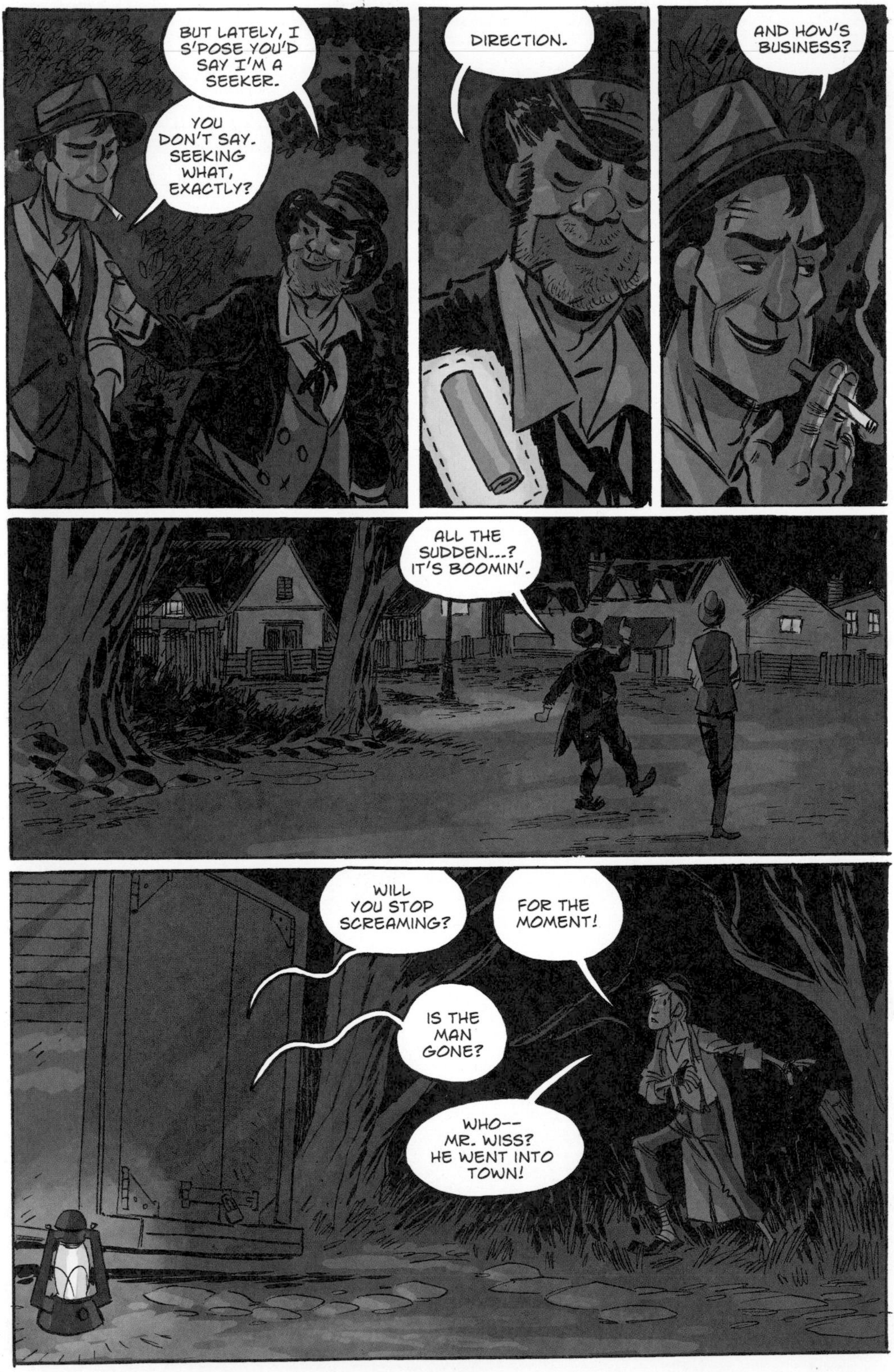
BUT LATELY, I S'POSE YOU'D SAY I'M A SEEKER.
YOU DON'T SAY. SEEKING WHAT, EXACTLY?
DIRECTION.
AND HOW'S BUSINESS?
ALL THE SUDDEN...? IT'S BOOMIN'.
WILL YOU STOP SCREAMING?
FOR THE MOMENT!
IS THE MAN GONE?
WHO-- MR. WISS? HE WENT INTO TOWN!

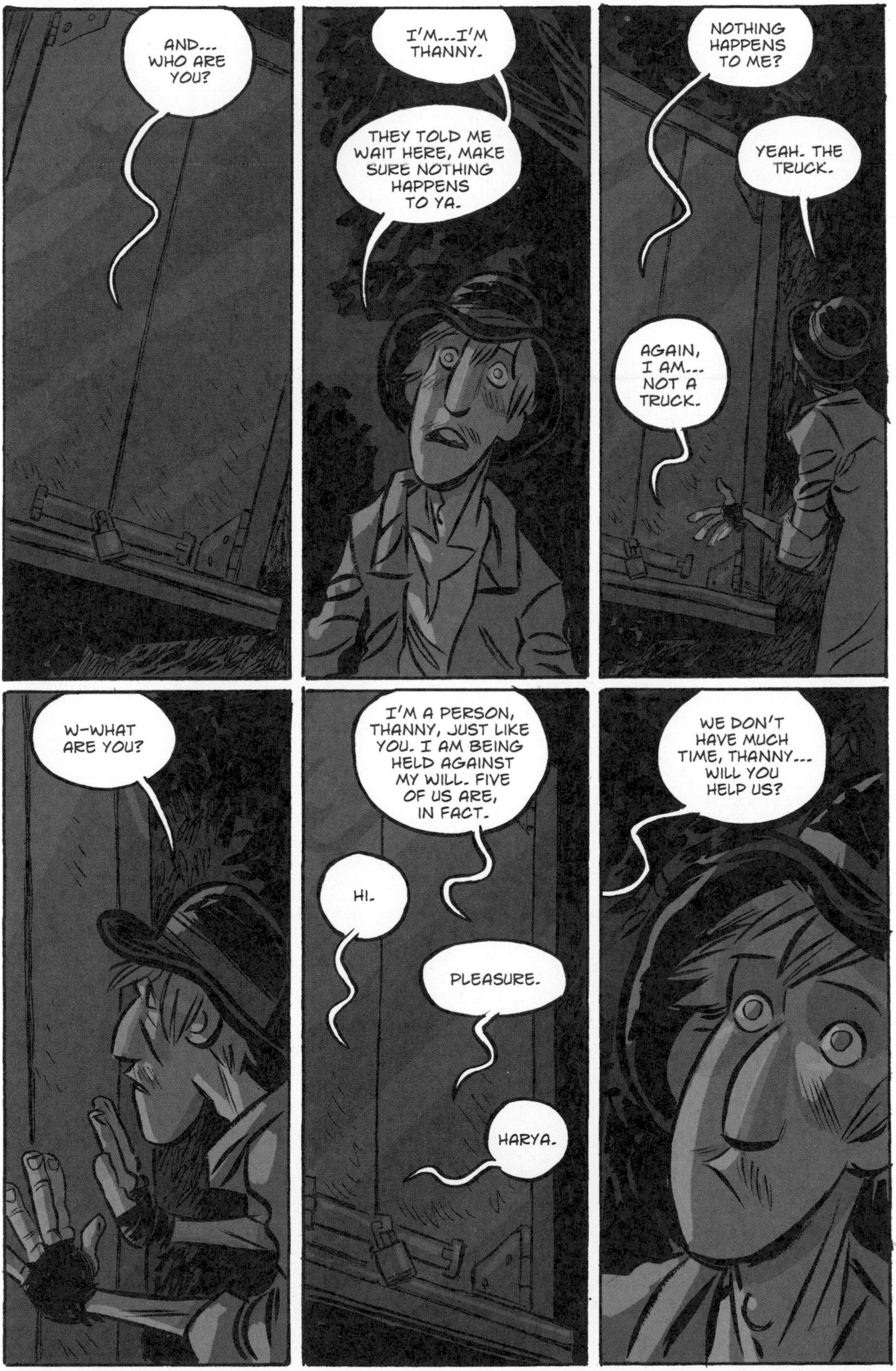
AND... WHO ARE YOU?
I'M...I'M THANNY.
THEY TOLD ME WAIT HERE, MAKE SURE NOTHING HAPPENS TO YA.
NOTHING HAPPENS TO ME?
YEAH. THE TRUCK.
AGAIN, I AM... NOT A TRUCK.
W-WHAT ARE YOU?
I'M A PERSON, THANNY, JUST LIKE YOU. I AM BEING HELD AGAINST MY WILL. FIVE OF US ARE, IN FACT.
HI.
PLEASURE.
HARYA.
WE DON'T HAVE MUCH TIME, THANNY... WILL YOU HELP US?

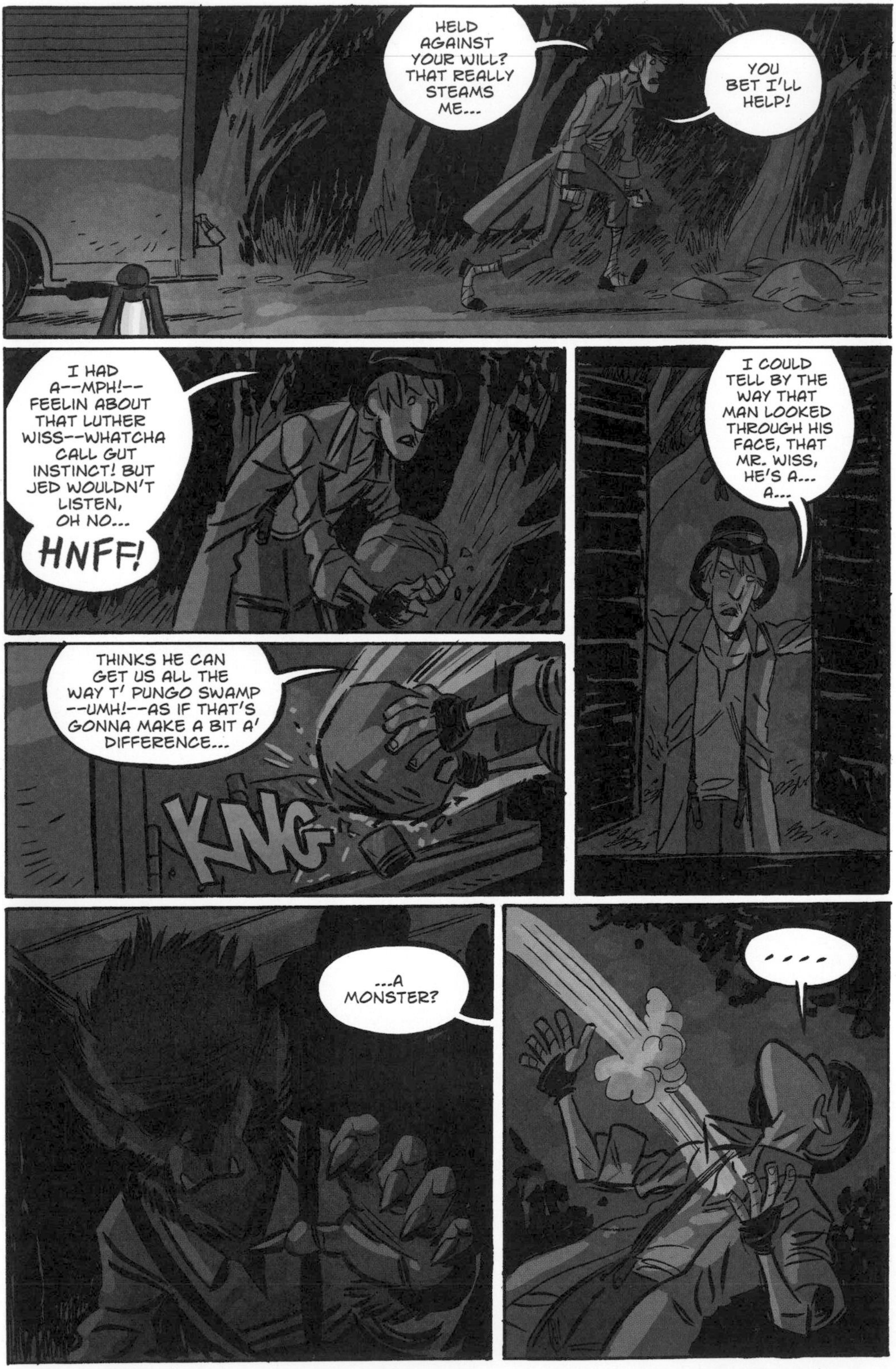
HELD AGAINST YOUR WILL? THAT REALLY STEAMS ME...
YOU BET I'LL HELP!
I HAD A--MPH!--FEELIN ABOUT THAT LUTHER WISS--WHATCHA CALL GUT INSTINCT! BUT JED WOULDN'T LISTEN, OH NO...
HNFF!
THINKS HE CAN GET US ALL THE WAY T' PUNGO SWAMP --UMH!--AS IF THAT'S GONNA MAKE A BIT A' DIFFERENCE...
KNG
I COULD TELL BY THE WAY THAT MAN LOOKED THROUGH HIS FACE, THAT MR. WISS, HE'S A... A...
...A MONSTER?
....

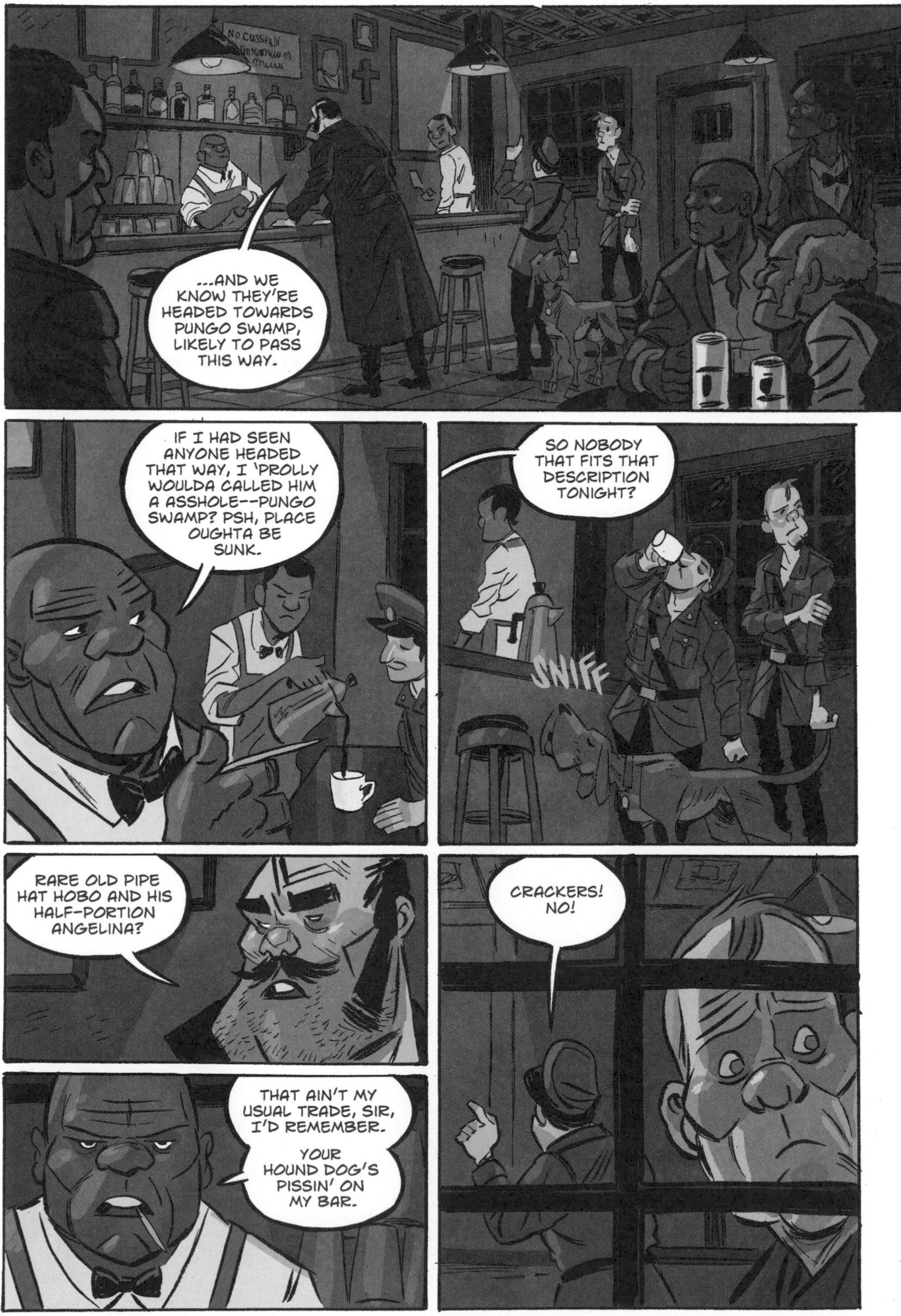
...AND WE KNOW THEY'RE HEADED TOWARDS PUNGO SWAMP, LIKELY TO PASS THIS WAY.
IF I HAD SEEN ANYONE HEADED THAT WAY, I 'PROLLY WOULDA CALLED HIM A ASSHOLE--PUNGO SWAMP? PSH, PLACE OUGHTA BE SUNK.
SO NOBODY THAT FITS THAT DESCRIPTION TONIGHT?
SNIFF
RARE OLD PIPE HAT HOBO AND HIS HALF-PORTION ANGELINA?
CRACKERS! NO!
THAT AIN'T MY USUAL TRADE, SIR, I'D REMEMBER.
YOUR HOUND DOG'S PISSIN' ON MY BAR.

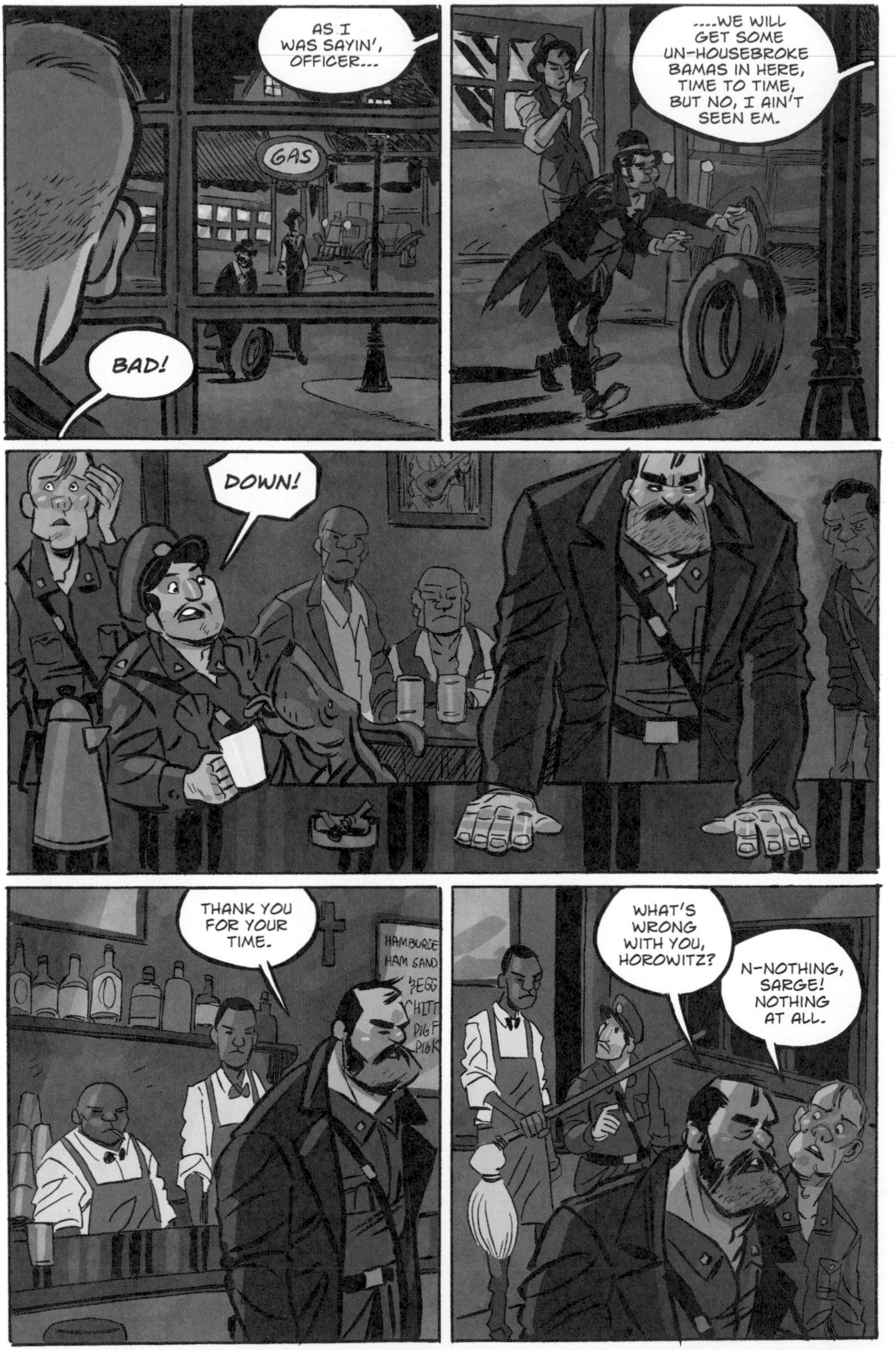
AS I WAS SAYIN', OFFICER...
BAD!
GAS
....WE WILL GET SOME UN-HOUSEBROKE BAMAS IN HERE, TIME TO TIME, BUT NO, I AIN'T SEEN EM.
DOWN!
THANK YOU FOR YOUR TIME.
WHAT'S WRONG WITH YOU, HOROWITZ?
N-NOTHING, SARGE! NOTHING AT ALL.

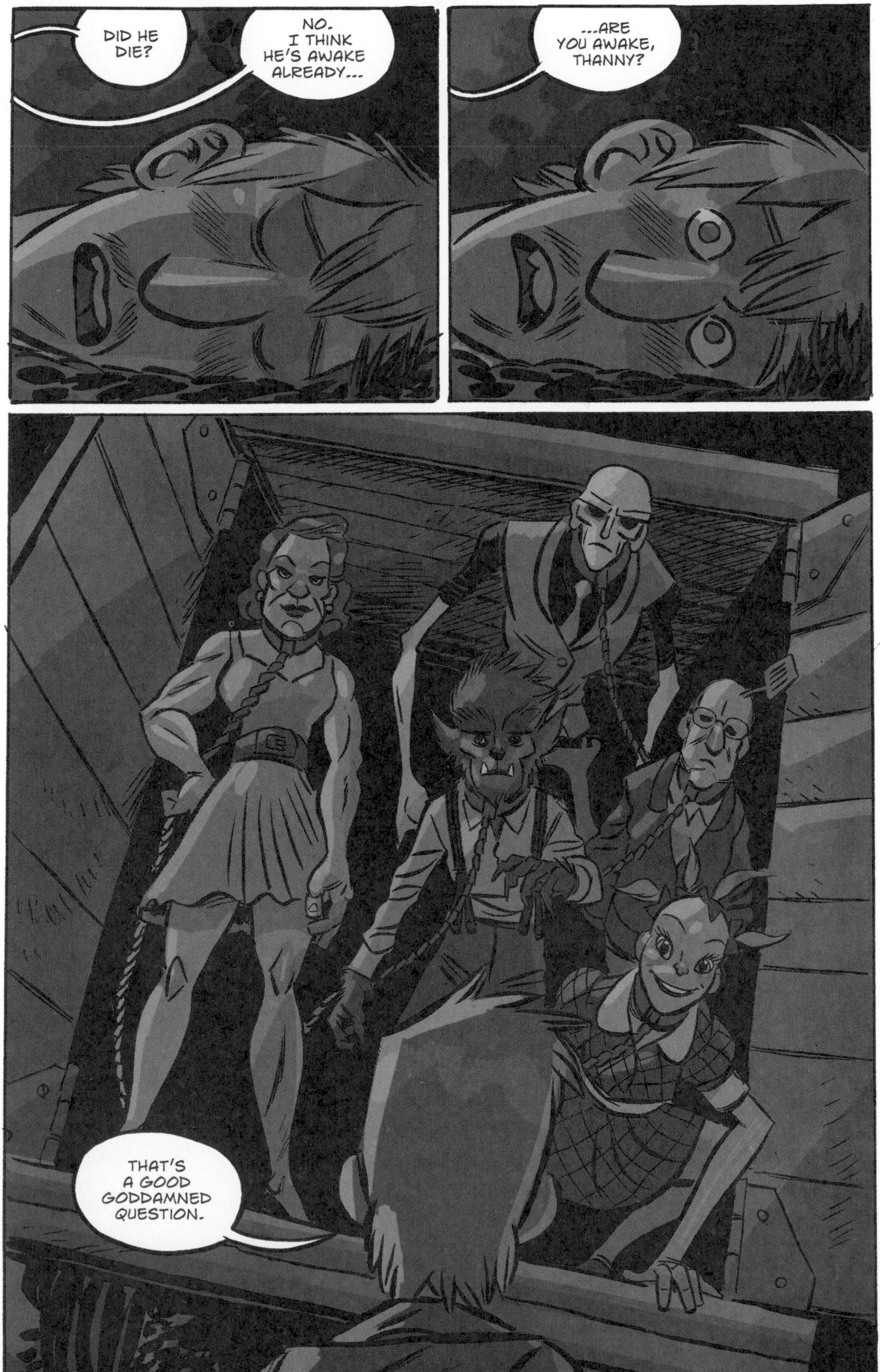
DID HE DIE?
NO. I THINK HE'S AWAKE ALREADY...
...ARE YOU AWAKE, THANNY?
THAT'S A GOOD GODDAMNED QUESTION.

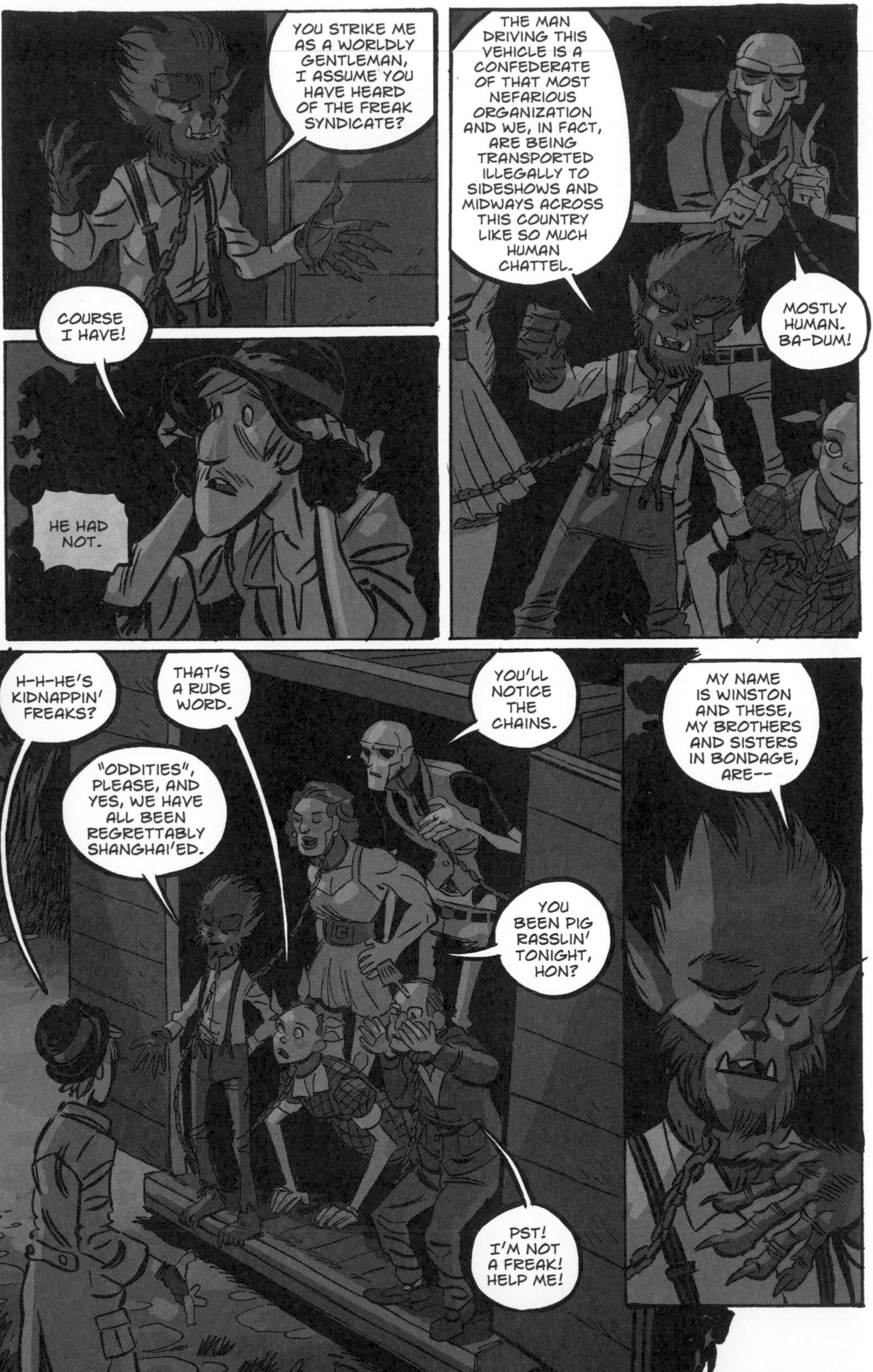
YOU STRIKE ME AS A WORLDLY GENTLEMAN, I ASSUME YOU HAVE HEARD OF THE FREAK SYNDICATE?
COURSE I HAVE!
HE HAD NOT.
THE MAN DRIVING THIS VEHICLE IS A CONFEDERATE OF THAT MOST NEFARIOUS ORGANIZATION AND WE, IN FACT, ARE BEING TRANSPORTED ILLEGALLY TO SIDESHOWS AND MIDWAYS ACROSS THIS COUNTRY LIKE SO MUCH HUMAN CHATTEL.
MOSTLY HUMAN. BA-DUM!
H-H-HE'S KIDNAPPIN' FREAKS?
THAT'S A RUDE WORD.
"ODDITIES", PLEASE, AND YES, WE HAVE ALL BEEN REGRETTABLY SHANGHAI'ED.
YOU'LL NOTICE THE CHAINS.
YOU BEEN PIG RASSLIN' TONIGHT, HON?
PST! I'M NOT A FREAK! HELP ME!
MY NAME IS WINSTON AND THESE, MY BROTHERS AND SISTERS IN BONDAGE, ARE--

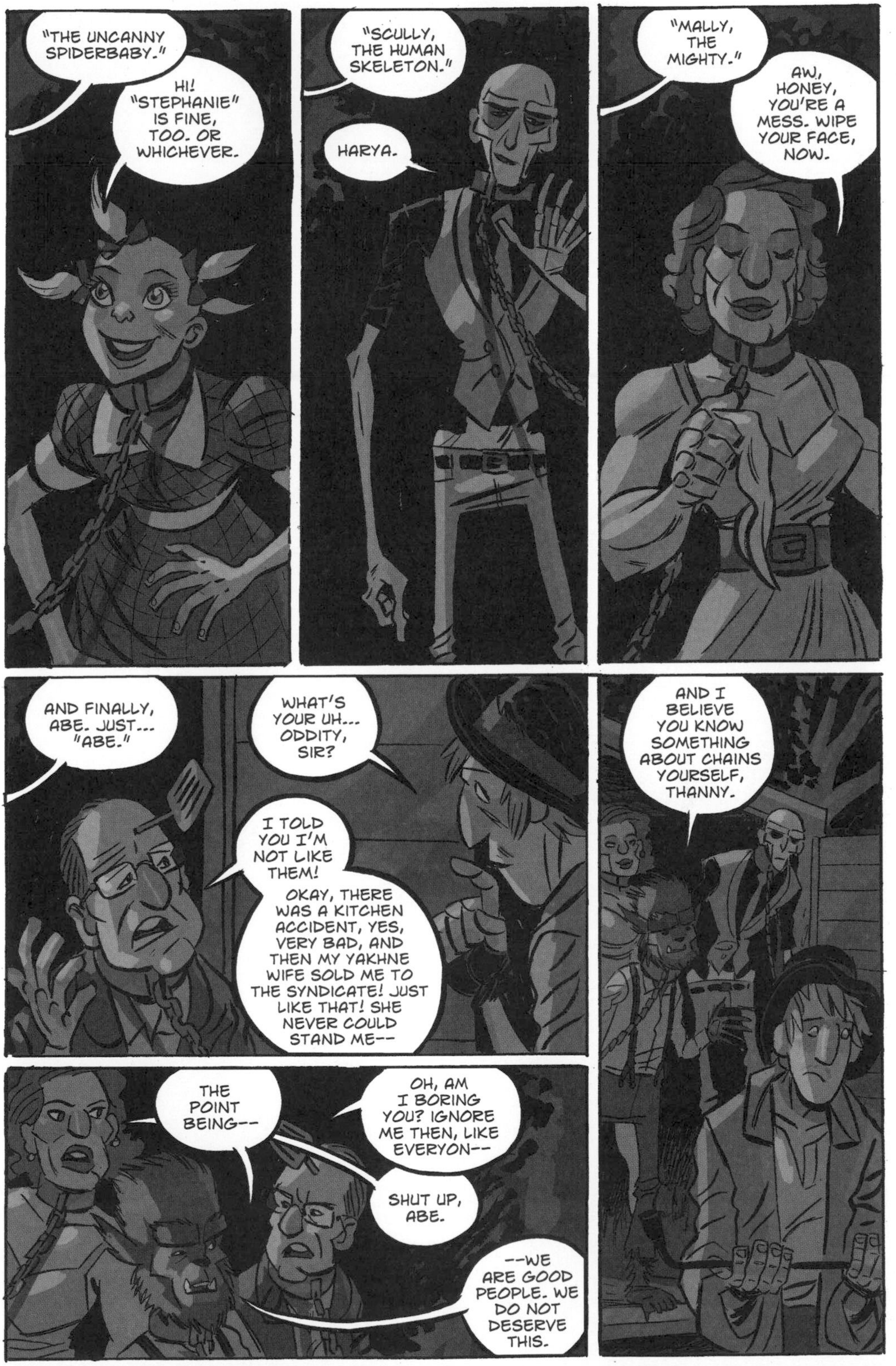
"THE UNCANNY SPIDERBABY."
HI! "STEPHANIE" IS FINE, TOO. OR WHICHEVER.
"SCULLY, THE HUMAN SKELETON."
HARYA.
"MALLY, THE MIGHTY."
AW, HONEY, YOU'RE A MESS. WIPE YOUR FACE, NOW.
AND FINALLY, ABE. JUST... "ABE."
WHAT'S YOUR UH... ODDITY, SIR?
I TOLD YOU I'M NOT LIKE THEM!
OKAY, THERE WAS A KITCHEN ACCIDENT, YES, VERY BAD, AND THEN MY YAKHNE WIFE SOLD ME TO THE SYNDICATE! JUST LIKE THAT! SHE NEVER COULD STAND ME--
THE POINT BEING--
OH, AM I BORING YOU? IGNORE ME THEN, LIKE EVERYON--
SHUT UP, ABE.
--WE ARE GOOD PEOPLE. WE DO NOT DESERVE THIS.
AND I BELIEVE YOU KNOW SOMETHING ABOUT CHAINS YOURSELF, THANNY.

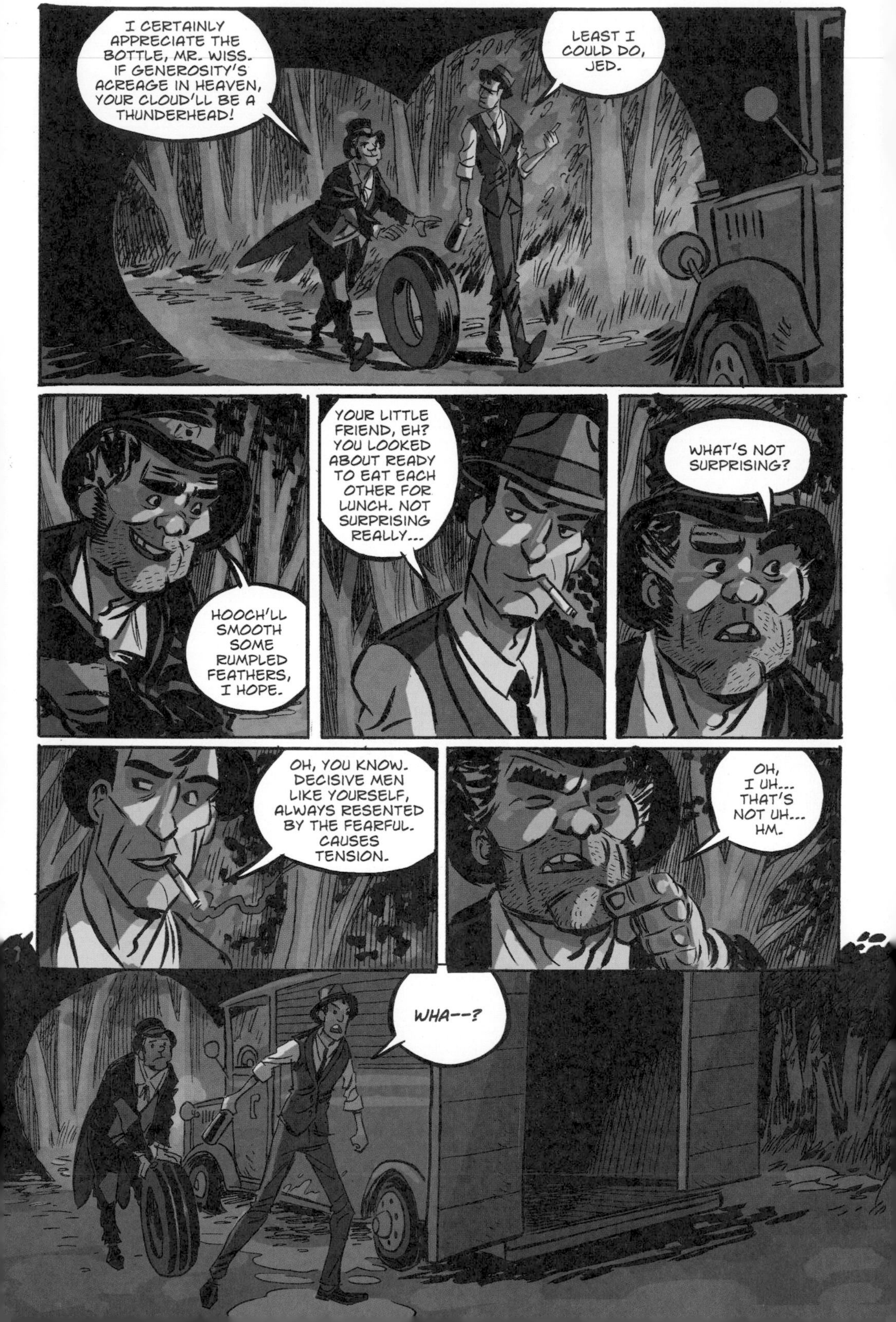
I CERTAINLY APPRECIATE THE BOTTLE, MR. WISS. IF GENEROSITY'S ACREAGE IN HEAVEN, YOUR CLOUD'LL BE A THUNDERHEAD!
LEAST I COULD DO, JED.
HOOCH'LL SMOOTH SOME RUMPLED FEATHERS, I HOPE.
YOUR LITTLE FRIEND, EH? YOU LOOKED ABOUT READY TO EAT EACH OTHER FOR LUNCH. NOT SURPRISING REALLY...
WHAT'S NOT SURPRISING?
OH, YOU KNOW. DECISIVE MEN LIKE YOURSELF, ALWAYS RESENTED BY THE FEARFUL. CAUSES TENSION.
OH, I UH... THAT'S NOT UH... HM.
WHA--?

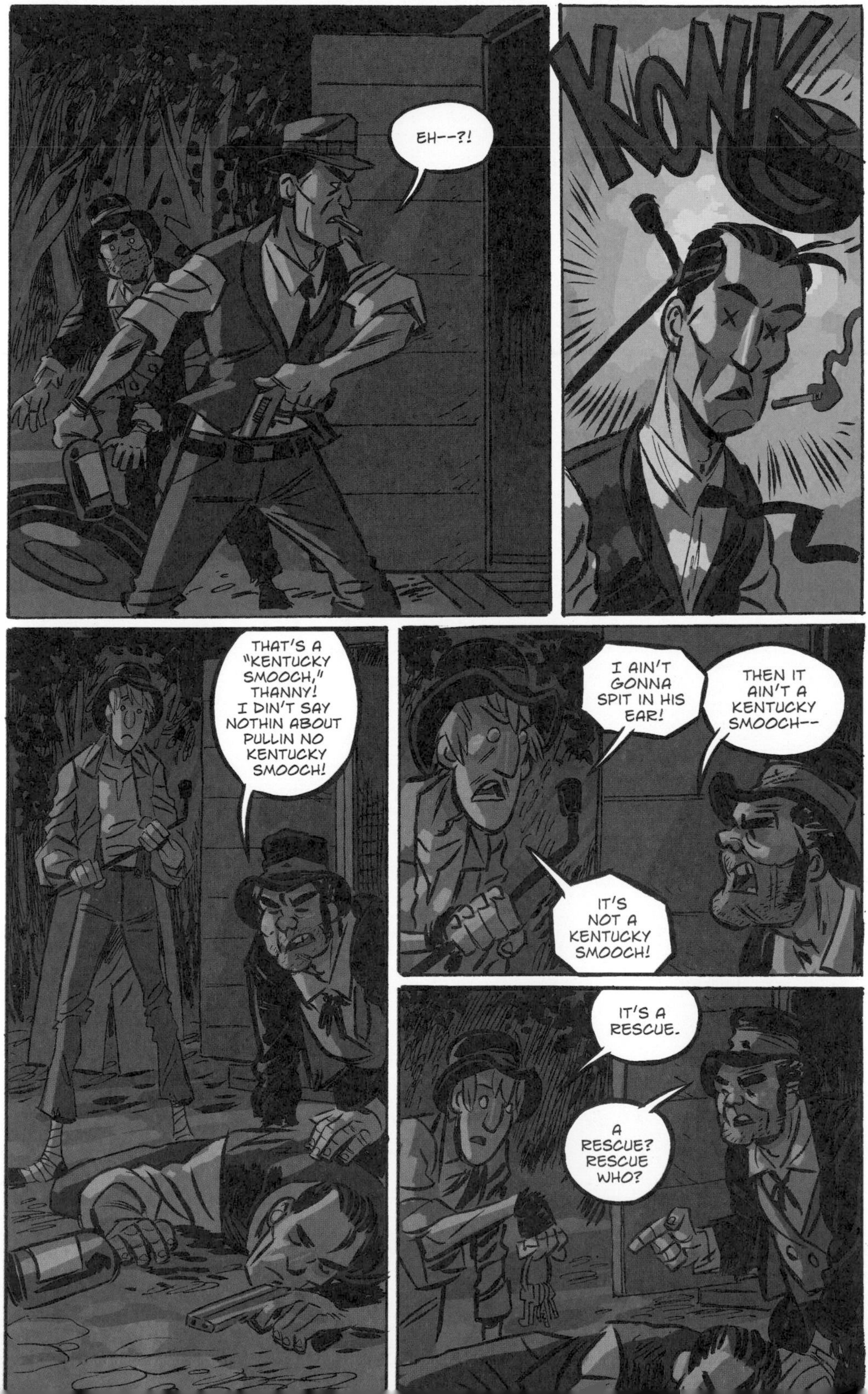
EH--?!
KONK
THAT'S A "KENTUCKY SMOOCH," THANNY! I DIN'T SAY NOTHIN ABOUT PULLIN NO KENTUCKY SMOOCH!
I AIN'T GONNA SPIT IN HIS EAR!
THEN IT AIN'T A KENTUCKY SMOOCH--
IT'S NOT A KENTUCKY SMOOCH!
IT'S A RESCUE.
A RESCUE? RESCUE WHO?

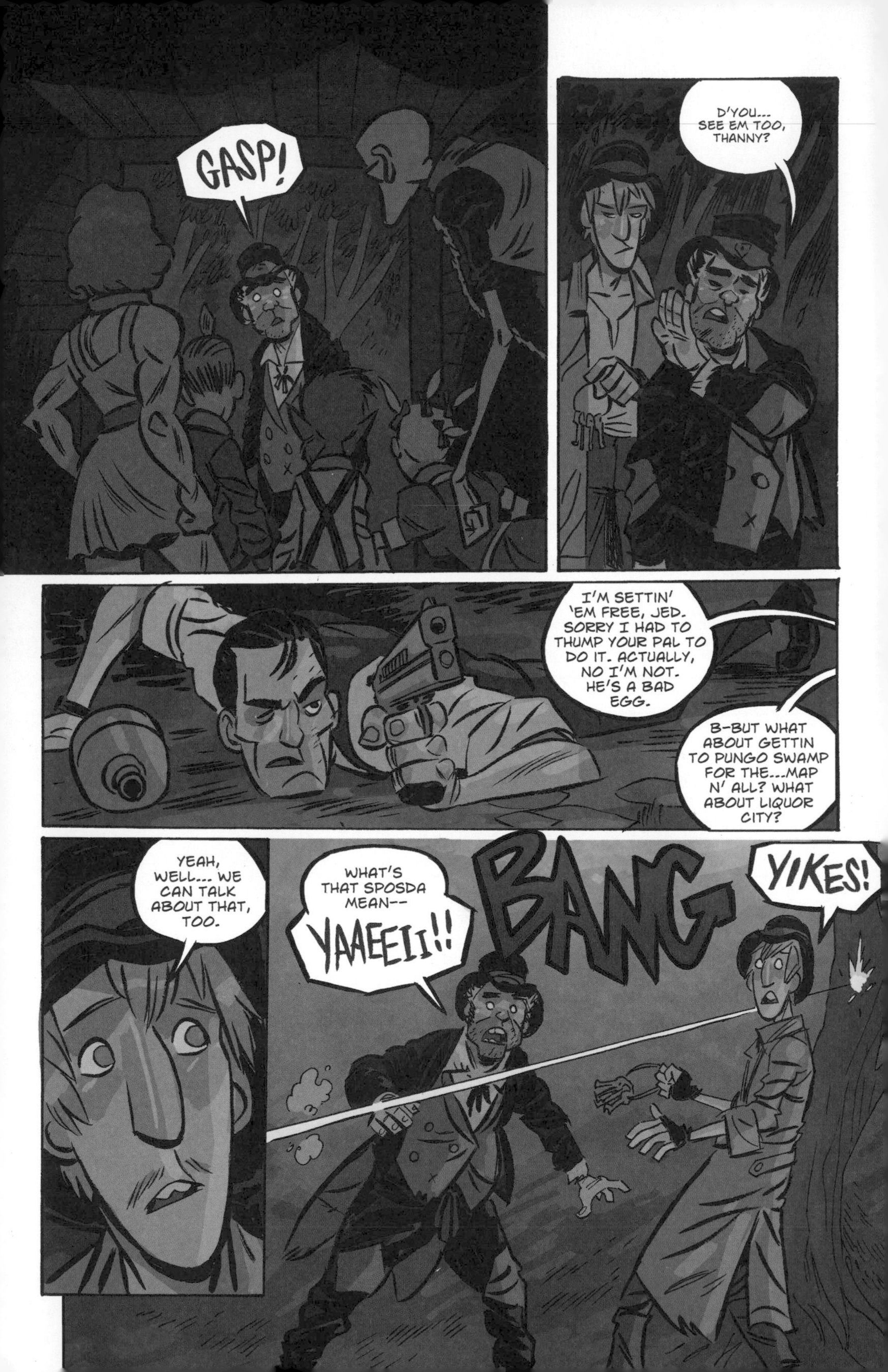
GASP!
D'YOU... SEE EM TOO, THANNY?
I'M SETTIN' 'EM FREE, JED. SORRY I HAD TO THUMP YOUR PAL TO DO IT. ACTUALLY, NO I'M NOT. HE'S A BAD EGG.
B-BUT WHAT ABOUT GETTIN TO PUNGO SWAMP FOR THE...MAP N' ALL? WHAT ABOUT LIQUOR CITY?
YEAH, WELL... WE CAN TALK ABOUT THAT, TOO.
WHAT'S THAT SPOSDA MEAN--
YAAEEII!!
BANG
YIKES!

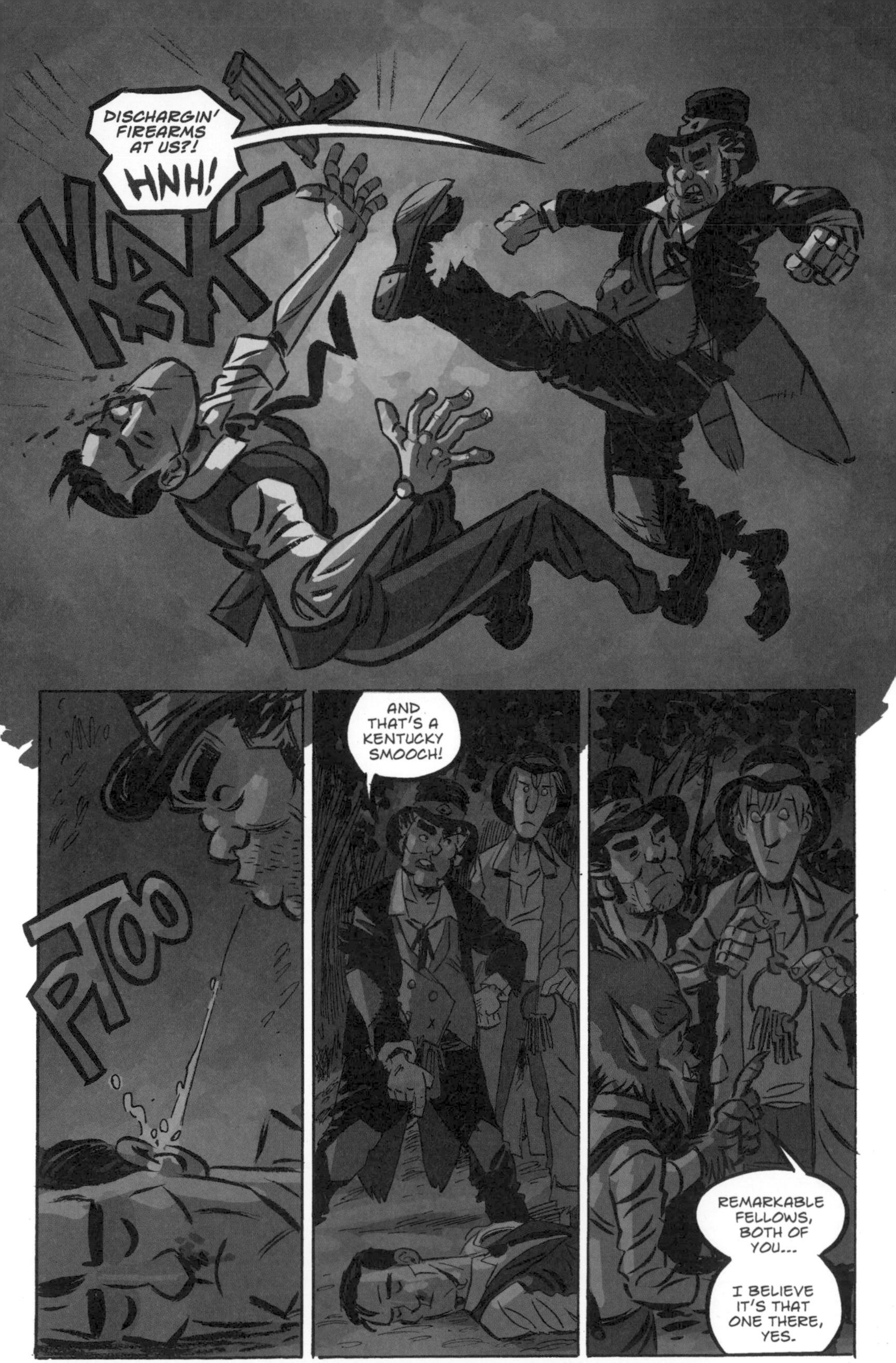
DISCHARGIN' FIREARMS AT US?!
HNH!
PTOO
AND THAT'S A KENTUCKY SMOOCH!
REMARKABLE FELLOWS, BOTH OF YOU...
I BELIEVE IT'S THAT ONE THERE, YES.

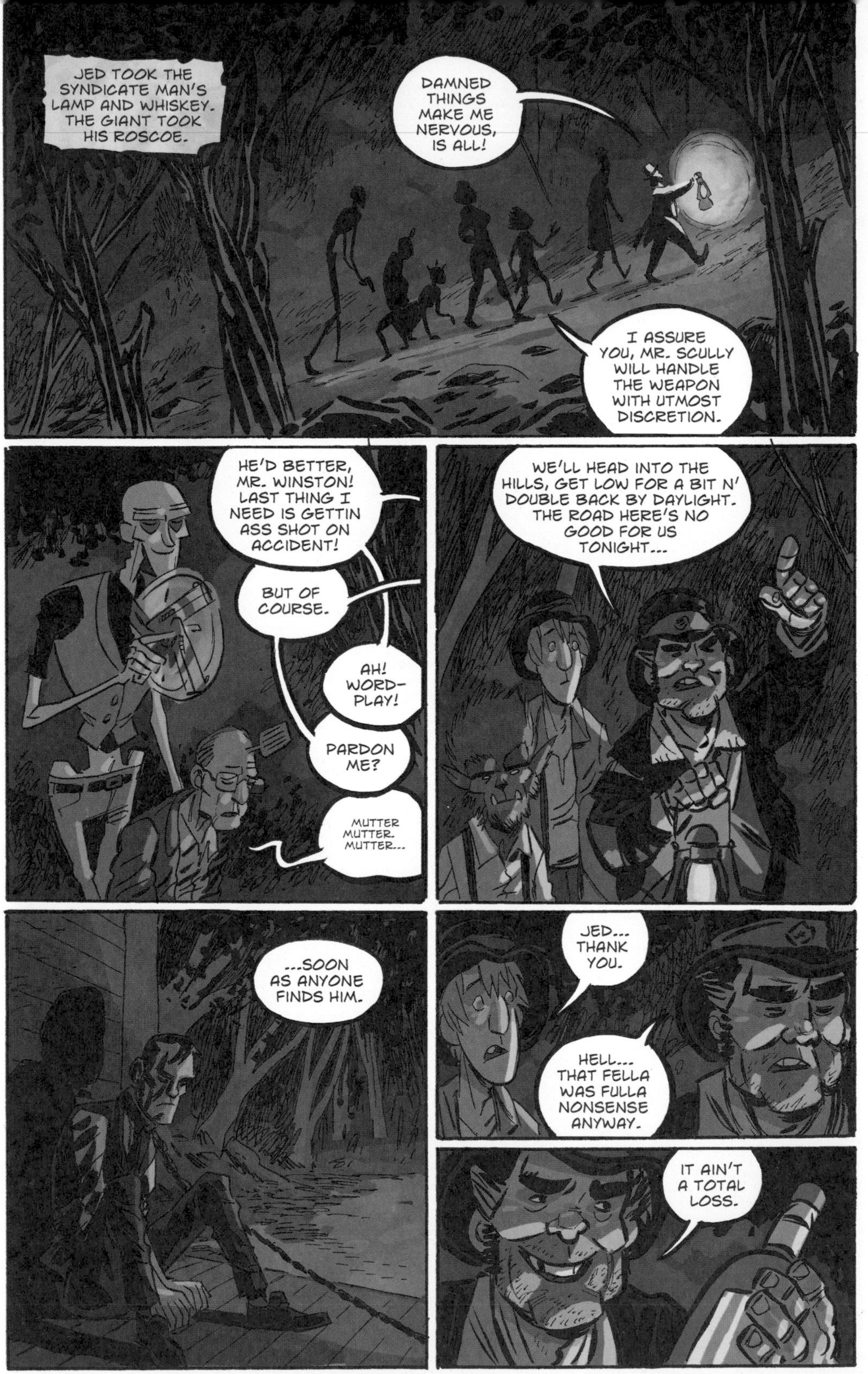
JED TOOK THE SYNDICATE MAN'S LAMP AND WHISKEY. THE GIANT TOOK HIS ROSCOE.
DAMNED THINGS MAKE ME NERVOUS, IS ALL!
I ASSURE YOU, MR. SCULLY WILL HANDLE THE WEAPON WITH UTMOST DISCRETION.
HE'D BETTER, MR. WINSTON! LAST THING I NEED IS GETTIN ASS SHOT ON ACCIDENT!
BUT OF COURSE.
AH! WORD-PLAY!
PARDON ME?
MUTTER MUTTER. MUTTER...
WE'LL HEAD INTO THE HILLS, GET LOW FOR A BIT N' DOUBLE BACK BY DAYLIGHT. THE ROAD HERE'S NO GOOD FOR US TONIGHT...
...SOON AS ANYONE FINDS HIM.
JED... THANK YOU.
HELL... THAT FELLA WAS FULLA NONSENSE ANYWAY.
IT AIN'T A TOTAL LOSS.

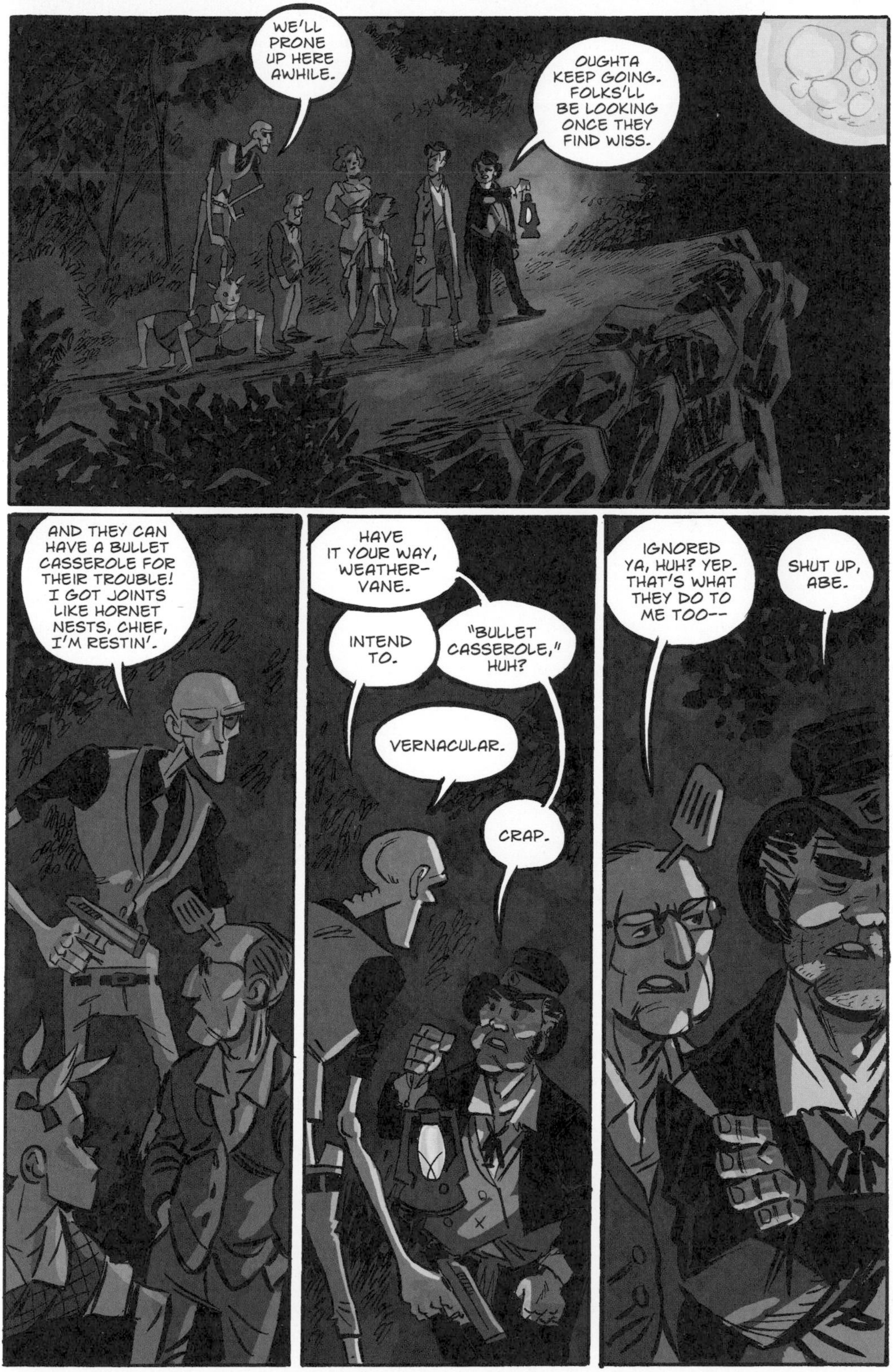
WE'LL PRONE UP HERE AWHILE.
OUGHTA KEEP GOING. FOLKS'LL BE LOOKING ONCE THEY FIND WISS.
AND THEY CAN HAVE A BULLET CASSEROLE FOR THEIR TROUBLE! I GOT JOINTS LIKE HORNET NESTS, CHIEF, I'M RESTIN'.
HAVE IT YOUR WAY, WEATHER-VANE.
INTEND TO.
"BULLET CASSEROLE," HUH?
VERNACULAR.
CRAP.
IGNORED YA, HUH? YEP. THAT'S WHAT THEY DO TO ME TOO--
SHUT UP, ABE.

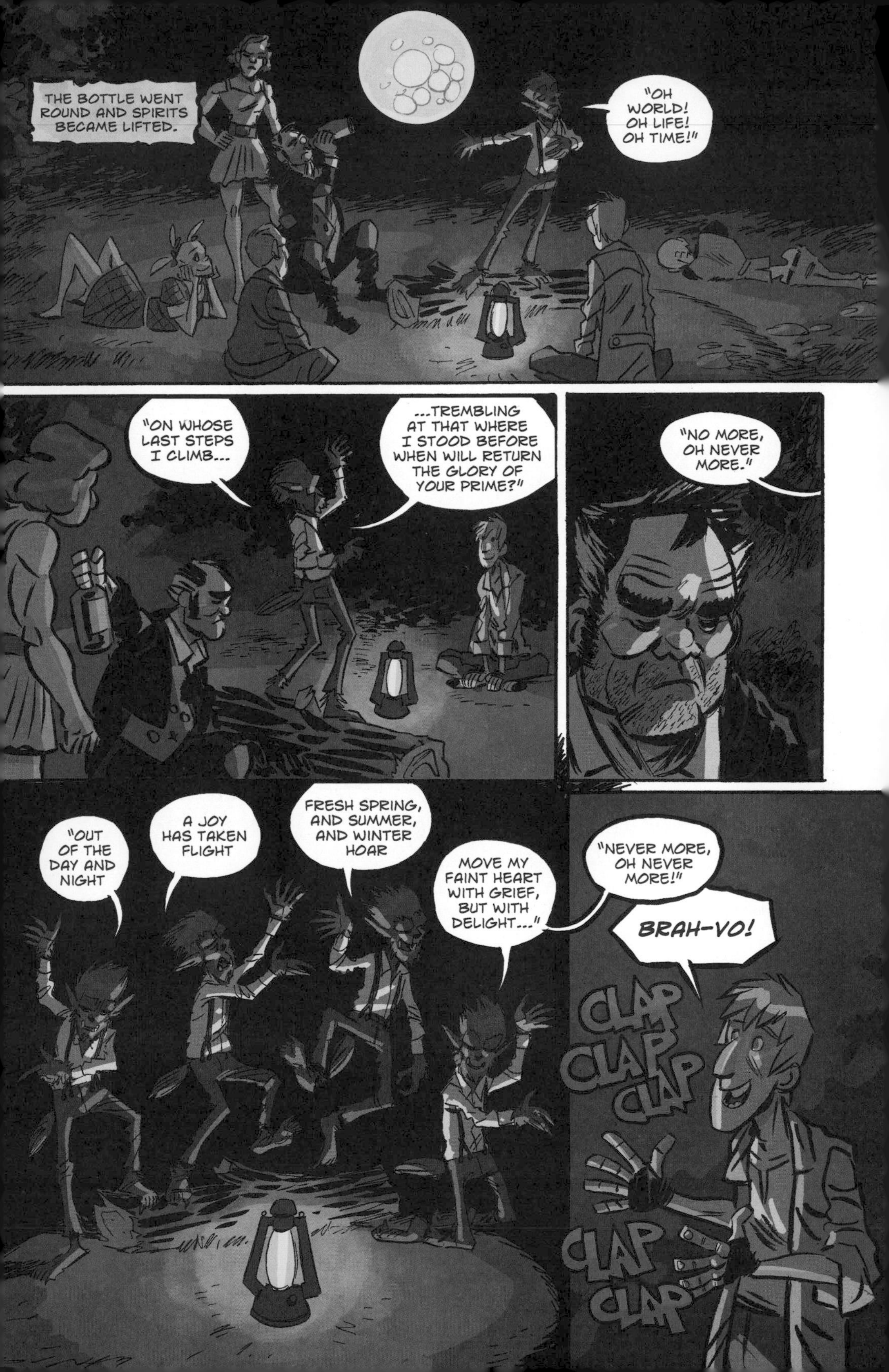
THE BOTTLE WENT ROUND AND SPIRITS BECAME LIFTED.
"OH WORLD! OH LIFE! OH TIME!"
"ON WHOSE LAST STEPS I CLIMB...
...TREMBLING AT THAT WHERE I STOOD BEFORE WHEN WILL RETURN THE GLORY OF YOUR PRIME?"
"NO MORE, OH NEVER MORE."
"OUT OF THE DAY AND NIGHT
A JOY HAS TAKEN FLIGHT
FRESH SPRING, AND SUMMER, AND WINTER HOAR
MOVE MY FAINT HEART WITH GRIEF, BUT WITH DELIGHT..."
"NEVER MORE, OH NEVER MORE!"
BRAH-VO!
CLAP CLAP CLAP
CLAP CLAP

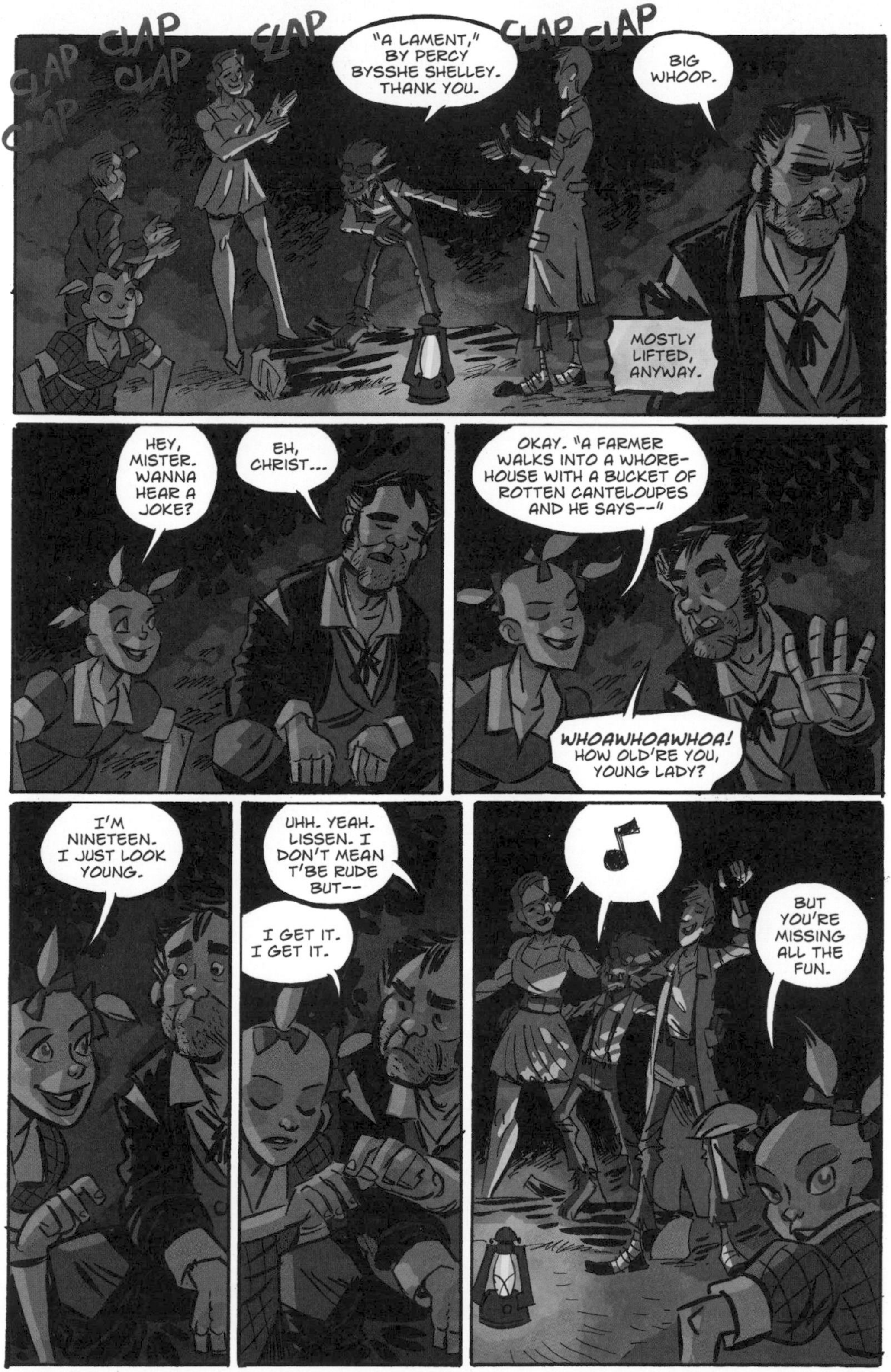
CLAP CLAP
CLAP CLAP
CLAP
"A LAMENT," BY PERCY BYSSHE SHELLEY. THANK YOU.
CLAP CLAP
BIG WHOOP.
MOSTLY LIFTED, ANYWAY.
HEY, MISTER. WANNA HEAR A JOKE?
EH, CHRIST...
OKAY. "A FARMER WALKS INTO A WHORE-HOUSE WITH A BUCKET OF ROTTEN CANTELOUPES AND HE SAYS--"
WHOAWHOAWHOA! HOW OLD'RE YOU, YOUNG LADY?
I'M NINETEEN. I JUST LOOK YOUNG.
UHH. YEAH. LISSEN. I DON'T MEAN T'BE RUDE BUT--
I GET IT. I GET IT.
BUT YOU'RE MISSING ALL THE FUN.

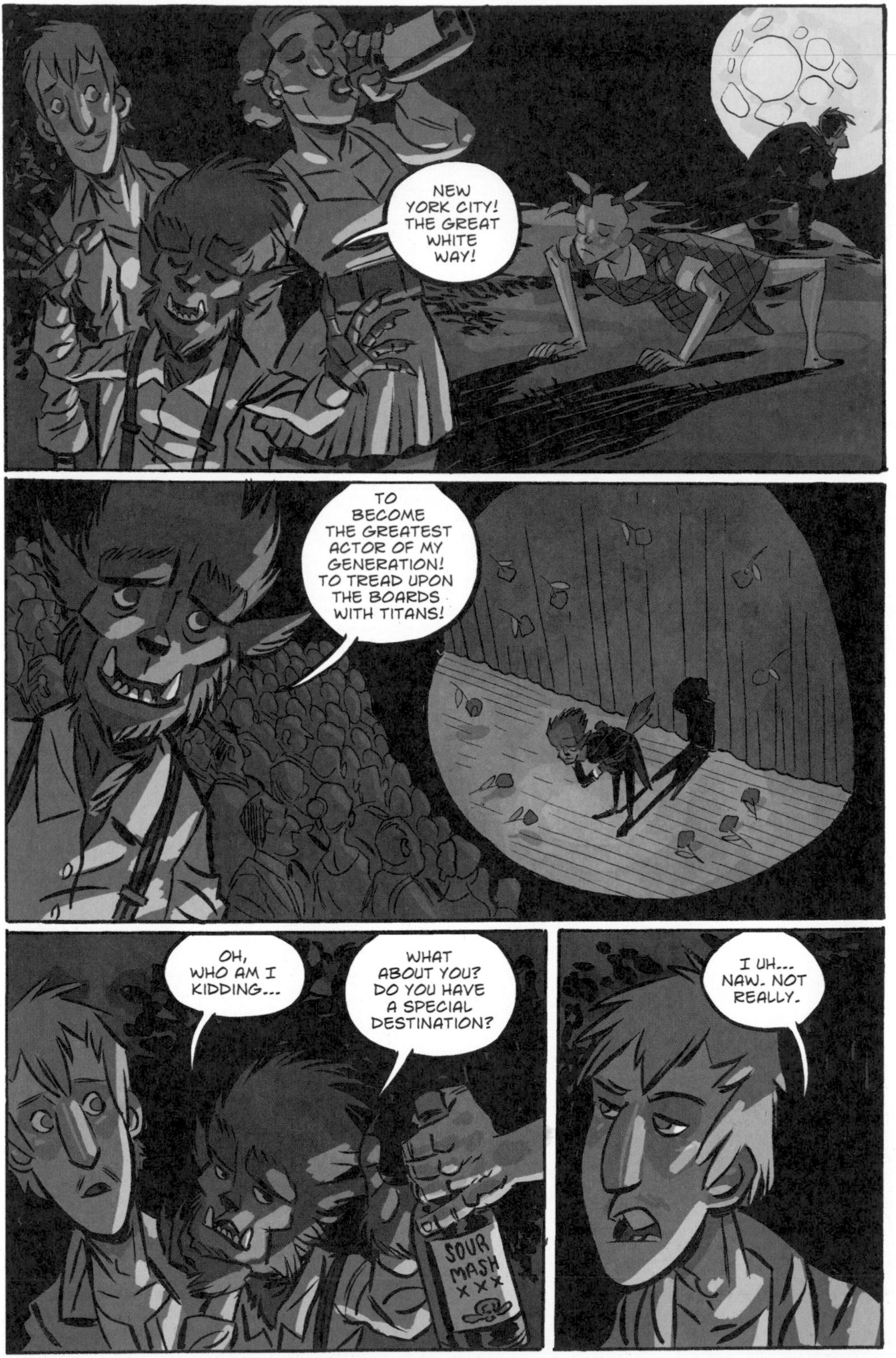
NEW YORK CITY! THE GREAT WHITE WAY!
TO BECOME THE GREATEST ACTOR OF MY GENERATION! TO TREAD UPON THE BOARDS WITH TITANS!
OH, WHO AM I KIDDING...
WHAT ABOUT YOU? DO YOU HAVE A SPECIAL DESTINATION?
SOUR MASH XXX
I UH... NAW. NOT REALLY.

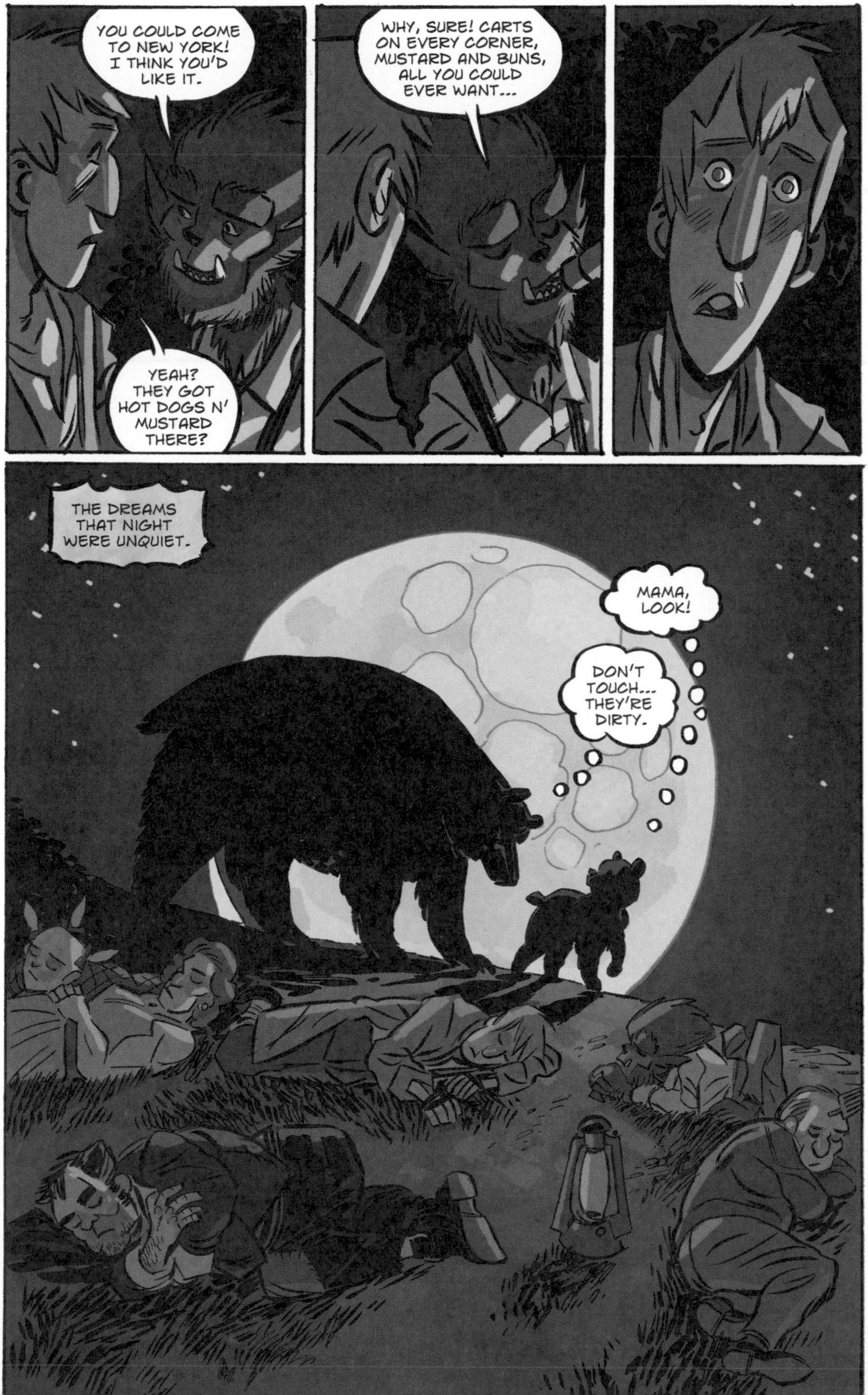
YOU COULD COME TO NEW YORK! I THINK YOU'D LIKE IT.
YEAH? THEY GOT HOT DOGS N' MUSTARD THERE?
WHY, SURE! CARTS ON EVERY CORNER, MUSTARD AND BUNS, ALL YOU COULD EVER WANT...
THE DREAMS THAT NIGHT WERE UNQUIET.
MAMA, LOOK!
DON'T TOUCH... THEY'RE DIRTY.

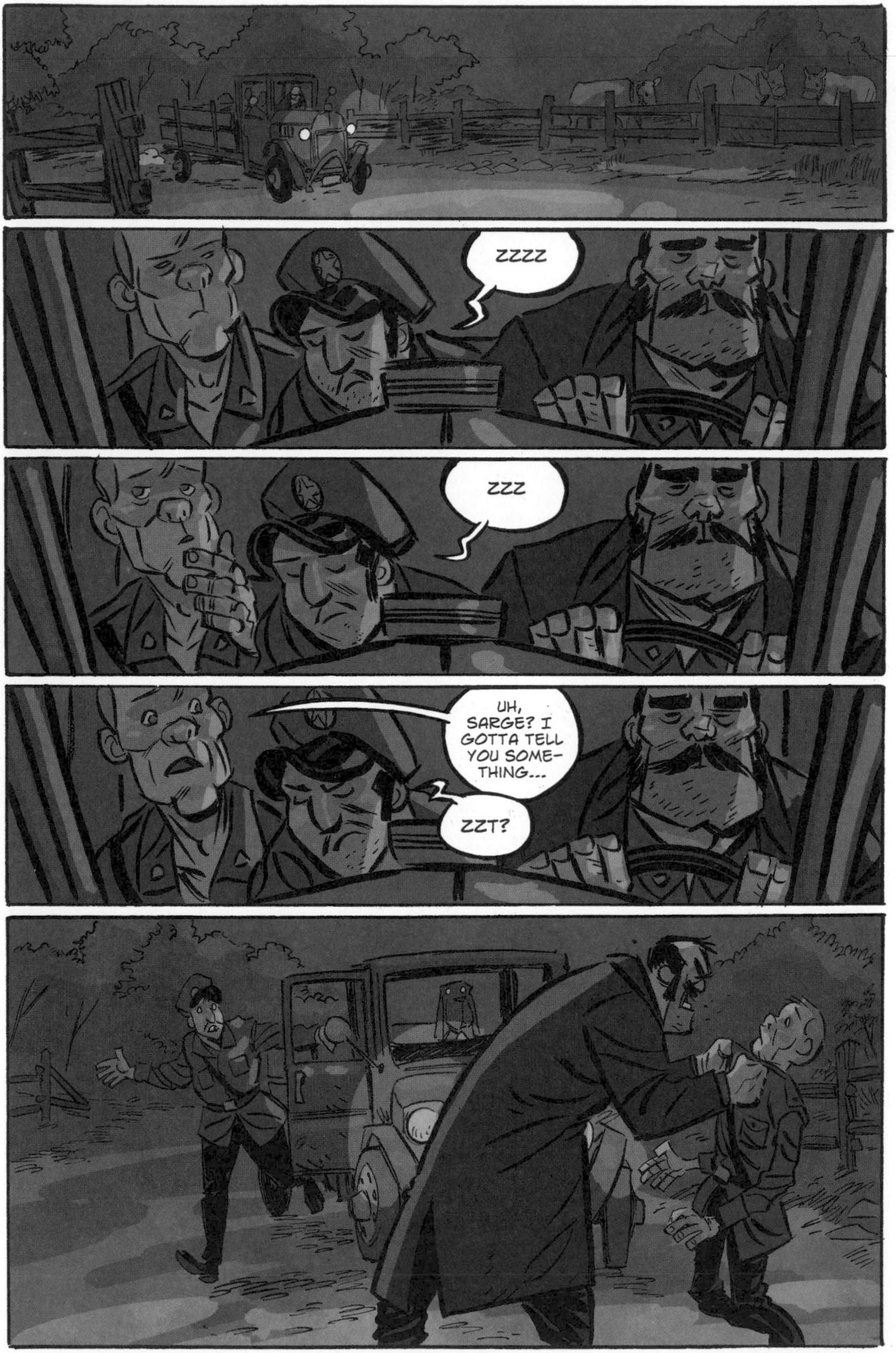
ZZZZ
ZZZ
UH, SARGE? I GOTTA TELL YOU SOME-THING...
ZZT?

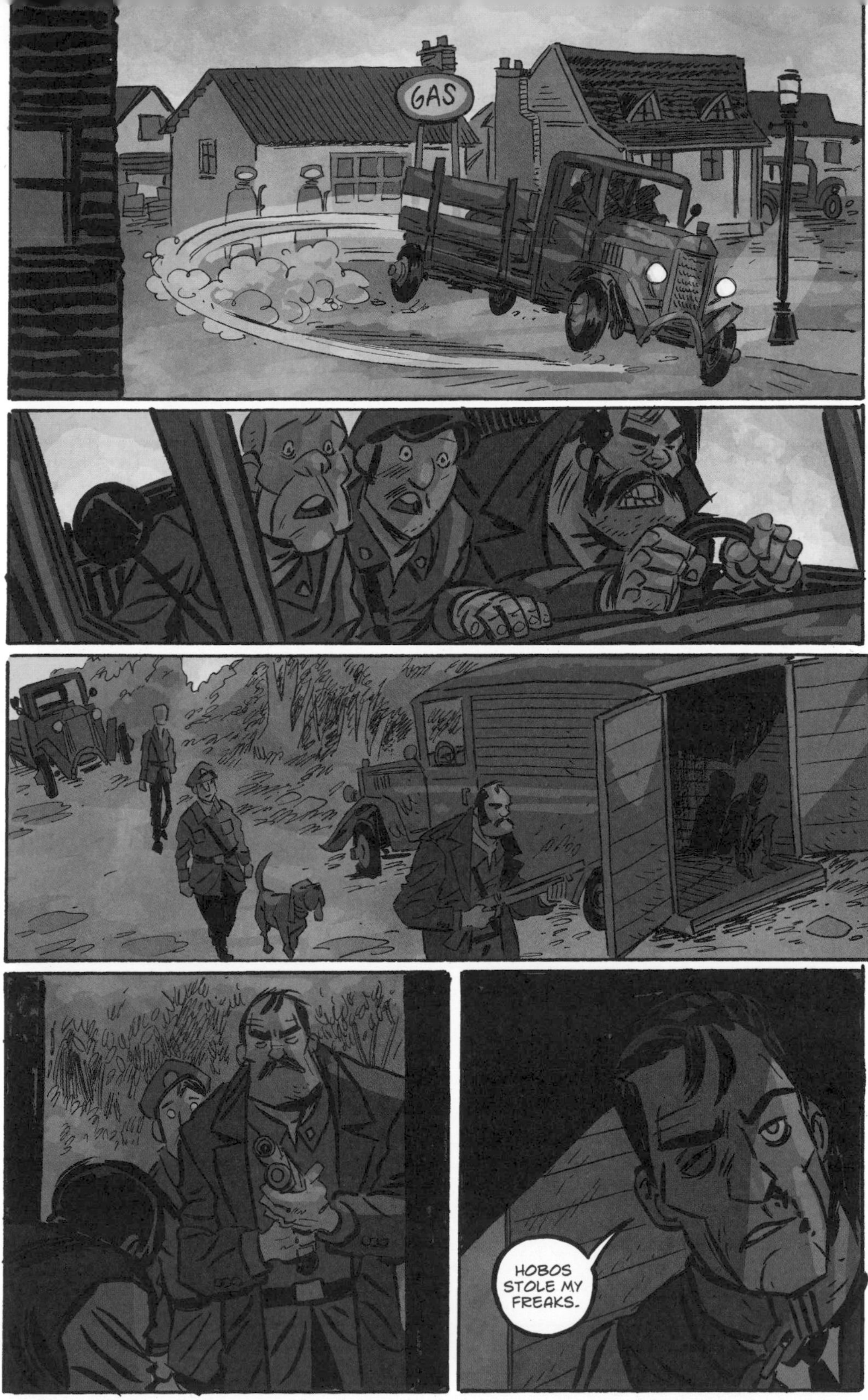
GAS
HOBOS STOLE MY FREAKS.

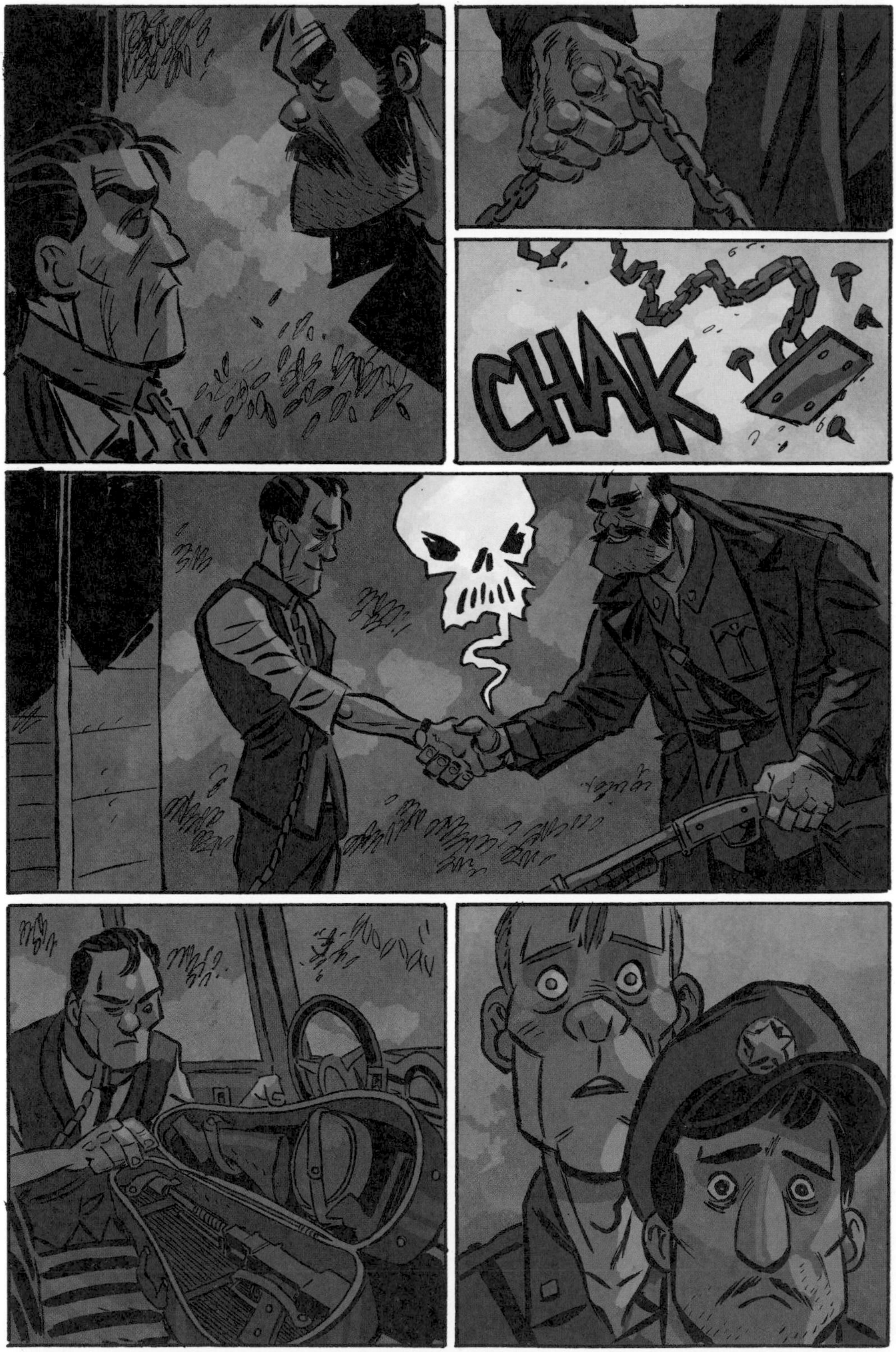
CHAK

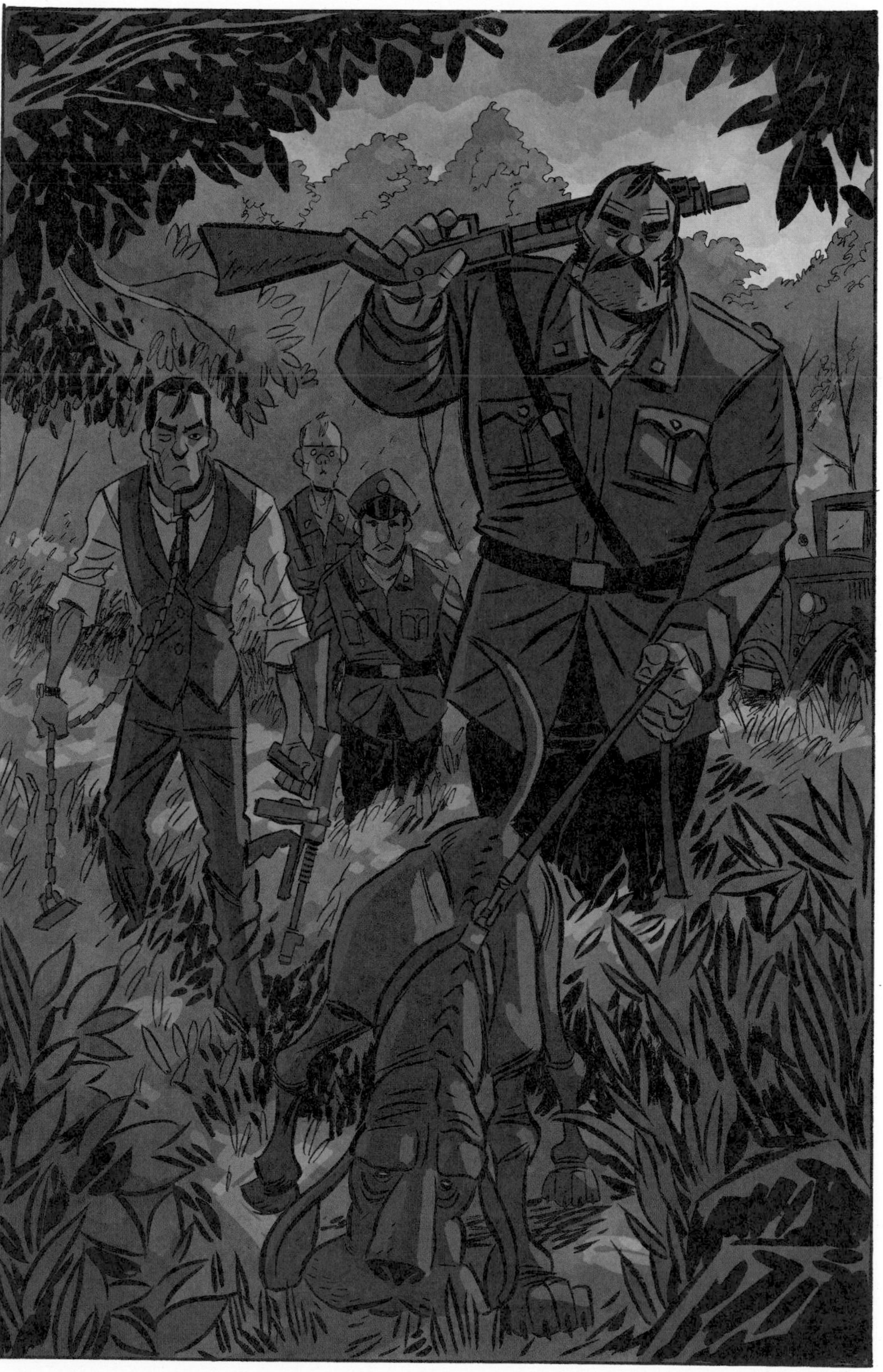

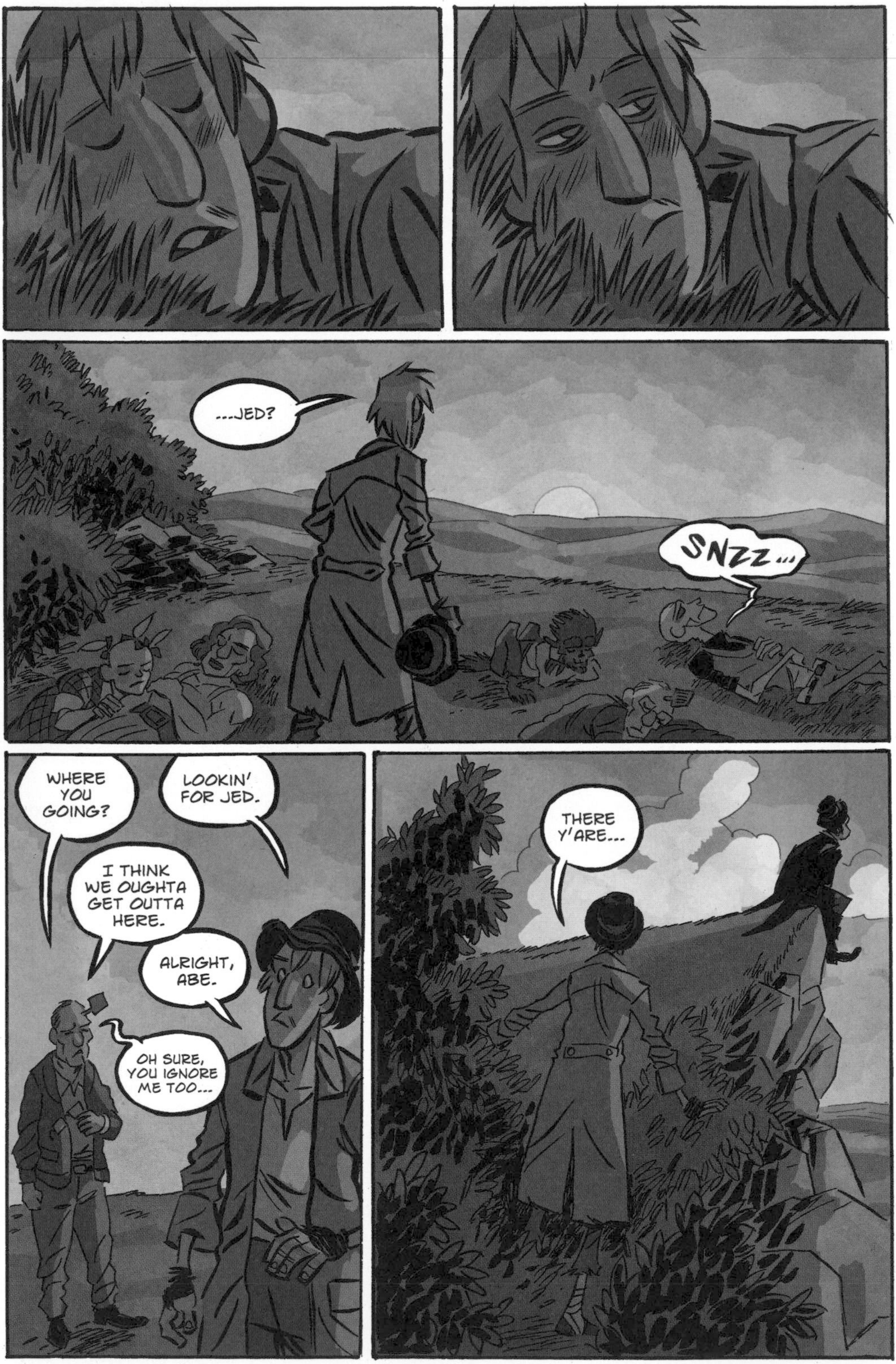
...JED?
SNZZ...
WHERE YOU GOING?
LOOKIN' FOR JED.
I THINK WE OUGHTA GET OUTTA HERE.
ALRIGHT, ABE.
OH SURE, YOU IGNORE ME TOO...
THERE Y'ARE...

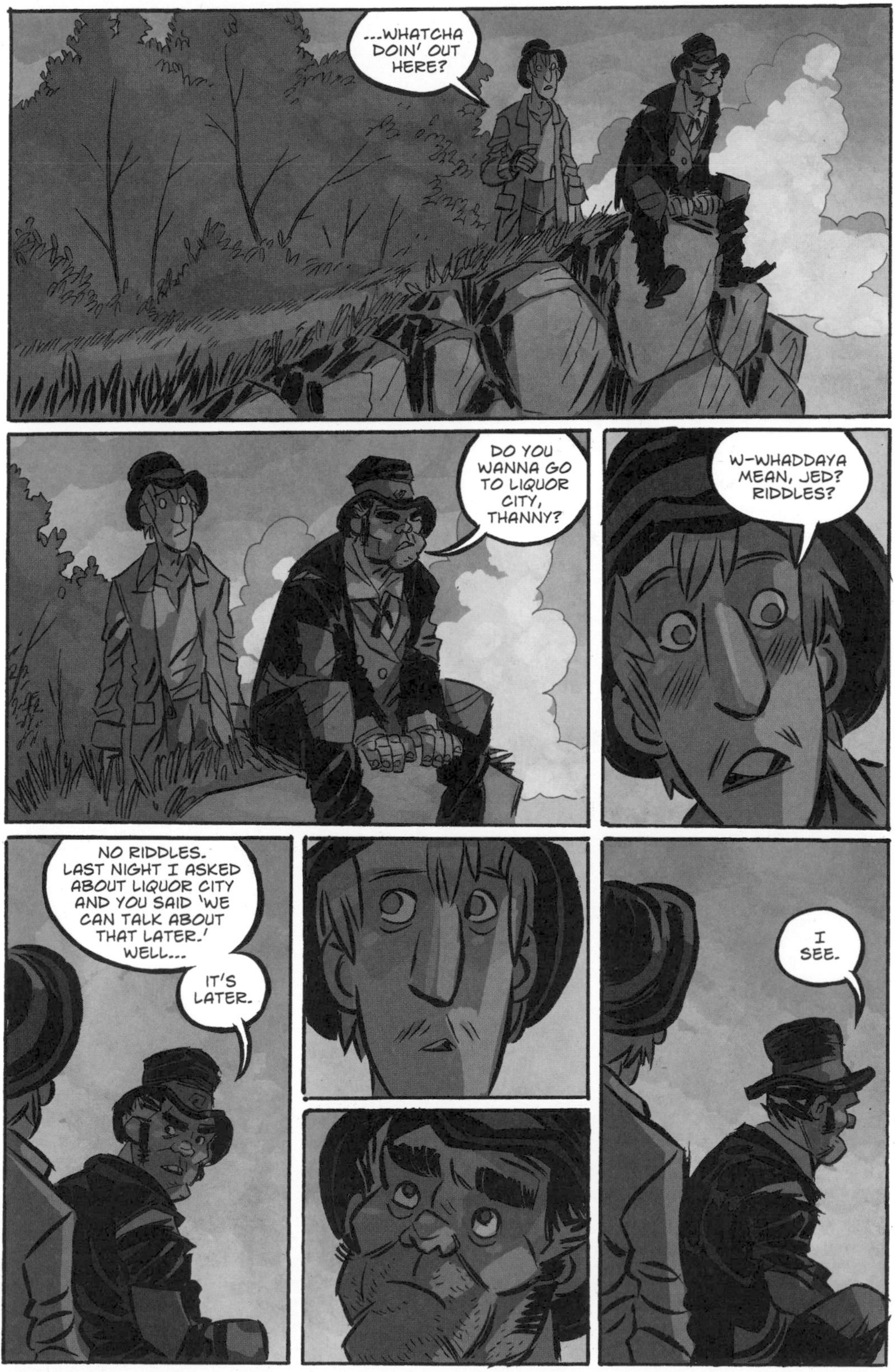
...WHATCHA DOIN' OUT HERE?
DO YOU WANNA GO TO LIQUOR CITY, THANNY?
W-WHADDAYA MEAN, JED? RIDDLES?
NO RIDDLES. LAST NIGHT I ASKED ABOUT LIQUOR CITY AND YOU SAID 'WE CAN TALK ABOUT THAT LATER.' WELL...
IT'S LATER.
I SEE.

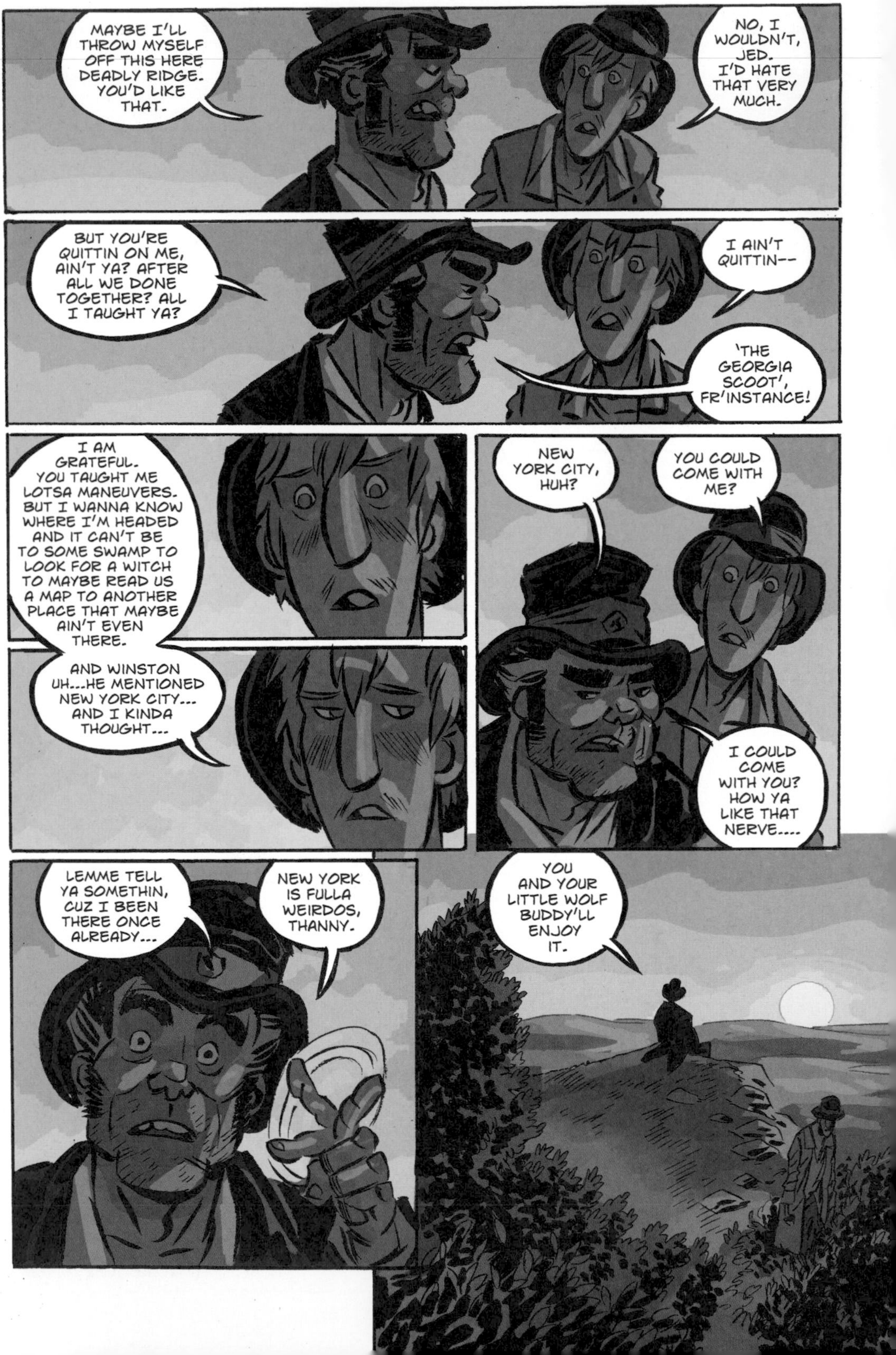
MAYBE I'LL THROW MYSELF OFF THIS HERE DEADLY RIDGE. YOU'D LIKE THAT.
NO, I WOULDN'T, JED. I'D HATE THAT VERY MUCH.
BUT YOU'RE QUITTIN ON ME, AIN'T YA? AFTER ALL WE DONE TOGETHER? ALL I TAUGHT YA?
I AIN'T QUITTIN--
'THE GEORGIA SCOOT', FR'INSTANCE!
I AM GRATEFUL. YOU TAUGHT ME LOTSA MANEUVERS. BUT I WANNA KNOW WHERE I'M HEADED AND IT CAN'T BE TO SOME SWAMP TO LOOK FOR A WITCH TO MAYBE READ US A MAP TO ANOTHER PLACE THAT MAYBE AIN'T EVEN THERE.
AND WINSTON UH...HE MENTIONED NEW YORK CITY... AND I KINDA THOUGHT...
NEW YORK CITY, HUH?
YOU COULD COME WITH ME?
I COULD COME WITH YOU? HOW YA LIKE THAT NERVE....
LEMME TELL YA SOMETHIN, CUZ I BEEN THERE ONCE ALREADY...
NEW YORK IS FULLA WEIRDOS, THANNY.
YOU AND YOUR LITTLE WOLF BUDDY'LL ENJOY IT.

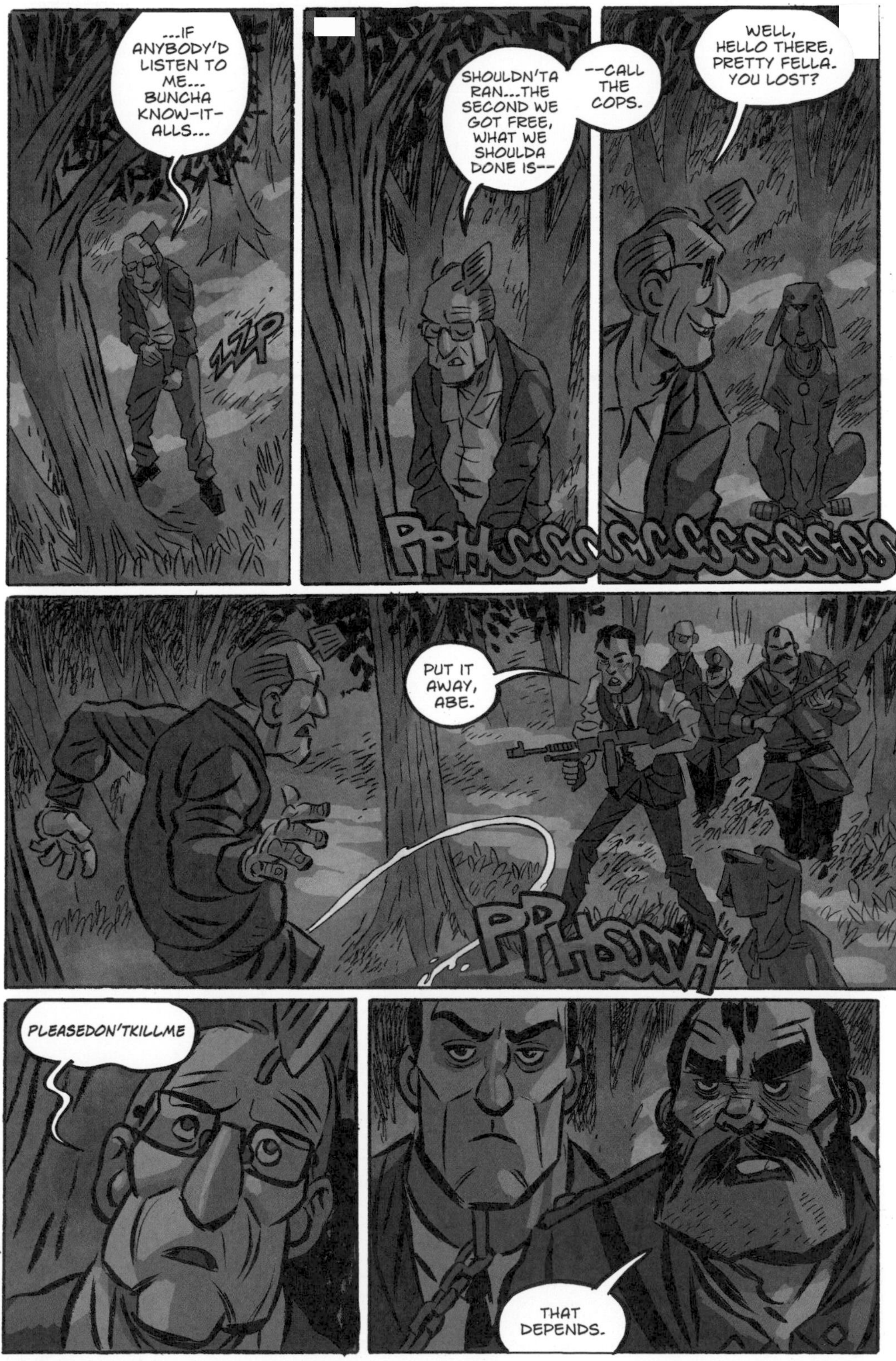

...IF ANYBODY'D LISTEN TO ME... BUNCHA KNOW-IT-ALLS...
ZZZIP
SHOULDN'TA RAN...THE SECOND WE GOT FREE, WHAT WE SHOULDA DONE IS--
--CALL THE COPS.
WELL, HELLO THERE, PRETTY FELLA. YOU LOST?
PPHSSSSSSSSSSSSSS
PUT IT AWAY, ABE.
PPHSSSH
PLEASEDON'TKILLME
THAT DEPENDS.

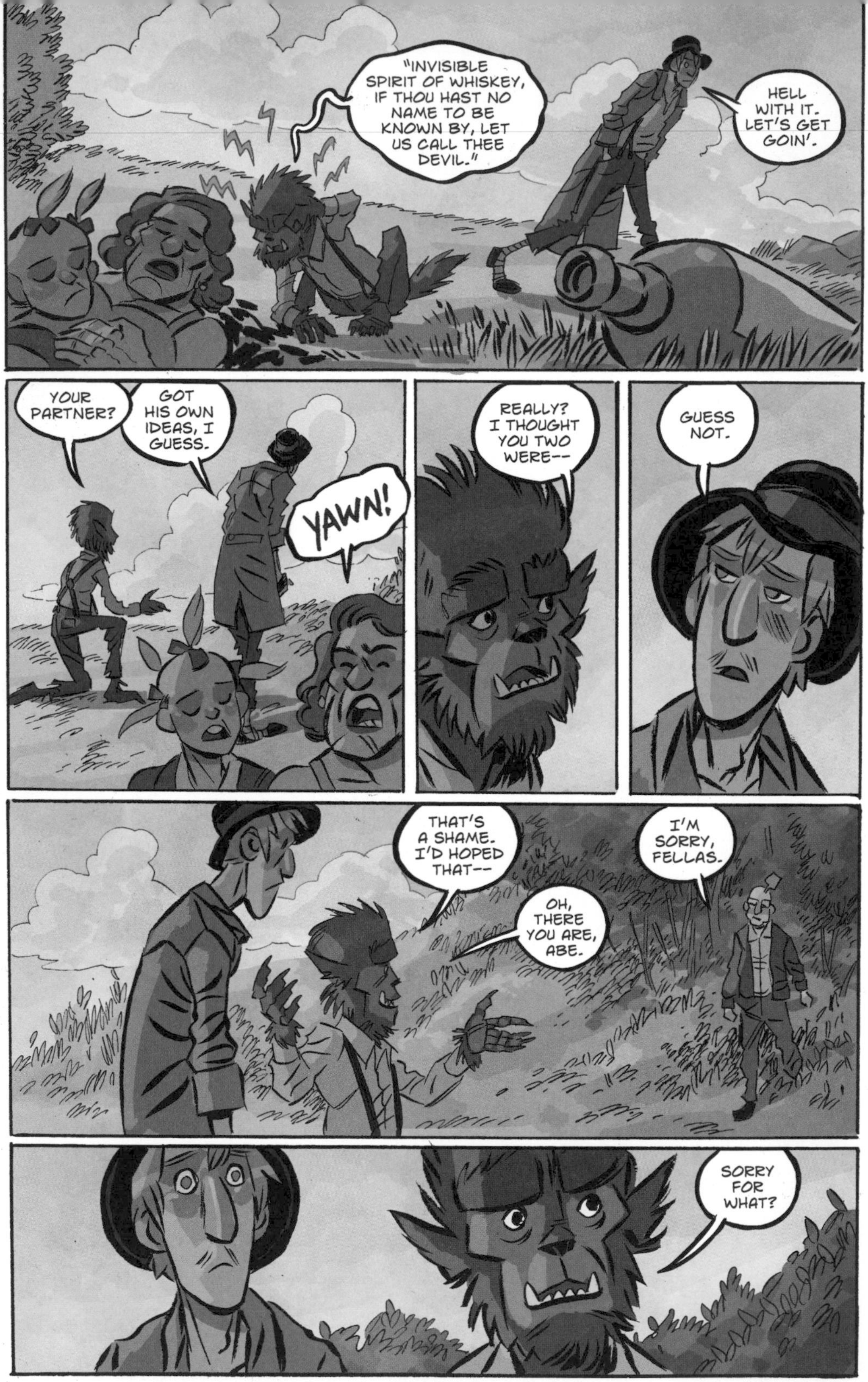
"INVISIBLE SPIRIT OF WHISKEY, IF THOU HAST NO NAME TO BE KNOWN BY, LET US CALL THEE DEVIL."
HELL WITH IT. LET'S GET GOIN'.
YOUR PARTNER?
GOT HIS OWN IDEAS, I GUESS.
YAWN!
REALLY? I THOUGHT YOU TWO WERE--
GUESS NOT.
THAT'S A SHAME. I'D HOPED THAT--
OH, THERE YOU ARE, ABE.
I'M SORRY, FELLAS.
SORRY FOR WHAT?

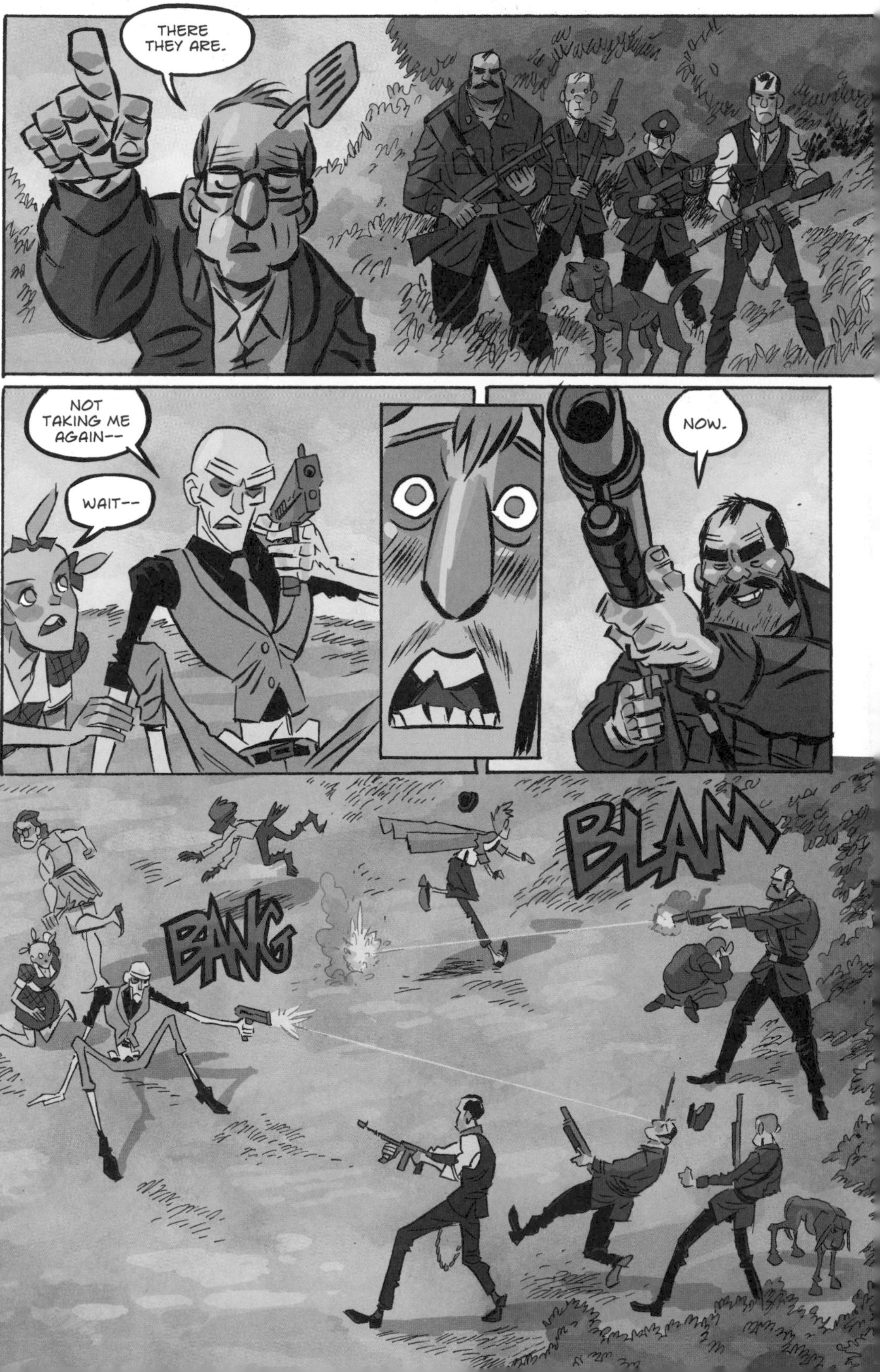
THERE THEY ARE.
NOT TAKING ME AGAIN--
WAIT--
NOW.
BLAM
BANG

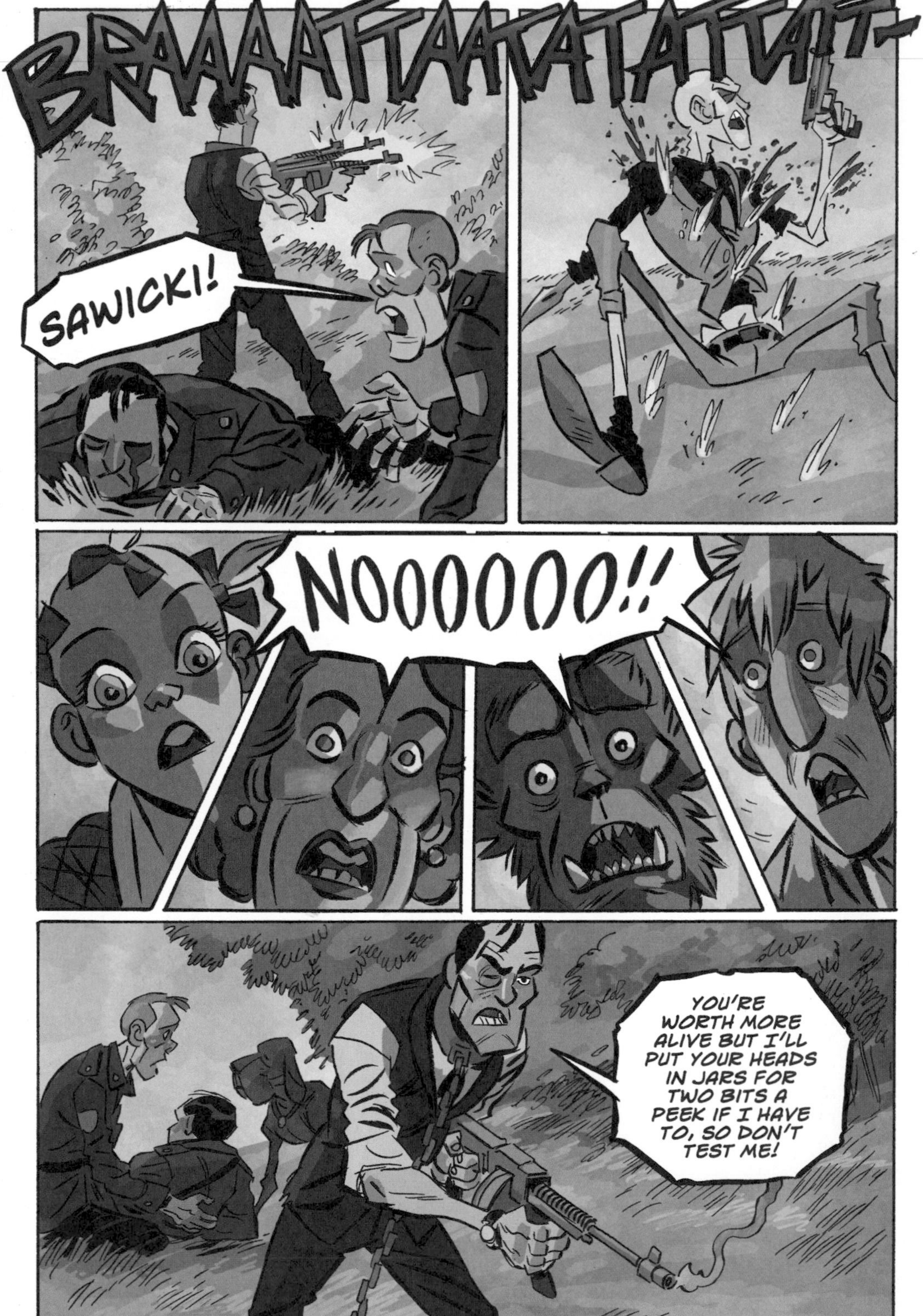
BRAAAATTAAKATATTATT-
SAWICKI!
NOOOOOO!!
YOU'RE WORTH MORE ALIVE BUT I'LL PUT YOUR HEADS IN JARS FOR TWO BITS A PEEK IF I HAVE TO, SO DON'T TEST ME!

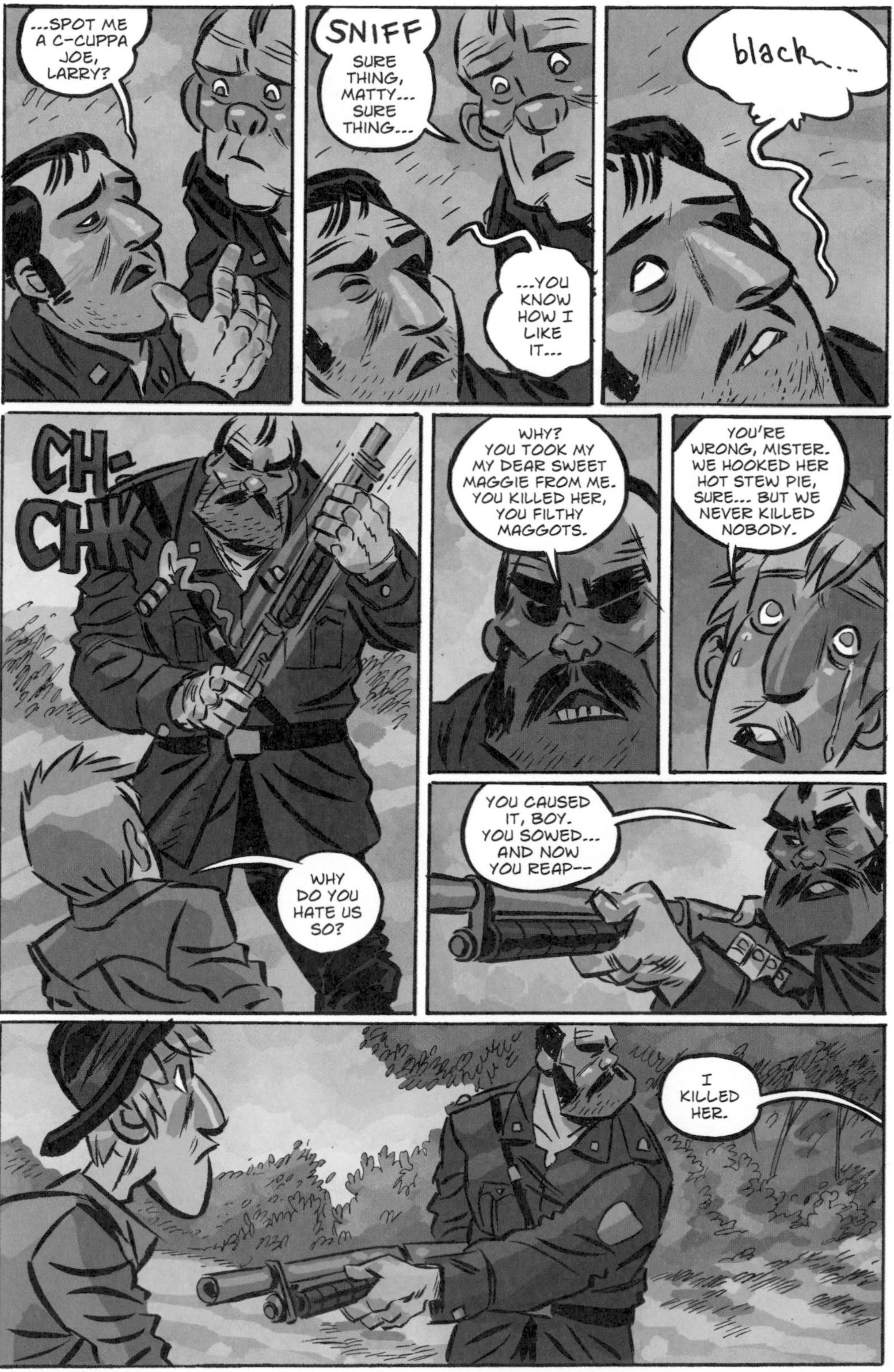
...SPOT ME A C-CUPPA JOE, LARRY?
SNIFF
SURE THING, MATTY... SURE THING...
...YOU KNOW HOW I LIKE IT...
black...
CH-CHK
WHY? YOU TOOK MY MY DEAR SWEET MAGGIE FROM ME. YOU KILLED HER, YOU FILTHY MAGGOTS.
YOU'RE WRONG, MISTER. WE HOOKED HER HOT STEW PIE, SURE... BUT WE NEVER KILLED NOBODY.
WHY DO YOU HATE US SO?
YOU CAUSED IT, BOY. YOU SOWED... AND NOW YOU REAP--
I KILLED HER.

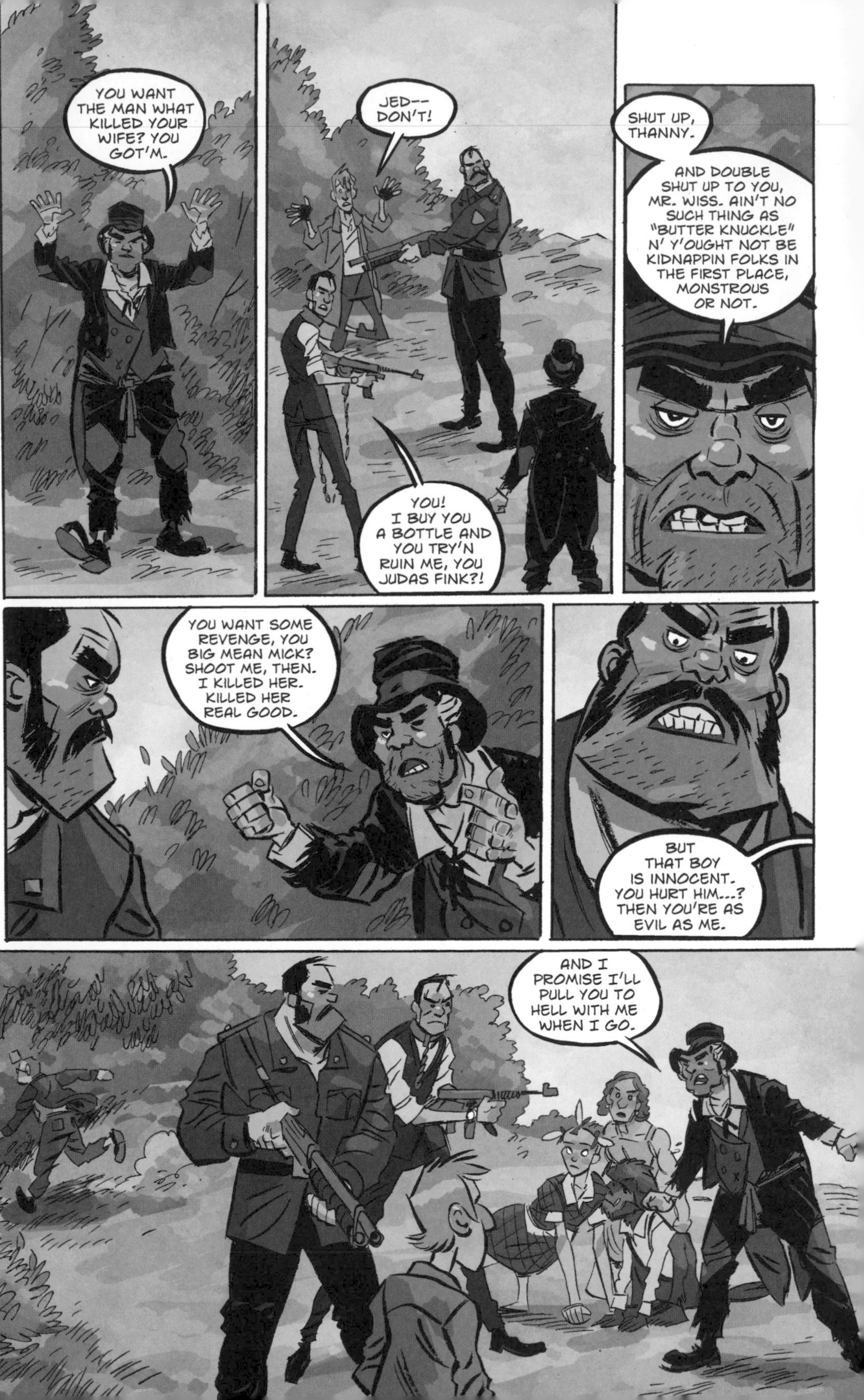
YOU WANT THE MAN WHAT KILLED YOUR WIFE? YOU GOT'M.
JED-- DON'T!
YOU! I BUY YOU A BOTTLE AND YOU TRY'N RUIN ME, YOU JUDAS FINK?!
SHUT UP, THANNY.
AND DOUBLE SHUT UP TO YOU, MR. WISS. AIN'T NO SUCH THING AS "BUTTER KNUCKLE" N' Y'OUGHT NOT BE KIDNAPPIN FOLKS IN THE FIRST PLACE, MONSTROUS OR NOT.
YOU WANT SOME REVENGE, YOU BIG MEAN MICK? SHOOT ME, THEN. I KILLED HER. KILLED HER REAL GOOD.
BUT THAT BOY IS INNOCENT. YOU HURT HIM...? THEN YOU'RE AS EVIL AS ME.
AND I PROMISE I'LL PULL YOU TO HELL WITH ME WHEN I GO.

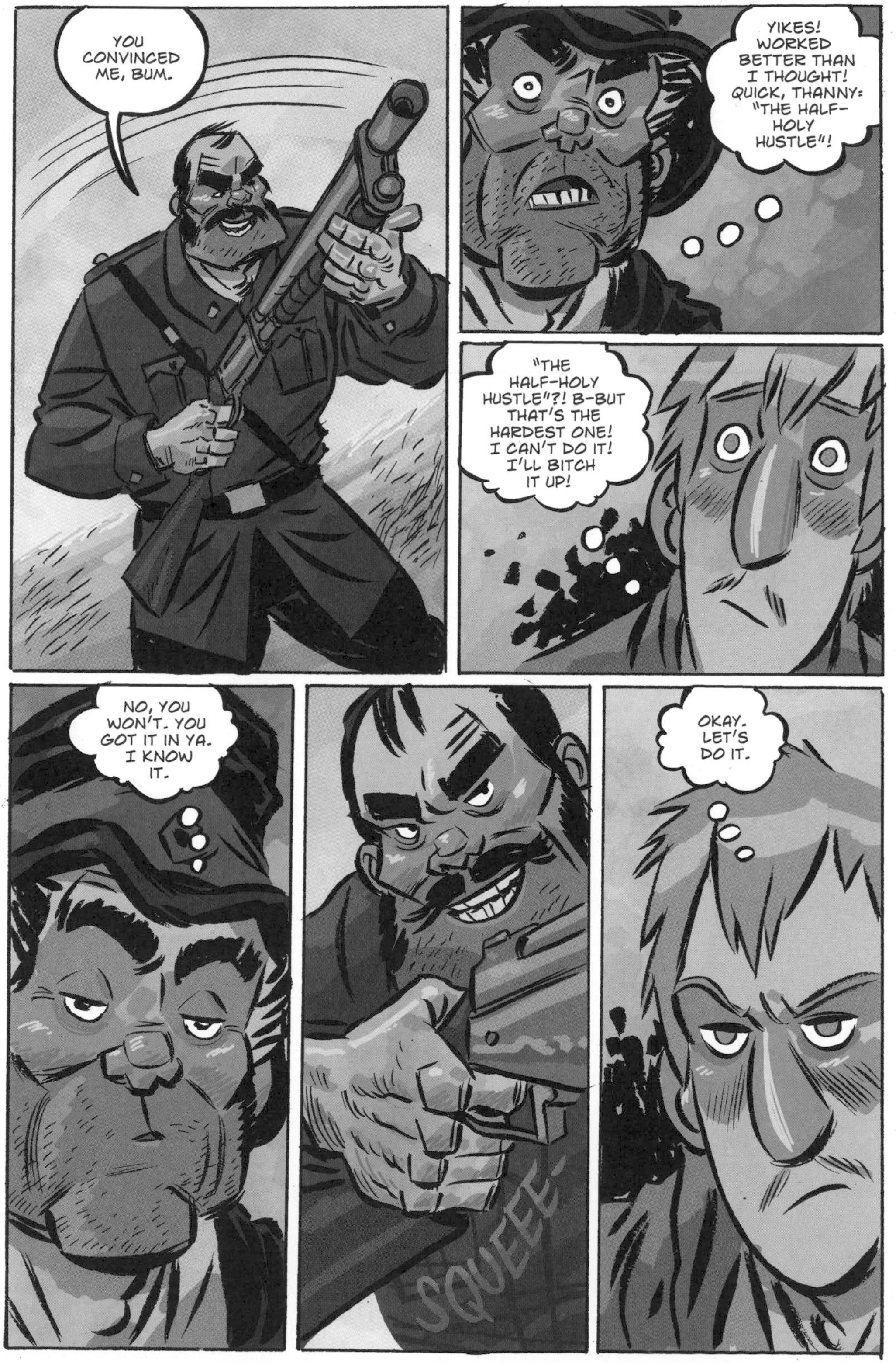
YOU CONVINCED ME, BUM.
YIKES! WORKED BETTER THAN I THOUGHT! QUICK, THANNY: "THE HALF-HOLY HUSTLE"!
"THE HALF-HOLY HUSTLE"?! B-BUT THAT'S THE HARDEST ONE! I CAN'T DO IT! I'LL BITCH IT UP!
NO, YOU WON'T. YOU GOT IT IN YA. I KNOW IT.
SQUEEE-
OKAY. LET'S DO IT.

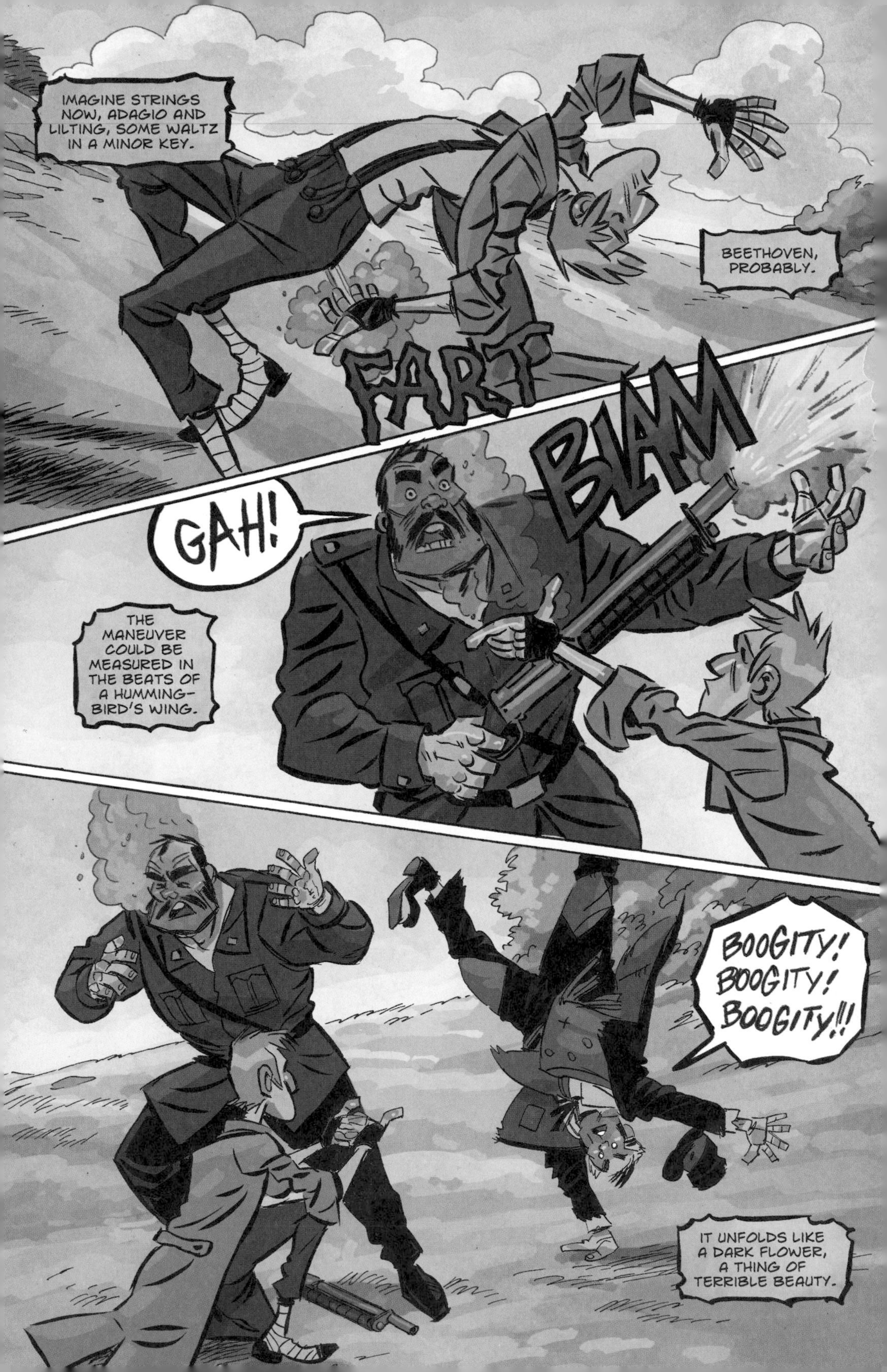
IMAGINE STRINGS NOW, ADAGIO AND LILTING, SOME WALTZ IN A MINOR KEY.
BEETHOVEN, PROBABLY.
FART
BLAM
GAH!
THE MANEUVER COULD BE MEASURED IN THE BEATS OF A HUMMING-BIRD'S WING.
BOOGITY! BOOGITY! BOOGITY!!!
IT UNFOLDS LIKE A DARK FLOWER, A THING OF TERRIBLE BEAUTY.

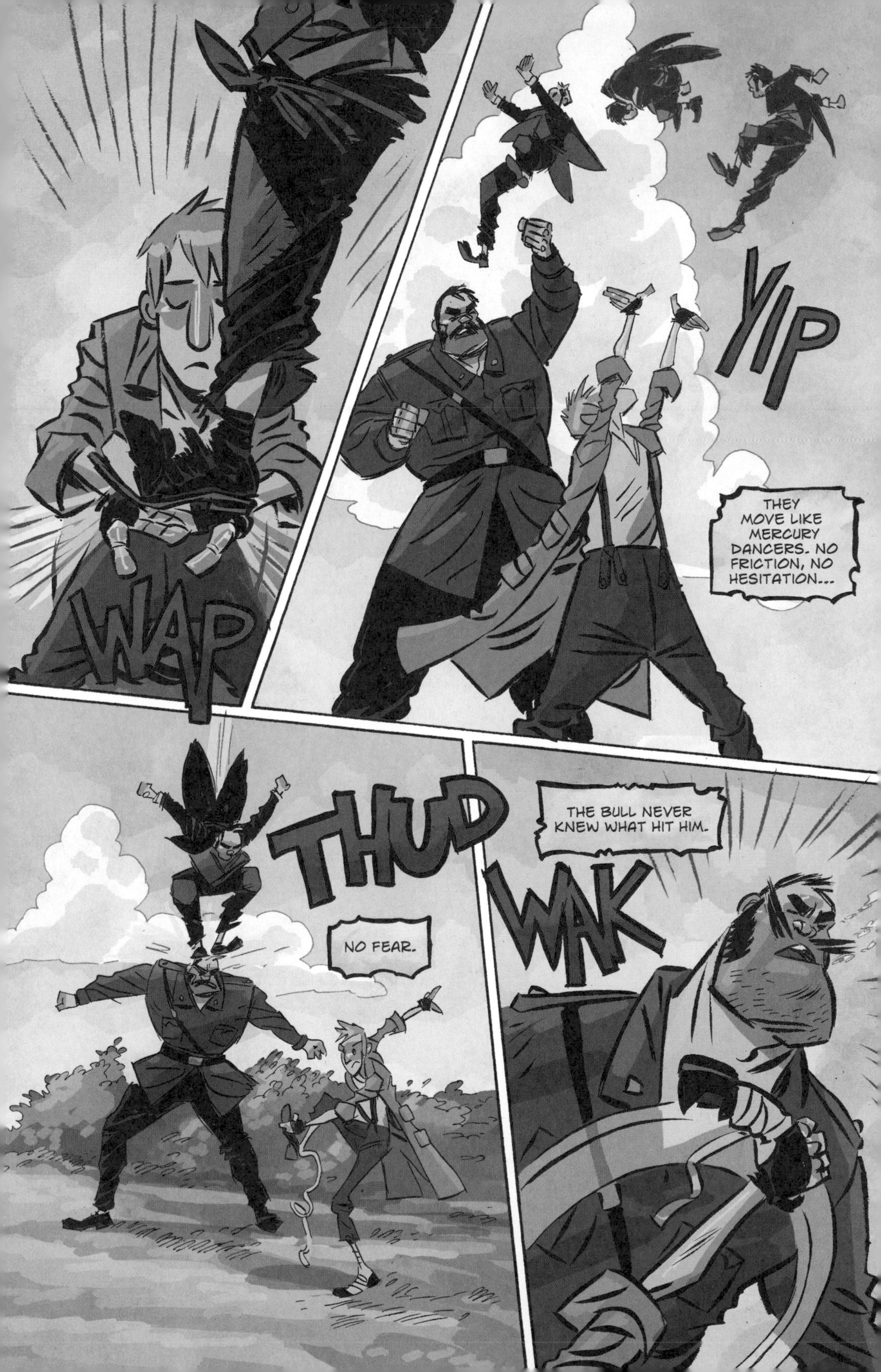
WAP
YIP
THEY MOVE LIKE MERCURY DANCERS. NO FRICTION, NO HESITATION...
THUD
NO FEAR.
THE BULL NEVER KNEW WHAT HIT HIM.
WAK

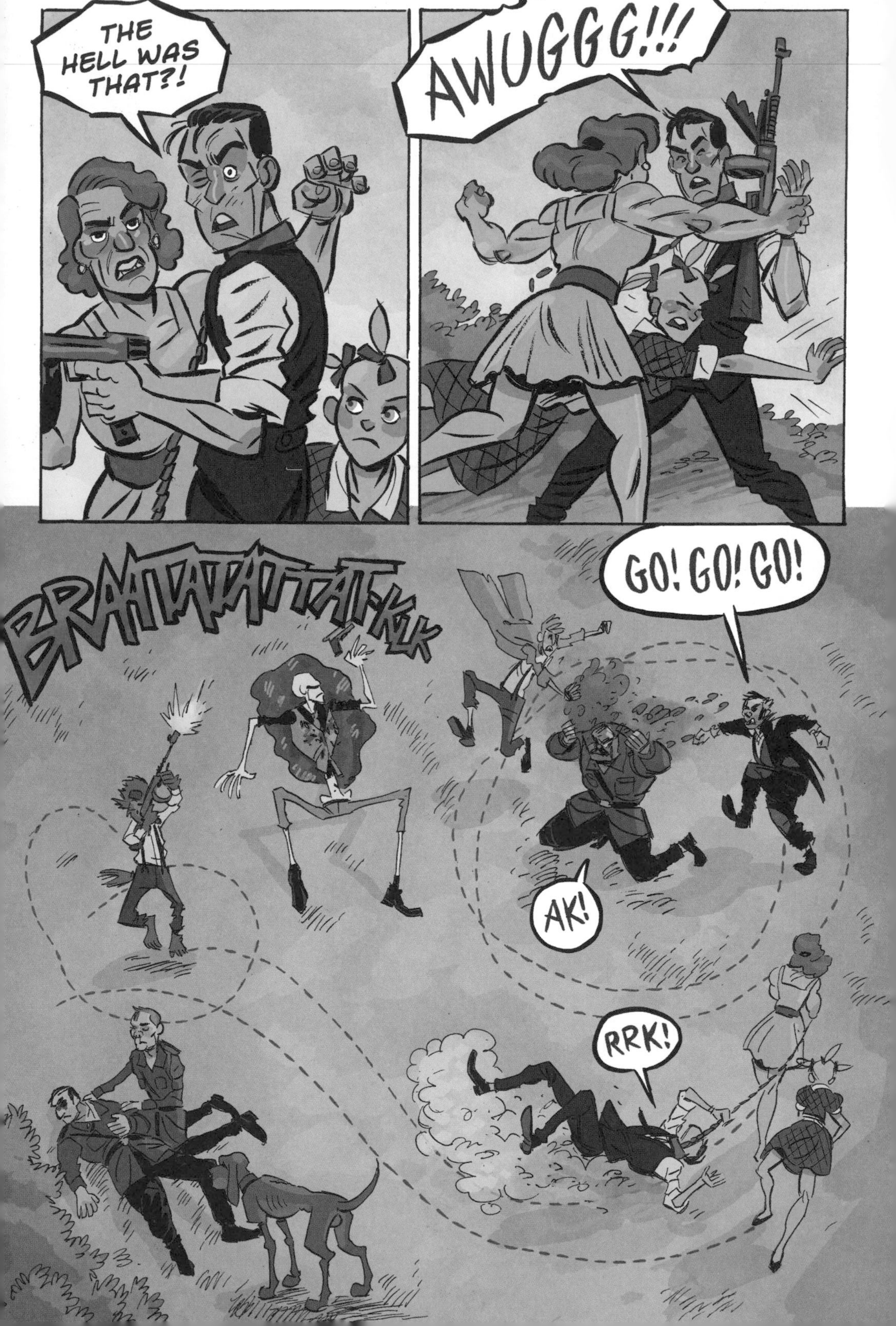
THE HELL WAS THAT?!
AWUGGG!!!
BRAATATATTATATKLIK
GO! GO! GO!
AK!
RRK!

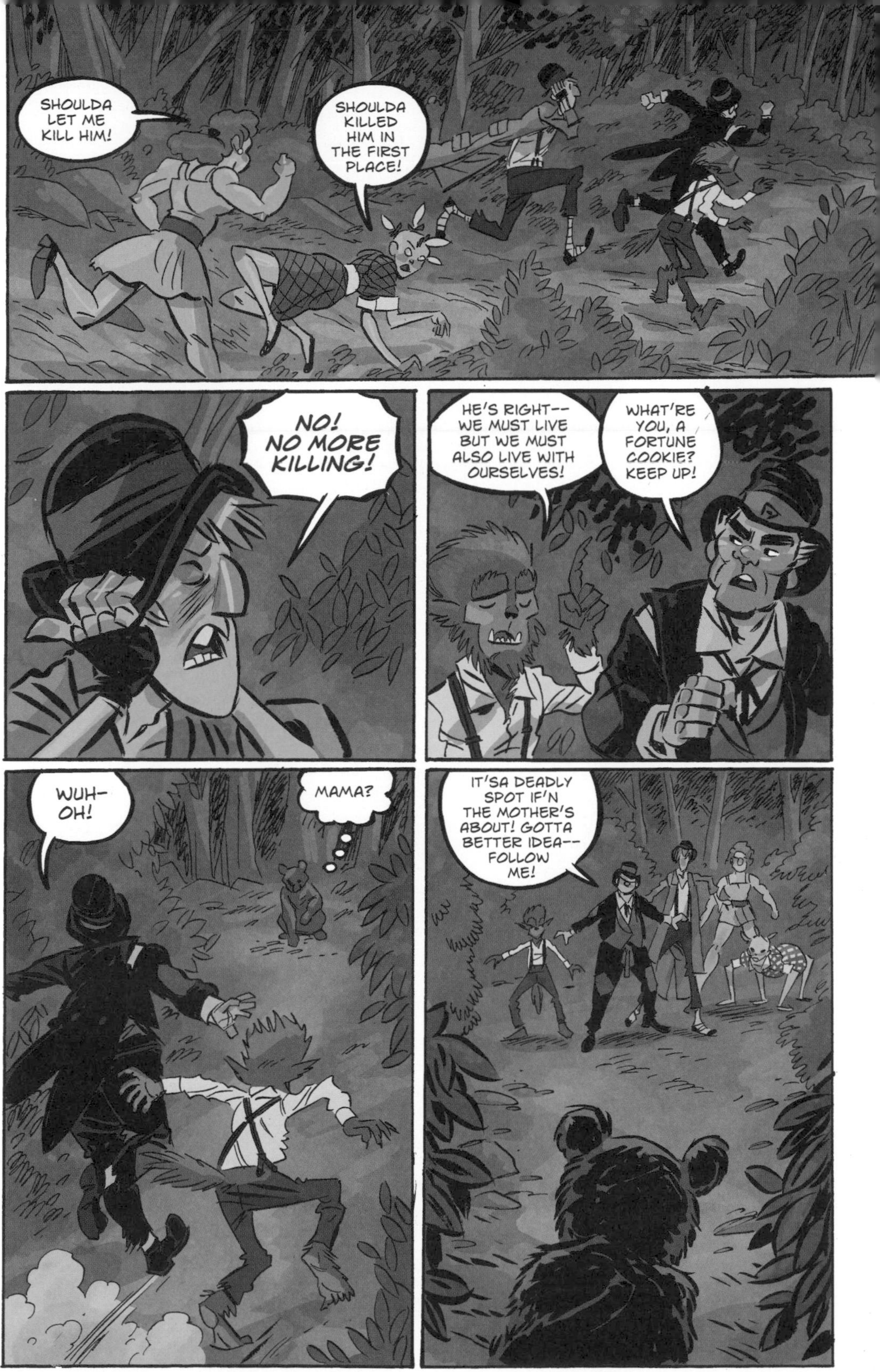
SHOULDA LET ME KILL HIM!
SHOULDA KILLED HIM IN THE FIRST PLACE!
NO! NO MORE KILLING!
HE'S RIGHT-- WE MUST LIVE BUT WE MUST ALSO LIVE WITH OURSELVES!
WHAT'RE YOU, A FORTUNE COOKIE? KEEP UP!
WUH-OH!
MAMA?
IT'SA DEADLY SPOT IF'N THE MOTHER'S ABOUT! GOTTA BETTER IDEA-- FOLLOW ME!

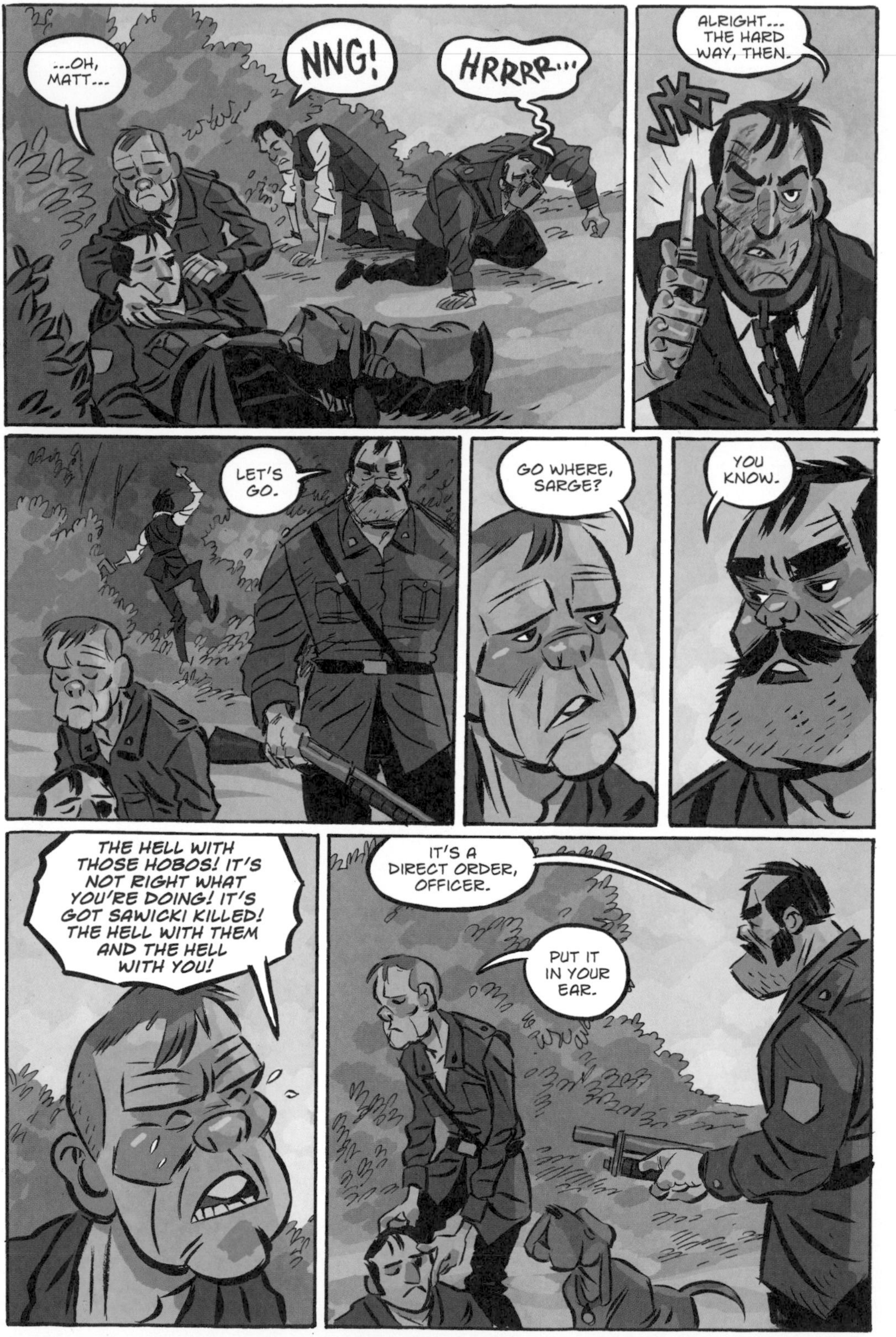
...OH, MATT...
NNG!
HRRRR...
ALRIGHT... THE HARD WAY, THEN.
LET'S GO.
GO WHERE, SARGE?
YOU KNOW.
THE HELL WITH THOSE HOBOS! IT'S NOT RIGHT WHAT YOU'RE DOING! IT'S GOT SAWICKI KILLED! THE HELL WITH THEM AND THE HELL WITH YOU!
IT'S A DIRECT ORDER, OFFICER.
PUT IT IN YOUR EAR.

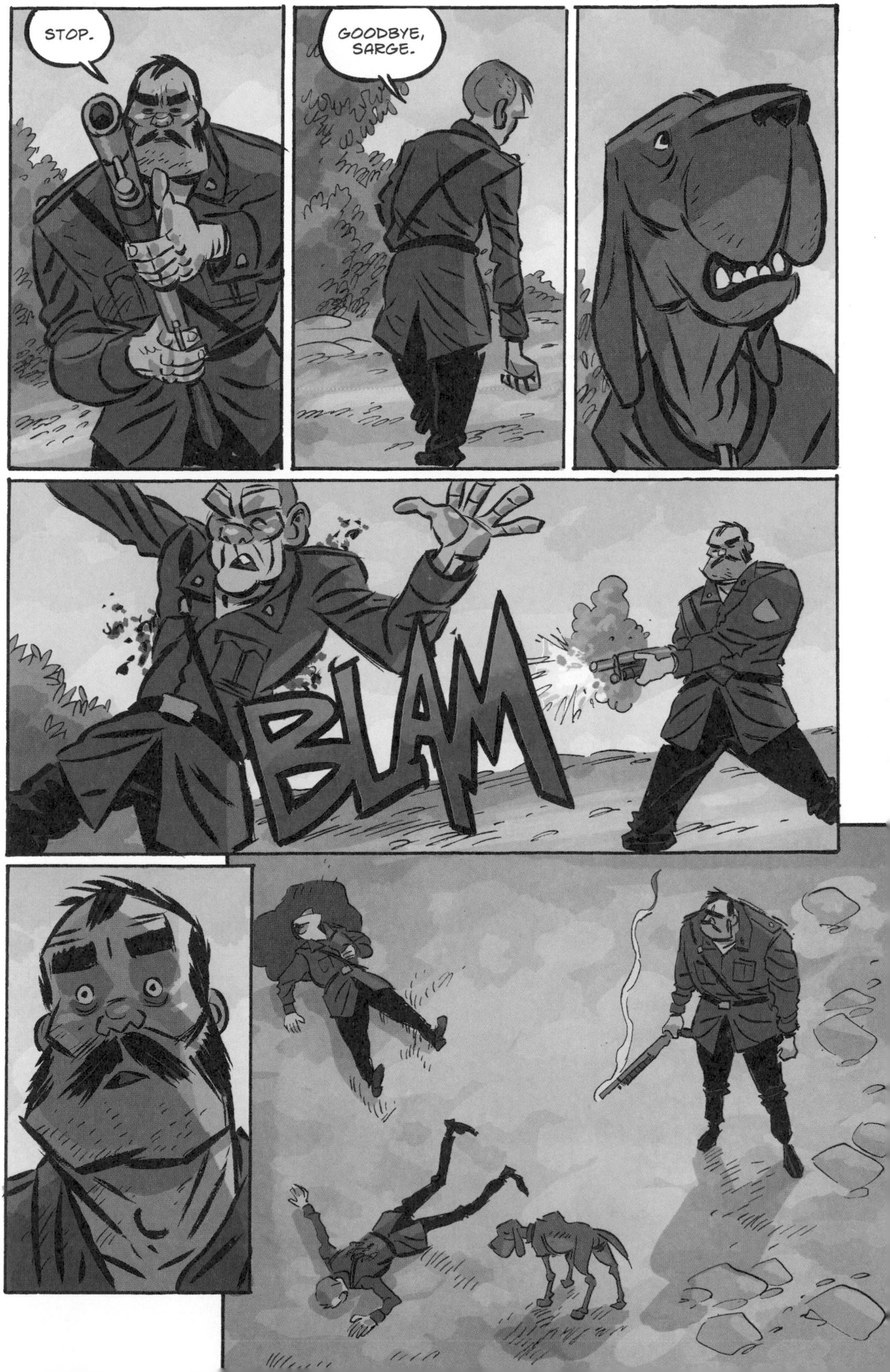
STOP.
GOODBYE, SARGE.
BLAM

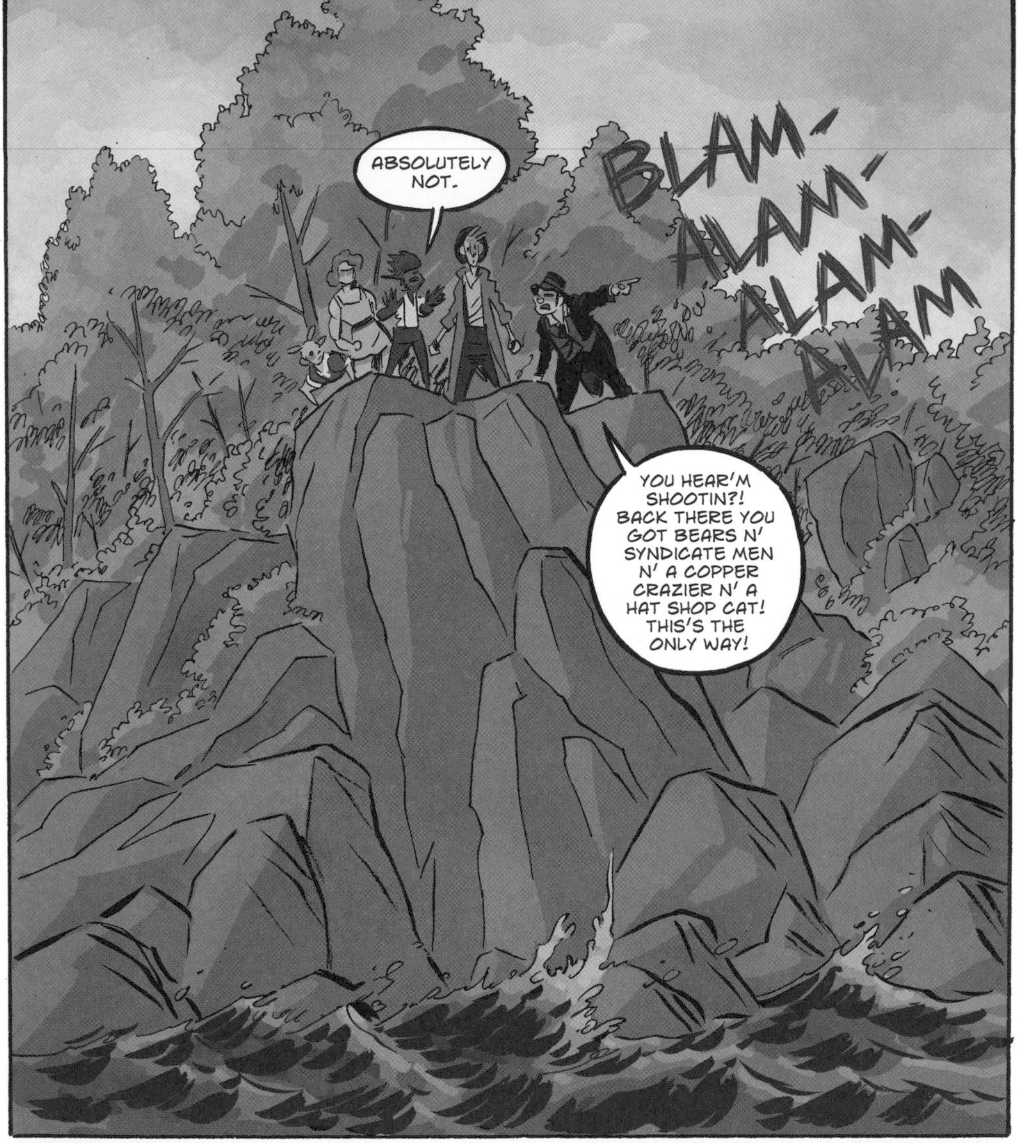
ABSOLUTELY NOT.
BLAM-ALAM-ALAM-ALAM
YOU HEAR'M SHOOTIN?! BACK THERE YOU GOT BEARS N' SYNDICATE MEN N' A COPPER CRAZIER N' A HAT SHOP CAT! THIS'S THE ONLY WAY!

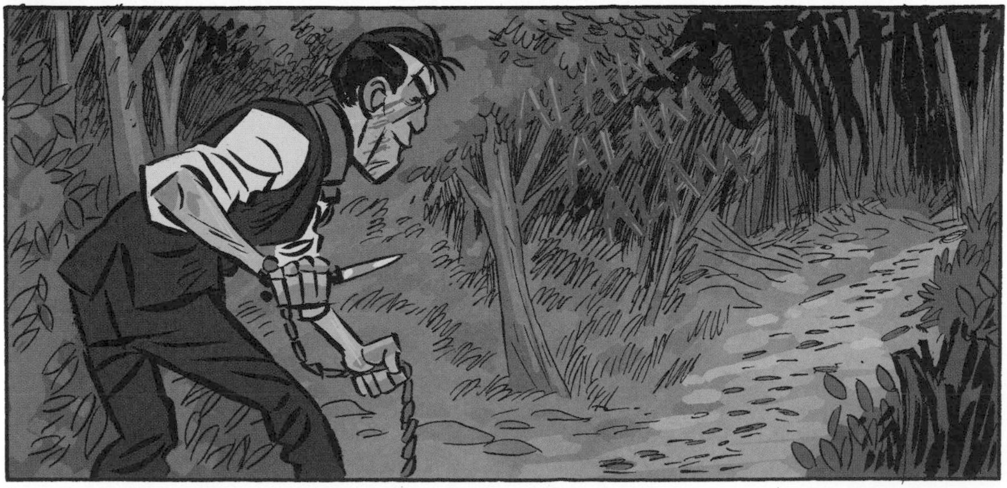

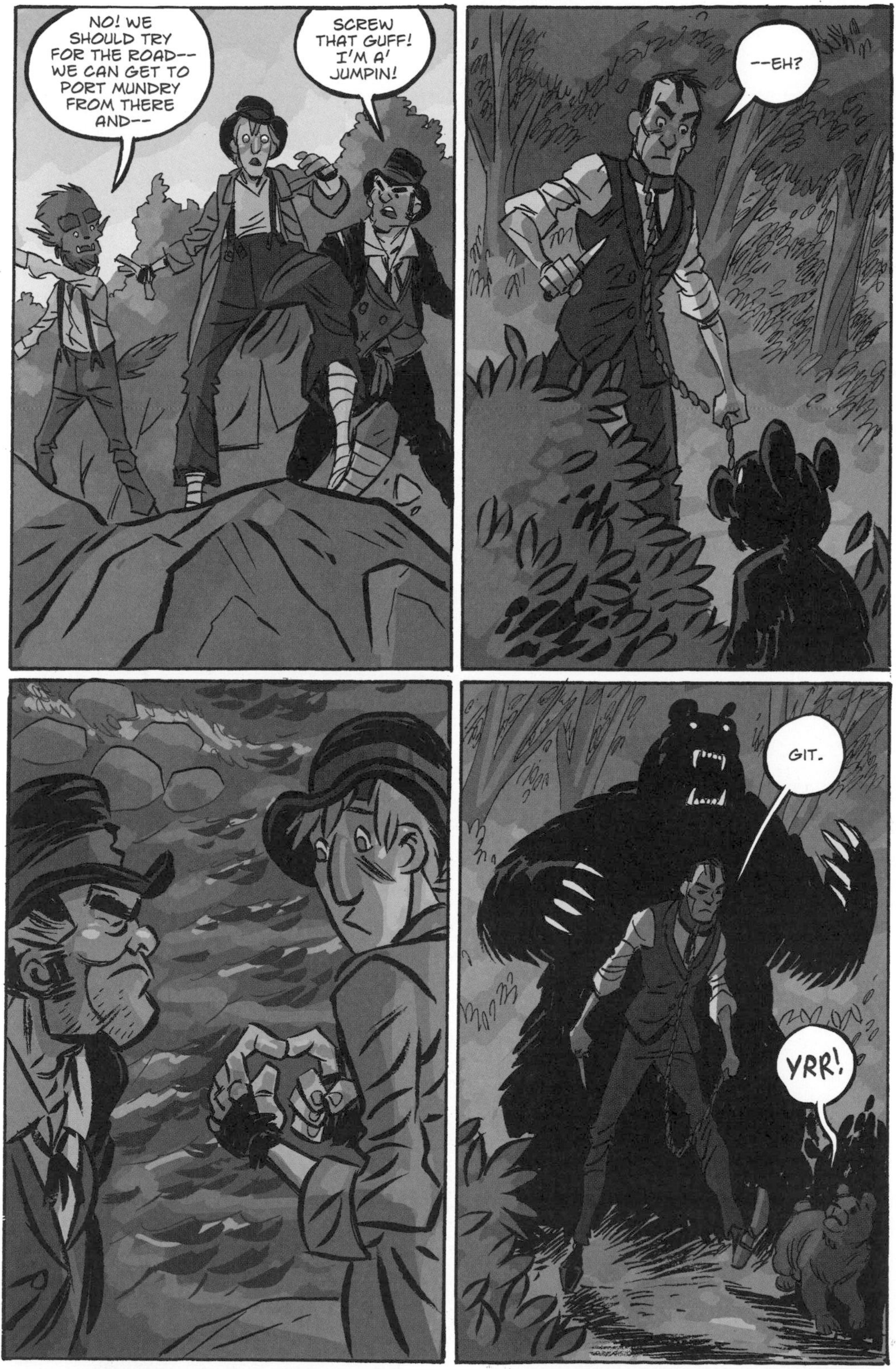
NO! WE SHOULD TRY FOR THE ROAD-- WE CAN GET TO PORT MUNDRY FROM THERE AND--
SCREW THAT GUFF! I'M A' JUMPIN!
--EH?
GIT.
YRR!

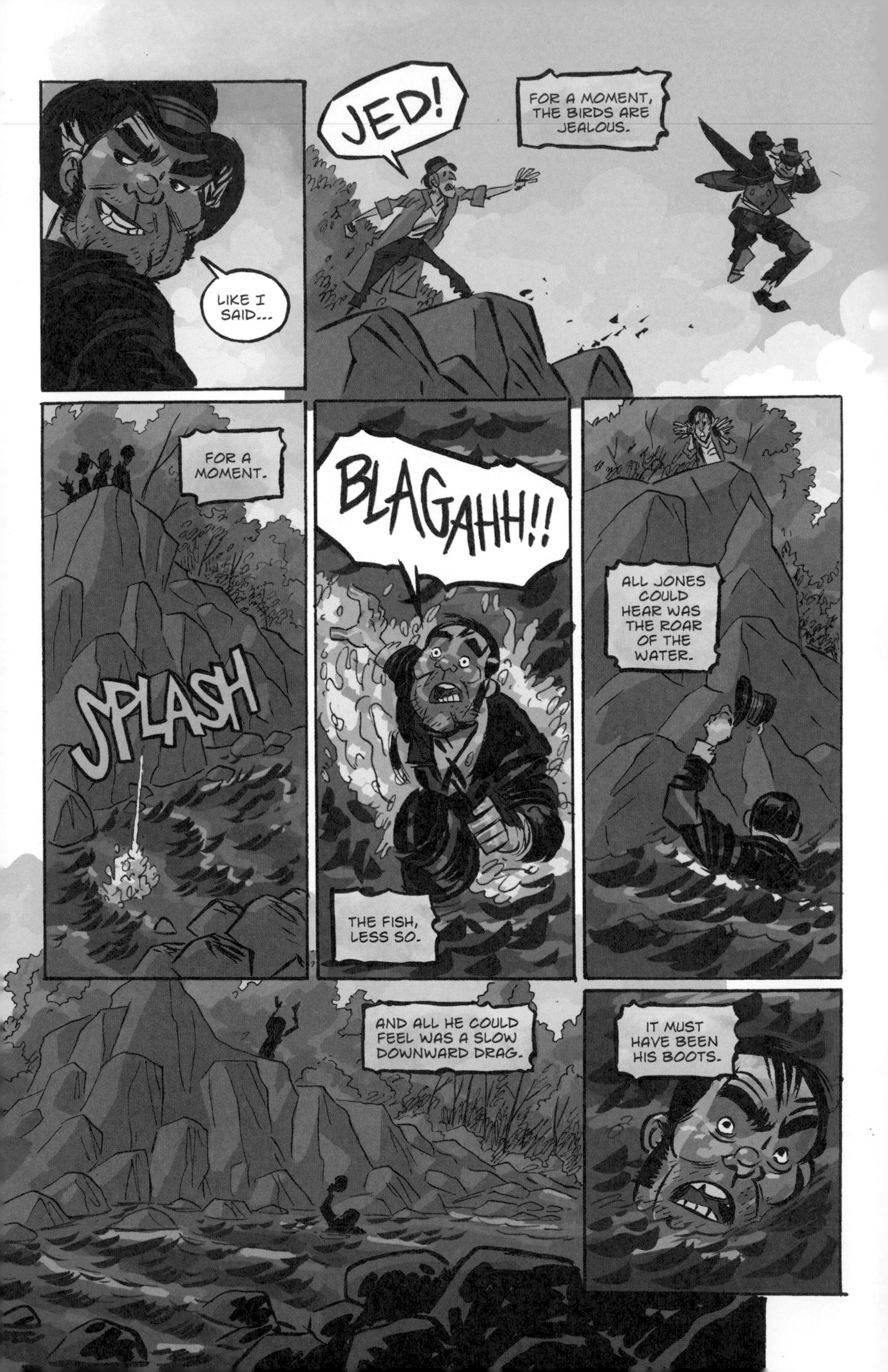
LIKE I SAID...
JED!
FOR A MOMENT, THE BIRDS ARE JEALOUS.
FOR A MOMENT.
SPLASH
BLAGAHH!!
THE FISH, LESS SO.
ALL JONES COULD HEAR WAS THE ROAR OF THE WATER.
AND ALL HE COULD FEEL WAS A SLOW DOWNWARD DRAG.
IT MUST HAVE BEEN HIS BOOTS.

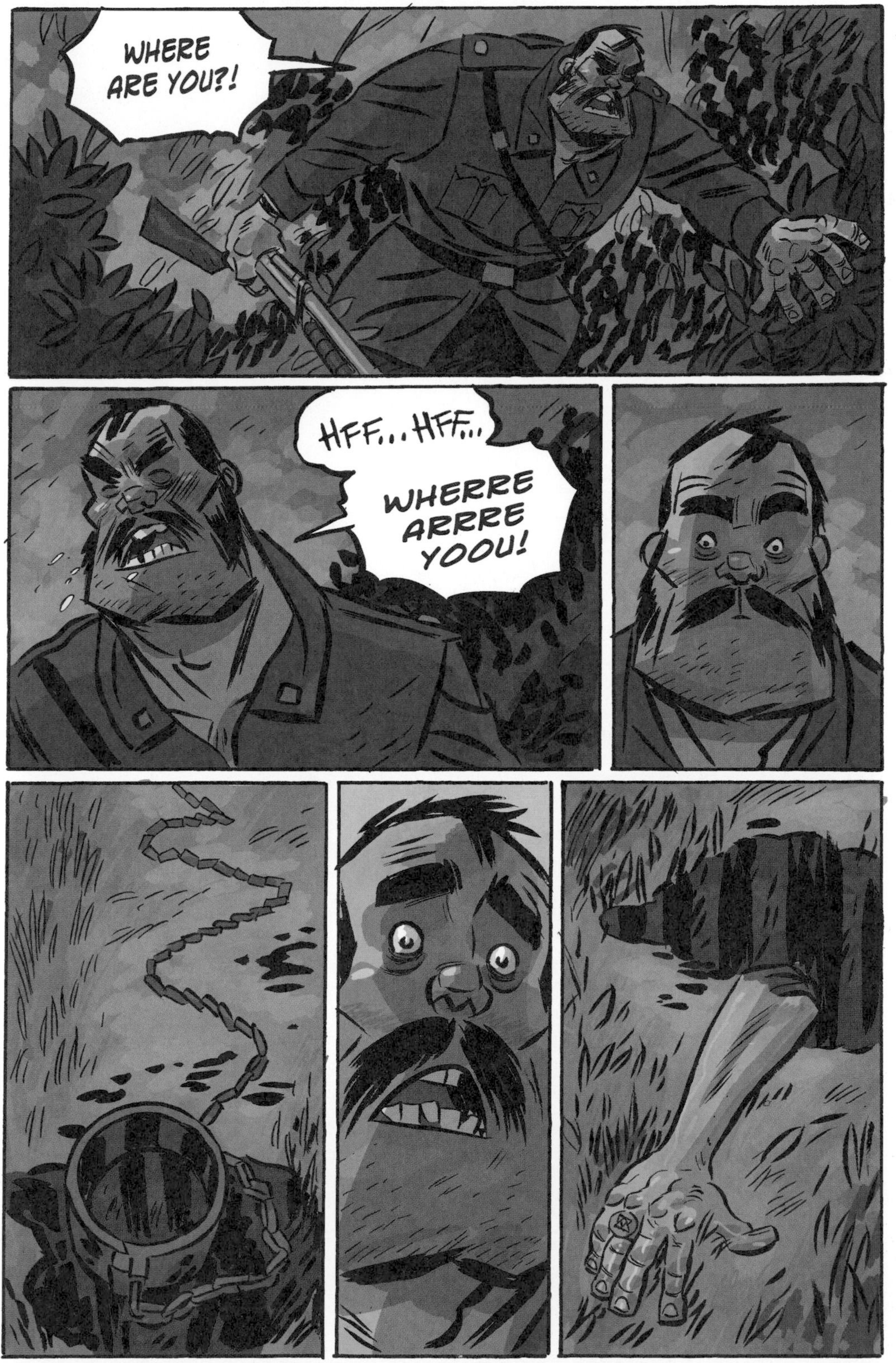
WHERE ARE YOU?!
HFF... HFF...
WHERRE ARRRE YOOU!

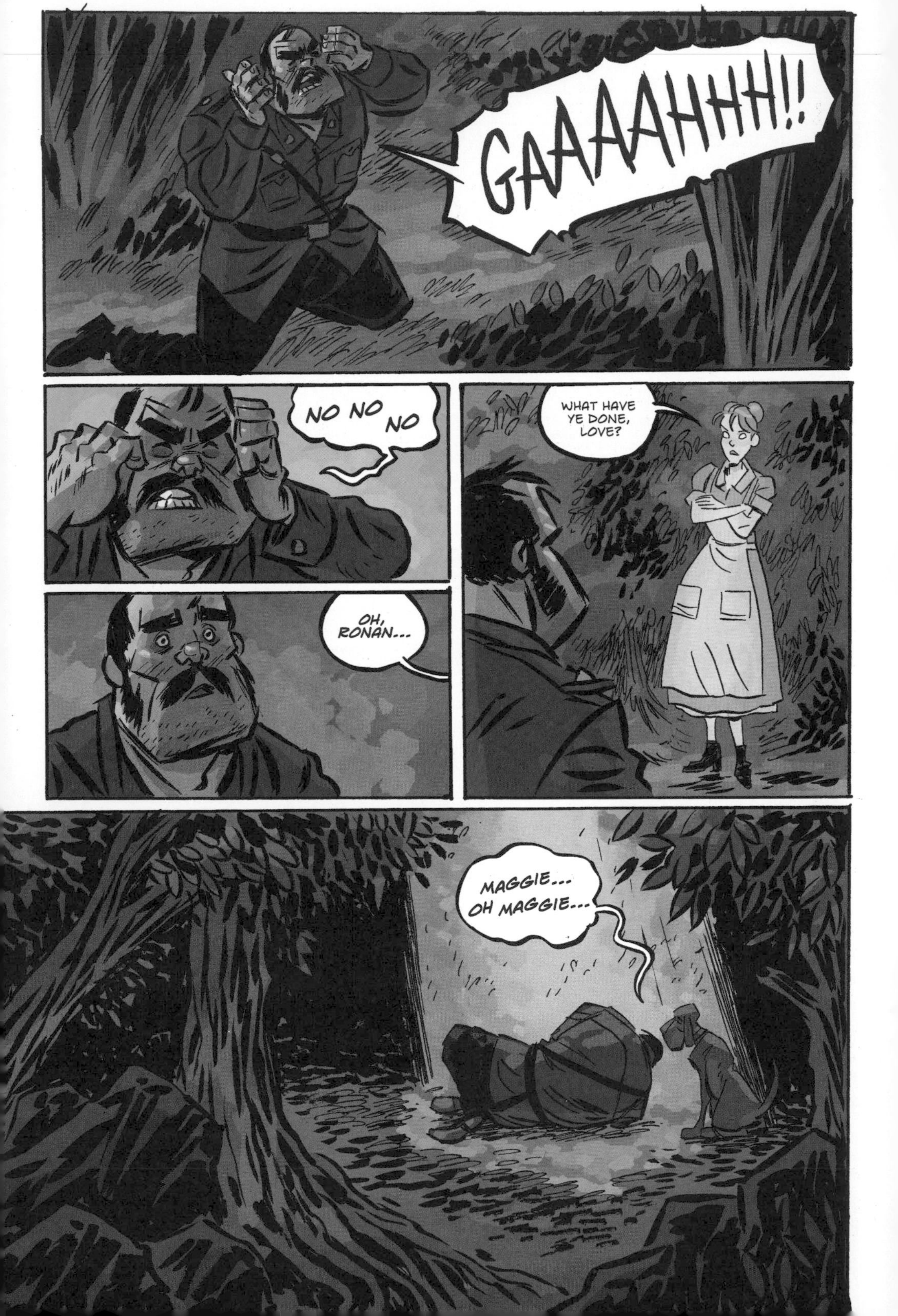
GAAAAHHH!!
NO NO NO
OH, RONAN...
WHAT HAVE YE DONE, LOVE?
MAGGIE... OH MAGGIE...

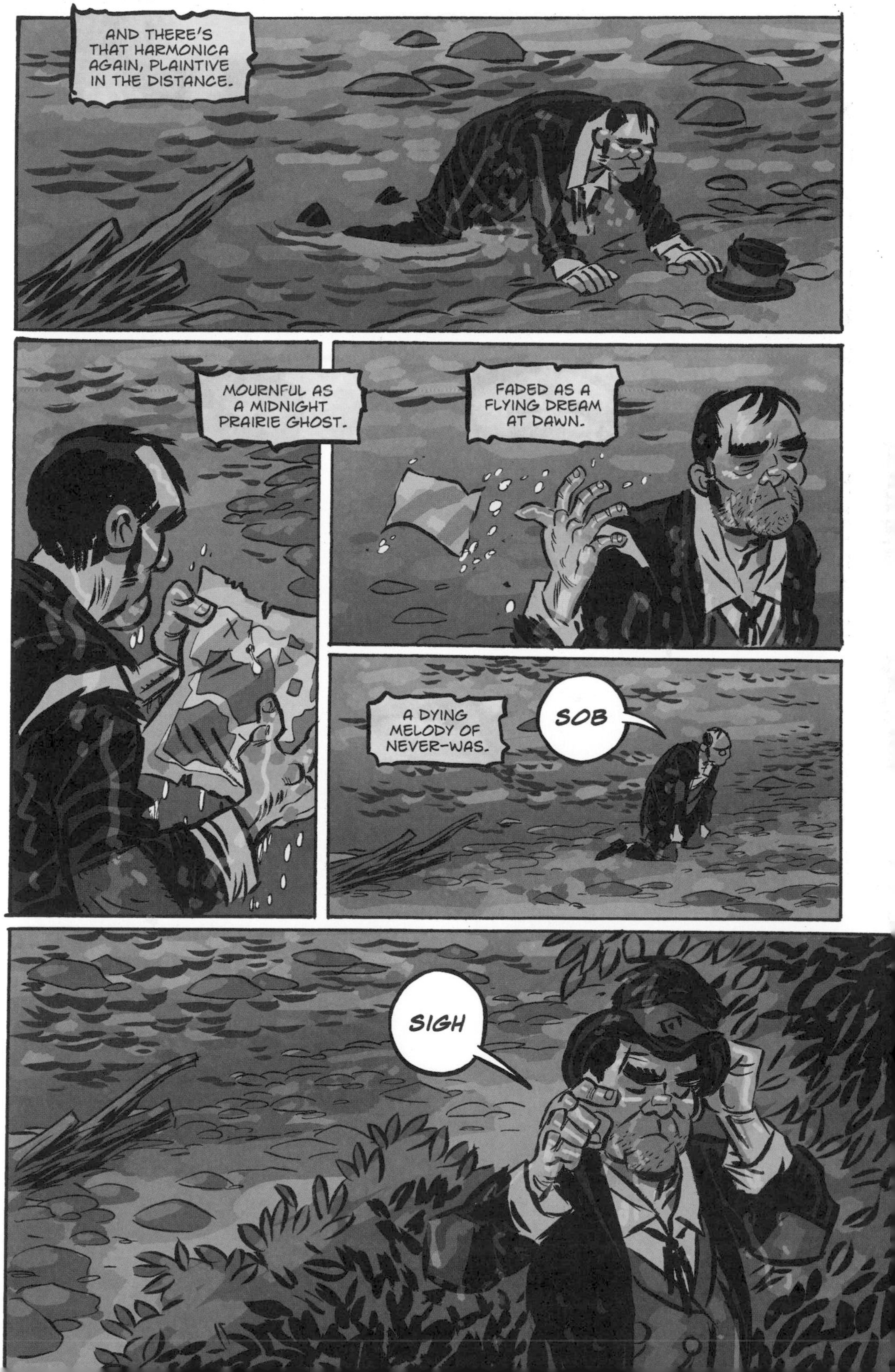
AND THERE'S THAT HARMONICA AGAIN, PLAINTIVE IN THE DISTANCE.
MOURNFUL AS A MIDNIGHT PRAIRIE GHOST.
FADED AS A FLYING DREAM AT DAWN.
A DYING MELODY OF NEVER-WAS.
SOB
SIGH

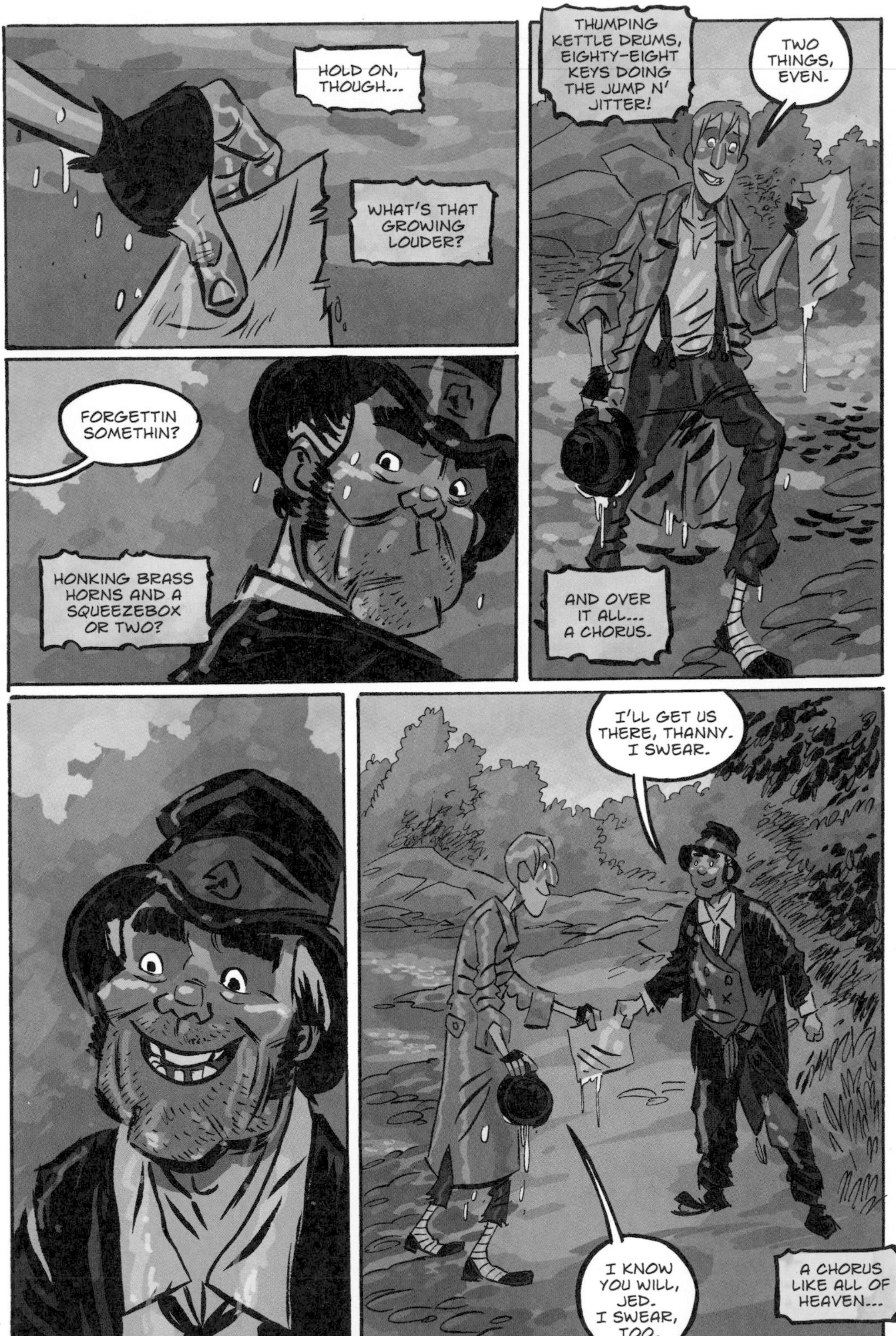
HOLD ON, THOUGH...
WHAT'S THAT GROWING LOUDER?
FORGETTIN SOMETHIN?
HONKING BRASS HORNS AND A SQUEEZEBOX OR TWO?
THUMPING KETTLE DRUMS, EIGHTY-EIGHT KEYS DOING THE JUMP N' JITTER!
TWO THINGS, EVEN.
AND OVER IT ALL... A CHORUS.
I'LL GET US THERE, THANNY. I SWEAR.
I KNOW YOU WILL, JED. I SWEAR, TOO.
A CHORUS LIKE ALL OF HEAVEN...

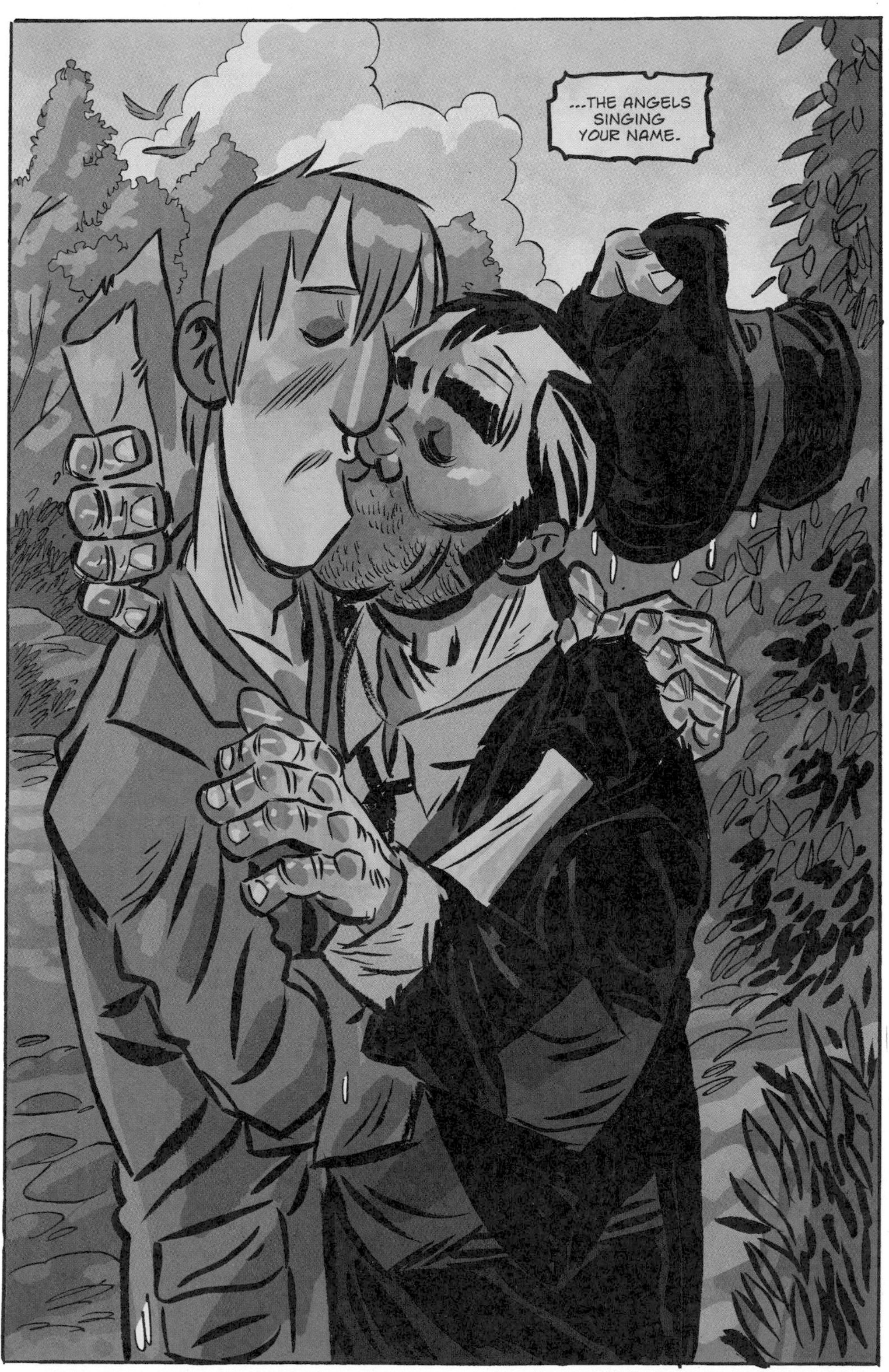
...THE ANGELS SINGING YOUR NAME.

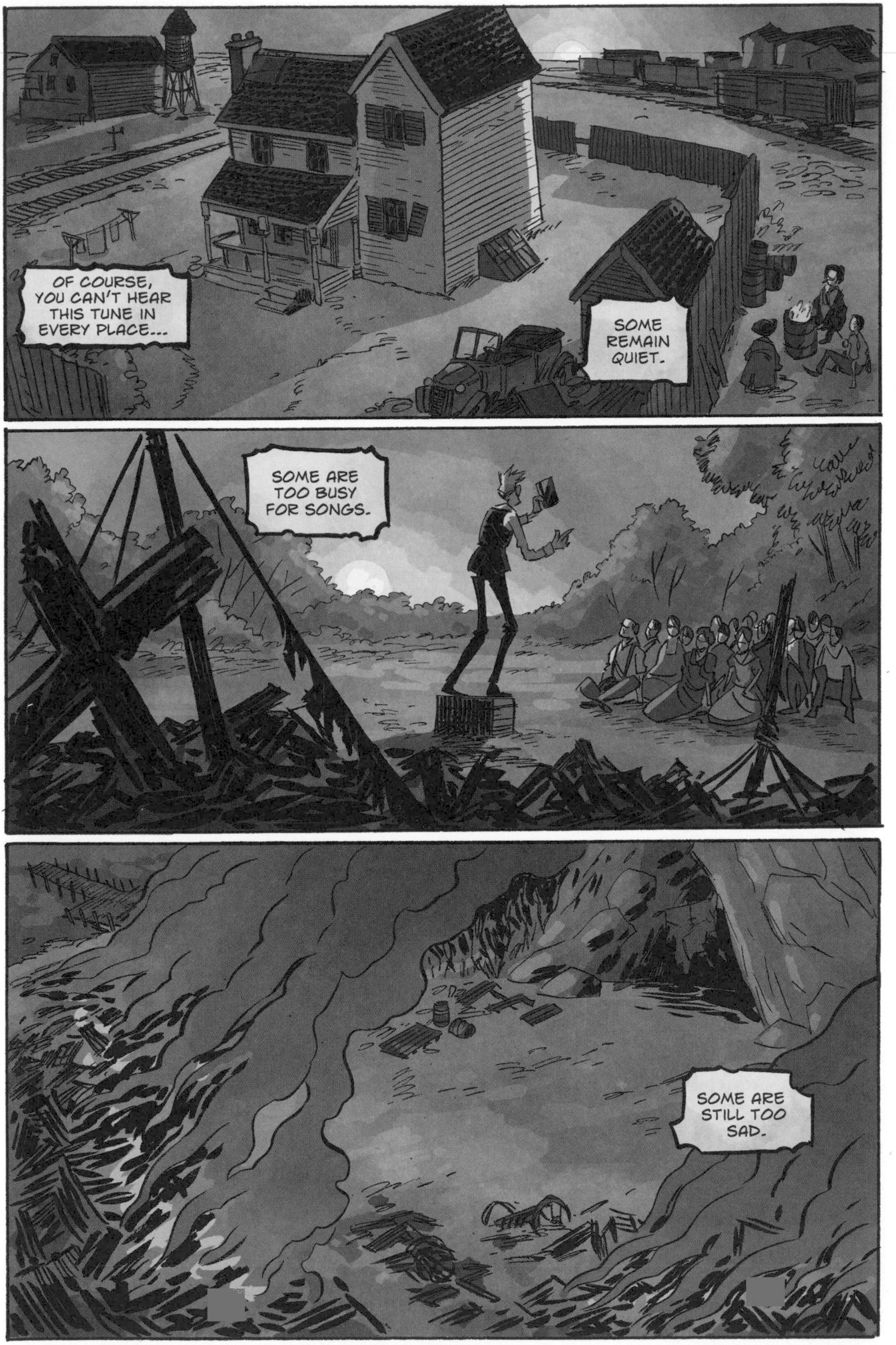
OF COURSE, YOU CAN'T HEAR THIS TUNE IN EVERY PLACE...
SOME REMAIN QUIET.
SOME ARE TOO BUSY FOR SONGS.
SOME ARE STILL TOO SAD.

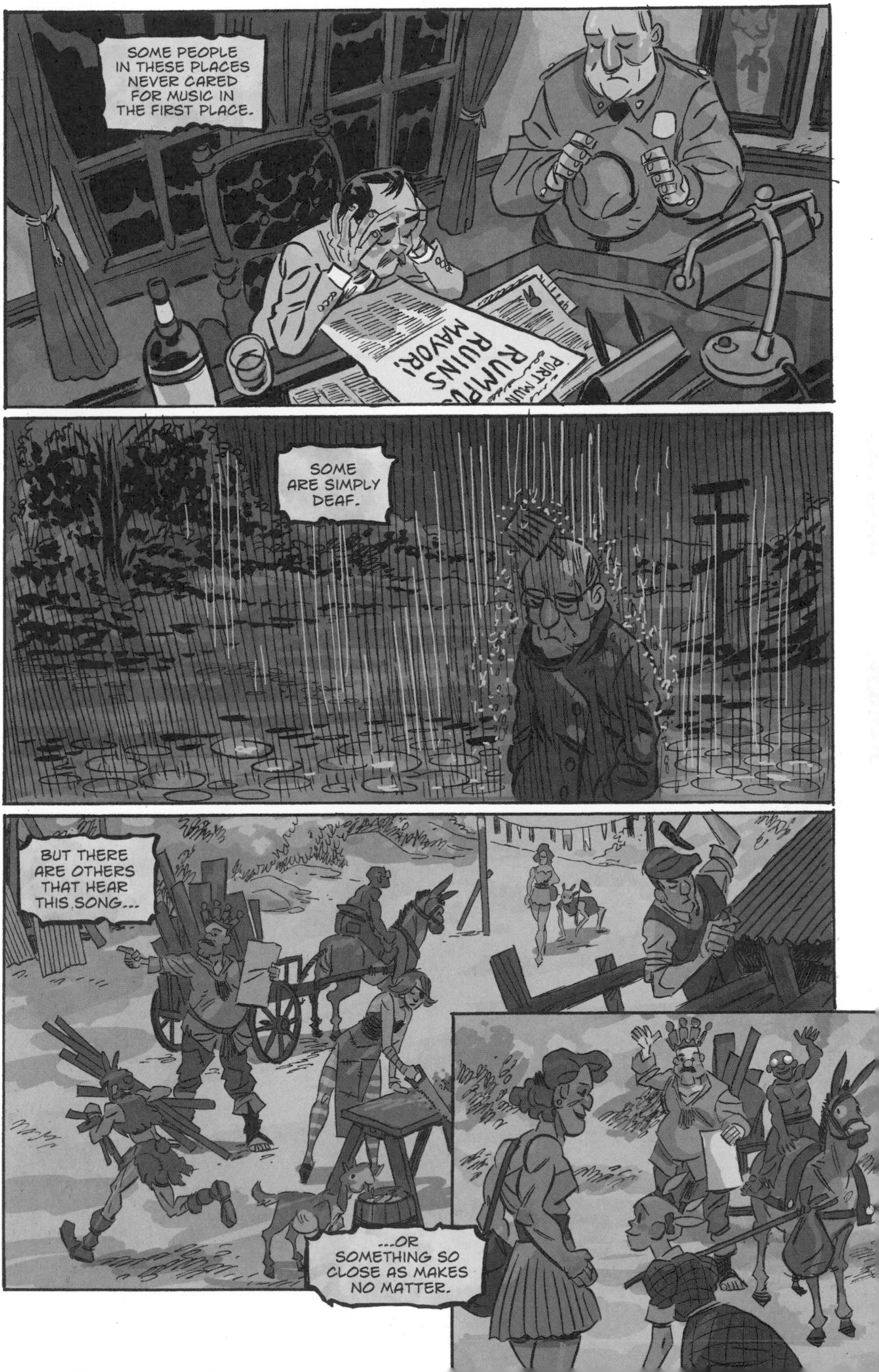
SOME PEOPLE IN THESE PLACES NEVER CARED FOR MUSIC IN THE FIRST PLACE.
PORT MUN
RUMPUS RUINS MAYOR!
SOME ARE SIMPLY DEAF.
BUT THERE ARE OTHERS THAT HEAR THIS SONG...
...OR SOMETHING SO CLOSE AS MAKES NO MATTER.

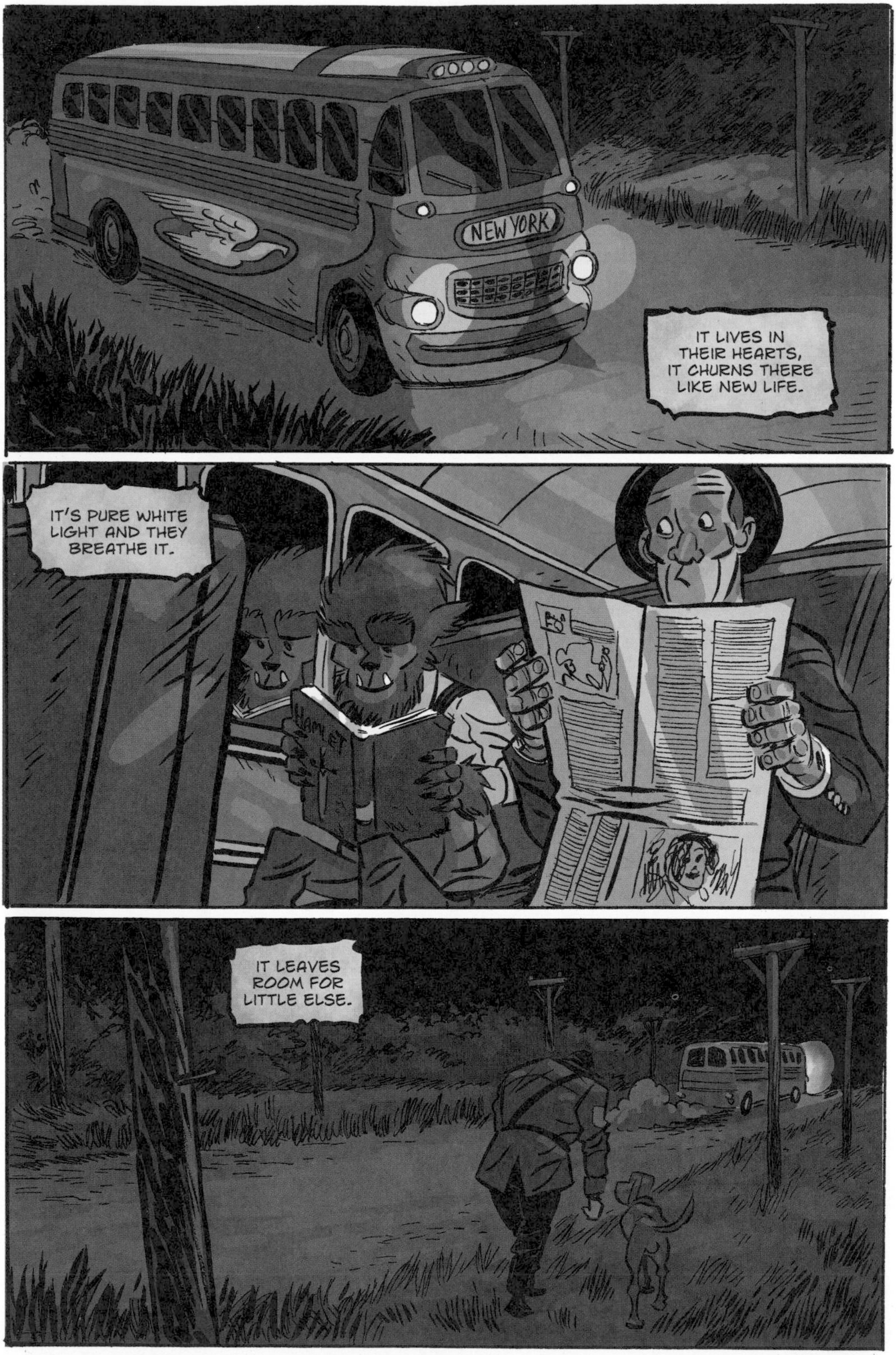
NEW YORK
IT LIVES IN THEIR HEARTS, IT CHURNS THERE LIKE NEW LIFE.
IT'S PURE WHITE LIGHT AND THEY BREATHE IT.
IT LEAVES ROOM FOR LITTLE ELSE.

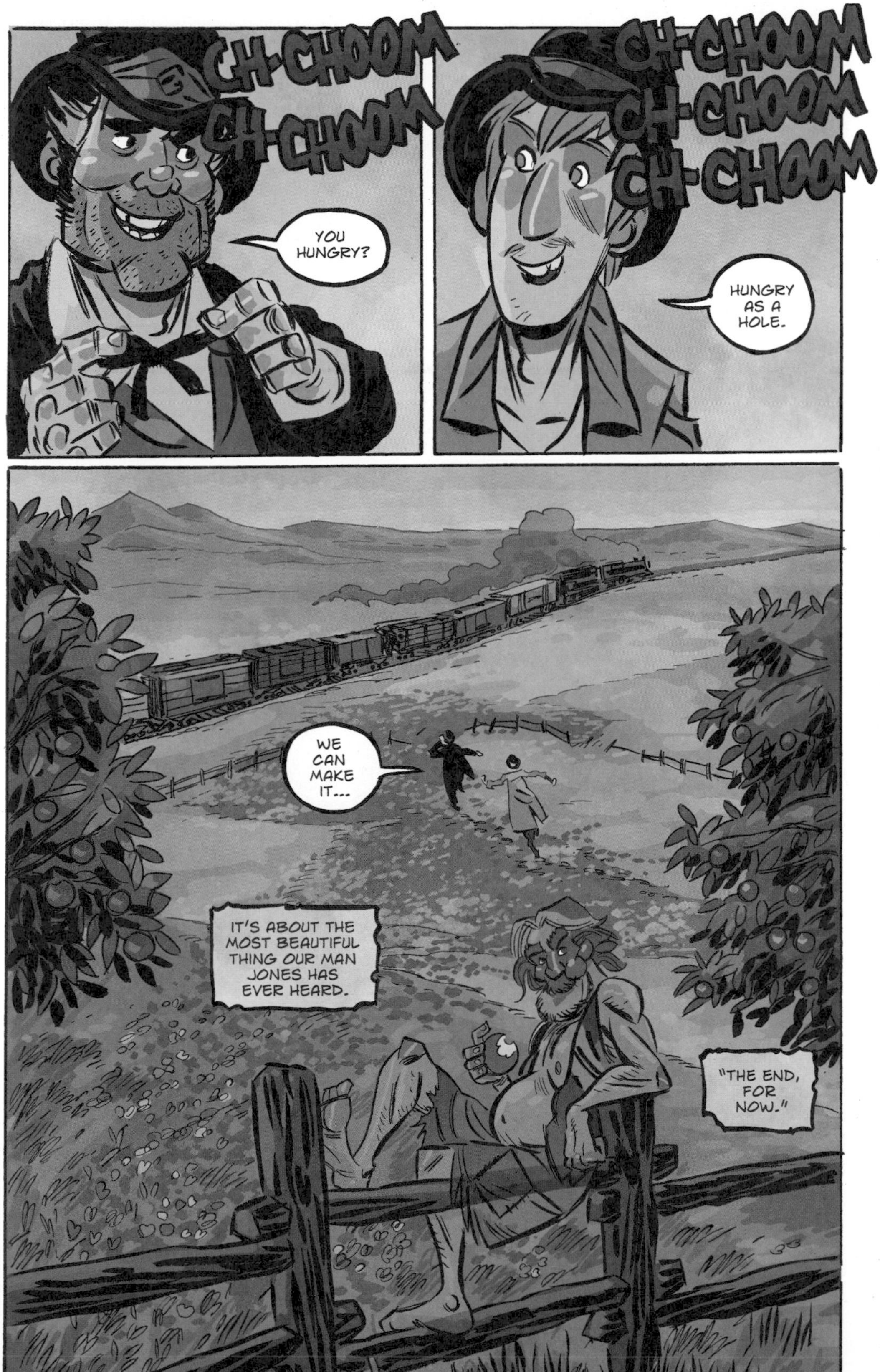
CH-CHOOM
CH-CHOOM
YOU HUNGRY?
CH-CHOOM
CH-CHOOM
CH-CHOOM
HUNGRY AS A HOLE.
WE CAN MAKE IT...
IT'S ABOUT THE MOST BEAUTIFUL THING OUR MAN JONES HAS EVER HEARD.
"THE END, FOR NOW."

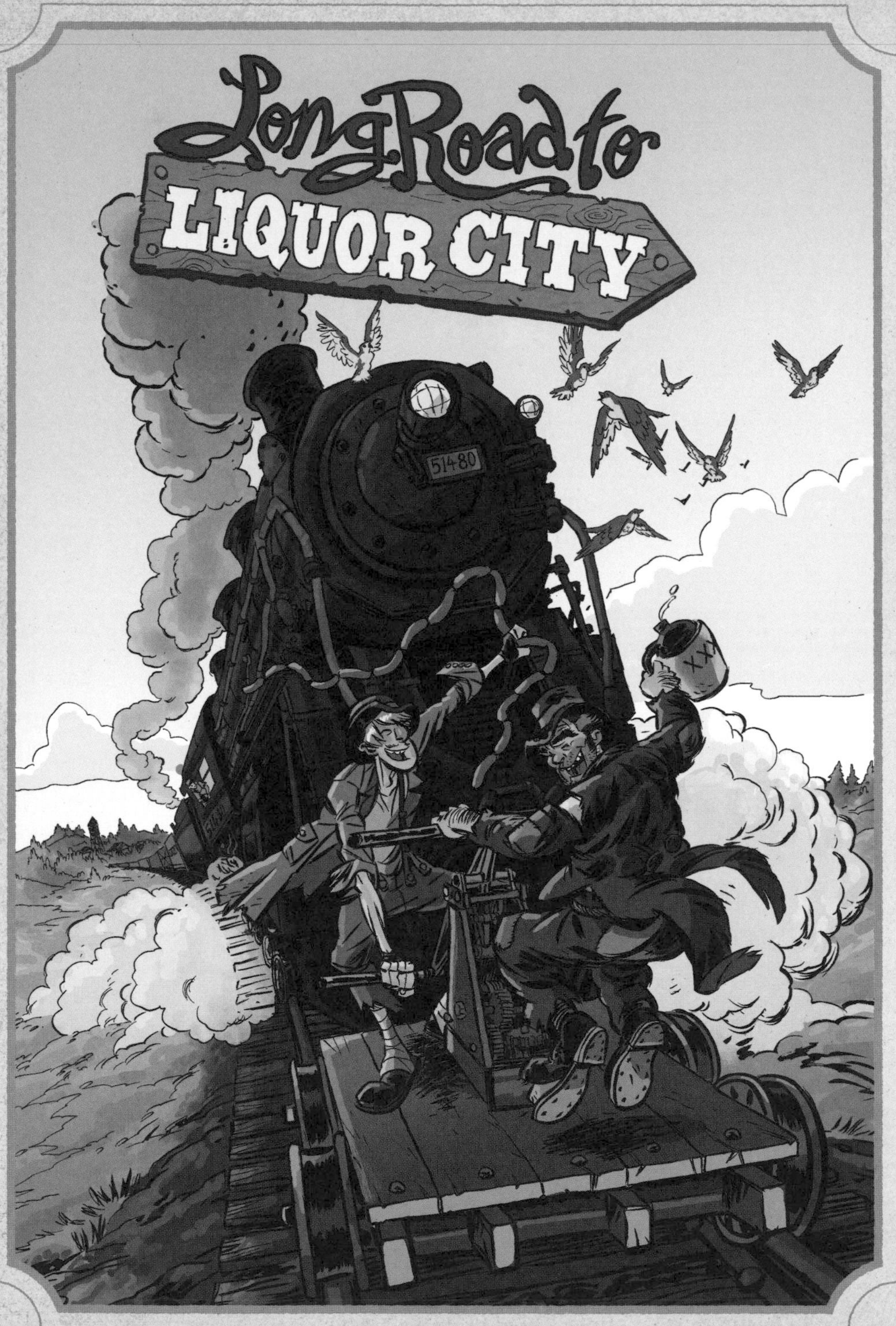
Long Road to
LIQUOR CITY
51480

Original cover and logo design by
JOE FLOOD

BONUS MATERIAL FROM

LIQUOR CITY

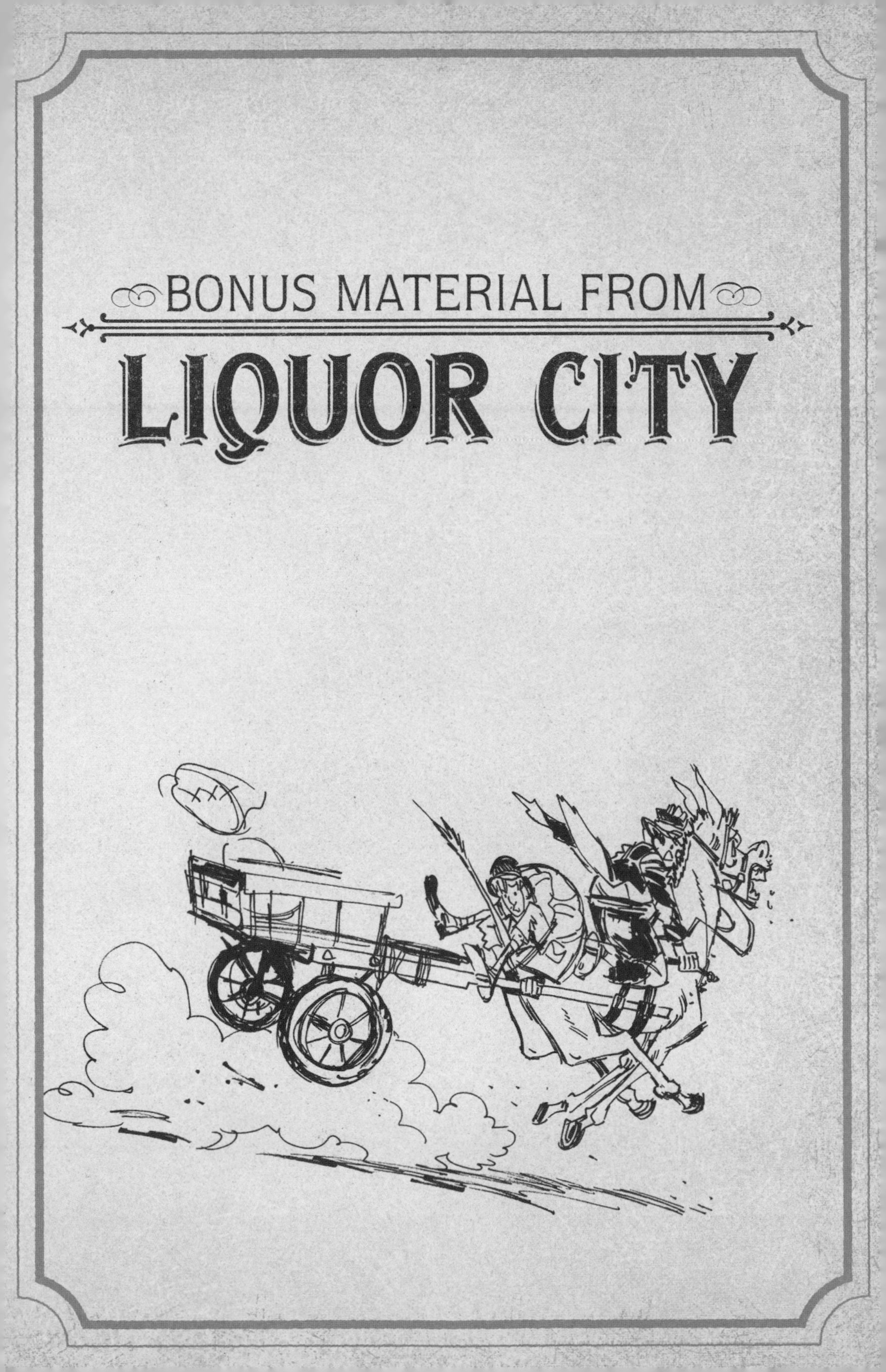

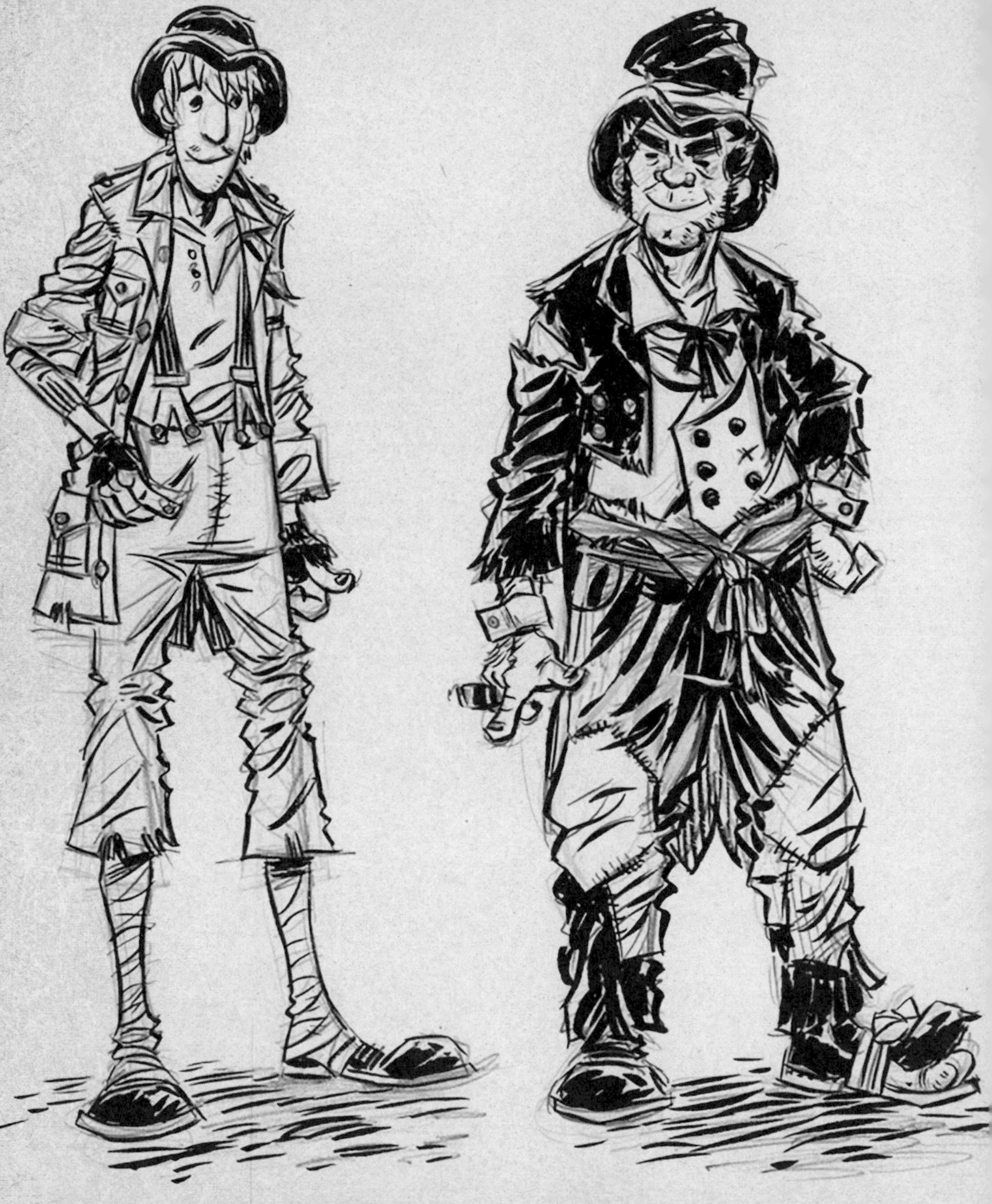

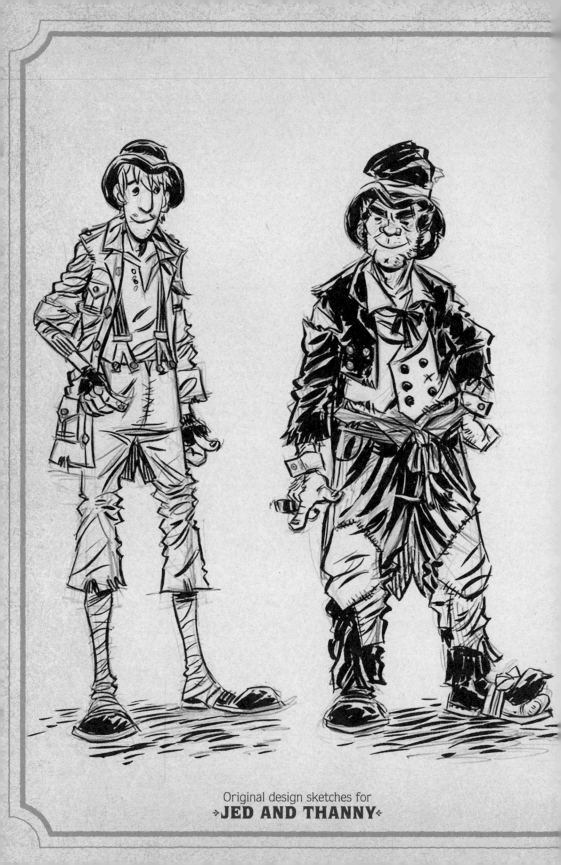

Original design sketches for
JED AND THANNY

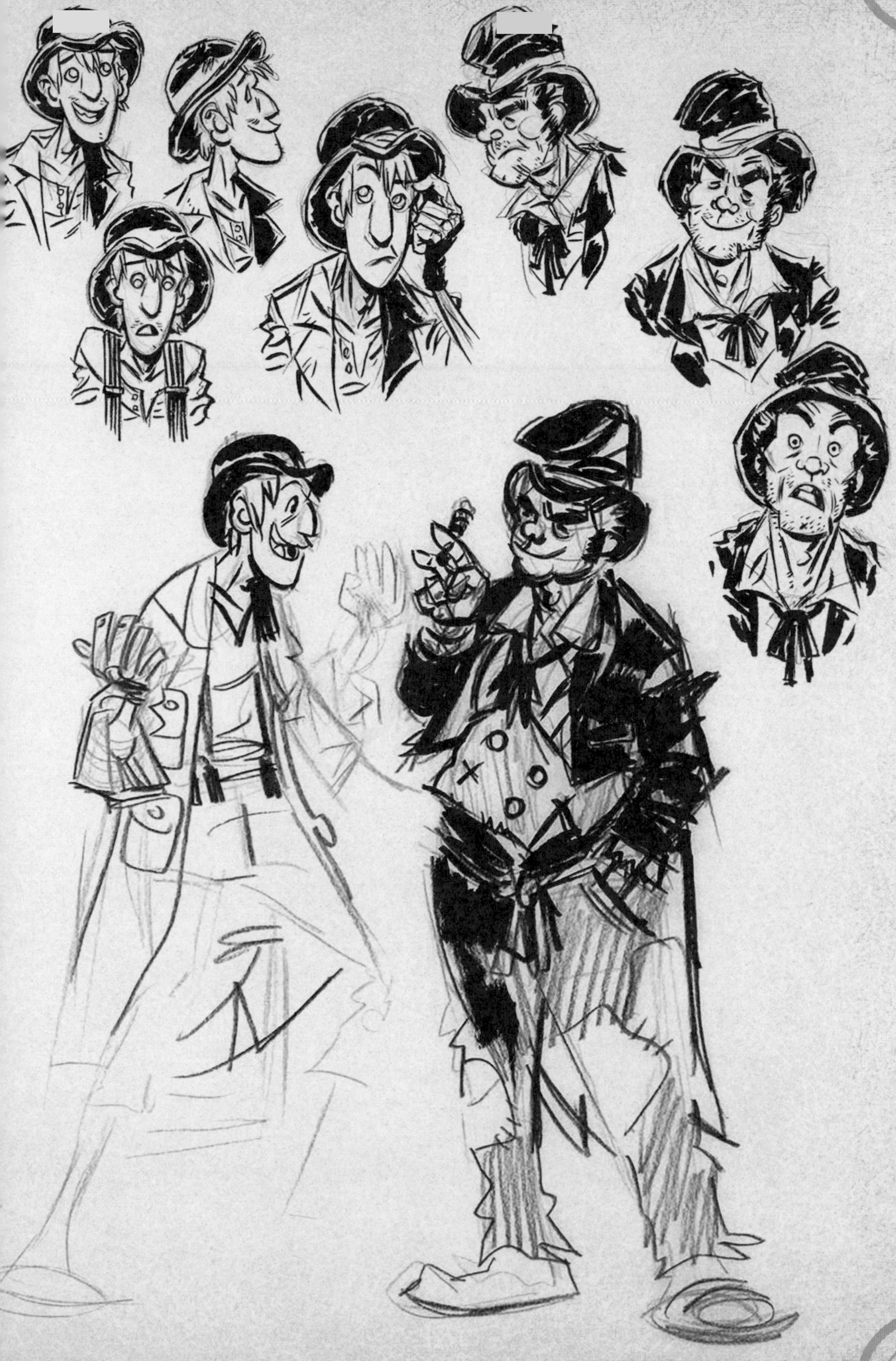

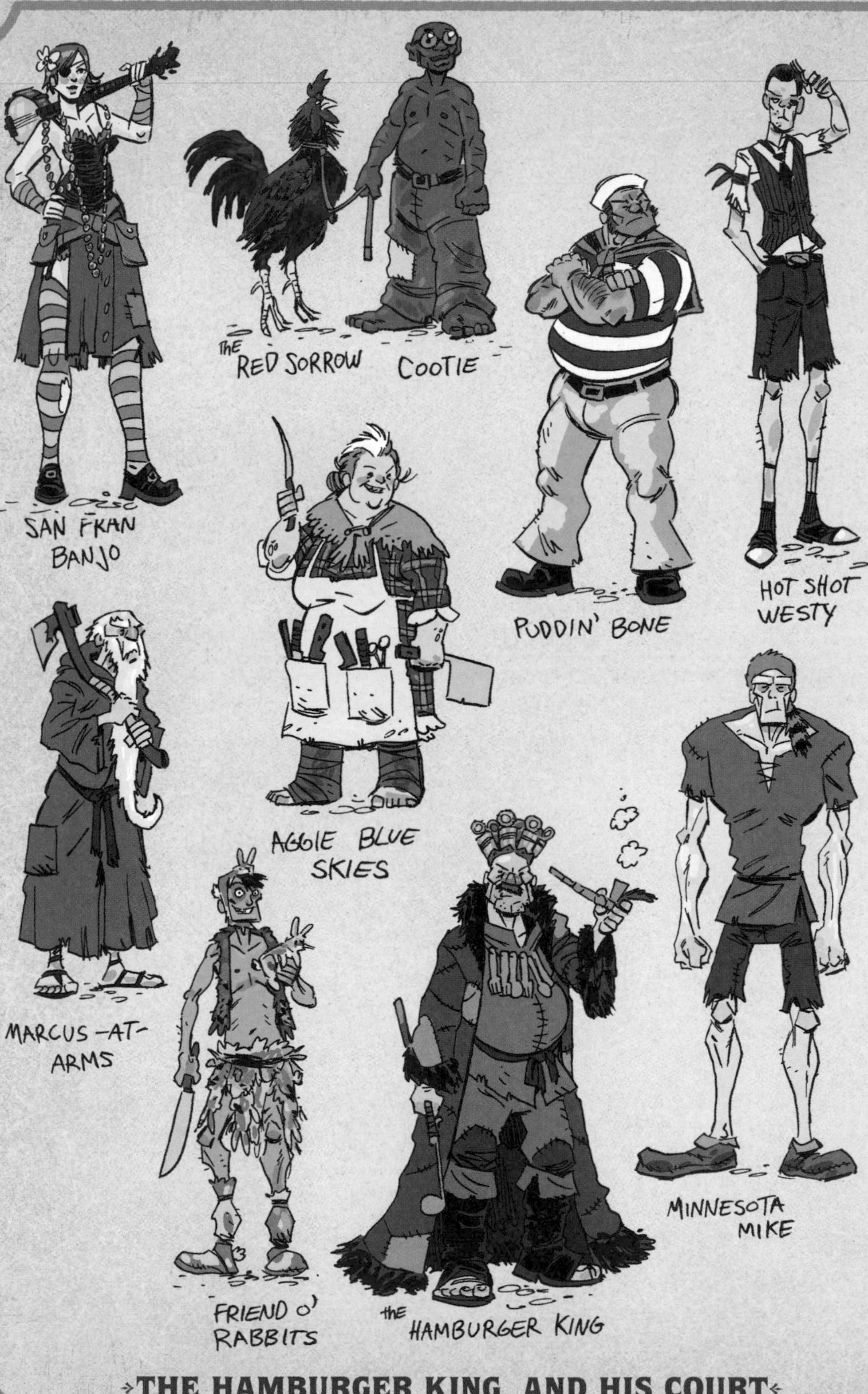
SAN FRAN
BANJO
THE RED SORROW
COOTIE
PUDDIN' BONE
HOT SHOT
WESTY
AGGIE BLUE
SKIES
MARCUS-AT-
ARMS
FRIEND O'
RABBITS
THE HAMBURGER KING
MINNESOTA
MIKE

THE HAMBURGER KING, AND HIS COURT

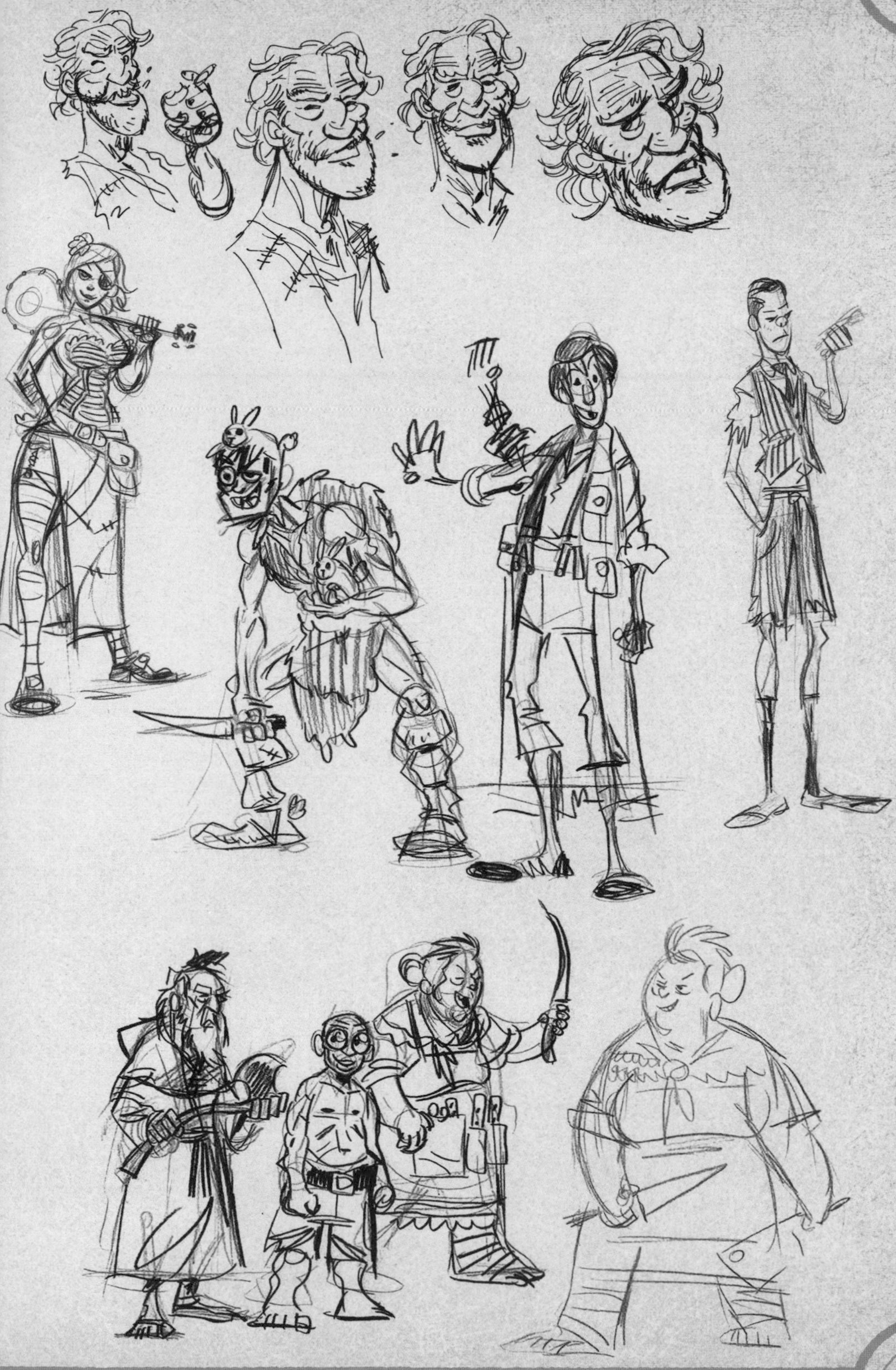

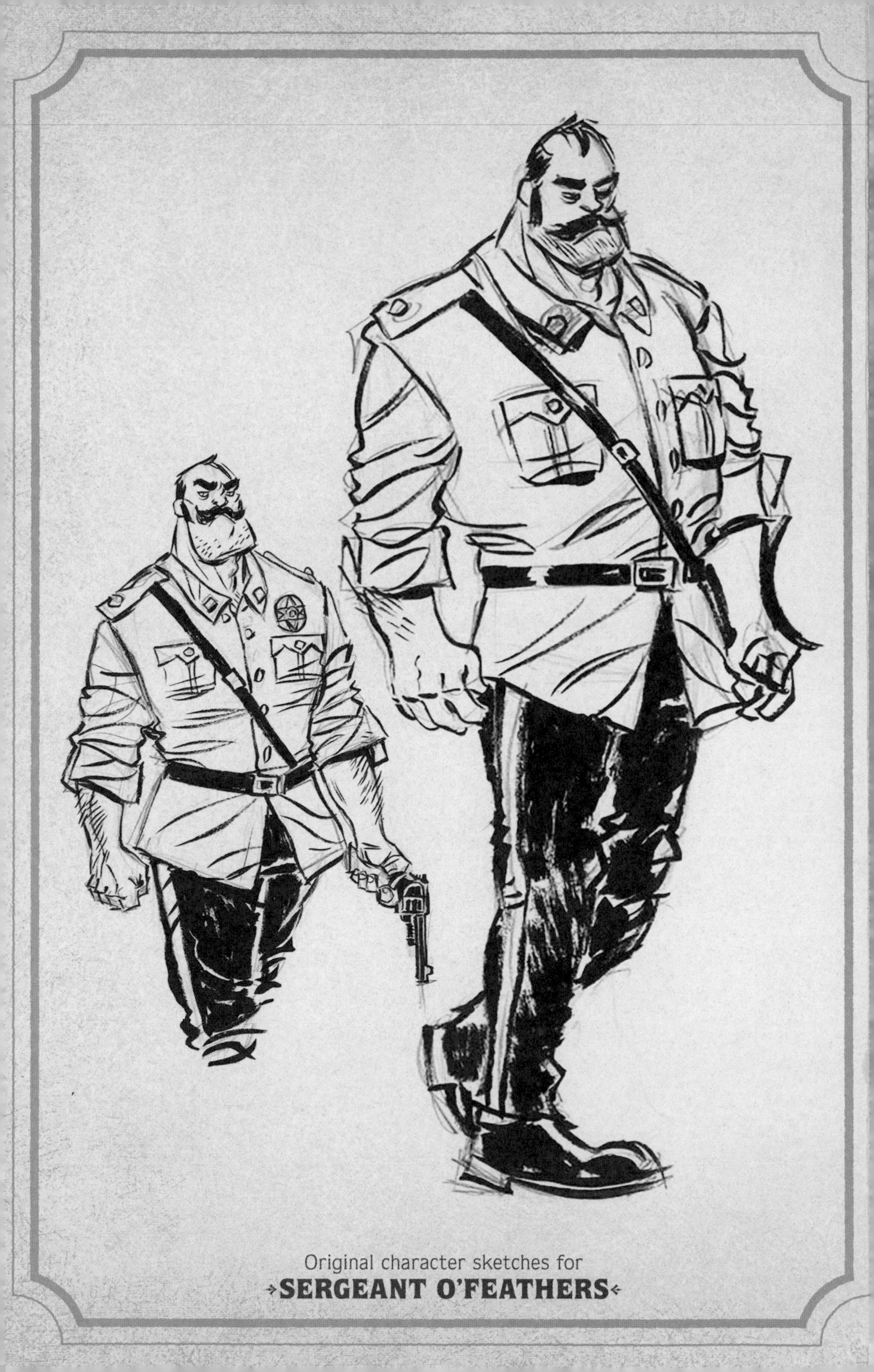

Original character sketches for
SERGEANT O'FEATHERS